SELECTIVE HISTORY
OF THEORIES
OF VISUAL PERCEPTION:
1650-1950

font H I K L M. J'eſtime en ſuitte, que les extremitez E & K, qui ſont au milieu des autres, ſe trouvent juſtement au bout des axes optiques, c'eſt à dire aux extremitez des lignes T E, V K, qui paſſent par les centres de la prunelle, de l'humeur cryſtaline, & du corps de l'œil, & que les autres ſont tellement rangées a-lentour d'elles, que l'on peut prendre ſeparé-

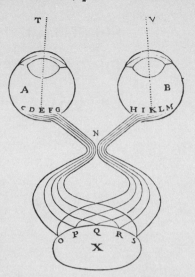

ment en certain ordre tous les filets de l'un des yeux, & les comparer avec ceux de l'autre pris dans le meſme ordre, pour en compoſer pluſieurs paires, que nous nommerons ſympathiques. Ainſi, commençant par les filets C, & H, qui ſont les plus avancez vers la main gauche, j'en fais une premiere paire; les autres paires ſont D I, E K, F L, G M. Enfin je me perſuade que les filets ſympathiques de chaque paire aboutiſſent à un meſme point de la partie du cerveau qui excite l'Ame à ſentir; comme vous voyez icy que la paire C H abou-

This page is reproduced from Jacques Rohault,
Traité de physique, *1671. The major problems which have plagued theories of perception from the time of Descartes to the present are represented in this single diagram.*

SELECTIVE HISTORY
OF THEORIES
OF VISUAL PERCEPTION:
1650-1950

NICHOLAS PASTORE

Queens College, The City University of New York

New York · OXFORD UNIVERSITY PRESS · London 1971 Toronto

Copyright © 1971 by Oxford University Press, Inc.
Library of Congress Catalogue Card Number: 75-129638
Printed in the United States of America.

PREFACE

In my opinion an examination of the literature on "perception" published since 1945 will disclose a multiplicity of theories and innumerable experiments for which the rationale is not always evident. A theory may burgeon and survive for ten years before fading away, and the body of experiments cited in support of it becomes irrelevant. The reasons for the life span of a theory are not well understood. The intellectual effort involved in trying to understand the theory and the experiments related to it would seem to be misplaced. A new theory, for all we know, will have a similar fate. When I became aware of considerations of this kind a few years ago, I thought that a study of the history of theories of perception would provide an understanding of present theories and would also help crystallize the problems which have been of permanent interest. However, I found that no book adequately dealt with the topic from a historical standpoint which would be of interest to the psychologist. My principal aim in writing this book was to fill this gap so that the reader might get some idea as to what past and present theories of perception are about.

I should like to state some of the principles that guided my selection of the theorists I have discussed in the text. One such principle originates in Helmholtz's classification of theorists as "empirists" and "nativists," a distinction which has remained in the scientific vocabulary since 1867. I have selected the development of empiristic theory before 1900 for investigation, beginning with Locke and terminating with Helmholtz himself. Thus I have ignored "nativists" in this period whose contributions were influential in shaping the history of the subject. I have made a further selection by choosing those empirists who seemed to be saying something different from what had been stated by Locke and Berkeley. Moreover, I have selected particular topics for discussion so as to preserve some sense of historical continuity.

I should wish to call the reader's attention to the fact that many of the theorists I have discussed, especially those belonging to an earlier period, did not explicitly formulate a theory of visual perception. For instance, the chapter on Descartes represents my interpretation of what the statement of his theory might have been if he had set down his own thoughts in 1971. Moreover, a theory, even when explicitly formulated, may reflect several important and interdependent interests which include epistemology, physiology, and psychology. The theorist may emphasize one or another, or he may so interweave his interests that detection of the prior interest and the central problem is made difficult. Thus interpretation again is necessary. As a precaution against error I have inserted interpretations of particular theories which were stated by others in the theorists' own period. I have included many quotations and extracts, some of which have been drawn from generally inaccessible sources, so that the reader may be in a position to evaluate the issues himself.

A few words on the general plan of the book. Following the introductory chapter, the theories of Descartes and Malebranche are included principally as historical context for the empiristic theories of Locke and Berkeley. The exposition of empiristic theory is continued through Chapter 10, completing the development of the theory as of 1900. In Chapter 11, and in part of Chapter 12 on William James, I describe some of the important criticisms of empiristic theory which had been stated before 1900. I continue this criticism in Chapter 13, adding some points of further evaluation to those which had already been cited. Following this, I have selected gestalt theory for extended treatment not only because this theory is the first nonempiristic theory but also because it provides the basis for understanding the development of other theories in the twentieth century. In Chapters 15 and 16 I have discussed theories which are representative of the critical reaction to gestalt theory, a reaction which I have evaluated principally from the standpoint of gestalt psychology. Perhaps I should say that I have freely borrowed those ideas of gestalt psychology expressed by Wertheimer, Köhler, Koffka, and other gestalt psychologists, which were relevant to understanding the development of theories of perception. For instance, Köhler's concept of the "constancy hypothesis" is introduced in Chapter 1 and becomes a major theme of this book.

I regard the inclusion of the criticisms of the Berkeleyan theory of perception by Condillac in 1746 and by Bailey a century later as a significant feature of this work. As far as I know this is the first systematic discussion of their point of view to appear in any text of psychology or philosophy. Furthermore, I have profited from a study of Bailey's works on perception. In particular, Bailey called attention to the implication of Berkeleyan theory that consciousness would have to be regarded as a delusion. Thus a theorist's attitude concerning the interpretation of consciousness from a theoretical standpoint becomes another major theme of this book. I should say that my appreciation of the significance of Bailey's work was only made possible by a prior acquaintanceship with gestalt psychology.

Professors John C. Baird of Dartmouth College and Walter Cohen of the State University of New York at Buffalo, who read the manuscript at the request of the publisher, offered thoughtful comments for revision which I accepted. For this I thank them. I am grateful to students who read many chapters of the manuscript and who suggested constructive changes. In this regard I am particularly grateful to Mr. Jeffry Luria. I also wish to thank Mrs. Silvia Greenberg, my colleague Dr. Mildred E. Hamilton, and Dr. Ruth Stark for their reading of the manuscript and helpful comments, and Mrs. Ruth G. Hollander and Mrs. Mimi B. Penchansky of the inter-library loan desk of Queens College who performed many valuable services gracefully and efficiently.

N.P.

January 1970
New York City

CONTENTS

SELECTIVE HISTORY
OF THEORIES
OF VISUAL PERCEPTION:
1650-1950

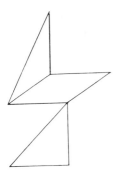

1 INTRODUCTION

The eye which is the window of the soul is the chief organ whereby the understanding can have the most complete and magnificent view of the infinite works of nature. Leonardo da Vinci

An important source of facts for any theory of perception is what we see in our everyday activities in directing our eyes to objects and in undertaking actions in relation to them. The scientist tries to understand and explain the descriptions we provide in terms of his knowledge of various subject matters. Other sources of facts are available to him which generally are inaccessible to others, such as those derived from laboratory investigation and case studies. He may formulate a theory that will give the facts, irrespective of their source, a coherency and consistency that are not apparent on casual observation. If the theory is a successful one, it becomes the basis for discovering other hitherto unsuspected facts. But however intricate its structure, however successful in accounting for some facts, and however consistent with other knowledge, the theory must ultimately satisfy the criterion of explaining those facts of perception which we describe. The same criterion would apply to the explanation of perception that might be proposed by a philosopher.

ERRORS OF SIGHT

From the time of early Greek philosophy much of the theoretical discussion of perception, especially before 1900, concerned "errors of sight" or "visual illusions." An important reason for the discussion of "errors," which pertain to the discrepancy between the characteristics of perceptions and the characteristics of objects, was to show that the sense of sight was untrustworthy in providing information about objects and in guiding our actions in relation to them. Of course, it was recognized that visual perceptions usually were nonerroneous or "cor-

Triumph of Alexander the Great, ceiling fresco, Museo degli Argenti, Palazzo Pitti.

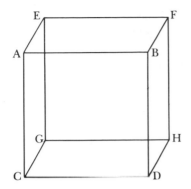

FIGURE 1.1. The Necker Cube.

rect" but it was pointed out that from the standpoint of perception alone there could be no way of deciding whether a particular perception was correct or incorrect. The following selection of traditional examples of "error" drawn from the early literature, which will be relevant to later discussion in this text, exemplifies these points.

Relative distance. Generally the sun, moon, and stars are seen as though at the same distance although their relative distances from the viewer are vastly different. Painters of the Renaissance were adept at representing columns and other objects on a curved ceiling, so that from below they would be perceived as though they were actual objects.

Solidity. Although the moon is a three-dimensional object, it looks flat. Painters can arrange pigments on canvas so that a sphere or a cube will be perceived. In reference to Figure 1.1, the "Necker Cube," we see the lines as a "cube" although the lines are drawn on paper. Moreover, a reversal in the perceived relative distances of faces ABCD and EFGH can be observed in continued inspection of the diagram.

Form. The actual square-like contour of a tower viewed from a distance looks somewhat rounded, the square-like form being perceived when the viewing distance is short. The artist paints ovals and diamond-like shapes, but we perceive circles and squares. Five profiles can be perceived in the accompanying reproduction of an eighteenth-century "puzzle picture."

Magnitude. The moon appears larger when it is at the horizon than when it is overhead, yet the physical size is the same in both posi-

Weeping Willow, 1795.

tions (moon illusion). The two lines in Figure 1.2 are of the same length but we see the vertical line as longer than the horizontal line (horizontal-vertical illusion).[1]

RETINAL IMAGES

Beginning with Leonardo da Vinci in the fifteenth century, artists, in that century and the century following, regarded the camera obscura as a convenient model for depicting the images that would be formed in the eye or in the "bottom of the eye." They discovered that pictorial representations should resemble the images of the camera obscura so that these representations would produce the same or similar perceptual effects as objects did. The images of the camera obscura often were described in relation to a room in which the only light entered through an aperture in the window; a person inside the darkened room was able to see the images of the objects outside the room depicted on the wall opposite the aperture. However, artists at that time constructed a small "dark chamber" since it was more convenient for observing the characteristics of images. The face opposite the aperture of this box was a translucent screen, and usually a convex lens was placed in front of the aperture. The scientist in this same period had also adopted the same model. However, the artist and scientist had incorrectly analyzed the optics of the formation of the images inside the eye. An important reason for their error was that when they did proceed correctly, they found that the images formed in the retina were upside down—hence they changed their analysis. For instance, Leonardo da Vinci introduced the concept of a double reversal of rays inside the eye in order to eliminate the inverted image and to get one that would be erect. Further, Leonardo, as the result of this error, was led to another error, namely, that of regarding some part of the eye other than the retina as the part that was sensitive to light. In 1604 Kepler, who had also adopted the conception of the eye as a camera obscura, resolved the problems of the optics of image formation inside the eye. He predicted on theoretical grounds that the retina is the place where images are formed and that they are inverted. The subsequent verification of his analysis in the observation of images of objects either in the excised eyes of dead animals and men or on the translucent screen of an "artificial eye," which was essentially a minia-

FIGURE 1.2. The horizontal-vertical illusion.

Robert Hooke's "picture-box," an early example of a camera obscura (1694).

ture camera obscura, led to the general scientific acceptance of the conception of the eye as a camera obscura.

Some of the properties of the images of the camera obscura, knowledge of these images being obtained by viewing them on the translucent screen or by geometric analysis, are depicted schematically in Figure 1.3. An image is usually a distorted or perspective representation of the object, a "line" in this diagram. Thus an image is flat, the measurements of its parts do not accurately represent the measurements of the corresponding parts of the object, and, in respect to two objects of the same size, the more distant one projects the smaller image. Furthermore, the size of the image is small relative to the size of the object, and the orientations of image and object are reversed. Finally, an image is ambiguously related to the object producing it; that is, an infinite number of objects may project the same image. These properties also are descriptive of the image of a two or three-dimensional object that has been placed in an appropriate spatial location. The representation of the object and the perspective changes in its image are not as easy to depict on paper as is the representation of the line and image of Figure 1.3. For the purpose of exposition, some of the properties of the images of a circle and a square will be considered. A plane parallel to the translucent screen will be called the frontoparallel plane, and the line perpendicular to the screen passing through the aperture will be called the line of sight (line ST in Figure 1.3).

When the plane of a circle is inclined at various angles in respect to the frontoparallel plane, it projects a series of images which are el-

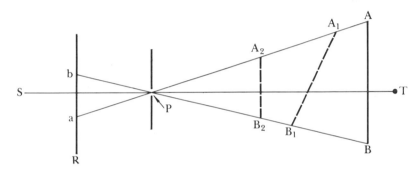

FIGURE 1.3. The camera obscura is schematically depicted in cross section, P representing the aperture, and R the translucent screen (the lens is not represented). An object such as the line AB was usually regarded as consisting of an infinity of point sources of light rays so that each point projected a corresponding image-point on the screen. The diagram only indicates the two image-points a and b of the image. Variation in the distance of AB from the aperture, which is not here shown, would produce a proportional variation in the size of the image. Lines A_1B_1 and A_2B_2 project the same image as does AB, as would any line connecting the two "rays." Thus the same image represents or can be coordinated with an infinity of external objects; this illustrates the concept of the ambiguous relationship of image and external object. Since the image is flat, there is no representation of the relative distance of the end points of the slanting line A_1B_1. Further, the measurements of the parts of the image which are projected by the corresponding unequal lengths of the parts A_1O and OB_1 of the slanting line are equal. Obviously, the orientation of an image is inverse to the orientation of the object.

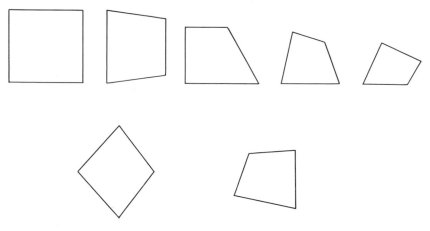

FIGURE 1.4

lipses of varying eccentricities. Only when the circle is in the fronto-parallel plane will it project the image of a circle. This is true even when the line of sight does not intersect the circle. Similarly, the image of a square is a square shape only when the objective square is in the frontoparallel plane. When the plane of the square is inclined in different ways in respect to the frontoparallel plane, the typical image is a quadrilateral of which the opposite sides converge although the corresponding sides of the square are parallel. The opposite sides also are unequal in length. Furthermore, this typical image does not have any right angle although the square has four right angles. Some of the images produced by a square, its spatial location having been changed in different ways, are depicted in Figure 1.4.

Inasmuch as the camera obscura is similar to the structure of the eye, the images formed in the retina would have properties similar to the images of the camera obscura. The fact that the retina is a curved surface was ignored most often in the discussion of the formation of the images on this surface, it being supposed that a section of the retina when made sufficiently small approximated a flat surface. The distortions and reversed orientation of an image were usually regarded as "defects" or "imperfections." [2]

EMPIRISTIC AND NATIVISTIC EXPLANATIONS

The retinal image traditionally was regarded as a defective representation of the object as well as the first step in the explanation of perception, since the image would be a physiological process of some sort. In this regard, two interrelated questions were asked. How could we see objects as we do? How could we obtain knowledge of the actual characteristics of objects? Although theories of perception before 1900, and to a lesser extent after 1900, dealt with these questions, the first question will be emphasized in this text. Empiristic and nativistic theories were two types of theories that developed in answer to this question. Proponents of empiristic theory supposed that "we learn to see" whereas proponents of nativistic theory proposed to explain the important features of perception in terms of innate physiological mechanisms. We shall describe the major assumption of empiristic theory which will help in the understanding of this theory as it is developed in this text, and exemplify nativistic theory in relation to the problem of the binocularly perceived three dimensions of an object. Much of the discussion of theories of perception has hinged on hypothetical statements concerning what the human infant might see independently of "training" or "experience." Such perceptions of the infant usually were referred to as "sensations" or as "original perceptions."

The Constancy Hypothesis:
The Assumption of Empiristic Theory

The content of the constancy hypothesis in reference to spatial characteristics refers to the conformity or correspondence of the spatial attributes of original perception and the retinal image. Before 1900 the major feature of this assumption, which was sometimes made explicit, was that any object would look flat or bi-dimensional to the infant. Originally, therefore, there would not be any perception of relative distance of objects nor any perception of motion when an object approaches or recedes. Obviously the perceptions of the adult are fundamentally different. The change from the original perception to the perception in the later life of the child as a result of training or experience defines what is meant by "learning to see." Although the implications concerning magnitude and form are inherent in the supposition of the original perception of flatness, they will be selected for further discussion because they are the basis for understanding further perceptual facts.

Magnitude. In accordance with the constancy hypothesis, when the retinal-image size varies with the approach or recession of an object, the magnitude of the originally perceived object would vary correspondingly. For instance, when a man whose distance from the infant has doubled, the area of the retinal image shrinks to about one-fourth of the area of the previous image, and the infant would perceive a similar shrinkage in size. However, in adult perception the man is seen as having constant dimensions. The fact that the adult sees an object as having the same size, notwithstanding variation in the magnitude of the retinal image, defines the concept of *size constancy*. The following is another illustration of size constancy but only in reference to the vertical dimensions of retinal images. The dimensions of the retinal images of a child and man are equal when the man is proportionately more distant. However, the man looks taller than the child. The constancy of size is related to perceived distance. For instance, the man also looks more distant than the child. If both man and child were to be perceived as being at the same distance, as might happen in some circumstances, they would be perceived as though equal in height.

The results of an experiment reported by R. W. Darwin in 1786 illustrate some of the concepts involved in the perception of magnitude. One looks at a black triangle placed on a large sheet of paper for about twenty seconds in bright light with one eye. When the eye is turned away the retinal area of the after-effects of stimulation remains constant. Upon directing the gaze to a distant and not so brightly illuminated wall, one sees the after-image of the triangle as though it were part of the wall. The seen size of the triangle is relatively larger. When a white sheet of paper, held in the hand, is interposed between the eye and the wall, the after-image is seen as though on the paper. In this instance, the size of the after-image shrinks considerably. When the paper is brought very close to the eye, the after-image size is only a fraction of what it was when the triangle was seen on the wall. One may also note, upon moving the paper to and fro, that the perceived size is directly correlated with perceived distance. Furthermore, each perceived size of the after-image corresponds to the perceived size of a suitably selected triangle that may be drawn on the paper, an illustration of what is meant by the ambiguity of retinal-image size in relation to the size of the external object.

Form or shape. Originally, perceived form conforms to the shape of the retinal image. If the image is a square or circle, the original perception is also a square or circle. Generally, the form of the original perception corresponds to the distorted perspective shapes of the image. By regarding the distorted shapes of Figure 1.4 as representations of original perceptions, we obtain an idea as to the way a square might look to the infant when the square has been moved about in various ways or when the infant's viewing position changes. Usually in adult perception, an object retains its form despite the distortion of the retinal image which is correlated with it. This particular fact defines the concept of *shape constancy.* For instance, the perceived shape corresponding to the square moved about in space is a square rather than a trapezoid or irregular quadrilateral. Shape constancy and perceived distance are interrelated, as when we see the square slanting in space. If all sides of the square were to appear equidistant, we would see a distorted shape.[3]

Nativistic Explanation

The explanation of the binocular perception of solidity is related to the explanation of single vision, or the seeing of an object as single although two images are formed in the retinas. Both explanations will be considered from the standpoint of the discoveries of Wheatstone in 1838, the significance he attached to his work, and the subsequent revision in nativistic theory to accommodate his discoveries to the physiological explanation of single vision.

In Wheatstone's time, as Wheatstone himself pointed out, the physiological explanation of single vision involved the concept of "corresponding" or "identical" retinal elements. According to this explanation, a retinal element in the left eye was paired off with an element in the right eye such that the prolongation of their fibers in the optic nerves met at the same place in the brain. A pair of such elements was referred to as "corresponding" or "identical." The correspondence was defined geometrically, the distance between the element and central reference point for one retina being equal to the distance of the paired-off element and central reference point for the other ret-

• •   • •

FIGURE 1.5

ina. The retinal distances were to be measured in the same direction from the reference points. For instance, if the distance for the left eye was measured toward the right in the direction of the nose, the distance for the right eye was measured away from the nose toward the right side of the head. The reference points represented the retinal elements that would receive the stimulation from the point of the external object when the optic axes are converged to that point. When the eyes are thus converged, other points of the object would stimulate corresponding retinal elements. Excitations would be transmitted along paired fibers and would be fused at common termini in the brain, each pair having its unique terminus. According to this explanation, we see the object single because a single "image" is formed in the brain. Other retinal elements were called "noncorresponding" or "disparate" because, when stimulated, a double object was perceived. Thus when we raise a forefinger and fixate some point on a distant wall, we see two forefingers. Wheatstone observed that this explanation presupposed the equality of the horizontal dimensions or "similarity" in the retinal images "projected" by an object. He pointed out that this supposition was only correct when the optic axes are parallel, as in viewing a very distant object, or when the axes are converged in looking at a drawing. In all other instances, the viewing of a sphere being a possible exception, the supposition is false. Nevertheless, we perceive the object as single although the anatomical explanation would predict that parts of it should appear double. Wheatstone further pointed out the important fact that the difference in the horizontal dimensions or "dissimilarity" of the retinal images is an essential condition for the binocular perception of solidity. He justified these conclusions by observations obtained with a stereoscope, a device invented by him.

The two pairs of dots of Figure 1.5, each pair stimulating only one eye, represent a simple version of the drawings Wheatstone inserted in the stereoscope. When the distances between the dots for each of the pairs are properly chosen and the eyes are converged so that "fusion" is obtained, two dots are perceived such that the right hand dot appears more distant than the left hand dot. The theory of correspond-

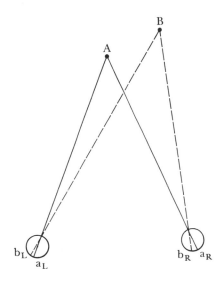

FIGURE 1.6. When the optic axes intersect at point A, a_L and a_R represent the corresponding retinal elements receiving stimulation from A and b_L and b_R, the noncorresponding retinal elements receiving stimulation from point B. According to the first revision subsequent to Wheatstone's discoveries, A would be perceived as single because corresponding elements are stimulated. The eyes move so that point B is fixated, the dotted lines now representing the new positions of the optic axes. Because of the rotation of the eyes, the corresponding elements occupy the previous positions of b_L and b_R. Point B is now perceived as single. The perceptual effect of seeing A as single continues while the optic axes are directed to B so that two points would be perceived simultaneously. The perceived relative distance would be the result of the change in convergence movements in fixating from a near to a more distant point of the object. In the second revision the eyes remain fixated at A. Although B stimulates noncorresponding elements, the difference between the distances $a_R b_R$ and $a_L b_L$, as measured along the arcs, is sufficiently small so that the excitations from those elements would be united into a single impression in the brain. Thus, without movements of the eyes being supposed, two points would be perceived simultaneously such that one appears more distant than the other.

ing points, however, would have led to the prediction that three dots should be perceived because, when the eyes are converged so that the left hand members of the two pairs of dots are perceived as a single dot, the right hand members necessarily stimulate noncorresponding points. Furthermore, two dots in the same plane are perceived when the distances for each of the two pairs are equal because corresponding points would be stimulated, a fact demonstrating the importance of dissimilarity in the two retinal images as a condition for the perception of depth. Depending on the nature of the drawings placed in the stereoscope, one sees convexity or concavity, planes intersecting in depth, and so on, as though an actual object in its three dimensions is being viewed. Since the drawings stimulating the retinas imitate the stimulation produced by viewing actual objects, the disparities in the images are important in perceiving the "real object" in its three dimensions. In other experiments Wheatstone showed that objects may appear double even when corresponding points are stimulated. His general conclusion was that "there is no necessary physiological connection between the corresponding points of the two retinae." Although he did not develop a theory to account for the results of his experiments, he seemed to favor an explanation of single vision and binocular depth in terms of psychological factors which presumably would be affected by past experience in the viewing of objects.

The anatomical explanation nonetheless was not abandoned, and it underwent two revisions to account for Wheatstone's findings (Figure 1.6). (1) The eyes were supposed to be capable of rapid movement so that each point of the object would be fixated successively. A point of the object was defined as the point of intersection of the optic axes. Such a point would stimulate corresponding retinal elements and, as a result, the point is perceived as single. When the eyes turned and another and more distant point was fixated, corresponding retinal elements again would receive stimulation, and so on. The lateral motion of the eyes would be accompanied by appropriate convergence movements such that the optic axes would intersect at points of the object which are at different distances from the eyes. The convergence movements of the eyes were regarded as the important factor in the perception of depth. The survey of all points would be so rapid that the viewer could perceive its three dimensions as though instantaneously. An experimental test, however, discredited this explanation. Depth was still perceived when a diagram in the stereoscope was illuminated by an electric spark; eye-movements could not have occurred during the brief interval of the flash.

(2) It was supposed that excitations of pairs of corresponding elements receiving stimulation would necessarily fuse on being transmitted to common termini in the brain. While the optic axes were and remained fixated or converged on the same point of the object, other points of the object stimulate noncorresponding elements and their excitations would arrive at slightly different places in the brain. Providing the disparity was not too great, physiological "forces" in the brain would combine the paired excitations into a single impression. Such retinal noncorresponding points were called "nearly corresponding points." The conscious concomitant of this unification is the perception of a point at a somewhat different distance relative to the perception of the point stimulating corresponding elements. This revision in contrast to the first did not rely on eye-movements, hence it was not invalidated by the results of the experiment with the electric spark. Although later modified to account for new experimental results the basic idea remained, namely, that innate anatomical structures are responsible for the binocularly perceived three dimensions of a three-dimensional object. This explanation was often cited as an example of the nativistic approach to perception.[4]

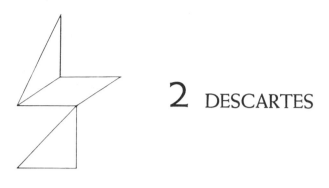

2 DESCARTES

And I have explained in the Dioptrics how all the objects of sight communicate themselves to us only through the fact that they move locally by the intermission of transparent bodies which are between them and us, the little filaments of the optic nerves which are at the back of our eyes, and then the parts of the brain from which these nerves proceed; I explained, I repeat, how they move them in as many diverse ways as the diversities which they cause us to see in things, and that it is not immediately the movements which occur in the eye, but those that occur in the brain which represent these objects to the soul. **Descartes, 1649**

Important contributions in mathematics, physics, physiology, philosophy, and psychology make Descartes a significant figure in the history of modern thought. In standard histories of philosophy and psychology he is described as the "father" of those subjects in the modern period. His conceptualization of what is usually termed the "mind-body problem" is the basis of this influence. The theory of perception set forth by Descartes was the first to examine the facts of perception in detail. The problems inherent in the theory together with various criticisms of it, have influenced the formulation of all major theories of perception from the seventeenth century to the present day.

We may consider in a preliminary way his conception of mind and body as "two distinct substances."

The "mind" was regarded as an unextended "thinking substance" that feels, perceives, thinks, and has sensation. The "unextension" of the mind meant that it is "indivisible" or nonspatial. It cannot be divided into parts; it has no length, width, or breadth, and occupies no space. The body, on the other hand, is extended in the three dimensions of space, is divisible into parts, and cannot feel. Thus the hand, considered as any other object in nature, cannot feel pain when receiving some "action" from the environment. The difference between the two substances is emphasized in Descartes's conception of the functioning of the body as a machine or automaton similar to a clock. The extended clock and its moving parts do not feel pain or pleasure.

The parts of the body relevant to the understanding of Descartes's theory of perception and sensation comprise the organs of sense and the nerves connecting them to the brain, the brain itself, the nerves from the brain to various muscles, and "animal spirits" or nervous fluids. In the center of the brain is a small organ, the pineal gland, which Descartes chose as the place that would receive impressions, or the place where images would be formed, when sensory organs are stimulated. All events up to and including the formation of an image were to be explained by physical laws similar to those governing the motion of planets or the operation of a clock. The gland is also the place where the mind is "located" or "joined to the body." As a result of this union the mind has a "sensation" or "perception of sense" when an image is formed in the pineal gland.[1]

THE MIND AND THE PINEAL GLAND

A prevailing view, opposed by Descartes, maintained that the mind was diffused throughout various parts of the body. The fact that feelings are usually localized in parts of the body, for example, a pain in the finger or the emotion of anger in the chest, was in part responsible for this conception. Since mind was responsible for a feeling, its presence was required in an affected part of the body. If mind did not extend to the finger, we ought not to experience pain in it. But since we obviously do, it followed that mind is present in the finger. Descartes rejected this opinion, citing as evidence the localization of pains and itches in those who have undergone the amputation of a limb. Thus when the arm is amputated, sensation is experienced in those places formerly occupied by fingers. The amputee may feel a pain or an itch in one "finger" or another. Evidence of this kind proved that mind is not present in the particular part of the body in which the feeling is localized in a normal situation. For if the presence of mind were necessary, the amputee ought not to continue to feel pain or an itch as though the limb were still there. On the basis of this and other evidence, Descartes arrived at the conclusion that the mind is in the brain. The selection of the pineal gland as the site of the mind was guided by the following considerations. He observed that all parts of the brain, except for the gland, are double, and that the organs of "external sense" are also double—two eyes, two ears, and so on. Although in looking at a single object two retinal images are formed, we nevertheless perceive *one* object. This proved that the two images are conveyed to the pineal gland, the only single organ in the brain, where they are combined into one brain image.[2]

Having proved the mind is joined to the pineal gland, Descartes referred to the gland as the "seat of the mind" or the "seat of sensation." For this reason, moreover, he said the "mind is in the brain" and the "mind understands, imagines, and perceives in the pineal gland." [3]

The pineal gland is also termed the "common sense." Stimulation of all the senses are conveyed to the gland where they cause "sensations in the mind," and for this reason the gland is referred to as the "common sense." In other words, each sense has no direct connection with the mind. If each sense did, we could not speak of a "common sense," nor could we say that the mind has a specific seat. The gland may be regarded as the central agency which receives sensory impressions from various organs, coordinates them, and sends out other impressions so as to enable the adaptive functioning of the body. Through the impressions the gland receives from stimulation of the visual sense, the mind is enabled to see objects. When an object rapidly approaches the eye, we may close the eyelid or raise an arm in protection by means of impressions from the gland to the appropriate muscles. Or when an object is relatively close to the eye the retinal image is indistinct; however, the shape of the lens changes so that a clear image of it is obtained and the result is that we see the object distinctly. Descartes cited these and many other coordinations, which he regarded as purely reflexive or automatic.

The psychophysical postulate. A significant feature of Descartes's theory of perception is the acceptance of the psychophysical postulate, which generally asserts a one-to-one correlation between the series of sensory perceptions and the corresponding series of brain events in the "seat of sensation." More particularly, however, Descartes asserts that there be as many diversities in the brain image as exist in some percept, and the converse. When the seeing of one object as more distant than another object is the sensory perception, the correlated brain image would then be so diversified so as to represent the number, size, and relative distance of the two perceived objects. Furthermore, whenever these same differences in the brain image recur, the concomitant sensory perception would again have the same diversification.

The postulate was supplemented by another principle, namely, that the cerebral image should possess as many differences as exist in the external objects. Thus the greater physical distance of one object from another object, relative to the viewer, would be correlated with a representation of that distance in the viewer's brain. The application of this principle is to be understood in reference to the machine-like functioning of the body. The stimulation from these objects will automatically produce the corresponding physical effect in the brain irrespective of the fact that the mind is united to the body.

Both the postulate and the principle were subordinate to a more general conception. Sense perceptions, as the consequence of physiological mechanisms, should convey correct information of the characteristics of external objects. Our perception that one object is more distant than another or our perception of "one" object should correspond to the physical relative distance of the two objects or the presence of a single object in space.

The occurrence of such correct perceptions requires a physiologically accurate representation of external objects in the brain. For the mind, limited by its location in the brain, can perceive only in relation to brain events. And if the correlation between such brain events and the characteristics of objects producing them were inaccurate or defective, perceptions would be incorrect. Thus if a single object determined two cerebral images, the consequent perception of a double object would erroneously represent the external fact. But by maintaining that one single image is produced, Descartes could then say that the perception of a single object is correct.[4]

The Formation of Cerebral Images

The physiological counterpart of a sensation, according to Descartes, is a cerebral image in the pineal gland. Stimulation of an external sense leads to its formation through the mediation of nerves. However, it can also have another source. For instance, in imagining how a thing looks, an image of it is formed at the gland. Descartes says that this image has its origin in the previous stimulation of sense and for this reason he calls it a "memory image." Moreover, he makes the interesting point, which we shall develop in the discussion of Malebranche, that the memory image is an "effigy" or copy of the cerebral image derived from sensory stimulation.

Descartes regarded the nerves as hollow tubes through which nervous fluids ("animal spirits") flow. When passing into muscles, they cause them to move in various ways. Moreover, the emission of the fluids at the surface of the gland also causes the mind to have sensation. Their flow, he said, is instigated and regulated by the motion of filaments which each tube contains. The optic nerve has a very large number of such filaments. One end of the nerve originates at an inner surface of the brain near the pineal gland; the other end spreads out to form the retina. The whole length of a filament (which is taut) moves when its end in the retina is stimulated by light. Therefore a motion in the retinal ending induces a similar motion at the opposite end in the brain. The movement of the filament is said to be similar to the motion of one end of a pencil when the opposite end is pushed. Light is regarded as an action of moving pellets which exert pressure on a retinal filament and causes it to move.

The motion in the retinal ending depends on two factors. First, the greater the number of pellets that strike it, the more vigorous the motion. This motion, upon being transmitted to the opposite end of the filament in the brain, causes a vigorous flow of fluid from the gland. And as a result we may have the sensation of a bright light. Second, the pellets from the same light source have a motion which depends on the quality of the source. For instance, the pellets have one kind of motion when the source is "red," and another kind when the source is "blue." The differences in motion cause the retinal endings to move in different ways, which in turn produce corresponding differences in the movement of the nervous fluids; consequently, we have the sensation of a red or blue light.

The retinal image. The "camera obscura" model was adopted by Descartes in discussing the formation of the retinal image. Following Kepler's proof that the image is of the same kind as the picture of the camera obscura, Descartes demonstrated its existence using the eyes of a dead animal and a "newly deceased man." This was important to establish experimentally, for the possibility existed that the image in the eye of a man or animal was not the same as the image in the camera obscura. Descartes explained at length that in the excised eye one could see not only the retinal image but also the "defects" inherent in it as a representation of external objects.

In noting the correspondence between the luminous points composing the external object and the projected points in the retinal image, Descartes observed that the spatial characteristics of the image "resemble" to some degree those of the object. Thus the order of the points in one is preserved in the other, and the shape of the image is similar to the shape of the object. But this resemblance is not exact and, for this reason, he proceeded to point out the "imperfections" or "defects" in the image. These include its reversal, changes in shape and size, curvature, and absence of any representation of relative distance. Another and important "defect" concerns the confusion of the retinal image. When the eye is fixated at one luminous point, only this point will project a clear image-point on the retina, all others projecting "confused" or indistinct image-points. The rays from the fixated point converge to one retinal ending whereas for the other luminous points, the convergence is not exact and as a result a number of endings are stimulated. For this reason, he says, only one point can be perceived clearly at a time.

The cerebral image. Descartes supposed the cerebral image to be the result of two component factors. One component relates to the flow of fluid from the gland as a function only of retinal stimulation. The second component relates to the movement of the eye and the changes in the shape of the lens. The transmission of their effects to the brain not only changes the direction of the flow of fluids but also causes the pineal gland to move. We shall suppose that a cerebral image is formed when the eye and its parts are completely stationary, and we shall first discuss its characteristics in relation to the characteristics of the retinal image.

When Descartes said that the retinal image is "traced out" at the surface of the gland, as he often does, this was merely a shorthand device summarizing the complex details of its physiological transmission. The mode of transmission is such that the defects in the retinal image are reproduced in the cerebral image. The seal-wax metaphor adopted by Descartes for the purpose of explaining the formation of images alone makes this clear. Initially the surface of a piece of wax is unformed or smooth. But when stamped it receives the imprint or impression of the design on the seal. The wax corresponds to the retina, and the seal to the pressures exerted by rays from luminous points. Thus Descartes spoke of "light rays pressing" an image of the object on the retina. The metaphor also applied to the formation or imprinting of the cerebral image, the surface of the gland being conceived as wax and the retinal image as the seal. Just as the defects in a seal are imprinted on wax, so too for the reproduction of the defects of the retinal image in the cerebral image. We may consider the defect of inversion of the retinal image in the same way. When a seal impresses a design on wax both the order and left-right locations of their respective parts are preserved. Since light rays cross inside the eye, the order and orientation of their pressures are the same as that of the impressed retinal image although inverse to the points of the external object. The orientation of the cerebral image then is the same as that of the retinal image and shares the same defect. The formation of a cerebral image did not imply that the surface of the gland should at all be deformed such as takes place in wax when imprinted by the seal, inasmuch as the image was regarded as a collection of motions of nervous fluids passing through the pores of the gland.[5]

The retinal image also consists of a group of motions, those of the retinal elements stimulated by light. These motions have an existence only while the retina is being stimulated by some object so that when the eye is turned to another object the previous image is no longer in existence and the retina is ready to receive a fresh one. The retinal filaments, in other words, move in direct response to the pressure exerted by light. By the time the eye turns to gaze at a new object, the original state of the filaments is restored and the retina can respond with a new set of motions. However, an after-image is an exception. When the sun

FIGURE 2.1. The diagram is a schematic top view for one eye. R and B represent red and blue light sources of such size that only two retinal endings, r_1 and r_2, would be stimulated; f_1r_1 and f_2r_2 represent two filaments of the optic nerve; C represents the inner surface of the brain; H represents the pineal gland, and p_1 and p_2 two pores at its surface. The pressure of light causes the two filaments to move, the motion of their endings at C causing the emission of fluids from the pores in the directions f_1 and f_2. The stimulations of r_1 and r_2 and fluid emissions from p_1 and p_2 respectively represent the retinal and cerebral images of R and B. It should be observed that the orientation of the cerebral image is the same as the orientation of the retinal image, but is reversed in respect to the orientation of the two light sources. (Diagram reconstructed from Descartes's *Man*.)[6]

is gazed at momentarily another object cannot be seen when the eyes are directed to it, instead one continues to "see the sun." Descartes interpreted this fact by saying that the pressure of light on the retina is so strong that the agitation of the filaments continues even when the eyes are turned away.

If the cerebral image, considered as a "copy" of the retinal image, were to be the immediate correlate of a sense perception, this perception would defectively represent the characteristics of external objects. Since this image would not contain the diversity necessary for representing those characteristics, neither could its correlated perception. Descartes postulated a one-to-one relation between a correct perception and its brain image and he wished to provide an explanation of sense perceptions in terms of physiological mechanisms. In order to achieve these goals the cerebral image could not be a copy of the retinal image and Descartes, in probably recognizing this problem, introduced various corrections of the defects or imperfections in the retinal image. The correction of this image implies a corresponding correction in the cerebral image, and this latter corrected image is the one that must be regarded as the immediate correlate of perception.

All the "means" of correction suggested by Descartes are physiological, for they reflect the structure and the machine-like functioning of the body. In this case the "mind" will have correct percepts because the cerebral images, which have the necessary diversity, reproduce the significant characteristics of external objects. The important means discussed by Descartes lie in the motion of the eyes. The physiological effects of this motion, instantaneously conveyed to the brain, cause the pineal gland to move toward or away from the eyes or from side to side. And the motion of the gland so alters the emission of fluids that their pattern has the necessary diversity. For instance, the back and forth motion of the gland is graded according to the distance of objects. This change produces a variation in the cerebral image so that it represents the physical distance and the perceived distance. The factors governing the formation of the image are intrinsic to the physiological functioning of the body. Since in Descartes's theory memory or factors of experience do not contribute to its formation, the theory is an early and first expression of nativistic theory.[7]

What Descartes proposes is most readily understood in relation to his explanation of single vision in terms of physiological mechanism. The retinas, he says, are joined to the inner surface of the brain by two separate optic nerves. Each filament in one nerve is paired off to a filament in the other nerve. Although the endings of a pair of filaments occupy distinct places inside the brain, they regulate the flow of nervous fluid from the same pore. Since all filaments are thus paired off, the two retinal images, upon being transmitted to the brain, determine one cerebral image. We may observe that there is one object in space, a double retinal image, one cerebral image, and the correct percept of a single object. Descartes did not include the two retinal images in his list of defects. If he had done so, his plan of the anatomy and functioning of the nervous system would have naturally led to its correction. The "means" which Descartes did specify, are to be understood in a similar way.

PERCEPTION

Several examples of the correction of the defects in the retinal images will be given in order to illustrate the role of corrective mechanisms, but without indicating their influence in the formation of the cerebral image except for the example pertaining to distance perception. The motion of the pineal gland is described by Descartes only in discussing the monocular and binocular perception of distance. Whether the moving gland is involved in the perception of contour and the perception of situation cannot be decided.

The indistinctness of the retinal image. We have noted that for the stationary eye one point in the image is distinct and that there is the clear perception of only a single point. According to Descartes, the ocular muscles turn the eye "promptly in all directions" so that these muscles "are able to apply it [the eye] successively to all points of the object in an instant, and thus enabling the soul to see them all distinctly one after the other."

Situation. The motion of the eye in fixating the points of an object successively apparently was intended to be the "means" for the correction of image reversal so that we would see an object upright or in its correct "situation." However, the explanation was not developed.

Distance. In monocular viewing the change in the shape of the lens is in proportion to the distance of an object. The nervous effects of such a change when transmitted to the brain cause a change in the position of the gland which is commensurate to the distance of the object. For binocular viewing the disposition of the eyes is inversely correlated with distance. The stimulation originating in the ocular muscles of the two eyes causes the gland to move through a distance proportionate to the external distance. The mental concomitant of shifts in the position of the pineal gland is the perception of one or another distance. However, the cerebral diversity produced by either accommodation or disposition of the eyes has natural limits. For an object at a distance exceeding "5 feet" there is no noticeable change in accommodation, and for an object at a distance greater than "200 feet" the optic axes are practically parallel. Hence objects exceeding the critical limits cannot produce changes in the brain image appropriate to their actual physical distances. For this reason Descartes asserts, in respect to binocular viewing, that the apparent distance of the sun and moon from the earth is about 200 feet. He points out that this limitation explains why they look as small as a "two-foot object" at a distance of 200 feet. Since the perceived distances are equal and since the sizes of the retinal images are the same, the perceived sizes are of equal magnitude.[8]

The means for the correction of the defects in situation and distance, according to Descartes, apply to all other spatial characteristics of objects. For the purpose of illustrating his point, we shall suppose that Figure 1.3 represents the monocular viewing of objects. When the eye successively fixates the points of line A_2B_2, the distance and situation of each point are correctly perceived by means of changes in the accommodation and rotation of the eye so that we perceive the magnitude represented by A_2B_2 rather than the magnitude represented by AB. In a similar manner we can perceive the lines represented by AB and A_1B_1. We observe in these instances how the mechanisms proposed by Descartes may overcome the ambiguous relationship between a given retinal image and the object projecting it.

External Reference

Material, nonfeeling entities such as nerves and other parts of the body, Descartes said, surround the mind which is localized in the pineal gland. Two problems that would seem to arise from this formulation may be considered. When a finger, which is a physical object, is hurt, we feel pain in it; when an object stimulates the retina we see the object at a distance or as external to the body. The latter problem is perhaps more significant because nerves do not extend from the body to the object.

To elucidate and resolve problems of this kind, Descartes concerned himself mainly with pain localization. He supposed that a single nerve originates in the brain and terminates in the fingertip after having passed through various parts of the body, and he further supposed that a hurt to the finger causes a motion in the filament of the nerve and the flow of nervous fluid at the pineal gland. The entire motion along the path, including the flow of fluid, is a physical event. At no point along the path can any feeling be localized, since it is only the mind that feels. But since the mind is at some distance from the injured finger, it would appear utterly impossible to feel a pain in the finger. Nevertheless, Descartes considered it possible to reconcile the "pain in the finger" to the hypothesis of the mind's location in the pineal gland, and he did so in terms of the principles of the "institution of nature" and of the "conservation of body," and the distinction between phenomenal and physical space. Incidentally, the phrasing of this distinction is not Descartes's own.[9]

Said Descartes, "Each movement of the gland seems to have been joined by nature to each one of our thoughts from the beginning of our life." This statement defines what is meant by "institution of nature." In the context of the quotation, "thoughts" refer to sensations, sensory perceptions, and emotions. Particular movements in the gland make us see, hear, or feel pain, and so on. Inasmuch as these motions are caused by stimulation of the senses—Descartes specifically excludes the effect of "custom"—the "institution of nature" has a meaning equivalent to the term "innate." "Thoughts," he also said, are "naturally joined" to the movements. The fact that pain is felt in the hand, in his view, is another example of the institution of nature. The movement in the nerves when a limb is hurt is naturally correlated with the feeling of pain in that limb.[10]

That particular constitution of man prevails, according to Descartes, which enables the avoidance of those objects which cause pain and the seeking of those which produce pleasure. Such actions tend to conserve the body. For instance, on accidentally touching a hot object we immediately retract the hand, rather than continuing contact with it; the prompt and appropriate action prevents further damage. The principle of the "conservation of the body" also suggests the biological advantageousness of pain localization itself. On feeling pain in the hand, the consequent retraction removes the hand from the source of the hurt. On the other hand, if pain were felt at any point in the nerve between the hand and the brain or in some other part of the body the necessary and prompt action might not be undertaken. For if pain were to be felt in the head or in the foot when the finger is hurt, the withdrawal of the hand is not guaranteed. Although Descartes generally assumes that the physical place of the damage to the body usually coincides with the feeling of pain in that particular part, he notes some exceptions. He conceives of an experiment where the nerve connecting the hand with the brain is hurt at some intermediate point; the ensuing pain, according to him, will be felt in the hand rather than at the locus of the damage. He proposes to explain the discrepancy in the following way. A motion in the filament of a nerve, irrespective of its origin along the pathway, always produces the same motion in the gland. Since this motion at the gland is the very motion which, in accordance with an "institution of nature," is responsible for the sensation of pain in the hand, the pain will not be felt at any intermediate point of the nerve.

We may observe, however, an apparent deviation from the principle of the "conservation of body," since the retraction of the hand may not relieve the pain when the hurt takes place at an intermediate point. Descartes, in fact, grants some exceptions to this principle, but he regards them as occurring in unusual circumstances. In any case, he points out that it is more biologically advantageous for pains to be localized in the peripheral parts of the body, for these are the parts most likely to be hurt by objects. Parenthetically, the localization of pain in cases of amputation is explained in similar terms. Thus, when the stump is stimulated it causes the same motion as did the stimulation of the limb when present, and the amputee feels "pain in the hand" although the hand is missing. We may observe that the conservation of body principle is a special case of the "institution of nature." For Descartes says, "nature teaches me that many bodies exist around mine, of which some are to be avoided, and others sought after." Since the teaching is natural, the principle represents an instance of the "institution of nature." [11]

The distinction between phenomenal and physical space is implied in Descartes's report and discussion of a girl who had a diseased right hand which required an amputation at the elbow to prevent further spread of the disease. On the day of the operation the surgeon blindfolded the girl in order to keep her ignorant of the radical treatment that was now necessary. After cutting off the limb at the elbow, he contrived an artificial limb of linen which he bandaged to the girl's arm to minimize subsequent emotional trauma. Thus the girl believed she still possessed a limb after the blindfold was removed. In the few weeks following the operation she reported "various pains, sometimes in one of the fingers of the hand which was cut off, and sometimes in the other."

Let us now suppose, although Descartes himself did not do so, that the surgeon asks her to point to the exact place of the pain. She proceeds to touch the dressing with a finger of the left hand and designates the very place where her aching right hand should have been. The surgeon may at first think that this is rather odd, especially if it is his first encounter with a fact of this kind. He knows that there is no nerve that extends from the arm to the place of pain indicated by the girl. The girl, so to speak, is localizing the pain in empty space. Consequently he may think of denying her experience of "pain in the hand" until he remembers that she does not yet know that the hand is missing, and that before the operation he accepted her report without question. No very good reason presents itself for denying her present experience. The validity of the girl's experience can be preserved by saying that pain is localized in phenomenal space or in the phenomenal hand. But the space she indicates with her left finger is a physical space from the surgeon's standpoint. The patient and surgeon are thus describing two different kinds of space as well as two different kinds of limbs. The distinction applies even when the limb is actually present because feeling could not be in it. Feeling, according to Descartes is always "in the mind." Hence the pain in the normal case also is localized in a phenomenal limb.

In saying that pain is in the mind, Descartes did not mean that the pain would ever be felt in close proximity to the pineal gland, nor even that the pain would be experienced as a mental effect in which the reference to the body is absent. As a physicist he traced the path of motion from the sensory organ to the pineal gland and he noted that since this path represents a sequence of physical events, pain could not be anywhere along this path. At the gland, however, a mental effect occurs which, in this instance, is pain. The pain therefore would be in the mind. This description of the physical events and the correlated "pain in the mind" can be regarded as a scientific description. However, the phenomenal aspect of "pain in the mind" can only be ascertained from the person who feels, and from his standpoint the pain is in the hand. In accepting this report of the person who feels, the hand may be described as "phenomenal." Hence, in the normal case, the phenomenal limb coincides with the physical limb whereas in the case of the amputee, the two limbs and two spaces necessarily cannot coincide since the physical hand is missing.[12]

Visual Sensation

In his analysis of pain localization Descartes said the "same is true of all the other perceptions of our senses."

Consider again the girl whose arm has been amputated. When the nerve endings in the stump are stimulated by pressure, the ensuing sensations are localized in the phenomenal limb. There is a measurable distance between the stump and the indicated place of pain. Similar facts would apply to the sense of sight when an object stimulates the retina. To the perceiver the sensation has a "thereness" in space, or he sees an object in what he regards as external space. We may consider a possible objection to this aspect of Descartes's theory. The sensation of pain is instigated by the direct contact of an external agent, and the pain normally is felt at some place on the surface of the body. The object of sight, on the other hand, is at some measurable distance from the body. The immediate physiological reaction to that object, due to the pressure of light, takes place in the retina. Consequently, by a parity of reasoning, the visual sensation ought to be felt as though in the retina. However, Descartes might reply by first pointing out that the girl localizes pain in the region formerly occupied by her right hand; the pain is not felt in the stump when stimulated. In this instance, one could even say that the pain has an external reference, a localization in apparent space resulting from an "institution of nature." Other senses would have their own institutions of nature. Thus when light stimulates the retina and a motion is transmitted to the pineal gland, the mind would have an externally referred visual sensation. Moreover, the objection ignores the principle of the conservation of the body. Suppose an external object is moving at a rapid velocity in the direction of the head and that it is perceived as though in the retina. Those actions necessary for averting injury to the body will not be undertaken. On the other hand, if the sensation "is related to the external object," injury can be avoided by appropriate reflex movements of the head or body. When on the edge of a cliff one step forward means disaster, hence seeing the edge "there in space" is advantageous to survival. Evidently Descartes regarded external reference as an attribute of visual sensation. Because of the importance of "external reference" in the history of perceptual theory, further aspects of Descartes's theory will be considered.

Descartes distinguishes three ways of "relating" perception or sensation. Having observed that one perception is related to "objects which are outside us," he writes,

> Thus when we see the light of a torch, and hear the sound of a bell, this sound and this light are two different actions which, simply by the fact that they excite two different movements in certain of our nerves, and by these means in the brain, give two different sensations to the soul, which sensations we relate to the subjects which we suppose to be their causes in such a way that we think we see the torch itself and hear the bell. . . .

Another perception such as pain or hunger "we relate to our body" as though "in our members," and not as though "in objects which are outside us." Still another perception "we relate only to the soul" as though "in the soul itself." The feeling of joy or anger exemplifies this type of referral. The first two perceptions concern a physical entity of some sort: torch, bell, or part of the body. A perception, which is "in the mind," corresponds to this entity, such as the torch "we think we see." But there is no clue whatever in the perception itself which betrays its subjectivity; the torch we see is a torch there in physical space. From the scientific or philosophical standpoint, however, the seen torch is subjective because it is "in the mind." But from the perceiver's standpoint, on the other hand, there is no subjectivity to the percept. The third percept is quite different. The relating of joy to the soul or self is so experienced by the owner of the feeling and is, from his standpoint, subjective. However, it is also subjective in a scientific or philosophical sense.

The manner of relating these perceptions is innate, for it reflects an "institution of nature." Movements in the brain as caused by the stimulation of one or another sense have as their direct conscious concomitants specific modes of referred sensation. These movements also determine differences in the qualities of sensation, whether of pain, color, or sound, and so on. Moreover, the stimulation of each sense produces a sensation unique to that sense irrespective of the way in which the sensory organ is stimulated. For instance, Descartes points out that when the eyes are closed and we press against an eye with a finger we see light and color but when a finger is inserted in an ear, the pressure causes us to hear sounds. By the same token the visual perception of distance and other visual perceptions are also to be understood in terms of an institution of nature. For those movements in the fluids or gland which are caused by stimulation of the retina and motion of the eye directly give rise to those perceptions.[13]

Finally, a natural correlation between perception and behavior already indicated in the principle of the conservation of body is presupposed by Descartes. When a friend suddenly thrusts his hand toward us, he says, our eyes automatically blink even though he intends no harm. The "spirits" at the pineal gland cause us to see his hand but they simultaneously flow to the muscles of the eyes, causing the lids to close. Similarly a dog on "seeing" a bird naturally runs to it. Descartes points out that natural correlations may be modified by custom or training; for instance, the dog can be trained to stop on seeing the bird.[14]

SEEING AND JUDGING

Descartes develops the distinction between seeing and judging in terms of several examples. For instance, two ships of different size when viewed from a distance will "appear equal in size" providing that the smaller ship is appropriately closer than the larger one. The perceived equality in size also means that they are perceived at the same distance. Knowledge of their difference in shape or color, however, enables us to "judge" their relative distance. For emphasis he points out that distance so judged is "not properly seeing." The phenomenal distance of the ships, in other words, is not affected by judgment.

This distinction is the basis of Descartes's exposition of the errors or "deceptions" of sense, for all the examples enumerated by him involve an error in the judgment of the characteristics of external things based on appearance. The "ancient" beliefs that the sun is larger than a star and that the sun and moon are of equal size, he points out, are instances of this type of error. He expounds on these errors so that, in guarding ourselves against supposing "external things always are as they appear to be," we may appreciate the importance of reasoning as the source of true judgments. Thus, the reasoning of astronomers shows the ancient beliefs to be false and demonstrates the truth of other conclusions. The example of the ships, of course, also indicates the unreliability of appearance. In this instance, however, the correctness of judged distance is not completely assured. The larger of the two ships may in fact resemble another and smaller ship in shape and color. Thus when the two ships appear to be of the same size we cannot make any certain inference in respect to distance; the two ships may be of the same size and at the same distance or they may be unequal in size and at different distances. Although we may have other information at our disposal, the judgment of distance has a probable character.

The "reasoning" of interest to Descartes is that which leads to certain conclusions as in mathematics. However, this consideration is not relevant to the previous point that perceptions are "correct," nor does it deny the possibility of some degree of agreement between the appearance of external things and the things themselves. For the "correctness" or agreement is regarded from the standpoint of behavior, enabling us to act so that pleasure is secured and pain avoided. The inferences that we do make thus have only a practical significance. For instance, when we see one object this percept is correct in the sense that our action in relation to it is appropriate. To be sure, in normal circumstances a single external object corresponds, but the judgment of the correctness of the percept is still practical. Thus Descartes points out that pressing one side of an eye causes us to see double. Although we are aware of the pressure in this experiment, it nevertheless serves to show us that the single appearance may possibly be deceptive in other circumstances.

A "deception" of sense has two aspects, a phenomenal fact or appearance and a judgment about a thing on the basis of the appearance. Descartes questions only the validity of the judgment; in his theory an appearance, a fact of consciousness, could never be questioned. When the girl whose hand has been amputated believes she possesses her hand upon feeling pain, she renders an erroneous judgment since the hand is missing. But the feeling of pain as though it were in the hand remains indisputable. And similarly for those events in which we see objects in a dream with the same vividness as when the objects are present. Thus he points out that if we did not distinguish between the dream and the waking state we would make false judgments about the presence of objects which mysteriously enter and depart from our room at night. In another example he says the person who hallucinates is often in this very predicament for he believes that objects in the environment are responsible for what are actually imagined voices and things.[15]

NATURAL GEOMETRY

Thus far Descartes's explanation of perception has been developed in terms of cerebral mechanism or the mechanical principles governing the operation of the body. Although for Descartes the mind was essential to perception, he regarded the mind as "passive" in respect to the events at the pineal gland. The mind merely has perception or sensation without the intervention of any special intellectual activity or operation such as reasoning. With one notable exception, this seems to be the point of view which Descartes expressed in various works beginning with his text on physiology, the *Treatise on Man,* written before 1635 but published posthumously in 1664 (its publication was suppressed by him), and the *Passions of the Soul* which was published in 1649 shortly before his death. However, "natural geometry," another "means" for correction of defects in the retinal image which Descartes had suggested, is a contradiction.

In the "geometric" explanation of perceived distance he attributed to the "mind" the ability of knowing the interocular distance and the size of the angles formed by the optic axes and the line joining the two eyes, and the ability of computing the distance of the point of intersection of the axes. He regarded this process as similar to the "reasoning" of surveyors who determine the location of an inaccessible point by means of triangulation.

For the purpose of visualizing what he said concerning the perception of "situation" we can refer to Figure 1.3. He attributed to the mind the ability of "transferring its attention" to all points along the lines *aA* and *bB* and their prolongations to "infinity." In relation to this posited ability he concluded, "objects can be seen in their true position notwithstanding the reversal of the picture imprinted in the eye." The explanation of single vision was similar: "when both our eyes are disposed in the same manner which is required in order to direct our attention toward one and the same location, they need only cause us to see a single object there, even though a picture of it is formed in each of our eyes."

In Descartes's explanations of similar facts which we have previously described, eye-movements, and the cerebral effects they caused, were regarded as sufficient for correcting the defects of retinal images. And this would also be the case for single vision, inasmuch as the proper disposition or convergence of the eyes was an essential condition to the formation of a single cerebral image. Although eye-movements also are invoked in the new explanation for seeing distance and for seeing an object single, they merely enable natural geometry to become operative; for instance, the movements could not be responsible for the reasoning process. It is analogous to a person who, although ignorant of the principles of geometry, can measure the base angles and included side of a triangle but is unable to compute the distance of the apex. In any case, since natural geometry is an "innate geometry," the "reasoning" or the "paying of attention" is not learned and sense perceptions could still be regarded as innate although the acts of mind are involved in their determination.

Natural geometry gives rise to other problems. External reference, seeing an object to be "without us," does not readily fall under the scope of natural geometry any more than does the "hearing of a bell." Descartes cited the change in the shape of the lens as a factor in the "seeing of distance" but its interpretation from the geometric standpoint, which he did not discuss, is not readily apparent. He had said that lower animals "see" objects which, if "see" is taken literally, would imply that they have abilities similar to human beings; but he regarded animals as incapable of reasoning of any kind.[16]

GASSENDI'S CRITIQUE

The unextended mind Descartes had said was joined to the extended body at the pineal gland and he also had said that the cerebral image, an extended entity, caused sensations in the mind. Descartes's contemporary, Gassendi, inquired into the nature of this relationship and developed two contrasting alternatives each of which he believed would be unpalatable to Descartes. But Descartes in his reply dismissed Gassendi's contentions with a brief counter-argument. (Gassendi's arguments and alternatives will be developed in reference to Figure 2.1.)

The mind is extended. Let us regard p_1 and p_2 and their separation as the cerebral image. Since the two parts in this image produce separable sensations, the mind is divisible into parts. Moreover, the separateness of the sensations means that the mind is extended, an extension which corresponds to the separation between the parts of the image. Since the form of a cerebral image comprises a spatial distribution of parts, the mind is shaped because sensations have a similar distribution. Moreover, the left-right relation of the two parts is reproduced in the mind and, as a consequence, a particular sensation may be to the left of another. "An idea," Gassendi concludes, "appears not to lack extension utterly." In his opinion the mind must be extended since it receives the "semblance of a body" (cerebral image) which is extended. Evidently Gassendi's argument is guided by the seal-wax metaphor, the image corresponding to the seal and the mind to the wax. We may observe that this argument supposes that sensations are simultaneous events, for if the mind attended to but one sensation at a given moment—such as might be represented by p_1—the argument is no longer valid. The next alternative, however, shows that the assumption of simultaneity is not essential.

The mind is a mathematical point. Gassendi anticipated a possible way out for Descartes from the consequences and conclusion of the previous alternative. It may be supposed that the seat of sensation is a "point," such as might be represented by pore p_1. In accordance with this assumption, all nerves converge to this point and stimulation in each nerve causes the emission of fluid from it. Since there is only one pore, there is but one sensation; hence the assumption of an unextended and indivisible mind seems to be immune from criticism. But this "point," Gassendi continues, must be a "physical point." Since such a point has extension, the same difficulty as in the previous alternative repeats itself. The pore, although very small, has a certain width and also has parts which compose its circumference. Therefore the sensation has extension and parts. However tiny the pore might be, it must still have some extension. Consequently it is necessary to suppose that the point is a "mathematical entity." Since this entity has no dimension the assumption of an unextended mind is saved although the mind is confined to a single dimensionless sensation at a given moment. Gassendi replies to this possibility by rejecting the assumption of the seat of sensation as a mathematical point as a "useless fiction." Nerves, he says, are material entities and not mathematical lines. Moreover, anatomical considerations prove that nerves do not converge to a single physical point.

At the basis of Gassendi's line of reasoning is the assumption that the characteristics of sensation and cerebral image are co-extensive. If the image has extension, there must be extension in the sensation (and mind); if the sensation has no extension, the image must be a mathematical point. The critique apparently did not trouble Descartes. In saying that "the mind is not extended," he wrote in reply, "my intention was not thereby to explain what mind is, but merely to proclaim that those people are wrong who think that it is extended." Obviously for Descartes the perception of extension or form did not require an extended or shaped mind.[17]

ROHAULT FRONTISPIECE

In the preface of his work which deals mainly with physics, Rohault stated that of the eminent philosophers whose names he credited at various places for their assistance, he omitted mentioning Descartes as the philosopher most helpful to him in order to avoid "perpetual repetition." His theory of perception closely follows Descartes's, both in examples and explanations.

The purpose of the diagram was to illustrate single vision; and its explanation was undertaken in order to refute two opinions of the period concerning the "principal organ of vision," and to demonstrate that some part of the brain was this organ. "Principal organ of vision" had the meaning of the place where visual sensations were excited by impressions. One opinion, according to Rohault, supposed that the retina was the principal organ, which he rejected because we should "always see the object double, when we look at it with both eyes at the same time." Another opinion held that the place "where the optic nerves met" was the principal organ. This was rejected because, as he said, anatomists had discovered that the two nerves were separated in some dead human bodies they had examined, yet when they were alive, "they saw things in the same manner as others do."

Rohault noted that the two impressions made on an external sensory organ "most probably" met in "one particular place in the brain" because we have "but one sensation only." He points out the difficulty in determining whether the pineal gland or some other part of the brain is the place where the impressions are united. The X in the diagram, not necessarily the gland, denotes the part of the brain which is the "immediate organ of vision" and where the two impressions combine into a single impression. Although it is not yet known, he says, "it is reasonable to think" that the number of filaments in the optic nerve of one eye is equal to the number of filaments in the optic nerve of the other eye. The ends of these filaments in the retina of each eye are arranged "regularly" on either side of the point of reference E for one eye, and K for the other eye. E and K, he continues, "are exactly at the ends of the optic axes, that is, at the extremities of the lines TE, VK. . . ." The filaments in the optic nerves are arranged in "corresponding" or "sympathetic" pairs so that the filaments of each pair are united at their point of origin in X. Having "supposed all this," he continues,

> I conceive that when we wish to look at an object, we turn our eyes to it in such a way, that the two optic axes meet at the point at which we principally direct our attention. Thus this point, acting by means of the lines [rays] TE and VK on the corresponding filaments E and K, form two impressions there, which are again joined together in only a single point,

namely, point Q. Similarly the part of the object which is at its right, shakes the corresponding filaments D and I, the impressions of which pass on to P. And again similarly, the part of the object which is at its left, acts on the corresponding filaments F and L, and their impressions reunite at the point R, and so for the others.

Rohault goes on to say that the points O, P, Q, R, and S, which exemplify a "material image" in the brain, excite a corresponding number of sensations in the "soul" at the same time. These sensations, according to him, compose a "spiritual" or "incorporeal" image and, in relation to this image, we see the object as single. Furthermore, when the optic axes are fixated at one point of a particular object, an object beyond this point will stimulate noncorresponding filaments. Since their impressions do not reunite in the brain, we see the remote object as double.

We may observe that the orientations of the brain image and external object are reversed. Rohault did not discuss this point, hence whether he would have considered this a problem in the explanation of the formation of the incorporeal image is not known. Nevertheless, having said that the number of sensations of the incorporeal image is equal to the number of points in the material brain image, he might have supposed that the order of sensations would correspond to the order of the points in the brain image. In which case points O and S would excite sensations in the mind so that their left-right order would correspond directly to the order of the points in the image but inversely to the order of the points in the object. In any case Rohault concerned himself only with the reversed orientations of retinal image and object in his explanation of "seeing the object in its true situation." His explanation was similar to Descartes's except for the substitution of the relating of "sensation" arising from an "impression" on the lower part of the retina to an upper point of the object for "transferral of attention." [18]

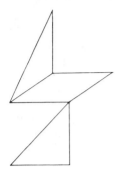

3 MALEBRANCHE

We see all things in God.   Malebranche, 1674

Malebranche, a philosopher and secular priest, wrote extensively on the "nature of sensations" and general facts of perception as outlined in the chapter on Descartes. His decade of study of these and related topics was inspired by Descartes's text on physiology, and culminated in *The Search After Truth*. This work in its first edition of 1674 and in subsequent editions became the important link between Descartes's and Berkeley's theories of perception. A basic goal in Malebranche's theory concerns the acquisition and discovery of truths about the nature of things. Malebranche said that the "notices of external things" supplied by the senses generally were regarded as a significant source of truths about things and he set out to contradict this popular view by demonstrating in many ways that the senses were "completely useless for the discovery of truth." He selected the visual sense and emphasized its errors because in the common belief this sense was regarded as the "noblest" of all senses. Therefore, to "destroy the authority" of this sense as a source of truth would imply a "general distrust of all the other senses." He then proceeded to show that the sense of sight was usually erroneous in representing the spatial characteristics of magnitude, figure, and motion of objects, but always erroneous in the attribution of light and color to objects. Since the senses were "false witnesses," the truth could only be attained through reason and faith in God. Although his discussion of error and its correction is generally similar to Descartes's, we shall later observe a significant deviation.

Malebranche's theory is set in the general framework of Descartes's philosophy and physiology. The unextended mind substance has its "principal residence" in a circumscribed part of the brain although not necessarily the pineal gland. The body is a machine and its nervous functioning consists in motions of nervous filaments and fluids; the motions or agitation of the retinal endings and nerves in other parts of the optical apparatus are conveyed to the inner brain, where they are again reproduced. The psychophysical postulate, the principle that there be as many diversities in the cerebral image as exist in external objects, and the principle of the conservation of the body are accepted. Moreover, he follows Descartes in the enumeration of defects in the retinal image and of their correction through eye-movements and other means. Malebranche's theory, however, is more detailed in the description of visual facts though not from the standpoint of a further delineation of cerebral mechanisms. But in contrast to Descartes, Malebranche introduced the concept of *natural judgments* and maintained that the explanation of all perceptual facts involved these judgments. Since the discussion of natural judgment is intricately embedded in a metaphysical and theological context, we shall first present several aspects of his theory by supposing its exclusion. In this way we may understand Malebranche's approach to sensation and phenomenal facts, notwithstanding a possibly obscure comprehension of the operation of natural judgment.

EXTERNAL REFERENCE

The concepts of "sensible qualities" and "modifications of the soul" provide a convenient approach in the understanding of Malebranche's opinion concerning external reference.

Sensible qualities. Color is defined as "that which one sees on looking at this paper, that is to say its apparent brightness." Color or light includes hues such as green or blue and also shades of gray. The "sensation of color" thus defined is a sensible quality. Tastes, smells, sounds, and pains are likewise sensible qualities. These qualities, Malebranche says, as other philosophers before him had said, are not descriptive of physical objects because they do not inhere in them. How can it be proved, he asks, that sensible qualities are not in the objects? He supposes, for the sake of argument, that the qualities are indeed in the objects and he examines the implications of this supposition; in finding them to be false, the supposition is declared to be false. In bright light objects have vivid hues; in dim light they may have no hues at all. If hues are in the objects there can be no variation in their appearance. When a man immerses one hand in hot water and the other in cold water and subsequently touches the same object with both hands, the object feels cool to one hand and warm to the other. The rare case of an individual is cited who saw yellow when viewing an object with one eye and green or blue when viewing it with the other eye. Since an object cannot possess contradictory characteristics at the same time, neither hot and cold nor color are in the object. And similarly, "salt is savory to the tongue and pricking and smarting to a wound." Stimulation of different senses by the same object does not produce the same sensation, hence the qualities of savoriness and pain are not in the object.

Malebranche cites other examples in support of his conclusion. For instance, a needle produces a sensation of pain when it pricks the finger, but there is no pain in the needle itself. A sensation of color has exactly the same status as that of pain although, in his opinion, not everyone understands the one as readily as the other. Malebranche expends considerable effort in order to make this example clear to the ordinary person because he has "prejudices" which incline him to believe otherwise. In looking at a paper, the ordinary person says that he sees its whiteness "spread" over the paper, the whiteness being regarded by him as coincident with the rectangularity of the paper. But according to Malebranche, he is completely "deceived," for the whiteness is a "sensation in the soul" and not in the paper.[1]

Modification of the soul. According to Malebranche, sensible qualities are only "modifications of the soul" since it has been proved that they could not be in objects nor modifications of objects. We may observe that Malebranche seems to be in agreement with Descartes if "modification of the soul" is interpreted as a mental effect. For instance, Descartes said that the feeling of pain was a "thought" and not in a limb. However, Malebranche's doctrine of modification has an additional meaning. Where Descartes regarded the pain "in the mind" as descriptive of a scientific fact, Malebranche supposed pain to be felt there. Or, at least, that is where the pain ought to be felt if a natural judgment did not intervene. What has been said of pain is true of all other sensible qualities. Therefore in the theory of Malebranche a visual sensation would not have the attribute of external reference. That color ought to be felt in the mind is borne out in his discussion of "passions." He said, "The feelings of love and hate, joy and sorrow, are not referred to the objects of those feelings. They are felt in the soul, and there they are. They are, then, good witnesses for they speak the truth." Since color also is a "sensation *in* the soul" it ought to be related to the soul in the same way as is a feeling. However, the color sensation is not a "good witness" since actually we perceive color as belonging to an object. For the purpose of exposition, a color sensation or any other sensation when considered as a mental state equivalent to passion will be referred to as a *mind-localized* sensation.[2]

In dealing with a controversy of the period Malebranche wrote:

> And a man would be laughed at among some Cartesians, that should affirm the soul grows actually *blue, red, yellow,* and that she is dyed with all colors of the rainbow, when she contemplates it. There are many who doubt, and more that don't believe, that the soul becomes formally *stinking* upon the smell of carrion, and that the taste of sugar, pepper, and salt, are properties belonging to her.

Sensible qualities, as modifications of the soul, characterize the soul itself. The soul becomes colored when external objects are seen, or it stinks when a carcass is smelled. Returning to a previous example the soul is white rather than the paper. And in being white one really ought to perceive the whiteness there.[3]

Natural Judgment

The basic principle of explanation of external reference, as well as other visual facts, is natural judgment. The source of the natural judgment is God. God instantaneously "excites" it in the soul when we open our eyes and look at objects or when any other sense receives stimulation. God produces natural judgments in the mind by reacting to the cerebral "vibrations" or "disturbances" which are conveyed to the "seat of sensation," and also joins them to sensation. To the cerebral excitation aroused by stimulation of the retina, the color sensation is joined to a natural judgment so that we see colors on external objects. To another cerebral excitation resulting from a hurt to the finger, the sensation of pain is accompanied by a natural judgment so that pain is localized in the finger. Natural judgment, Malebranche also says, is "confused" with sensation so that the soul cannot distinguish between them. Furthermore, as the result of this confusion the "soul herself" is inclined to attribute the source of judgment to sensory factors but this attribution is false. Sensation is a sensory event because it is "only peculiar to the senses" whereas the judgment is nonsensory because its origin is God.

Malebranche's prolonged discussion of natural judgment and explanation of the referral of sensation to object is too complicated for a brief and accurate description. Nevertheless, the critical importance of natural judgments is apparent, since without them color, pain, and other sensations, would be mind-localized. We shall select for discussion a problem and its resolution, as stated by Malebranche, because of its historical interest.

Because pain is localized in the finger when pricked by a needle and warmth is felt in the hand when not too distant from a fire, Malebranche was led to consider why we ordinarily do not feel or judge colors to be inside the eye. He realized that although in each instance the nerves in the sensory organ are "vibrated," the mental effects are diverse. By way of explanation he cited our sensibility or insensibility of the vibrations as a factor. For instance, our general insensibility of vibrations either in the retina or optic nerve was said to be important in the externalization of color.

Said Malebranche, "Because we are insensible of any vibrations caused by visible objects in the optic nerve, which is in the bottom of the eye, we think this nerve is not vibrated at all, nor covered with the colors that we see. On the contrary, we judge these colors are spread only on the surface of the external objects." He undertook an experimental demonstration of his thesis that colors are spread over the retina. An eye was removed from an animal and when he looked at the back part of this eye under proper conditions, he saw the "colors of objects . . . spread upon the bottom of the eye although depicted there in reverse." On the basis of this result he concluded, "we ought to judge or feel colors in the bottom of our eyes in the same way as we judge that warmth is in our hands." In order to account for the "spreading of colors" over objects, he considered a candle which was placed at such a distance that it produced "feeble" sensations of light and color. These sensations, he says, "so little concern the soul that she judges they do not belong to her, nor that they may be inside her self, nor even in her own body, but only in objects." For this reason he said, "we unclothe the light and colors in our soul and in our own eyes for the sake of adorning outside objects with them." On the other hand, when sensation is relatively strong, as in looking at a candle close to the eyes, "the soul judges that the light is not only in the candle but also in the eyes." What Malebranche seems to mean is this. The distant candle, for instance, produces a weak excitation which gives rise not only to a feeble sensation but also the right sort of natural judgment joined to it so that color is seen on the candle.[4]

OTHER VISUAL FACTS

Judgments of divine origin are essential for making us see distance, size, and so on. To each percept there must correspond some difference in the cerebral image, for otherwise the appropriate natural judgment cannot be elicited. "God," says Malebranche, "can only act in our soul to make us see objects on the occasion of images traced out in our eyes and changes which take place in the body." If there is no alteration in the sensory organs, he also notes, there can not be any change in "our sensations." [5] God, in other words, can only act on the mind insofar as there is some change in the body mechanism. The diversification of the cerebral image is brought about by changes either in binocular or monocular viewing, the size of the retinal image, and other factors to be indicated below.

Distance

In binocular viewing the triangle formed by the eyes and a point in the object where the "two rays" (sides) meet is one of the surest means "we have for judging the distance of objects which are not too far away." When the angle of the optic axes is large the object is seen as close but when small the object is seen as very distant. Monocular viewing is said to be inferior to binocular viewing for the seeing of distance because one side and one base angle of the triangle are missing. In this instance "the soul cannot make use of her natural geometry for judging the distance" of the object. He suggests that the reader try the experiment of inserting a stick sideways through a ring which is turned endwise with one eye open and then with both eyes open, and discover for himself that the task is impossible in monocular viewing but simple in binocular viewing. The "disposition of the eyes" in fixating a point on the object, he says, is one of the "best and universal means" for judging distance.

In speaking of judgment, Malebranche did not mean that the mind itself does the judging, inasmuch as the judgment is a "natural judgment." A particular disposition of the eyes elicits the natural judgment appropriate for seeing the particular distance of the object. Another disposition of the eyes will make us see another distance through mediation of still another natural judgment. However, the disposition of the eyes is the same when they are directed at clouds or at very distant objects, such as the sun and moon. Since in this case the means for the elicitation of the natural judgment are not available, we "see the sun and moon" as though in the clouds.[6]

Size

Having pointed out in a discussion of size constancy that the height of the retinal image doubles when an approaching man moves from a ten to a five-foot distance, Malebranche continues: "But because the impression of distance decreases in the same proportion as the other increases, I see him always of the same stature." The natural correlation between perceived distance and perceived size is presupposed since "impression" relates to physiological mechanism. The muscular change of the disposition of the eyes produces a change in the brain which causes the man to be seen as approaching. But this change in the brain at the same time so compensates for the other change in the brain, which originates in the increase of retinal image size, that the man is perceived as constant in size. In another example, he supposes the retinal image size of a "child" at a distance of ten feet is the same as that of a "giant" at a distance of thirty feet. The perceived size of the giant, Malebranche says, is three times that of the child. It is obvious to him that the size of the images could not be the factor causing the difference in perceived size because the images in themselves could not cause the necessary differential change in the state of the brain. Thus he concludes that there must be other variable factors which would cause changes in the brain so as to account for the difference in perceived size. One such factor is the cerebral change arising from the disposition of the eyes in looking at the child and then at the giant.[7]

Malebranche's explanation of the moon illusion also supposes the natural correlation of perceived distance and perceived size. The retinal image of the horizontal moon, he says, is accompanied by images of terrestrial objects lying between the viewer and the moon, whereas this is not the case for the retinal image of the zenith moon. The presence of other retinal images causes us to see the horizontal moon as somewhat more distant than the zenith moon. As a consequence of the increase in perceived distance, the moon is also seen larger. Malebranche further comments that a man believes that he merely sees the horizontal moon as larger, "without thinking there is any judgment in his sensation." But it is "indubitable," he continues, that without natural judgment he "would see it smaller." And should this be the case, both moons would be perceived at the same distance. Malebranche cites personal observation and experiment in support of his explanation of the illusion. In viewing a distant steeple from behind a wall so as to intercept the view of intermediate objects, the steeple appeared to him "both as little and at no great distance." When viewed away from the wall, the distance being the same, the image size of the steeple was the same. But in this instance the steeple appeared to him to be more distant and larger. The images of intervening houses and fields, therefore, were responsible for this perception of distance and size. Malebranche blackened a piece of glass with a candle flame to such a degree that, when held before the eyes and the flame looked at, the glass only obscured the perception of objects about the flame. Malebranche then viewed the rising sun with the smoked glass held close to his eyes, and he reported that the sun appeared closer and smaller. But when he again viewed the sun without the glass, the intervening objects were seen distinctly and as a consequence the sun appeared more distant and larger.

Régis, a contemporary of Malebranche, explained the illusion by supposing that the differential refraction of light rays would cause the retinal-image size of the horizontal moon to be greater than that of the zenith moon; the perceived size, therefore, would correspond to the image size. This explanation was set in opposition to the explanation advanced by Malebranche, who replied with an extensive critique and further justification of his explanation. He pointed out that the assumption of differential refraction led to self-contradictions and that, in any case, astronomers had proved that the image size of the horizontal moon is in fact slightly smaller.

We may observe, however, that Malebranche and Régis agree in respect to the basic assumption that perceived size is a function only of retinal-image size, providing that the natural judgment Malebranche presumed to exist did not intervene.[8]

Solidity

The retinal image of a cube, says Malebranche, is similar to a cube "painted in perspective." Consequently, "the sensation we have of it ought to represent the faces of the cube unequal, since they are unequal for a cube in perspective." But a natural judgment supervenes and as a consequence we "see them all equal."

This judgment presupposes the natural correlation of perceived distance and perceived size. Thus, the vertical edges of an oblique face project unequal retinal-image lengths. The difference in the perceived distance of the edges would so compensate for the inequality in image length that they would be perceived to be equal in size. Malebranche's explanation also presupposes that without any natural judgment the sides of the cube would be perceived as though depicted on a flat surface.[9]

Visual Direction

Malebranche concerns himself with the interpretation of what today is referred to as a "pressure phosphene." When the left side of an eye is pressed with a finger, both eyes being closed, light will be perceived on the right side. The apparent direction of the light-sensation is opposite to the feeling of pressure exerted on the eyeball. The problem as probably understood by Malebranche may be stated as follows. We know that the finger is responsible for both the felt pressure and the sensation of light. Thus if one believes that the sensation or "pressure phosphene" should be experienced on the same side where the finger presses the eye, then it becomes necessary to explain why the effect is opposite. Malebranche explains the phenomenon thus:

> The pressure of your finger on the left side produces the same effect on your eye as a luminous body on the right whose rays were to pass the pupil and the transparent part of the eye would produce. . . . Thus, God makes you experience the light on the side on which you see it because He always follows the laws which He has established in order to keep His procedure perfectly uniform. . . .

God in this example refers to a natural judgment. Pressure on one side, whether produced by light or by the finger, causes us to see the light on the side opposite. This is what Malebranche means by uniformity. If God's procedure were not uniform we might see the light on the left side when the finger presses on the left side of the eye, and on the right side when light rays produce pressure at the left side.[10]

In discussing the moon illusion, natural judgment being absent, it is evident that Malebranche presupposed the constancy hypothesis, as was also the case in the description of the "sensation" of the cube. If Malebranche had offered descriptions of the sensational counterparts of those other percepts which involved distance, the constancy hypothesis would have been the basis for them. Thus, without natural judgment the perception of distance would be impossible. Therefore, as a man approaches we would see him grow larger in size. Moreover, without God the pressure phosphene would be sensed on the same side as the finger pressing against the eye. These and other consequences were evident when Malebranche stated the special assumptions necessary to explain seeing on the premise that the natural judgments appropriate to given percepts are excluded.

"I open my eyes in the middle of a field," he says, "and in that instant, I see an infinity of objects, some more distinctly than others, and all quite different either in their shapes, or in their colors, or in their distances, or in their motions, etc. I see among others about a hundred feet from me a large white horse galloping to the right." The following (paraphrased) assumption would have to be made by the viewer if God were to be excluded in the explanation of those perceptions: that the viewer has an exact knowledge of physiology, optics, geometry, and the ability to perform an infinite number of reasonings in an instant.

Having stated this basic assumption, Malebranche proceeded to delineate a number of further assumptions to explain "seeing only a single object," namely, the horse galloping to the right. A few of these assumptions will be stated in an abbreviated form: (1) The viewer must know that light rays, reflected from the unknown object (horse), travel in straight lines and that they are refracted by the lens of the eye to form an image on the retina. (2) The viewer must know that the image is reversed on the retina, and that the retina is a concave surface. Knowledge is also necessary of the fact that two lines, which represent light rays, will intersect inside the eye. In this way the viewer knows that a stimulated point on the right side of the retina represents a point to the left. (3) From the retinal images of the horse and other objects, the viewer is able to deduce the distance of the horse. (4) The viewer's awareness that it is a big horse hinges on knowledge of the physical distance, size of the retinal image, diameter of the eyes, and a certain theorem from Euclidean geometry. (5) In order to "see that it is white," Malebranche essentially states that the viewer must be familiar with Cartesian physiology.[11]

These are some of the assumptions that must be made to explain the perception of a "large white horse galloping to the right." Other reasonings and judgments are necessary, Malebranche adds, in order to explain the larger number of objects that can be seen at the same time. In his view, the necessary reasonings and judgments are performed by God. We may ask a question which Malebranche himself did not ask. What would a person see without a God to perform the reasonings and computations? The first four assumptions imply that the horse would be seen upside down, at no distance, and of a size corresponding to the size of the retinal image. Assumption 5 implies that the soul rather than the horse will be perceived as white. The person does not have the knowledge of physiology that would lead him to suppose that a cerebral image is formed when the retina is stimulated. Since he has no knowledge of the body whatever, he merely feels the whiteness as a modification of the soul. Since in fact the viewer cannot perform these reasonings and form the necessary judgments, Malebranche concluded, "Only God can give us the various perceptions we have of objects." Or also, "We see all things in God." Natural judgments therefore represent the infinite reasonings and knowledge of God in having perceived cerebral images. God unites the judgments with sensations in our mind, thus causing us to perceive as we do.

The role of natural judgment cannot be tested experimentally. Although we may suppose that observation of the infant might provide the opportunity for such a test, it is impossible because the soul is already united to the body at the time of birth. And insofar as the infant is physiologically mature, the "vibrations" or stimulation of certain nerves will instantaneously elicit the appropriate natural judgment. Consequently, he may feel pain as though in the hand and he may see whiteness or color as though in an external object. Moreover, the infant would not have any awareness of the role of judgment. Therefore in later life, even on the premise of perfect recollection, there can be no consciousness of judgment. Nor could the adult himself have any awareness of a natural judgment in his present experience. Although he may be able to deduce the involvement of judgment, it is nevertheless not a fact of consciousness. The action of natural judgment is automatic and instantaneous, and operates outside the level of awareness. Therefore in Malebranche's theory visual perceptions are, in the main, innate. But this does not mean that judgment is given once and for all by God at or before birth; if such were the case, his continuing presence would be unnecessary. On the contrary, his constant intervention is required in every act of seeing throughout life. For only God can perceive the brain images and perform the infinite number of reasonings.

Acquired Percepts

Malebranche's theory allows for the influence of experience in the modification of percepts. Although only a few examples are provided, they give some relevant insights into his over-all theory of perception. The context of the discussion of the influence of experience concerns the physiological basis of memory and an exposition of the psychophysical postulate. As Descartes had already indicated before him, a cerebral image leaves behind a replica or "memory image." Malebranche, in using this notion, also refers to it as a "vestige" or "trace." He observes that some people see a "face in the moon": "two eyes, a nose, and a mouth." The large number of times that the human face has been seen, he says, is responsible for this perceptual fact. The frequent and attentive viewings of the face leave "traces of it deeply imprinted in the brain." In looking at the moon, the cerebral image which it evokes meets with the "opposition" of the memory image of the face. The latter image, in being deeply imprinted or embedded, sidetracks the flow of some of the "animal spirits" from the cerebral image. As a consequence of the merging of the parts of the cerebral and memory images, a face in the moon is seen rather than just "irregular blotches."

Malebranche also introduces the degree of "resemblance" between the cerebral image of the moon and the trace of the human face as a factor facilitating the arousal of this particular trace rather than any other trace. The "apparent magnitude" of the moon does not much differ from that of an average head placed at the right distance and, in respect to this particular characteristic, the impressions in the brain of the image of the moon and the trace of the head are similar. Moreover, the nose, mouth, and eyes as represented in the trace have connections among them which correspond to parts of the image. He further observes that the strength of a memory image depends on idiosyncratic factors so that not everyone may see a face in the moon. Others may even see a "man on horseback." Malebranche also explains by means of interaction of trace and image the fact that some people see various animals in cloud formations even though there is "little resemblance" between the shapes of the clouds and the animals.[12]

We may observe here Malebranche's adherence to the principle that a given percept and its characteristics must have corresponding representations in brain mechanism, although in these instances the mechanism comprises a combination of cerebral and memory images. Furthermore, the effects of experience would be quite limited since the modification of a percept is mediated by a trace. The trace could not possess any characteristics not already contained in the cerebral image of which it is a replica. Thus, if a person were to look at the moon without ever having perceived human faces, it would be impossible for him to perceive a "face in the moon." For a similar reason it would have been theoretically impossible for Malebranche to uphold the view that the perception of distance is acquired. If the cerebral image does not have a representation of distance, its trace likewise not having any such representation, the possibility for the acquisition of the perception of distance is nonexistent.

MIND AND BODY

The invocation of divine intervention for explaining the mundane facts of seeing objects was essential to Malebranche, his conceptualization of mind and body being the reason for it. Descartes had sup-

the feeling is in the mind, the place where the pain would be felt if the judgment did not intervene. The girl's belief that she still has her hand, he says, constitutes a second erroneous judgment. And similarly for visual facts such as external reference.[14]

The acceptance of the psychophysical postulate is an important common feature in the theories of Descartes and Malebranche. Although the latter expresses the postulate by including God in the relationship of mind to body, it nevertheless is equivalent to Descartes's version. And it is in the delineation of cerebral mechanism that their nativistic approach can be understood. The advent of empiristic theory, on the other hand, was accompanied by a loss of interest in the detailed description of the physiological correlates of either original or acquired perceptions. In emphasizing "psychological" factors, it was quite natural to ignore physiology. It was not until the nineteenth century, in the empiristic theory of Bain, that the physiological basis of perception was again treated in any detail.

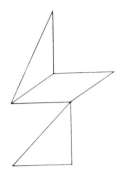

4 LOCKE AND MOLYNEUX

When we set before our eyes a round globe . . . it is certain that the idea thereby imprinted on our mind is of a flat circle. . . .
Locke, 1690

Locke's *An Essay Concerning Human Understanding* (1690), principally concerned with philosophical questions, opposes the "received doctrine, that men have native ideas, and original characters, stamped upon their minds in their very first being." This doctrine supposed innate principles and innate memory images to be the basis of knowledge and morality. In Locke's contrary view, the original state of the mind is conceived as a *tabula rasa:* "a white paper, void of all characters, without any ideas." Locke then asks a few questions and provides a simple answer. "How comes it to be furnished? Whence comes it by that vast store which the busy and boundless fancy of man has painted on it with an almost endless variety? Whence has it all the *materials* of reason and knowledge? To this I answer, in one word, from EXPERIENCE." In his theory ideas enter the mind primarily through stimulation of the external senses and also through faculties of the mind such as memory and judgment.

Stimulation of a sense elicits "motions" in the nerves which upon being conveyed to the seat of sensation immediately excite "ideas in the mind." Such ideas are called "simple" or also "ideas received by sensation" and they include space, color, sound, taste, and so on. In general, "sensation" refers to the physical events terminating in the seat of sensation, and occasionally to a psychic fact or idea. However, the context of sensation decides the meaning intended. The ideas derived from sensory stimulation are "stored" in memory to be subsequently revived by the mind. The idea of memory is regarded as a copy of the corresponding idea of sense except for the fact that it is fainter. For instance, the remembered idea of a sound is not as vigorous as the sound we hear when the ear is stimulated. The faculty of "the judgment" pertains to the ability of the mind to compare ideas received through sense or through memory and to discern differences and similarities among them. Through such operations as comparing or judging, the faculty of judgment can create new ideas. The reception of these ideas is what Locke means by experience. However, the simple ideas are the basic materials of knowledge for without them the mind is a clean slate and, therefore, the ideas of memory and the formation of new ideas impossible. Since, according to Locke, all knowledge must come to the mind through ideas received by sensation, the notion of innate ideas is false.

We may observe that Locke's theory, as a theory of knowledge, implies no necessary commitment to an empiristic approach to visual perception. A simple idea, depending on its definition, could include distance or any other characteristic as an original perception of sight. And indeed this seems to be the position generally adopted by Locke in the *Essay* except for the attribute of solidity. It is in the clear and decisively stated assumption that the simple idea is bi-dimensional, and in the suggested explanation of the acquisition of solidity that Locke makes his single most important contribution to the history of theories of perception. His discussion, occupying but a few pages, is the common thread serving to unite all empiristic theories that were subsequently elaborated. Locke's influence, however, also includes the notion of "resemblance" and the Molyneux problem, which generally pertain to a theory of knowledge but which we shall discuss only insofar as they are relevant to perceptual theory.

SOLIDITY

Locke's critique of Malebranche's "opinion of seeing all things in God" provides insight into Locke's theory concerning the perception of solidity which Locke expressed in the *Essay*. He states the Malebranche thesis that sensation is a modification of the soul or mind whereas *idea* is perceived in God, and he advances a number of reasons which in his opinion render the appeal to deity superfluous in the explanation of visual perception. He finds the distinction between sensation and idea quite vague and questions the very notion of modification. Moreover, if sensation is presumed to be a modification of the mind, he can find no cogent reason for not so regarding idea. "When we see and smell a violet," says Locke, "we perceive the figure, colour, and scent of that flower." But he fails to see where Malebranche stipulates a "rule" that enables him to assert that the color and smell of the violet are sensations in the soul whereas the shape of the violet is an idea in God. If the figure, color, and scent are regarded as ideas then Malebranche should say "as I see the figure of violet in God; so also I see the colour of it, and smell the scent of it in God." But Locke observes that Malebranche does not allow this "absurdity," for he says that the figure of the violet only is in God and not its color and smell. Locke then finds "no reason why the action of one of our senses is applied only to God, when we use them all as well as our eyes in receiving ideas." On the other hand, "If the figure, colour, and smell are all of them 'sentiments,' then they are none of them in God, and so this whole business of seeing in God is out of doors." * Thus, according to Locke, all the senses are on the same footing. If God is not necessary to explain one sense, there is no compelling necessity for his intercession in explaining some other sense. "I think the perception we have of bodies at a distance from ours," claims Locke, "may be accounted for, as far as we are capable of understanding, by the motion of particles of matter coming from them and striking on our organs." The motions excited in the organs are transmitted to the seat of sensation where they "produce ideas in our minds." But he concedes that he cannot explain or understand how motions in the brain can cause ideas. He, therefore, supposes that God, "whose ways are past finding out," is

* In this context, *sentiment* has the meaning of sensation, and figure has the meaning of *idea* or perceived form.

necessary for their explanation. God as the "original cause" has "appointed" the motions in the brain to be the cause of the ideas. Evidently Locke does not suppose the active presence of God as the causal agent of either ideas or sensations. Thus when looking at a series of objects in succession, according to Locke, our different perceptions are directly caused by "motions" in the brain. Therefore, Locke can conclude that color and form are produced "in our minds" as a simultaneous unitary event and that Malebranche's separation of them, one being in the mind and the other in God, is an unnecessary hypothesis.

We may observe that Locke, in having supposed perceived form to be in the mind, must cope with the problem of an extended mind. He argues that Malebranche himself may have had the same problem even in his conception of modification. Locke says that he has the simultaneous sensations of white and black in looking at a paper, of hearing someone singing, of the warmth of a fire, and so on. The mind that perceives, "one immaterial indivisible substance," apparently requires subdivision into the "distinct parts" corresponding to the sensations. In any case the hypothesis of an extended mind is not uncongenial to Locke, "I shall here only take notice how inconceivable it is to me, that a spiritual, *i.e.* an unextended substance, should represent to the mind an extended figure, *v.g.* a triangle of unequal sides, or two triangles of different magnitudes." In the *Essay*, however, as will be observed subsequently, Locke inclines to the acceptance of the hypothesis of the unextended mind in explaining the perception of solidity.[1]

The rejection of natural judgment, inasmuch as its origin is in God, is the logical implication of Locke's critique. Although not made explicit, the intention is clear in the further objections to Malebranche. It is this rejection, moreover, which forms the basis for Locke's empiristic approach.

In contesting an interpretation conferred by Malebranche on the change in the apparent size of objects when viewed through a magnifying glass, Locke thinks this fact

> . . . would persuade one that we see the figures and magnitudes of things rather in the bottom of our eyes than in God: the idea we have of them and their grandeur being still proportioned to the bigness of the area, on the bottom of our eyes, that is affected by the rays which paint the image there; and we may be said to see the picture in the retina, as, when it is pricked, we are truly said to feel the pain in our finger.[2]

Although Locke seems to suggest that the retina is the experienced locus of the "seen retinal picture," we shall stress the assumption that the "pictures" or "ideas" are "proportioned" to the corresponding retinal images. For instance, since the third dimension is absent in the image, it would also be absent in the idea. Furthermore, in quoting and opposing Malebranche's opinion that "we see all its sides equal" in looking at a cube, he asserts this is a "mistake." The "true idea" of the cube is quite different from the present idea, the former serving to "excite" the latter through "custom." But the "true idea" is the same as the sensation of the cube in perspective hypothesized by Malebranche.

Evidently, Locke's opinion of the true idea of the cube as a flat object with unequal sides was arrived at by the rejection of natural judgment as a causal factor in perception. Moreover, we may observe that custom is substituted for natural judgment and the "seeing of all things in God" is exchanged for the seeing of the retinal pictures. We turn to Locke's *Essay* for the further elucidation of the original and acquired ideas of a solid object. Says Locke:

> We are further to consider concerning perception, that the ideas we receive by sensation are often, in grown people, altered by the judgment, without our taking notice of it. When we set before our eyes a round globe of any uniform colour, v.g. gold, alabaster, or jet, it is certain that the idea thereby imprinted on our mind is of a flat circle, variously shadowed, with several degrees of light and brightness coming to our eyes. But we having, by use, been accustomed to perceive what kind of appearance convex bodies are wont to make in us; what alterations are made in the reflections of light by the difference of the sensible figures of bodies; —the judgment presently, by an habitual custom, alters the appearances into their causes. So that from that which is truly variety of shadow or colour, collecting the figure, it makes it pass for a mark of figure, and frames to itself the perception of a convex figure and an uniform colour; when the idea we receive from thence is only a plane variously coloured, as is evident in painting.[3]

The substance of Locke's explanation of perceived convexity is contained and implied in the quotation since in the sections that follow Locke explains why adults do not notice the flat appearance. We may first comment that the "idea imprinted on the mind" represents the "true idea" in Locke's previous discussion of the cube and that the "judgment" can create the new idea corresponding to the acquired perception of convexity or figure.

Its acquisition, supplying some detail of our own, may be conceived as follows. When the globe (ball) is used or handled by the child, he observes a variation in its distribution of light and shade, though still presenting a flat circular appearance. He learns that it is one and the same object which causes the variation and also, that this object is convex. In such ways he may acquire the idea of convexity which, in representing the actual dimensional characteristics of the objective cause, is responsible for the alteration of the original appearance. Concurrently, moreover, he also learns that each original appearance is the "mark," "sign," or "token" of the acquired idea. The child has so many opportunities to exercise and establish the habit that the idea of convexity is "excited" by the "token" automatically. Thus whatever may be the viewing position of the globe, the specific token corresponding to it nevertheless arouses the perception of convexity. In asserting that the "idea received by sensation is altered by judgment" Locke, in effect, supposes that the idea formed by the judgment is substituted for the other idea. The same considerations apply to the cube so that the child learns to see it as a solid object of intersecting planar surfaces with all edges of the same length.

Locke proposes two reasons to explain why the original appearance is not noticed. One reason lies in the strength of the habit established through "frequent experience" which is "performed so constantly and quick" that only the "idea formed by our judgment" is noticed. This is especially true, according to Locke, for those habits acquired in early life. By way of example he notes, "How frequently do we, in a day, cover our eyes with our eyelids, without perceiving that we are at all in the dark!" Presumably, in early life there would have been an awareness of periods of intermittent darkness.

The assumption of mind as a special substance distinct from the body is the basis for the second reason. Thus he says, "Nor need we wonder that this is done with so little notice, if we consider how quick the actions of the mind are performed. For, as itself is thought to take up no space, to have no extension; so its actions seem to require no time, but many of them seem to be crowded into an instant." Actions of the body extend over time and, therefore, are successive. Now if the actions of the mind are similarly successive, the apparent implication is that the idea of sense ought to be noticed since it precedes the idea of judgment. But the simultaneity of their actions precludes this implication. By way of evidence he points out that we may see all the parts of a mathematical demonstration "with one glance." Yet a long time may be necessary in putting it into words and explaining it step by step to another person. Thus just as the intermediate steps are not noticed in the first glance, so for the steps antecedent to the perception of convexity. Locke, however, fails to explain why the instantaneity of the actions of the mind confers the advantage to the acquired perception rather than to the original bi-dimensional appearance. In any case these are some of the reasons which explain the non-noticing of the idea of sense and which justify the general conclusion that the judged idea is "apt to be mistaken for a direct perception." Incidentally, Leibniz wrote an extensive commentary on Locke's *Essay* and disagreed with many of its basic premises, but assented to the over-all discussion of the globe in saying "nothing is truer." [4]

The painting of an object is the only reason advanced to justify the certainty that the original appearance of a globe is a flat colored circle, but Locke does not explain how it is relevant. However, if he thought that the original appearance of the painted depiction of a globe is necessarily flat, he would have presupposed the point at issue. Hence, it would seem that the decisive factor is the assumption that the idea originally imprinted in the mind by the physical globe corresponds to the bi-dimensional spatial characteristics of the retinal image, as he intimated in his critique of Malebranche. Thus the globe and its painting, in producing similar retinal impressions, are both originally perceived as flat.

We may further consider the implication of Locke's view that the cerebral motions in the seat of sensation, rather than the retinal imprint, are the immediate cause of the idea received by sensation. It ought to be the case that the cerebral imprint should be bi-dimensional because this is the entity interposed between retinal image and idea. Although the phrase "idea imprinted in the mind is of a flat circle" already suggests such a possibility, Locke's metaphors are somewhat more decisive. In the *tabula rasa* conception of the mind the slate is clean; before experience nothing is yet stamped or marked on it. Since the first inlet of the markings is through the senses, they are inscribed on a flat surface. Locke refers to the "understanding" as a "dark room" which is "not much unlike a closet wholly shut from light." Light enters the chamber through the senses. He considers the "pictures" formed on the wall opposite the apertures (the senses). If the pictures but stayed on the wall, he says, "it would very much resemble the understanding of a man, in reference to all objects of sight, and the ideas of them." Thus since the wall is flat, so are the pictures. In effect, he is supposing the pictures to be the ideas received through the sense of sight. And if the rear wall is regarded as the seat of sensation, the cerebral images are necessarily flat.[5]

It should be observed that since the globe and cube are the prototypes of all three-dimensional objects, Locke supposes that the world of objects is originally perceived as outline forms of light and color in a plane. Furthermore, it should be observed that the development of his theory is guided by the constancy hypothesis and by the supposition that the "true ideas" are altered by operations of the mind. Finally, his explanation implies that the "operations" are always present in the perception of solidity because the original idea imprinted in the mind is regarded as a necessary condition for exciting the idea of the judgment. The fact that the judged idea has been previously formed through learning is not critical, since the presence of the original idea as a "token" is still required. The language at the beginning of the long quotation, stating that the original idea and its alteration are not noticed by "grown people," in itself conveys this implication; the very fact that the idea is not noticed means that it is present.

An important and unanswered question in Locke's explanation concerns the ability of the mind to create new ideas. The simple idea of the globe or cube, whatever the viewing position, is bi-dimensional, and the idea of it in memory is also bi-dimensional. The way in which the mind could form the idea of convexity from these materials is not apparent. Locke, we may add, did not appeal to the "sense of touch" as others were to do subsequently.

RESEMBLANCE

In the discussion of the concept of "resemblance" Locke points out that motions from "external objects" so affect the senses as to cause other motions in the nerves which, in continuing to the seat of sensation, produce in the mind those ideas which we have of objects. The topic of interest concerns the relationship of idea to the object corresponding to it. He distinguishes between the primary and secondary qualities of the characteristics of objects. The primary qualities which include shape, size, and number are, he says, "in the things themselves, whether they are perceived or not." But when they are perceived, the ideas are "resemblances" of them. For purpose of illustration we may consider the globe and cube, and the acquired visual ideas of them. Their respective perceived contours are a circle and a set of connected straight lines; moreover, the perceived surfaces are respectively convex and intersecting planes. When at the same distance their perceived sizes, depending on actual size, may be approximately the same or quite different. Since there are two objects, a corresponding number of ideas are produced in the mind. In each instance the ideas resemble the qualities of the objects. Locke maintains that the ideas of these same primary qualities are also perceivable through the sense of touch; therefore, the concept of resemblance applies equally to the ideas derived through touch and the qualities. He further maintains that there is a "common idea" between the ideas perceivable through sight and touch.

The ideas of secondary qualities are the "sensible qualities" we have already discussed in the Malebranche chapter, Locke himself using the same phrase. Such ideas as color and pain are also produced by stimulation of sense but they have "no resemblance" to the corresponding qualities in the objects. He uses a line of argumentation similar to that of Malebranche, including similar examples, to contradict the common belief that sensible qualities characterize both the idea and the object. The same fire at one distance produces the "sensation of warmth" and at a closer distance, the "far different sensation of pain." Neither sensation, therefore, is "actually in the fire." The fact that one hand may feel warm and the other hand cold when both are immersed in the same water serves as a further justification for this conclusion. Such opposite ideas, however, are not produced by primary qualities. Thus on feeling the same "figure" we do not get the "idea of a globe" with one hand and the "idea of a square" with the other. The presence of a sensitive organism or intact sensory organs is required for the appreciation of secondary qualities. Thus a person blind from birth cannot have color sensation nor can he form any conception of it. If he is asked what color is, upon having described color sensation to him, he may very well say that it is like the "sound of a trumpet." On the other hand, if given the opportunity to feel a statue, he can form some conception as to what the sighted individual sees. This is possible because the extension of the statue as a primary quality is "really" in the object and is thus perceivable through another sense.

The distinction between primary and secondary qualities and the concepts of "resemblance" and "common idea" had already been discussed and accepted by many philosophers before Locke. Moreover, Locke, in discussing "qualities" and "resemblance," did not indicate whether the idea obtained through the visual sense was to be regarded as a simple idea or as an acquired idea. It seems, obvious, however, that "acquired idea" was intended. For if the globe and cube were originally perceived as flat, there would be no resemblance between ideas and the third dimension of objects.[6]

MOLYNEUX'S PROBLEM

At the suggestion of his friend Molyneux, Locke published a letter received from the former, traditionally known as Molyneux's problem, in a revised edition of the *Essay*. The problem, together with Molyneux's negative answer and Locke's concurrence in it, was inserted into the text in a section immediately following the long quotation pertaining to the original appearance of the globe.

> 'Suppose a man *born* blind, and now adult, and taught by his *touch* to distinguish between a cube and a sphere of the same metal, and nighly of the same bigness, so as to tell, when he felt one and the other, which is the cube, which the sphere. Suppose then the cube and sphere placed on a table, and the blind man be made to see: *query*, whether *by his sight, before he touched them* he could now distinguish and tell which is the globe, which the cube?' To which the acute and judicious proposer answers, 'Not. For, though he has obtained the experience of how a globe, how a cube affects his touch, yet he has not yet obtained the experience, that what affects his touch so or so, must affect his sight so or so; or that a protuberant angle in the cube, that pressed his hand unequally, shall appear to his eye as it does in the cube'.—I agree with this thinking gentleman . . . in his answer to this problem; and am of opinion that the blind man, at first sight, would not be able with certainty to say which was the globe, and which the cube, whilst he only saw them; though he could unerringly name them by his touch, and certainly distinguish them by the difference of their figures felt.[7]

Both Locke and Molyneux presuppose that the resighted man must have the opportunity of simultaneously seeing and feeling the objects so that he can later distinguish them on the basis of sight alone. More important for our purpose is the further supposition that he would at first see both objects as flat. This is implied by Molyneux when he says that the resighted man "has not yet obtained the experience . . . that a protuberant angle in the cube, that pressed his hand unequally, shall appear to his eye as it does in the cube." The immediate context of the letter in the *Essay* indicates that Locke surely would maintain that the man, on first seeing, would perceive the globe and cube as contoured flat surfaces in the plane of the table top. Thus he would merely see a circular contour and, depending on the position of the cube, a square contour. Since the third dimension which he had felt is absent in his new ideas received through the visual sense, it may well be impossible for him to identify the objects with "certainty."

Their contemporary Synge, who contested the negative answer, supposes the man while blind can form two distinct ideas of the objects arising from their felt differences. The globe is perfectly smooth and the man, in running his hand over it, feels no interruptions in its parts. The cube, on the other hand, has sharp breaks in its otherwise smooth surfaces. In passing his hand over it, he successively feels an edge, the point of an angle, and so on. The two tactual ideas he has formed correspond to the characteristics of the objects. In recovering his sight and in merely looking at them, he sees that the globe is "alike on all sides" whereas the cube is "not alike in all parts of its superficies." Thus he is able to form, according to Synge, two distinct visual notions. Since these notions are "agreeable" only to the tactual ideas corresponding to them, Synge concludes that "by his sight alone he might be able to know, which was the globe, and which the cube." His argument obviously presupposes the "agreement" or similarity between visual notions and tactual ideas, thus insuring the possibility of correct visual identification. The ambiguity in Synge's solution is such, however, that it may be interpreted as supposing the original perception of the objects in their three dimensions. And if this be so, it could be the basis for the opposite answers to the Molyneux problem by Synge and by Molyneux and Locke.

The correspondence of Molyneux and Locke, posthumously published in 1706, includes the solution proposed by Synge and their opinion about it. Molyneux writes to Locke, "You will find thereby, that what I say, of its puzzling some ingenious men, is true: and you will easily discover by what false steps this gentleman is led into error." Locke in turn concurs in his reply, but they fail to correct or indicate Synge's "false steps." [8] Thus we do not know whether the difference in assumption toward the original perceptions of sight is in fact the basis for the disagreement of the protagonists. In any case, the history of the controversy concerning the problem shows that the Synge solution could be the basis for a positive answer even on the assumption that the original ideas of sight are bi-dimensional.

Leibniz in his critique of Locke's *Essay* proposes a solution to the query with an affirmative answer. He removes Locke's restriction that the man know the objects "at first sight" on the grounds that he might be "dazzled and confused by the novelty" and he stipulates that the man be instructed that the globe and cube are the cause of his visual "appearances." In other respects, however, his solution is similar to that of Synge. Leibniz, on the other hand, explicitly supposes that the man's first clear visual perceptions are bi-dimensional. For when he explains the reason for the "instruction" he says that without it the man could think that his appearances "might come from a flat picture upon the table." Apparently for Leibniz, given his conditions, the "appearances" of circular and square contours may provide sufficient information for the correct visual identification of the objects. [9]

MOLYNEUX

In 1692 Molyneux published the first text on optics in the English language, *Dioptrika Nova,* which is important for its influence in the development of Berkeley's theory of perception either through acceptance or protest of its ideas pertaining to visual perception. Molyneux advanced an assumption, well known in his period, which here will be associated with his name and labeled *Molyneux's Premise* by virtue of its subsequent general significance in the evolution of empiristic theory. It states:

> For *distance* of it self, is not to be perceived; for 'tis a line (or a length) presented to our eye with its end toward us, which must therefore be only a *point,* and that is *invisible.*

The geometrical part of the premise can be visualized by referring to Figure 4.1. Point L denotes an external luminous point source, R the retinal element stimulated by L, RL a line directed endwise to the eye.

FIGURE 4.1

In actuality RL represents a ray of light but discussion is considerably simplified by regarding the line and all points as mathematical entities, as supposed by Molyneux. Any point on RL, L' for instance, projects the same point R. Therefore, longitudinal distance is not represented in the particular element R. Moreover, there is no representation of relative distance on the retina since the lengths RL and RL' collapse to the same point R. From such retinal considerations Molyneux draws the conclusion, the essential aspect of the premise, that distance is "invisible" or not "perceivable." The content of the premise is similar to the result of the following experiment in which the subject is blindfolded. Force is exerted at one end of a rigid rod by someone else, the other end touching the forearm. The pressure will be felt locally and obviously not related to the opposite end. Moreover, the length of the rod cannot be judged on the basis of the feeling of pressure. Molyneux himself supposed, of course metaphorically, that a light ray is a "stick" delivering an impulse to the retina.[10]

We may consider whether the premise implies the localization of sensation in the retina since, at one point, Molyneux says that the representation of an object painted on the retina is "there perceived by the *sensitive soul*." However, somewhat later this implication is retracted—" 'tis not properly the eye that *sees*, it is only the organ or instrument, 'tis the *soul* that *sees* by means of the eye." In any case, we may observe that the premise exemplifies the constancy hypothesis. And when each retinal element is considered from the standpoint of the premise, solidity as an attribute of sensation is denied.

Molyneux stated the premise for the purpose of showing the importance of "natural" and "acquired" means in the perception of distance. He considered two cases in the discussion of the first "means," the objects being relatively close. In binocular viewing, he said, "their distance is perceived by the turn of the eyes, or by the angle of the optic axes." In respect to monocular viewing the external object was regarded as a point luminous souce. The rays of light diverging from this source, he noted, form angles with the plane of the pupil. And when the source is somewhat more distant those angles increase in size. The "visual faculty," according to him, can appreciate the differences in angles and thus "apprehend" the distances of the light source. In respect to the second "means," he supposed the importance of acts of judgment "acquired by exercise." These include the faintness of colors and knowledge of magnitudes as the "*chief* means of apprehending the distance of objects." [11]

Another point of interest concerning Molyneux's opinion about perception is the explanation of the erect appearance of objects which attributed to the mind a natural ability of "hunting back" along each ray of light from the point of retinal stimulation to the corresponding point of the object. Since the rays cross inside the eye, the object is seen erect. Further, single vision was explained similarly—the mind "hunting" along each of the two optic axes to their point of intersection.[12]

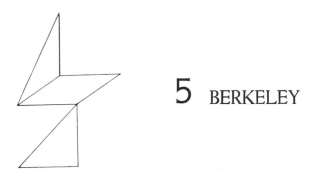

5 BERKELEY

I say, neither distance nor things placed at a distance are themselves, or their ideas, truly perceived by sight. Berkeley, 1709

Berkeley's *Essay Towards a New Theory of Vision* was "one of the most brilliant psychological works which has ever been written," said Höffding in his history of philosophy of 1894. Many other philosophers before and after have expressed a similar opinion. The *Essay* published in 1709 developed an empiristic theory of visual perception which came to dominate all discussions of the subject at least through the end of the nineteenth century, achieving widespread acceptance among philosophers, psychologists, and physiologists. The degree of acceptance of the theory, which was to be called "Berkeley's New Theory of Vision" or "Berkeleyan theory," apparently was nearly universal among philosophies in 1842, for in that year J. S. Mill, a proponent of the theory, said:

> The doctrine concerning the original and derivative functions of the
> sense of sight, which, from the name of its author, is known as Berkeley's

71

"Theory of Vision," has remained, almost from its first promulgation, one of the least disputed doctrines in the most disputed and most disputable of all sciences,—the science of man. This is the more remarkable, as no doctrine in mental philosophy is more at variance with first appearances, more contradictory to the natural prejudices of mankind. Yet this apparent paradox was no sooner published, than it took its place, almost without contestation, among established opinions: the warfare which has since distracted the world of metaphysics has swept past this insulated position without disturbing it. . . .

Berkeley defined the purpose of his investigation at the beginning of the *Essay* thus, "My design is to show the manner wherein we perceive by sight the distance, magnitude, and situation of objects: also to consider the difference there is between the ideas of sight and touch, and whether there be any idea common to both senses."

The execution of the "design" was shaped by arguments against the accepted or "received" doctrines of "natural geometry," "resemblance," "common idea," and also by arguments against the possibility of a positive answer to the Molyneux problem. These arguments, except for the one pertaining to natural geometry, essentially deal with various epistemological issues and are developed for the purpose of refuting Locke. This particular phase of Berkeley's theory is conspicuous in the late sections of the *Essay*. Natural geometry and the objections to it, which are expressed in the sections dealing with the perception of distance, magnitude, and situation, are directed to Descartes and Molyneux. Still another argument, and one which pervades the *Essay*, pertains to demonstrating the importance of the "sense of touch" in visual perception.

My tripartite discussion of Berkeley's theory generally follows his "design." However, common terms and concepts are defined in the section "distance and magnitude" although applicable to other aspects of the theory; his various arguments concerning natural geometry are summarized in this section. This section concludes with a discussion of "further points in Berkeley's explanation." It may seem odd that what may be regarded as a summary of the principal points of Berkeley's theory should follow "distance and magnitude" rather than the final section of the "design." Some of the reasons for the separation are given in the section "situation." Berkeley's investigation of the ideas of sight and touch are discussed under the heading "form" for emphasis, because the apparent disavowal of an original perception of form is what is significant for a theory of vision. The original perception of form ("visible figure") was assumed by Berkeley in discussing the perception of distance, magnitude, and situation. The chapter ends with the "Cheselden Case" which was thought by Berkeley and others to represent an experimental verification of the theory.

DISTANCE AND MAGNITUDE

In the critique of "natural" or "innate" geometry Berkeley pointed out that we ought to be conscious of the "means," such as lines and angles, which had been posited in the "geometric" explanation of perception. By way of refutation he stipulated the "evident" criterion that "no idea which is not itself perceived can be to me the means of perceiving any other idea." He illustrated the criterion by noting, "We often see shame or fear in the looks of a man, by perceiving the changes of countenance to red or pale." The emotions, however, are not directly perceived by sight because they are "in the mind" of that man and hence "invisible," only the "redness or paleness" being directly perceived. But if the redness or paleness were not perceived, the indirect perception of the emotions would be impossible. The changes in color are clearly intended to correspond to the means presupposed in natural geometry. In opposition Berkeley argued emphatically throughout the *Essay* that no one is or ever can be conscious of the means and as a result the geometric explanation of distance and other perceptions is invalid. For instance, he says, "Everyone is himself the best judge of what he perceives, and what not. In vain shall any man tell me, that I perceive certain lines and angles, which introduce into my mind the various ideas of distance, so long as I myself am conscious of no such thing." [1] In this passage Berkeley seems to restrict the criterion to his own personal consciousness but in other discussion it is evident that he was referring to the consciousness of any one, for the geometric means are of a universal character. This appeal to consciousness is adapted to the many problems discussed in the *Essay*. In dealing with the problem of upright vision, he quoted Molyneux's explanation *in extenso* and rejected it, since consciousness of "impulses, decussations, and directions of the rays of light" is supposed. Moreover, the explanations of perceived distance advanced by the "celebrated Descartes" and by Molyneux, involving the perception of either the angle of the optic axes or the angles of light rays at the pupil, are rejected for the same reason. He further observed that these means could only have been introduced by "mathematicians and opticians," who then unwittingly suppose that others have the same knowledge of mathematics and optics they possess. For a point of emphasis Berkeley indicates that "brutes," "children," and "idiots" perceive as well as those who have studied optics and geometry. Obviously, this type of personal knowledge is irrelevant for understanding the processes involved in visual perception.[2]

In thus combating the "received doctrine," Berkeley eliminated the traditional "means" for correcting the defects in retinal images. This in itself is an important contribution to the subject for it clearly establishes the point that percepts are to be explained only in relation to events taking place in the organism beginning with stimulation of the retina. Rays of light and their intersection are extrinsic physical events and they cannot be included in a physiological or psychological explanation of perception. The intersection is at some distance from the retina and for this reason alone it has no explanatory significance whatever. Its existence is surmised only by the student of optics and, further, it does not even have a counterpart in retinal stimulation. The stimulating effects of light rays on the retina produce other physical events which, of course, are physiological. However, there is no phenomenal light in the retina nor is there any phenomenal direction. Thus the hypothesis that the mind could trace an impulse on the retina along some ray or line to its source in the external object is meaningless. Moreover, any "reasoning" presupposing the psychic existence of those rays necessarily must be excluded as a cause of a percept since in fact they are nonperceivable. The important problem with which Berkeley himself must cope lies in the formulation of an alternative to natural geometry for the correction of defects in retinal images, the starting point of the visual process.

Berkeley did not consider physiological events in the retina or brain as relevant in the understanding of visual perception, hence the formation of cerebral images, the psychophysical postulate, and the principle of cerebral diversity, as described by Descartes, were of no interest to him. In his view, the "mind" could no more have direct knowledge of physiological events than it could have of light rays and of intersections. It was already conceded, argued Berkeley, that physiology could not explain why cerebral motions should give rise to one rather than some other sensation nor why those motions should give rise to any sensation whatever. It was obvious to Berkeley that the mind, which perceived ideas and sensations, was the essential factor for the understanding of mental events. Moreover, he maintained that the philosophical or psychological investigation of mental characteristics should be restricted to idea and sensation. It is for this reason that his theory of visual perception is regarded as "psychological."

An alternative to natural geometry may be considered which, although rejected by Berkeley, nevertheless is relevant in understanding the development of his theory. The geometric "means" could perhaps be saved by translating them into sensations arising from the motion of the eyes. Sensation of convergence, for example, is graded directly with the magnitude of the angle of the optic axes but inversely with the distance of the object. The sensation of convergence might then be considered as innately connected to visual sensation so that distance is directly perceived, awareness of lines or optic axes thus becoming an unnecessary supposition. Berkeley disagreed with this interpretation although he conceded that such sensation is perceivable. There is no "natural or necessary connection," he said, "between the sensation we perceive by the turn of the eyes and greater or lesser distance." The "connection," in his opinion, is acquired through experience. A similar consideration applies to the "confused appearance" due to the blurring of the retinal image when an object is relatively close and to "faintness" when an object is distant.[3]

Characteristics of visible objects. By "visible object" Berkeley refers to the psychic effect of retinal stimulation, neither memory nor judgment contributing to its formation. In respect to its specific characteristics such as size and shape, Berkeley speaks of "visible magnitude" and "visible figure." The visible object is also defined as the "proper," "primary," or "immediate" object of sight.

The characteristics Berkeley attributed to the visible object presuppose the constancy hypothesis. Immediately following the statement of the "design" of the *Essay,* the *Molyneux Premise* is quoted with but a slight change in wording. Whereas Molyneux had restricted the conclusion of the premise to those distances of objects which rendered "natural means" ineffective, Berkeley, on the other hand, removed the restriction and maintained that distance is always "of itself invisible." In the last chapter it was pointed out that the premise implies the constancy hypothesis not only in respect to distance but also in respect to the third dimension of an object. The acceptance of this hypothesis is rather clear when somewhat later in the *Essay* Berkeley says, "There is, at this day, no one ignorant that the pictures of external objects are painted on the retina or fund of the eye; that we can see nothing which is not so painted; and that, according as the picture is more distinct or confused, so also is the perception we have of the object." Although here Berkeley is explicit only in respect to the psychic effects of confused and distinct retinal images, in other discussions he supposes the visible object to be two-dimensional and that its size varies as the external object approaches or recedes. Moreover, the change in size represents a denial of an original perception of longitudinal motion. In respect to the moon illusion he maintains that the sizes of the visible objects corresponding to the two positions of the moon are the same. The constancy hypothesis as expressed through the acceptance of the *Molyneux Premise* is the important assumption underlying Berkeley's conception of visible objects and theory of perception. The conception of *minimum visibile* is a further illustration of this hypothesis.[4]

"There is . . . a *minimum visibile*," writes Berkeley, "beyond which sense cannot perceive." Imagine a very small object which can just be seen and that if made smaller, can no longer be seen. This perception exemplifies a *minimum visibile*—a sensation "just perceived and next door to nothing." Berkeley also refers to this entity as a "visible point." The expanse of this point must be quite small since a particle of dust can be seen under the right viewing conditions. This concept is derived from the science of the time. It was known that if the angle between two stars was less than 30″ of arc they would be seen as one. Some observers with acute vision could see the stars as distinct entities when the angle was slightly greater than 30″, but for others an angular separation of up to 60″ or one minute was required. Although expressing some uncertainty in respect to the magnitude of a "visible point," Berkeley accepts the visual angle of 60″ as its tentative measure. The science of the period also supposed a one-to-one correspondence between the points of the retinal image and the points of the external object and a similar correspondence between the retinal image and the visible object, suppositions also accepted by Berkeley. Thus he estimated the moon's diameter to be "about thirty visible points." This estimate supposes the 60″ arc as the magnitude of a visible point, for the angular subtense of the moon is ½° or 30″. In general Berkeley defines the magnitude of any visible object in relation to the "number of visible points" of which it consists. If the number be large or small, the visible magnitude is correspondingly larger or smaller. The correspondence of the points of the visible object to those in the retinal image also exemplifies the constancy hypothesis. The visible points vary in hue and in brightness and a particular grouping of them corresponds to the size and shape of the retinal image.[5]

The phenomenal locus of the visible object. After some discussion of the role of "experience" or "judgment" in the perception of distance Berkeley contrasts two predictions as to what a born blind man ought to perceive immediately after restoration of sight. According to the "common supposition" of natural geometry such a man should "perceive distance by sight." But in having proved this theory to be "false" he sets forth his own prediction and justification in the following noteworthy passage from Section 41 of the *Essay*.

> From what hath been premised, it is a manifest consequence, that a man born blind, being made to see, would at first have no idea of distance by sight: the sun and stars, the remotest objects as well as the nearer, would all seem to be in his eye, or rather in his mind. The objects intromitted by sight would seem to him (as in truth they are) no other than a new set of thoughts or sensations, each whereof is as near to him as the perceptions of pain or pleasure, or the most inward passions of his soul. For, our judging objects perceived by sight to be at any distance, or without the mind, is . . . entirely the effect of experience; which one in those circumstances could not yet have attained to.

The premise to which he alludes in the first line is the *Molyneux Premise*. By "idea of distance by sight" Berkeley means that which we ourselves see in looking at objects. A star, we would say, seems to be very far away, and some other object very near. The "idea" also includes the external reference of an object. The newly sighted man then will have no such idea of distance, all objects will 'seem to be in his eye or in his mind.' Berkeley also uses the term "outness," introduced in the English language by him and widely adopted, as the equivalent; the hypothetical man would not perceive the "outness" of a visible object. The phenomenal locus of a visible object or visual sensation in or touching the eye will be called eye-localization of sensation for the purpose of convenience. The possibility of eye-localization of sensation already had been suggested in restricted contexts by Malebranche, Locke, and Molyneux. In the chapter on Descartes it was noted that "in the mind" has a twofold meaning, one from the standpoint of the scientist and the other from the standpoint of the perceiver (in this instance, the re-sighted man). When Descartes expressed himself in a similar way he meant sensation to be "in the mind" only in the sense of a mental ef-fect which, in the present context, is the concomitant of a series of physical events beginning with retinal stimulation. Malebranche, on the other hand, indicated its mind-localization on the premise that natural judgment did not intervene. Berkeley often uses the phrase "in the mind" with Descartes's meaning. Thus he may say that the "visible object is in the mind" but without implying the phenomenal subjec-tivity of this object. The above quotation and its context, however, suggest that he intended Malebranche's meaning. An object would "seem to be . . . in his mind" in the sense that it is felt in the mind or experienced as subjectively as are the "perceptions of pain or plea-sure."

Since Berkeley gives two apparently different predictions without expressing a preference, one may suppose an indecisiveness as to what the hypothetical man of the quotation should perceive. The fact that in his writings on vision the two predictions are often coupled, "in his eye, or rather in his mind," would suggest an indecisive attitude as a matter of principle. Although the reason for contraposing two alterna-tives was not explained, "in his mind" probably represents his inten-tion.[6]

Berkeley's Explanation

From the standpoint of the present day, Berkeley's explanation of the learning of specific percepts will seem vague. Some of the steps in the learning process are merely indicated and other steps, essential to an understanding of explanation, are omitted. It is of interest that Berkeley anticipated difficulty in the appreciation of his theory. He said a "true theory of vision" could not be readily explained by words. Ordinary language is not well suited for the communication of truth and the attempt to circumvent this language, as in fact he did, may give the impression of "seeming contradictions" to the "unwary reader." He continues:

> I do, therefore, once for all, desire whoever shall think it worth his while to understand what I have written concerning vision, that he would not

stick in this or that phrase or manner of expression, but candidly collect my meaning from the whole sum and tenor of my discourse, and, laying aside the words as much as possible, consider the bare notions themselves, and then judge whether they are agreeable to truth and his own experience or no.

Obviously, he did not expect the understanding of his theory to be easy. Perhaps the active participation of the reader in understanding it is justified because the *Essay*, as he said, propounded a new and radical theory. In that case the innovator is not bound to eliminate linguistic inconsistencies or even to supply all the steps of an explanation, the interested reader himself performing these tasks on careful scrutiny. But in view of the relatively large body of literature that has arisen in the interpretation of the *Essay*, the difficulty is probably intrinsic to the theory. Accordingly, explanations in this chapter will be dealt with in a general way, deferring further elucidation to the followers of Berkeley. The example below of an infant "learning to see" is adapted from a contemporary of Berkeley who had accepted many of his basic ideas; Berkeley provides no example of the learning of any percept as is presumed to occur in infancy or childhood.[7]

Berkeley's theory relied on the importance of the sensations of touch, these sensations being regarded as the means for the correction of the defects in the retinal pictures. Berkeley includes under the sense of touch all motions of the body which bring it in contact with an object—the motion of the arm and the motion of the whole body in walking to an object. Also included are the motions of the hand in palpating an object. Through these motions, knowledge of the real characteristics of objects is obtained: their externality, relative distance, size, motion, and so on. The motions of the body produce sensations which are "perceived by the mind" and Berkeley refers to them as "tangible ideas" ("tactual ideas" to many of his followers). Other motions of the body not properly belonging to the sense of touch, such as eye-movements and the sensations they cause, are also regarded as important. However, these sensatons have a subsidiary role in Berkeley's theory since tangible ideas are the primary spatial factor.

All tangible ideas are regarded as the "mediate," "secondary," or "improper" objects of sight. Though giving the impression that such objects belong to the sense of sight, Berkeley doesn't quite mean this. The mediate "objects" cannot belong to the "sense of seeing" because they are only "perceived and measured by touch." They become connected to the primary objects of sight (visible objects) through experience and hence are the "secondary objects of sight."

The definition of other basic terms will facilitate the exposition of Berkeley's theory. *Visible ideas* and *visible appearances* are synonymous with the primary objects of sight. Visible sign refers to the attributes of the visible object. One type of sign refers to spatial attributes such as size and figure, and another type of sign refers to qualitative appearances such as confusedness, distinctness, vigorousness, and faintness. After a sign has been "connected" to a tangible idea the sign is said to "suggest the tangible idea" or also to "signify" the tangible idea.[8]

Distance. Let us suppose that an infant is in the arms of his mother and that her face represents his first visible object. He flails his arms about and in so doing touches her face, thus acquiring the tangible idea of its externality. Since he is simultaneously seeing and touching, the visible object tends to be connected to the tangible idea. After further practice the connection or association becomes so strong that the visible object very quickly suggests the tangible idea without the infant's experiencing the visible object to be either mind or eye localized. In such ways the face becomes externally referred at some but as yet undefined distance, that is, the infant cannot perceive the varying distance of the face when his mother moves toward or away from him.

Three of the "means" cited by Berkeley for the acquisition of perceived relative distance are of immediate relevance: "sensation of convergence," "confusion," and "straining." These means, of course, would have no "natural connection" to the degree of perceived distance. The acquisition of a connection will be indicated only for convergence sensation, it being similar for the others.

Suppose that the mother's face is first at one distance and then at another distance from the infant; corresponding to these distances there would be two distinct tangible ideas derived from the motion of the hand in reaching out and touching the face and two distinct convergence sensations. In the repetition of these events the connections between convergence sensation and the tangible idea of distance are acquired. Moreover, the convergence sensations elicit the tangible ideas appropriate to them, thus enabling the perception of relative distance. "This disposition or turn of the eyes is attended with a sensation," said Berkeley, "which seems to me to be that which in this case brings the idea of greater or lesser distance into the mind." When a raised forefinger is brought close to the eye one observes that the appearance of its contour becomes confused or blurred, and likewise for the infant when mother's face approaches him. Since the degree of confusion is inversely proportional to physical distance, the tangible idea being directly proportional, this "medium" elicits the perception of distance. The confused appearance, however, may be prevented by "straining" the muscles of the eye which control the shape of the lens so that distinct vision becomes possible. Since the degree of straining is inversely proportional to distance, its sensation is the third medium for the elicitation of perceived relative distance. This sensation replaces the confusion, thus, "aiding the mind to judge of the distance of the object."

Of these three means, only confusion is a visible sign since it pertains to the appearance of the visible object whereas the others are muscular sensations. These means are Berkeley's substitutes for the mind's ability to appreciate those lines and angles supposed in natural geometry in the perception of distance.

The infant's perception of relative distance is limited to the tangible idea derived from the extension of the arm. However, the infant matures and is able to walk to objects. Since the muscular feelings are directly proportional to the length of walk, this in turn being also directly proportional to physical distance, the child obtains a corresponding tangible idea of distance. As before, a connection between the tangible idea and "means" or "signs" must be acquired. The three previous means, however, are effective for relatively short distances only, and for this reason Berkeley introduced the degree of distinctness and the degree of vigorousness of the visible appearance as visible signs of perceived distance. When an object is at a distance of four or five feet its retinal image is distinct but at longer distances it becomes increasingly indistinct or obscure, and there is a corresponding change in its appearance. The light rays entering the eye are greater or fewer when the distance of the object is intermediate or remote; the visible appearance is accordingly vigorous or faint. These "signs," having been experientially connected to the corresponding tangible ideas derived from locomotion of the body, increase the range of perceived distance. For instance, the "sign" of faintness was regarded as responsible for perceiving an object as very distant. Berkeley cites other "signs" (e.g., visible size) as determinants of perceived distance, but we shall not discuss them.[9]

Size. The qualitative appearance of visible objects, such as their color, varies according to the nature of the corresponding physical objects and this fact will be presupposed except for the hypothetical example cited below. The magnitudes of objects are measured by the sweep of the hand, thus producing the tangible ideas of magnitude corresponding to them. Since such an idea after learning is suggested by the visible magnitude, perceived magnitude is accounted for. In this way the problem of the indeterminate relation of visible magnitude to "real magnitude" is resolved. We may consider two objects different in size but at the same distance. The visible and unequal magnitudes suggest perceived relative magnitude by virtue of their correlation to their respective ideas. And the same may be true even when the relative distance is such that the physically larger object produces a visible magnitude smaller than that of the closer but smaller physical object. Thus the visible size of the human face can be smaller than that of some toy. But in having learned of actual size through touch, the child perceives the face as larger than the toy. The previously mentioned degress of distinctness and vigorousness also can serve as signs for suggesting the tangible idea of magnitude.

In some circumstances signs have a double function; they can suggest not only the tangible idea of size but also the tangible idea of distance. For instance, when a child perceives two visible appearances of the same size but one being fainter than the other, he learns to relate them to the distance and size of the objects through the mediation of corresponding tangible ideas. But since the "visible extensions" are the same, the degree of faintness signifies differences in magnitude. One object, therefore, is perceived as larger and more distant than the other. Berkeley's explanation of the moon illusion follows this principle. The density of the atmosphere between the observer and the moon is greater when the moon is in the horizontal rather than in the zenith position, thus producing a differential absorption of light rays. Having pointed out this factor, Berkeley supposes the visible appearance of the horizontal moon is fainter than the appearance of the zenith moon. Since faintness suggests a greater magnitude, the moon's "appearance is enlarged." This same sign, however, also causes the moon to be perceived as more distant. He rejected the common opinion that the interjacent objects between the observer and moon cause it to be perceived as more distant, a distance perception which is said to have an increase in perceived magnitude as a natural correlate, because the illusion did not disappear when the view of those objects was blocked off by a wall.

Berkeley recognized that the signs of magnitude were not sufficient to account for all instances of perceived size, as exemplified in size constancy, and for this reason he introduced preconceived ideas ("prenotions") as an important determinant. To make his point he noted, "a picture equally great, equally faint, and in the very same situation shall, in the shape of a man, suggest a lesser tangible magnitude than it would in the shape of a tower." We may observe that since the signs of magnitude are identical and the visible magnitudes the same, in the absence of any preconceived ideas the suggested tangible magnitudes of the tower and man should be equal. In ordinary language this means that the man and tower would be perceived as having the same size. However, since they are perceived unequal in size, the difference in visible shape is the critical factor. In the interpretation of the passage it is important to realize that visible shape, in Berkeley's theory, is not a sign of tangible magnitude, and that in this context "tangible magnitude" means "tangible idea of magnitude."

The connections between tangible ideas of real magnitude and visible signs presumably are acquired when the man and tower are viewed from a closer distance. Concurrently, the notion or conceived idea is developed that the distinction in visible shapes represents the tangible ideas of magnitude. In the conditions of the present viewing situation, those previously conceived ideas are aroused by their respective visible shapes and as a result the tower has a perceived size larger than that of the man. Berkeley, however, did not refer to the fact that the tower is also perceived as more distant. Antecedent to the acquisition of preconceived idea the two objects would be perceived at the same distance because the signs of distance are also the signs of magnitude, the objects being remote and on a level ground. Thus, this other fact too should be explained. Recourse to the tangible idea of distance, a hypothesis consistent with other aspects of Berkeley's theory, would be necessary.[10]

The importance Berkeley attributed to the sense of touch is evident in his speculation concerning a hypothetical "unbodied spirit," which was presumed to "see perfectly well, *i.e.,* to have a clear perception of the proper and immediate objects of sight, but to have no sense of touch." By virtue of an inborn and permanent sensory defect this "spirit" could not have "any idea of distance, outness, or profundity . . . either immediately or by suggestion." Since Berkeley presupposed that the "mediate" objects of sight or the tangible ideas are never available to this "spirit," evidently it cannot learn to perceive, and only the previously described characteristics of visible objects can ever be descriptive of its state of consciousness. In our view the hypothetical being might correspond to a person whose senses are intact but who is so intellectually retarded that he can never learn the meaning of any written word, although he sees those same marks which have acquired meaning for the normal person.[11]

Further Points in
Berkeley's Explanation

The language metaphor. Berkeley maintained percepts are acquired in the "same manner" as are the meanings for spoken or written words. When the child learns to read, words are originally mere marks on paper. In scrutinizing them he may notice that some are larger than others or that some have straight lines while others do not. Through learning, however, he connects the meanings to the marks corresponding to them. With frequent and long practice the words (signs) suggest their meanings so readily that his attention immediately passes from the sign to the significate; in this rapid shift of attention the sign may not even be noticed. Thus, in the reading of a passage we tend to be conscious of the meaning rather than the specific characteristics of letters, whether italicized, capitalized, and so on, but especially so in later recall of the meaning. The association of meanings to sounds is acquired in the same way and the results are similar. Thus we pay attention to the meaning rather than to the peculiarities of sounds. It is quite possible for a multi-lingual person to recall the content of a conversation without recalling the specific language used.

What is true for the language of words is also true, according to Berkeley, for the "Language of Vision." To achieve this parallel, substitute *visible idea* for "word" and *tangible idea* for "meaning." For instance, the degree of confused appearance (a visible idea) denotes a corresponding degree of the tangible idea of distance after the appropriate connections have been acquired; before learning, however, it would have suggested no tangible idea. The metaphor, moreover, is responsible for the phraseology of "visible signs" and "things signified" when respectively referring to the "immediate" and "mediate" objects of sight. Berkeley often uses the metaphor for resolving problems which arise in his theory, and also for establishing the reasonableness of the theory. It was in reference to the metaphor that Voltaire, who introduced Berkeley's theory in France in 1738, said "We learn to see precisely as we learn to speak and to read." [12]

Tangible idea "superadded" to visible idea. Before learning, as in the case of the hypothetical man of Section 41 of Berkeley's *Essay,* visible and tangible ideas are unrelated and separate entities. But while looking and touching objects, the corresponding visible and tangible ideas are united in a "connection." However, the connection is such that the ideas, although closely united, are unaltered. They are then still separate entities and retain the same identities they had before their participation in the formation of the connection. The connection thus conceived defines what Berkeley means by the "superadding" of tangible to visible ideas. We shall use the term "adjunctive" as a synonym although "superadd" has another shade of meaning. One idea, therefore, is adjoined to the other. The phraseology of the visible idea "suggesting" the tangible idea has the same implication. In short, a visual perception is a visible idea plus a tangible idea.[13]

Visible ideas not noticed. From the preceding discussion it is evident that visible ideas generally do not change during the individual's life and that they are always present as a component of a perception. In ordinary circumstances of viewing objects, however, there is no awareness of them. But a visible idea like any other idea is perceived by the mind and presumably there ought to be consciousness of it. Berkeley explains this fact by supposing that the visible ideas are "not noticed" and advances two justifying arguments. One argument concerns the principle of the conservation of body. External objects cause pleasure or pain through direct contact with the body. In this way the tangible idea of their pain or pleasure-producing quality is obtained. A visible object in itself does not hurt nor does it convey any information of this quality. But when connected with tangible idea, it suggests the quality of pain or pleasure. The tangible idea is "principally attended to" because it is more useful to do so for the purpose of regulating our actions. Thus we can "attain those things that are necessary to the preservation and well-being" of the body and "to avoid whatever may be hurtful and destructive." And this is still true when the object is at a distance and we do not touch it. By attending to the tangible idea we can anticipate or "foresee" the consequences of an action and thus maximize survival. Attention, on the other hand, to the visible object would reduce the chances for survival. When not too far from the brink of a precipice, he says, a person is more likely to survive by attending to the edge and its apparent distance. In thus being anticipated, the danger can be avoided through immediate and appropriate action.

The second argument refers to a factual observation based on the language metaphor. The non-noticing of the peculiarities of sounds or marks and the paying of attention to meaning is regarded as important substantiating evidence. The perception of the signs obviously is essential for the suggestion of meaning and sometimes, especially when asked to do so, we become aware of a spelling error or some other peculiarity. Such facts are presumed to apply to the relationship of visible to tangible ideas, for Berkeley regards the two types of learning as similar. However, he recognizes that the verification of the visible sign in a perception may be difficult if not impossible.[14]

Tangible or tactual ideas are the distinctive content of visual perceptions. Since the visible idea suggesting the tangible idea is typically unnoticed, what we ordinarily consider to be a visual perception is therefore a tangible idea. Thus, the visual perceptions of distance and solidity represent tactual or tangible ideas as the distinctive content of visual consciousness. This statement refers to the perception not only after its formation in early life, but also to the present act of looking at objects. A connection is a relationship which necessarily requires two terms. Since any acquired perception incorporates two ideas, the continued presence of the visible idea as the antecedent term of a connection or suggestion is essential. For instance, in the present act of looking at a three-dimensional object, the bi-dimensional visible object suggests the tangible idea of three dimensions but we are conscious only of the tangible idea. We may again consider the "unbodied spirit" in this regard for the purpose of emphasizing an important aspect of Berkeley's theory. The visible ideas of the hypothetical being are identical to those of the infant in the absence of tangible ideas and also of the adult who has acquired all connections. The consciousness directly attributable to visible ideas is therefore the same in the infant, adult, and hypothetical being. Evidently, the actual awareness of the adult in looking at objects is tactual or tangible, the visible ideas being unnoticed.

Berkeley anticipates and answers an objection to his theory which can be developed as follows. It may be objected that to "disentangle" the primary or immediate from the secondary or mediate objects of sight is impossible. Thus we cannot ever see the flatness of the globe nor can we ever feel the globe as though in the eye, notwithstanding our full attention to such possibilities. The evidence for the separability of the two types of objects is then not sufficiently persuasive. Indeed the introspective evidence seems to prove that the percept is a single or unitary event, and also that the percept belongs wholly to the "visive faculty." The color of the globe is conceded to be a characteristic of the primary object. But its convexity and externality are also as immediate as the color, for on opening our eyes the three characteristics are perceived in the same instant. Since color is exclusively visual, so are the other two characteristics. Hence the percept is apparently unitary. Moreover, we cannot recall the time when things looked otherwise than they do now. We may then conclude that the thesis we learn to perceive is incorrect.

This objection when evaluated in reference to the language metaphor would not be cogent. In early life, sounds and their meanings were obviously separable events although in the present the meaning cannot be disunited from sound. Moreover, we cannot recall the time when the spoken word was devoid of meaning, nor can we even imagine the way in which we perceived sounds before they acquired meaning. A foreigner who has not learned the English language, Berkeley points out, perceives the sounds quite differently than we perceive them. The "Language of Vision" must be understood in exactly this fashion.

The decisive aspect of Berkeley's answer, however, rested on the implications Berkeley inferred from the *Molyneux Premise*. This premise guaranteed the imperceptibility of distance by the sense of sight. The idea of distance had to be nonvisual although suggested by an antecedent visible sign. And a visual perception, therefore, encompassed two distinctly separable events. Berkeley acknowledged the persistent difficulty in appreciating this necessary conclusion and he proposed to explain why. We "confound" the primary and secondary objects of sight or fail to "discriminate" between them. The former "alone are seen" whereas the latter "are not *seen*." In confusing one object for the other we believe that distance itself is seen, or that "we have a very great propension to think the ideas of outness and space to be the immediate object of sight." Berkeley advanced the reasons for the confusion in the following passage.

> But nothing, certainly, does more contribute to blend and confound them together, than the strict and close connexion they have with each other. We cannot open our eyes but the ideas of distance, bodies, and tangible figures are suggested by them. So swift, and sudden, and unperceived is the transit from visible to tangible ideas that we can scarce forbear thinking them *equally* the immediate object of vision.

It is interesting to observe that the unperceivability of the swift and sudden transit deemed responsible for the confusion of the two types of objects was anticipated by Locke in his explanation of the perceived solidity of the globe. The usual belief that the "idea of distance" is a visual datum or that it is a proper and immediate object of the sense of sight is strikingly described by Berkeley as a "prejudice" or "mere delusion." [15]

SITUATION

The explanation of the "perception of the situation of objects," which is discussed at length in the *Essay*, has been separated from the concluding comments of the previous section because of the ambiguity of the "true solution" proposed by Berkeley. Berkeley's problem seems to arise from his rejection of Molyneux's geometric explanation of the "erect appearance of objects." Since the image is inverted and since Berkeley supposes the spatial characteristics of the visible object to correspond to it, he must then contend, as it were, with an upside down appearance. However, the question of the orientation of the appearance was meaningless to Berkeley, and for this reason he could not subscribe to the opinion that the relationship of that appearance to the orientation of the external object presents a problem for theoretical interpretation. If we suppose this to be the case, there is still another problem. Thus, on seeing an object to the left and then closing our eyes, we can correctly reach for it or point to it. Our perception apparently provides information as to the actual distribution of objects in space.

The hypothetical man of Section 41 of the *Essay* was introduced by Berkeley in stating his opinion and for clarifying the intricate issues entailed by image-reversal. The man on first seeing and in having had tactual experience of objects while blind, "would not think the things he perceived by sight to be at any distance from him, or without his mind." He would be unable to render any "judgment" of their situation for he would regard those things as "intangible" or as of a "spiritual nature" similar to thoughts, desires and passions. In the same way that we do not say that an emotion is to the left or above another emotion, so also in respect to the visible objects perceived by him. Evidently Berkeley supposes that the hypothetical man would perceive the visible objects as mind-localized. Statements of position can only be asserted in reference to those things "perceivable by touch" and not to those which are intangible or spiritual. Since this man has not yet learned to correlate the visible objects to those ideas already available to him through touch, no judgment pertaining to the orientation of a perceived object is possible. Berkeley explained the acquisition of correct judgments as follows. The man while blind acquired the tangible ideas of up and down. By moving his hand across the body of an upright man he learned that his feet were contiguous with and resting on the earth and that his head was away from the earth. In reference to his own body position he learned that the head was in an "upper" and the feet in a "lower" situation. But on gaining his sight the visible appearance of the upright man does not directly suggest the tangible ideas, for he has not yet experienced any connection between them. When the connection has been formed through simultaneous looking and touching he can then judge the head to be "upper" and the feet "lower." In continuing his explanation Berkeley invoked eye-movements as the essential factor in the visual judgment of situation. He says:

> And this seems to me the true reason why he should think those objects uppermost that are painted on the lower part of his eye. For, by turning the eye up they shall be distinctly seen; as likewise they that are painted on the highest part of the eye shall be distinctly seen by turning the eye down, and are for that reason esteemed lowest.

Thus the judgment of situation is made possible through the action of the eye which enables the physical object to stimulate the most sensitive area of the retina. When looking at a man's feet and turning the eyes up, we judge the feet to be closer to the physical earth and the head more distant. And for a similar reason, should the man be standing on his head, we would know that his head is closer to and his feet more distant from the physical earth. For eye-movements to serve as a guide to judgment, however, they must have been previously connected to the sense of touch or motion of the hand for reasons similar to those already discussed, as in the case of convergence sensation as a medium for the perception of distance. Berkeley indicates that in the absence of eye-movement the transferral of tactual judgment to the "ideas of sight" could not take place. Thus, eye-movement is the essential factor and in his explanation it is the "true reason."

Berkeley developed another but overlapping "solution" in relation to the supposition that the retinal images are directly perceived, a supposition which implies an identity between images and visible appearances. From this supposition the further consequence is inferred, namely, that the appearance is upside down. Thus, there arises the problem of explaining the "erect appearance" of objects. Molyneux's geometric explanation implicitly supposes the inverted appearance, although the mind, by virtue of its ability to trace rays, would perceive an erect appearance. Berkeley adopts the supposition for the purpose of determining whether the upside down appearance is a logical consequence. The gist of his analysis is that any ascription of orientation to the visible appearance is, in fact, meaningless. In this case the problem of erect appearance is no problem at all.

For the sake of argument he supposes the hypothetical man to be viewing another who is standing on his feet. He perceives the visible feet to be contiguous to the visible earth and the visible head to be opposite either the visible feet or the visible earth. These relationships, in accordance with the supposition, are identical to the positions of the retinal images. These relationships correspond to the actual physical facts but the hypothetical man who perceives only visible appearances cannot have any knowledge of this correspondence. Thus, supposing he could do so, he would say that the visible head is opposite the visible earth, but he could not judge the physical head to be opposite the physical earth. Although any attribution of orientation to the visible appearance is not necessitated by the supposition, the problem

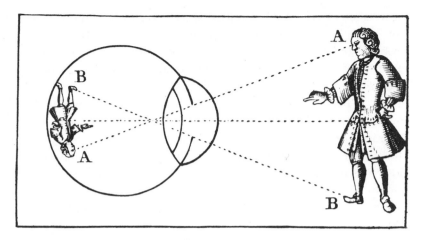

FIGURE 5.1. Voltaire's diagram that was intended to illustrate the theoretical problems arising from an upside down retinal image (1738).

still remains as to the way in which we do come to judge the situation of objects. The basis of judgment, as in the previous solution, rests on the sense of touch and eye-movement.[16]

In stating and developing his arguments, especially in reference to the "true reason," it is evident that Berkeley did not suppose any alteration in the appearance of things. It may possibly be true that eye-movement is important but this factor pertains to judgment, the knowing whether an object is erect or inverted. In discussion of distance and magnitude, however, Berkeley was concerned with the question of changed appearance. For instance, the problem in the moon illusion is to explain the difference in phenomenal size, it being supposed that the visible sizes are equal. In this instance the question of how we know the moon's physical size is constant in its upward transit was irrelevant.

FORM

Berkeley's investigation of an "idea common to sight and touch" led to the repudiation of the possibility of any common idea. In contrast to Locke, Berkeley argued that the two kinds of ideas are "heterogeneous," that there is no similarity, resemblance, agreement, or anything in common between them. This doctrine of "heterogeneity," a basic theme which is often regarded as Berkeley's significant contribution in the *Essay,* is linked to a prolonged discussion of the Molyneux problem and Locke's concept of "resemblance" of visible idea and external object. The problem, as often pointed out in contemporary philosophy, is the focal point in the development of Berkeley's theory of vision. Whenever Berkeley wished to clarify the distinction between the immediate and mediate objects of sight or to elucidate the meaning of some theoretical issue, he returned to the problem as stated in its classic form by Molyneux or to some variation of it. Thus the discussion of each of the four main subdivisions of the *Essay* is related to the hypothetical man of the Molyneux problem. He maintained throughout the *Essay* that the answer is necessarily negative. Although apparently sharing Locke's "solution" to the problem, actually he did not share it because he held that Locke, having presupposed a common idea, should have given a positive answer. Also in opposition to Locke, Berkeley denied any resemblance or similarity of visible idea and external object. On the other hand, he supposed a resemblance or similarity in respect to the properties of tangible idea and external object. This premise was typical in Berkeley's time and neither Locke nor Leibniz would have disagreed.[17]

For the purpose of clarifying some of these concepts we may consider a three-dimensional object moving toward or away from an observer. The visible object is flat; it increases or decreases in size without any apparent longitudinal motion; and its appearance may be confused, distinct, or faint. Obviously, there is no resemblance or similarity between these characteristics of the visible object and those of the external object. By touching the object, however, the tangible ideas of its real characteristics are obtained: that it is of the same size and in motion, three-dimensional, and of the same sharp edge. Since the tangible ideas of these properties resemble the properties of the object, visible and tangible ideas are heterogeneous. Furthermore, any judgment as to the nature of the physical object based upon visible ideas only, if a judgment were possible, necessarily would be erroneous. For instance, at most the object would be judged as variable in size and not one of the same-sized object in motion.

It would appear, however, that the heterogeneity for which Berkeley argued is contradicted by everyday experience. Thus in having obtained the tangible ideas of a disk and sphere of the same diameter with eyes closed, the correct identification of the two objects is surely possible when subsequently seeing but not touching them. Evidently, judgments derived from the visual perceptions of flatness and convexity are comparable with those previously obtained through touching. However, in Berkeley's theory, the conclusion would not follow because a visual perception is the combination of visible object adjoined to tangible idea. Therefore, the basis of the correct visual judgment would lie in the tangible idea which is common to the visual perception and to the tangible judgment derived with eyes closed. Moreover, since the visible ideas of the two physical objects are identical (flat circles of the same size), prior to experience, as in the hypothetical man of the Molyneux problem, correct identification would be impossible. Finally, the resemblance between the perception of convexity and the actual convexity of the sphere is tangible.

However, the analysis of the standard Molyneux problem is different because the visible ideas of the globe and cube are distinct, a circle for one and a square for the other. In Berkeley's "solution" the answer was necessarily negative because, as he said, there is no idea in common between the ideas of sight and touch. Visible and tangible ideas are to be regarded as two distinct "sorts" or "species." They cannot be compared, nor would the hypothetical man of the problem even think of comparing them. Should this man be asked to identify the "two bodies he saw placed on the table," Berkeley said, he would think the question was "downright bantering and unintelligible." A later example provided by Bourdon serves to clarify what Berkeley is getting at. Suppose, says Bourdon, a man who is born deaf and who "by sight" distinguishes a violin from a flute. The man is now given his hearing and, on hearing the sounds of the instruments with eyes closed, he is asked to try to recognize the instruments on the basis of their sounds. The man, said Bourdon, would be "bewildered." According to him, the man of the Molyneux problem would be similarly bewildered when he experiences visual sensations for the first time.[18]

Berkeley advanced several "arguments" to refute Locke's "common idea" and to demonstrate heterogeneity. One such argument in syllogistic form states:

> Light and colors are allowed by all to constitute a sort of species entirely different from the ideas of touch; nor will any man, I presume, say they can make themselves perceived by that sense. But there is no immediate object of sight besides light and colors. It is therefore a direct consequence that there is no idea common to both senses.

The major premise affirmatively includes light and colors as peculiar to the visual sense, but also implicitly, the ideas of primary qualities such as form. Since the minor premise seems to exclude the ideas of primary qualities, reserving them exclusively to the sense of touch, the conclusion of heterogeneity necessarily follows. Berkeley seems to suggest that light and colors are to be regarded as ideas of secondary qualities, in which case figure or form would be an attribute only of tangible ideas and not of visible ideas. An independent justification of the minor premise is necessary for the syllogism to be meaningful, for should it include an idea of a primary quality the conclusion would no longer follow. But some philosophers have doubted whether Berkeley in fact established the premise on independent grounds. Nevertheless, the syllogism may be accepted for the purpose of examining some of its implications.[19]

The minor premise denies any resemblance or similarity between visible ideas and external objects. The novelty of this phase of Berkeley's theory may be contrasted to the resemblance which is implicit in the previous discussion of visible figure in the section "characteristics of visible objects." Thus a globe and cube project retinal images which have the shapes of a circle and square. Since these shapes give rise to circular and square-like visible figures, there would be some degree of resemblance between the shapes of visible figures and external objects. This limited degree of resemblance (the visible figures are flat), is now rejected by Berkeley. The hypothesis of nonresemblance in itself would suffice to establish a necessary negative answer to the Molyneux problem. Further, it is evident in Berkeley's discussion of the problem that heterogeneity hinges on the question of resemblance. If the hypothetical man should see a curve and an angle in his first act of vision, says Berkeley, he might be able to find some similarity between his visual judgments of those part-forms and his tangible ideas of globe and cube. Therefore, in order to assure heterogeneity, Berkeley may have disallowed any discriminable difference in visible forms which resemble the external forms.

The importance of the implications of the negative answer to the Molyneux problem perhaps merits further consideration from a somewhat different standpoint. In 1746 Condillac objected to Berkeley's solution and proposed his own which, supposing a common idea, led to a positive answer. Having interpreted the light and colors of Berkeley's theory as being unextended or nonspatial, he argued that the hypothetical man of the problem would see them as "concentrated in a point" and that he would "judge that all nature is only a mathematical point." He maintained, on the contrary, that the light and colors must be extended in three dimensions. His objection is given here because it was stated by an influential philosopher and not because of its possible validity. However, Berkeley's opinion expressed in a notebook, and first published in the nineteenth century, is of interest in this regard. In alluding to the Molyneux problem, he wrote, "All things to a blind man at first seen in a point." Although this statement is not explained and "point" not defined, nevertheless there would seem to be some agreement with Condillac's interpretation. But Berkeley in the writings published in his lifetime did not refer to the immediate object of sight as an apparent single point. On the contrary, he said many visible points could be perceived at the same time, a few clearly and the others confusedly.[20]

In any case, that Berkeley would have denied the original perception of bi-dimensional forms such as might be represented on paper by a circle or square is implied in his discussion of Locke's opinion pertaining to the original perception of the globe as a variously shadowed flat circle. Berkeley cited this opinion and also paraphrased Locke's explanation of the alteration of the flat circle into a "solid" by an act of judgment and said, "From all which we may conclude that planes are no more the immediate object of sight than solids. What we strictly see are not solids, nor yet planes variously coloured—they are only diversity of colours. And some of these suggest to the mind solids, and others plane figures. . . ."[21]

In the following passage, Berkeley again implied that the perception of form is acquired and indicates the way in which it might develop.

> Add to this that whenever we make a nice survey of any object, successively directing the optic axis to each point thereof, there are certain lines and figures, described by the motion of the head or eye, which, being in truth perceived by feeling, do nevertheless so mix themselves, as it were, with the ideas of sight that we can scarce think but they appertain to that sense.

Although the explanation was not elaborated, Berkeley suggested that the motion of the eye or head traces out a shape corresponding to the external shape and that the successive sensations derived from this motion are responsible for the perceived shape. And he also suggested that because of the confounding of the visible ideas and the feeling of motion, the shape perceived through feeling is mistaken for a direct visual perception.[22]

Furthermore, it would seem that Berkeley presupposed a "point theory" of visual sensation. The optic axis, he said, is directed to "each point" of the object. Inasmuch as the optic axis represents a geometric line with one end related to a point in the object and the other end to a point on the retina, the size of the sensation would correspond to that of a geometric point. But a "geometric point" is not essential to the explanation nor to the meaning of "point theory."

It would seem obvious that Berkeley introduced the axis as a fiction to facilitate an understanding of how perceived shape might arise from experience because the axis is not perceivable. Further, the size of the objective point, although undefined, could not be a geometric point which, through the mediation of light, would produce retinal stimulation. Thus this point would have a definite physical size such that a *minimum visibile* or "visible point" corresponds to it. When the optic axis is directed to one such point of the contour of the object, other points to the left or right and above or below the fixation point will also give rise to visible points. However, only those visible points corresponding to the contour are relevant in the development of perceived shape. The successive fixation of the points of the contour produce a series of corresponding visible points but they do not directly give rise to perceived shape, for the perceived spatial arrangement would represent the path described by the motion of the eye or head. Since only one visible point for a given fixation of a point of the contour is relevant in the determination of perceived shape, a "point theory" of visual sensation is implicit in Berkeley's explanation.

THE CHESELDEN CASE

In 1728 the first report in a scientific journal on what a born blind individual sees subsequent to the removal of the cause of blindness, was published by the operating surgeon Cheselden. The fact that he was regarded as "one of the most celebrated anatomists and surgeons of the eighteenth century" and the further fact of publication in the *Philosophical Transactions of the Royal Society,* the English journal of the time reporting significant discoveries in science, undoubtedly enhanced the value of the report. The principal points of historical interest in this case (which is reproduced in the appendix) concern the boy's thinking that all objects touched his eyes as those which he felt touched his skin, the boy's behavior in relation to the cat and dog, and the boy's first seeing pictures as flat but seeing them in relief two months after the operation. In 1733 Berkeley defended his theory of vision against adverse criticism and he appealed to this case as a confirmation of it. After having briefly quoted and paraphrased the Cheselden data in which he noted these points, he said, "Thus, by fact and experiment those points of the theory which seem the most remote from common apprehension were not a little confirmed, many years after I had been led into the discovery of them by reasoning." [23]

Although Berkeley failed to say how the data confirm his theory, we may suppose that he was referring, among other things, to the following. First, he has said that learning occurs so early in life that grown-up individuals have no recollection of it. The Cheselden boy, in being able to recall and communicate his first visual impressions, provided information as to what an infant might see. The fact that his visual perceptions ultimately were similar to those of a child who developed normally indicates that the course of learning is the same for both. Second, when Berkeley stated the hypothesis in Section 41 of the *Essay* that a resighted man "would at first have no idea of distance by sight," all objects seeming to him to be in the eye or in the mind, he contrasted it to the hypothesis based on natural geometry. The fact that the boy said objects touched his eyes demonstrates the correctness of his hypothesis and the falsity of the other. Since his hypothesis rested on the *Molyneux Premise,* the data also confirm its validity. That the boy said "touching" the eyes, rather than "in" the eyes or "in" the mind, could have been interpreted by Berkeley so as to be consistent with his hypothesis. The discussion of the possibilities of reinterpretation will be deferred to later chapters. Third, the boy's inability to identify the cat and dog known to him by touch may be considered as an experimental verification of the negative answer to the Molyneux problem. Finally, the learning of the perception of the solidity or relief of pictures is indicated in the report.

The usual interpretation given to the boy's initial seeing of pictures as flat by followers of Berkeley's theory was that he saw all objects as though in a plane. But it is doubtful that Berkeley himself would have agreed with this interpretation since he had repudiated the Locke assumption that the original perception of a globe or cube is flat, maintaining that "planeness" is also a learned perception. However, many of his followers combined the Locke assumption to that feature of Berkeley's theory which stressed the importance of the "sense of touch."

The mathematician R. Smith in his work on optics of 1738 included a chapter, "Concerning Our Ideas Acquired by Sight," in which the principal features of Berkeley's theory are stated and in which the Cheselden case is quoted in its entirety as evidence for "learning to see." Smith asked Jurin to comment on his whole work and his remarks were included in the appendix. Jurin concurred with Smith's interpretations of that chapter and added observations of his own. Jurin refers to Locke's explanation of the perception of solidity for the purpose of illustrating the general importance of the "association of ideas" in the acquisition of percepts and supposes that Locke relied on the sense of touch. Berkeley, he says, gave a similar explanation in a somewhat different language, visible ideas exciting the tangible ideas customarily connected with them. He goes on to say, much in the same vein as did Locke and Berkeley, that the transition from visible to tangible ideas is so imperceptible and instantaneous that an act of judgment or memory is confused with a "bare sensation of sight." Almost everyone thinks that a globe is seen as "convex" and a cube as "angular" when in fact they are judged to be so. He continues, "The truth of this doctrine has been so well demonstrated by Mr. Locke and the above mentioned ingenious writer [Berkeley], and is so clearly confirmed in this very chapter, particularly by the curious observations of Mr. Chesselden, as to put the matter out of all doubt."

Evidently for Jurin the Cheselden data decisively established the validity of the theories of Locke and Berkeley. Voltaire in the same year also quoted and interpreted the Cheselden case in a similar vein. The importance of this case is attested to by its republication and translation, either *in toto* or substantially so, and also its citation and discussion in numerous texts in optics, philosophy, physiology, and psychology from 1738 until the end of the nineteenth century. Generally, it established the empiristic approach as factually supported in respect to external reference, and the perception of form, solidity, magnitude, and distance. Other corroborating cases of restored vision were reported toward the beginning of the nineteenth century and later, but the Cheselden case remained the most frequently cited source. It ranked as the most celebrated case study in the history of science until the early case studies of Freud came along at the beginning of the twentieth century which established the viability of psychoanalytic theory.[24]

6 CONDILLAC

How can sensation extend beyond the organ which feels and circumscribes it? Condillac, 1754

In the *Treatise on the Sensations* (1754), influential in shaping eighteenth-century French philosophy and psychology, Condillac proposed to demonstrate that all knowledge and operations of the mind are derived through sensory stimulation. This is what Locke himself set out to do in his *Essay,* according to Condillac, but he was inconsistent since he supposed that operations intrinsic to the mind were another source of ideas. Condillac, on the other hand, proposed to eliminate the inconsistency by showing that such operations as attention, comparing, and judging have their exclusive origin in simple ideas or, in his equivalent term, sensations. Memory in general consists in the revival of simple ideas or "remembered sensations" which, depending on the conditions, may have the vivacity of sensations arising from immediate stimulation of the senses. All knowledge represents various combinations of simple ideas which he names "complex ideas." Any visual perception is likewise regarded as a complex idea. Such considerations underlie his basic thesis that "we have learned to see, to hear, to taste, to smell, [and] to touch."

He acknowledged that the thesis is so contradictory to common opinion that it might not be readily understood. Therefore, he expounded it in relation to the fascinating conception of an animated statue who is successively endowed with each one of the senses of smell, hearing, taste, sight, and touch singly, and then in various combinations. The reader is advised to "enter into its life, begin where it begins, have but one single sense when it has only one." In short, he "must fancy himself to become just what the statue is." Essentially the statue represents a series of hypothetical individuals, some of whom are endowed with only one sense and others with various combinations of senses. Ideal conceptions or models are frequently advanced for the purpose of understanding complex phenomena. Thus our present perceptions and conceptions may be so contaminated with experience from infancy without our being aware of it, or our prejudices with respect to the origin of our perceptions may be so ingrained that we are unable to judge the true nature of sensation. Condillac's statue then serves the useful purpose of disentangling the learned and unlearned components in perception. We may observe that Berkeley's "unbodied spirit" and Locke's *tabula rasa* conception of the mind and even the Molyneux problem are earlier instances of such models. And, what is immediately important to us, the statue provides the opportunity for understanding the nature of sensation and the acquisition of perceptions as conceived by an important follower of the Berkeleyan theory.

In an evaluation of Locke's theory, Condillac comments that Locke erroneously supposed the sense of sight, independently of touch, was the basis for the discrimination of form and size, and the perception of distance. He believes Berkeley had the right approach when he states that "sight alone could not judge of these things." When elaborating his own theory, it is evident that Condillac refers to that aspect of Berkeley's theory which seemed to deny an original perception of form. But only a few years earlier in 1746 Condillac criticized and rejected Berkeley's theory because visual sensation would have to be regarded as a "mathematical point." At that time he pointed out other difficulties in Berkeley's theory and he maintained that the perceptions of size, form, depth, and direction were immediately given by the sense of sight. He now describes his earlier views as "prejudices" and adopts

Berkeley's theory without any apparent reservation. He explains the shift in theoretical orientation in terms of his abandonment of the prejudice that the visual sense could be regarded as independent of the sense of touch and of his present realization of the interdependency of the two senses. However, as long as the belief in the independency of the two senses is held, he says, it is impossible to overcome the conviction that seeing things of various shapes and at various distances is exclusively visual perception. For the judgments or ideas derived from touch are so thoroughly "mixed" in visual sensation that we remain unaware of them. He tells us that the conception of the statue was important in making him aware of his prejudices, and in eliminating them. Moreover, in order to enable his readers to more readily abandon their own prejudices, he has decided to endow the statue with smell as the first sense. This sense is to be regarded as the prototype for the other senses, particularly the visual sense. And for this reason the discussion of the sense of smell is more prolonged and detailed than for the others.

We may remark that in the new theory Condillac supposed the original awareness of objects to be a "point." In later life the statue has complete recollection of its early experience and says, ". . . before I had the use of my members [arms, legs, etc.] I was ignorant that something might exist outside myself. What do I say? I did not know that I was extended: I was only a point when I was reduced to a uniform feeling." Moreover, after some preliminary learning in how to see has taken place, Condillac indicates that only the "diameter of a line" will be seen. Although Condillac apparently presupposes that the "diameter" is a mathematical point, this particular feature of the theory is not further developed.[1]

Malebranche affords a direct approach to understanding Condillac's theory of sensation. He was the first philosopher, said Condillac, "to have observed that our sensations are mixed with judgments." This was a step in the right direction, but he was in error in attributing these judgments to God. To be sure judgments were always intertwined with sensations; however, they have been acquired in the experience of the individual. Although rejecting the divine origin of judgment, Condillac retained the conception of sensation as a modification of the mind.

SENSATION

Impressions on the external senses are propagated to the "common sense" and, as a consequence, the mind has sensations which are "only modifications of the soul." And for this reason Condillac says, "we perceive nothing but what is in ourselves." Since only the sensations are in the self, and not the external object, they must be the "object" or qualities which we perceive. From this line of thinking Condillac concluded: "were a man limited to smell he would be smell, were he limited to taste he would be taste; to hearing, noise or sound; to sight, light or color." These senses in themselves "give us no awareness of external objects." We observe here the omission of the sense of touch. At this point in the development of his theory, Condillac is merely considering the nature of original consciousness when touch is excluded, for he regards this sense to be responsible for the awareness of objects. And for this reason he can also assert that a man limited to the other senses would not know that he has a body. Likewise the man would not even perceive sensation as though in the eyes because he could not "suspect there is a space." The body, the eyes, their parts, are also objects in space; and learning is required to discover their existence.

It is apparent that Condillac, in accepting Malebranche's doctrine of sensation (as sensible qualities) also supposed that sensation ought to be experienced in the soul or mind. Thus, in writing of the first sensations of which the statue is conscious, Condillac said:

> If we give the statue a rose to smell, to us it is a statue smelling a rose, to itself it is smell of a rose. The statue therefore will be rose smell, pink smell, jasmine smell, according to the flower which stimulates its sense organ. In a word, in regard to itself smells are only its own modifications or modes of being. It cannot suppose itself to be anything else, since it is only capable of sensations.

In respect to color sensation the "statue discerns" that it is red or green when it first notices the sensation. The soul, in other words, becomes colored according to the sensation which modifies it. We may observe that the assumption of a mind-localized sensation is vividly expressed.

Condillac also alluded to *Molyneux's Premise* in justification of his opinion that visual sensation could not possess the attribute of external reference. He supposes a man, limited to the sense of touch, who has learned that he has a hand. Upon grasping a stick for the first time, the man has a sensation in the hand. With experience in touching objects with the stick, however, he learns to refer the sensation to the opposite end. And thus the man comes to feel objects at a certain distance in space. The same is true when a light ray is regarded as a "stick," one end of this "stick" having its origin in the external object and the other end touching the retina. "The eye feels the impression of the rays," says Condillac, "just as the hand feels the impression of the stick which it holds by one of its ends." After learning, however, the impression comes to be felt at the opposite end of the ray, that is, at its point of origin in the object. Although Condillac apparently implies that the impression originally is felt in the eye, he does not quite mean this, for in his view knowledge of the eye as an object in space is at that time absent. In this example he supposes the referral of sensation to the eye has been learned in order to emphasize the necessity of the acquisition of external reference.[2]

We may now consider the problem of form. Two premises were the basis of Condillac's discussion of this problem and the related problem of extension. He said sensation is and must be "unextended" and he developed the implications of this hypothesis in his theory of sensation. On the other hand, the second premise, which supposed mind to be an unextended and indivisible substance, remained implicit in his treatment. Much as Condillac tried to prove that sensation is "unextended," his efforts were unavailing. Thus it would seem that the premise concerning the nature of mind was the actual basis for his belief. Although the implications of both premises are equivalent, the summary of Condillac's discusson of form-sensation will be related to the first premise.

The statue which originally perceives only light and color does not have the ability of perceiving two colors at the same time. For if the statue did have this ability, the line separating the colors would have extension. Thus Condillac expounded the view that the mind experiences a single sensation at a given time and that this sensation is "simple" or "uniform." To have said that sensation is not simple would be equivalent to the mind's experiencing two sensations simultaneously, and the premise of "unextended sensation" would be contradicted. However, Condillac noted a difficulty arising from the fact that the various parts of a retinal impression are simultaneous. Thus if sensation is directly determined by this impression, it will also have parts and the same difficulty repeats itself. Condillac resolved this difficulty by supposing that the mind could direct its "attention" to one sensation at a time. But we may observe that this resolution does not quite escape the difficulty. For in being aware of the one sensation to which attention is directed, the other and unattended sensation is simultaneously present to the mind. Probably for circumventing this difficulty, Condillac adverts to the "mixing up of color sensations" into one uniform or blended color. For the purpose of clarifying this and another point to follow we may consider the sense of smell. An odor does not have the characteristic of extension and, of course, is not divisible into parts. If two odoriferous substances stimulate the olfactory sense at different times, there are two odors. But when they simultaneously stimulate this sense the two odors blend into a single odor, its components being indistinguishable. Condillac, in having developed these points concerning odor, is led to consider the question of why odors do not acquire the characteristic of extension as do color sensations. He points out that the apparatus of the eye has the special property of focusing an image on the retina so that each point of the image is relatable along a straight line to a given point on the object. He observes that if the olfactory sense possessed this property, odors too could be shaped through learning.

Besides philosophical considerations, "evidence" also helped determine Condillac's theory of sensation. For instance, the Cheselden data were cited by Condillac as proof of his theory; he said the boy had no immediate visual awareness of external things and was also unable to perceive forms. The fact that the boy said objects touched his eyes was not regarded as a contradiction. It is true that eyes are external things but, as we shall observe shortly, Condillac contends the boy's localization of sensation in the eyes was acquired.[3]

PERCEPTION

In affirming sensation to be mind-localized and in denying form-sensation, all visual percepts must be acquired. Moreover, since there is no immediate distinction in original consciousness between seeing, smelling, tasting, and so on, some learning process is necessary for the discrimination and allocation of sensations to the appropriate senses.

The mode of acquisition, intricate and not always too clearly set forth, involves remembered sensations, the "habit" of successively attending to sensations, and the habit of comparing and judging sensations. We will ignore Condillac's discussion of them. In any case the sense of touch is critical for all these acquisitions. And we may comment that the awareness of external objects through this sense, the statue being limited to touch only, is also learned. Generally we shall suppose this accomplishment to have been achieved in the discussion of visual percepts. The hand, regarded as a "graving tool" delineating the shapes and externality of objects and thus "engraving all in memory," is the important agent for the acquisition of percepts.

Condillac essentially divides the world in two, the inner world of sensation completely apart from and unrelated to the other world of objects. As a consequence he is led to wonder how sensation can "extend beyond the organ which feels and circumscribes it." The mind as the source of sensation is, as it were, encapsulated; how then can it reach out to the other world so as to become aware of external things? In his answer, access to objects is provided through touch, for this is the "only sense which of itself can judge of externality." It is the "bridge of passage" between the inwardly experienced states of the mind and the external things, the gap being closed by the reach of the arm in touching the object. By means of touch or the motions of the arm in reaching for and palpating an object, the mind learns that it has a body, that there are external objects at some distance, that these objects have magnitude, form, and solidity. After this learning has been achieved, "touch teaches the other senses to judge external objects." And through this instruction "we learn to see" the "distance, situation, figure, size and motion of objects." We shall indicate the mode of learning for a few of these percepts.

External Reference and Distance

"Perhaps by chance, or perhaps from pain," says Condillac, the statue "passes its hand over the external surface of the organ of sight." The statue notices that colors instantly disappear and re-appear in the various motions of the hand. It then "ceases to consider them as modes of its own being" and judges them to be in the same place where the hand feels the eyes. The colors are felt in "contact with the eyes," a process similar to the statue's learning to feel "at the ends of its fingers the objects which they touch." In thus being localized the colors now seem to be extended because the surface of the eye is extended. Since antecedent to any experience of touch the colors appear unextended, tactual knowledge is critical for its apparent extension. Condillac does not imply that color itself actually becomes extended as a result of this learning. He asks us to consider the fact that pain is sometimes felt along the entire arm. Since pain is felt in each of its parts we may (incorrectly) think the pain itself is extended. But in discussing this example he arrives at a different conclusion. In using the arm we have learned it is extended and we have also learned to notice its different parts. Moreover, we have learned to relate the pain to these parts, a fact which then makes us think that the pain itself is extended. Color, therefore, remains as unextended after learning as it was before learning.

The colors felt in the extension of the surface of the eye do not as yet possess form, for the statue has merely touched the eye and not the external objects. In order to perceive shapes the actual objects must be touched, and this the statue has not yet learned in this stage of its development. For the same reason it does not even have the awareness of things "outside," its total awareness being confined or limited to the colors contiguous with the eye. Furthermore, and still for the same reason, the statue cannot pay attention to one or another color, nor can it discriminate colors. The statue, in short, perceives a uniform expanse of a blended color even though this blend contains other colors which, as yet, remain unperceived. This is similar to the infant who has not learned to localize pain-sensation in different parts of his body. Suppose that two parts of his body are hurt and that each hurt leads to a pain-sensation. The infant experiences a single uniform feeling of pain. When he acquires a differentiated knowledge of his body as the source of sensations, he can discriminate and relate them to the affected parts of the body. The body in respect to pain-sensation has the same status as does an external thing in respect to color sensation.

Eye-movements are necessary for the statue's analyzing the uniform color expanse into its constituent colors. When the eyes are fixed in gaze, one particular color becomes vivid. When the eyes "shift mechanically" another color becomes vivid, and so on. The statue thus learns to "discriminate" several colors successively. In paying attention to a particular color, the statue is able to remember the preceding color to which it had previously directed its attention, and in this way the statue can learn to discriminate several colors at one time. The "aid of memory," says Condillac, is essential for the simultaneous discrimination of colors. At this stage of its learning, however, the statue merely perceives a "chaos of shapes" or of objects "jumbled together in the greatest confusion," for the colors have not yet been externalized to things. Moreover, the chaos of light and color is perceived in the surface of the eye.

These and other points may be understood in relation to the following example suggested by Condillac but which we have modified. Imagine a number of concentric spheres whose center is inside the eye. Further, imagine various shapes to have been drawn on the surface of the outermost sphere and projection lines to have been also drawn from each of their points to the center. These shapes will become successively smaller as the innermost sphere represented by the corneal surface is approached. The "luminous surface" perceived by the statue is "equal to the exterior surface of the eye." Since its extension is very small, all shapes depicted on it can very well appear jumbled up and chaotic to the statue. Considered from this standpoint, learning is essential not only for the discrimination of colors but also for their ordering so that they should correspond to the positions of the shapes on the outermost surface. We may remark that Condillac also asserts the statue sees the eye's exterior surface as "immense." Perhaps there is no contradiction because he supposes the statue is unable to see the limits of that surface and, for this reason, it may appear very large. If the innermost sphere completely circumscribed the statue, an impression that the statue could achieve by motion of its eye in all directions, the surface would appear as immense as the outermost surface.

In moving the hand toward or away from the eyes the statue sees a surface which becomes "either more luminous or more obscure." The statue observes the motion of its hand is the "cause of these luminous changes." In knowing the "distance its hand can move" the statue realizes that the perceived surface must be at some distance from it. When now the hand is moved across an object which it touches, it sees a color disappear and reappear. By further observing that the moving color replaces the other, "it will come to think that the unmoved color is on the object, and the moving color is on its hand." This judgment is reinforced in many experiments in touching the same or other and differently colored objects. In reference to this type of acquisition,

Condillac concludes, "This judgment will become natural and it will see colors no longer on the surface of its eyes but at a distance on its hand and on the objects which its hand touches." Having thus far accounted for the perceived externality of colors, Condillac next considers the learning of their perceived relative distance. The motion of the hand from the eyes to objects or from objects to the eyes, and the similar motion in carrying an object to or away from the eyes, are the basis for this achievement. Through such motions the statue is able to "measure distances," thus learning to "connect visual impressions with the distance known by touch." As a consequence says Condillac, "It will see the objects, sometimes near, sometimes far away, for it will see them where it touches them."

The distances thus perceived, however, are limited by the reach of the arm of "two feet." More remotely placed objects are perceived as though at this distance and also perceived as though on a concave spherical surface whose radius is the same two feet. For perception of greater distances, movement of the body is necessary. In trying to reach a distant object the statue discovers it cannot touch it and that it must move its body in order to establish contact. Since the different body-motions correspond to the physical distances of objects, the range of perceived relative distance is increased. When the statue realizes the significance of the visual signs of faintness and indistinctness in relation to the motion of the hand and body, it learns to perceive even greater distances. After this learning has been achieved distant objects no longer appear as though disposed on a near spherical surface.

In discussing the acquisition of other percepts we shall suppose the position of the statue to be stationary, thus limiting its perceived distance to two feet. We shall further suppose that objects whose characteristics must be perceptually learned are disposed along an imaginary physical surface of a radius of two feet. With objects so placed, the statue will perceive two-dimensional splotches of unshaped chaotic colors in the extension of an apparent spherical surface. We should observe that this apparent surface conceptually represents the outward projection of the previous luminous surface in contact with the eyes and, for this reason, the characteristics of one correspond to the characteristics of the other. Finally, we shall suppose, as does Condillac, that each percept is acquired independently of another.[4]

Form

Condillac selects a triangle as the object having the simplest form to be learned by the statue. The statue successively attends or judges each of the sides, these acts being guided by the motion of the eyes and hand. Thus the statue studies the visual impression of a side as its eyes track it by following the motion of the hand along its side. It judges this and the other sides to be straight lines. In having learned three successive judgments, it must also learn a fourth judgment in order to discover the way in which the three parts are "united." Without this further judgment the three parts could as well be arranged in parallel lines, a longer straight line, as in the form of a triangle. These successive judgments, performed very rapidly through continued practice, enable the statue to perceive the triangular form as a "whole." Condillac observes, however, that the statue is not aware of the succession of judgments and he offers two explanations for it. The succession is so rapid that it is not perceived. But Condillac, in noting the fact that we can "see many things at once," turns to another explanation. He says, in referring to the statue, that "it recalls in a moment all the judgments it has successively formed." The instantaneous recollection suggested by the "in a moment" apparently then explains the simultaneity of multiple percepts and also eliminates the problem of succession. This same "aid of memory," he points out, is necessary to "perceive the simplest shape as a whole." The perceptions of other forms, such as that of a "square" or a "circle," are learned in similar ways. We wish to point out that a memory factor is presupposed in the very learning of a perception. When the eyes move from one side of the triangle to another side, the perception of the former side must be retained in memory while the latter is being looked at. This memory factor is a prerequisite to the "aid of memory" supposed by Condillac.

In the above explanation we have merely adverted to the fact that the hand guides the motions of the eye without advancing the reason for it. Condillac explains the necessity for this guidance in the context of the inadequacy of eye-movements and other factors but excludes touch. He says:

> Now I cannot imagine what sort of need would induce our statue to form all the judgments necessary for obtaining the idea even of the simplest shape. Moreover, what lucky accident will direct the motion of its eyes so

that they can follow its contour? And even if they were able to follow it, how would the statue assure herself that she will not continually pass from one shape to another? By what means will she be able to judge that three sides, which she has seen one after the other, form a triangle? It is much more likely that her visual sense, only obedient to the action of light, will wander aimlessly through a chaos of shapes: a shifting scene whose parts vanish one after the other.

Here Condillac asserts that the eyes alone are incompetent to follow the contour of any particular object. They could stray, as it were, from the part of one object to the part of some adjacent object or from part to part of the same object in an unorderly fashion. Thus if the statue were able to perceive parts successively, it might unite the part of one object with the part of some other object. Obviously an ordering principle is essential, and for this reason Condillac says the hand must guide the eyes.[5]

Solidity

After the eyes have learned to follow outlines, the statue will see the globe and cube as flat surfaces when it first looks at them. By touching their different parts, the hand feels them to be in relief. The tactual judgment of convexity changes the visual impression so that the "globe takes the same relief." The statue has so firmly united the visual impression with the tactual idea of convexity that it will "no longer see what it is often said it ought to see." A similar consideration applies to the perception of the cube.[6]

Visual Direction and Single Vision

We shall return to the previous supposition that the chaos of colors is perceived at the corneal surfaces. Although the statue may perceive one or another color through acts of attention, it does not see any color as having a determinate place on the surface. However, the motions of the hand in touching objects above or below enable the statue to refer the sensations from its eyes to their appropriate places on the apparent surface. Thus the statue "sees" as above that which it has judged to be above. Through such actions, too, the statue is able to relate the sensations from the two eyes to the single object it touches and in the very same place. Thus the statue sees a single and erect object although the image inside the eyes is double and upside down.[7]

The basic framework of Condillac's thinking may be stated thus. Sensations are modifications of the mind. Since the mind is unextended the sensations do not have the attributes of extension, externality, magnitude, form, position, and order. In becoming related to the spatial properties of things through the sense of touch, the colors are externalized and "spread out" over them. It is through the specific motions of the hand that we learn to see colors as possessing form, size, and so on. The process is similar to the artist who has before him a series of colored pigments. By paying attention to each he notices their diversity, but these colors do not yet constitute a painting. By spreading them in certain ways over the canvas with his brush, he is able to achieve the representation of form, size, and distance. But without his physical canvas and brush, which are extended material objects, no representation is possible.

It is important to observe that the "learning to see" in Condillac's theory refers only to changes in states of consciousness and appearances. Sensation is at first mind-localized and then localized at the eye's surface. In the next step in learning, sensation is referred to objects. The appearance of the globe undergoes a change from flatness to one of convexity, and likewise for all other perceptual facts. All such changes are produced through what he supposes to be the transforming power of ideas derived from motions of the hand. Such learning has taken place so early in life that we have no recollection either of the original states of consciousness nor of the very process of learning itself. Judgments are so mingled with sensation in the present that we can no longer "feel colors in the eyes." The Cheselden Case would not contradict the thesis of an original mind-localization of sensation because the boy, Condillac points out, was not totally blind, being able to see colors in very bright light. In the period of partial blindness the boy had already learned to refer color sensations to his eyes, and after the operation he learned to refer them to external objects. Condillac's description of the boy's learning is similar to what has been said about the statue's learning to see.[8]

The exalted power attributed to the sense of touch is evident when Condillac relates the early recollections of the statue. The statue recalls:

I open my eyes, and I see at first only an obscure haze. I touch, I move forward, I touch again: a chaos gradually unravels itself to my gaze. Touch in some way decomposes the light; it separates the colors, distributes them on objects, separates a luminous space, and in this space of sizes and shapes, leads my eyes up to a certain distance, uncloses to them the road through which they must fly far and wide over the earth, and ascend up to the heavens: before them, in a word, it unfurls the universe.[9]

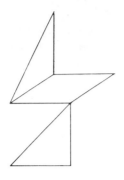

7 REID, HAMILTON, MÜLLER

How the immaterial can be united with matter, how the unextended can apprehend extension, how the indivisible can measure the divided,—this is the mystery of mysteries to man. Hamilton, 1846

Reid was a philosopher of the last half of the eighteenth century, and Hamilton and Müller were respectively a philosopher and physiologist of the first half of the nineteenth century. Generally they accepted the Berkeleyan-type explanation of perception except for several divergences, some of which will be noted. Although the problem of form will be emphasized in this chapter, their opinions concerning other perceptual issues which were to become the subject for controversy will be indicated.

REID

Reid is best known in the history of philosophy and psychology for the distinction of sensation from perception. Discussion of his conception of "original" and "acquired" perceptions and his agreement or disagreement with Berkeley's theory, serves as a convenient point of departure for developing this distinction.

Original Perceptions

According to Reid, the original perceptions which are determined by the "laws of nature" or "laws of our constitution" comprise visible figure, magnitude, and direction. "The objects which we see naturally and originally," he says, "have length and breadth, but not thickness, nor distance from the eye." Thus he supposes that the original perceptions are bi-dimensional and without external reference. In his further description of these objects the acceptance of the constancy hypothesis is fairly explicit, for he supposed that "visible" figure and magnitude correspond to the perspective changes and other attributes of the retinal image. For instance, he asserted that the sum of the angles of a "tangible" triangle is 180° whereas the sum for a "visible" triangle exceeds 180°. Here he supposes that the retinal image of the external flat triangle, in being depicted on the spherical surface of the retina, consists of curved sides; for this reason the sum of the angles of the visible triangle is greater than 180°. When the "tangible" triangle is made sufficiently small, he also said, the sum of the angles of the visible triangle will be almost 180°. Moreover, when he spoke of the "appearance of things to the eye," a common phrase in his writings, he was referring to the correspondence of the properties of the appearance to the properties of the retinal image.

Reid said that his conception of visible figure and magnitude was the same as Berkeley's but that he diverged when he included direction as an original perception. In not accepting Berkeley's solutions of the problem arising from the inversion of the retinal image, he explained the erect appearance of objects in terms of the "law of visible direction." This law, adapted from his predecessor Porterfield, was defined by Reid thus: "Every point of the object is seen in the direction of a right line passing from the picture of that point on the *retina* through the centre of the eye." This law also exemplifies what he meant by a "law of our constitution." Since the projection lines intersect in the eye, the erect appearance of an object is to be regarded as an original perception. Reid advanced no specific statement as to what the phenomenal locus of the original appearance might be. But in view of his acceptance of the Cheselden data, objects touching the eye, we may presume that the boy's perception would have defined this locus.

Acquired Perceptions

External reference, distance, size, solidity, and the constancies of size and shape are among the acquired perceptions which Reid specifically cited. Generally, Berkeley's empiristic explanation is followed. For instance, "We learn to perceive by the eye, almost everything which we can perceive by touch. The original perceptions of this sense, serve only as signs to introduce the acquired." The explanatory details in respect to the formation of associations or connections are similar to those already indicated in the chapter on Berkeley. Of particular interest is a special assumption in the empiristic approach to solidity which Reid made explicit. Having assumed that the original perception of a globe is a flat colored circle, he continued, "But when I have learned to perceive the distance of every part of this object from the eye, this perception gives it convexity and a spherical figure; and adds a third dimension to that which had but two before." We may observe that Reid supposes that the distance of every part of the globe must be perceived, a factor which previous theorists failed to specify. He did not, however, define "part" nor did he supply the details that might account for the way in which its perceived distance is acquired. He introduced this example for the purpose of illustrating the importance of distance perception in the learning of "many other" perceptions. In another context he adopted the usual features of Berkeleyan theory in the learning of distance perception: palpation, faintness, confusion, sensations arising from converging the eyes and the straining the muscles of one eye. Presumably these factors would be operative in the learning of the perception of the convexity of the globe.

The original perceptions, according to Reid, resemble the external objects they represent. The resemblance may be imperfect as in the case of a circle or square viewed obliquely but nevertheless, there is still some degree of resemblance since one visible figure is bounded by a curved line and the other by straight lines. The resemblance is "still more imperfect" in viewing solid figures because "visible extension" has "two dimensions only." However, "it cannot be said that the visible figure of a man, or of a house, hath no resemblance of the objects which they represent." Clearly the resemblance to which Reid refers in this instance pertains to the bi-dimensional form or contour of the man or house. Thus Reid disagreed with an important point in Berkeley's theory, namely, the nonresemblance of visible and external figure.[1]

SENSATION AND PERCEPTION

The distinction between sensation and perception which Reid proposed cannot be readily stated since no explicit definition of sensation was provided. In acknowledging his failure to say what sensation is, he proceeded to supply many examples of what it is not. In this way he hoped that a clear meaning of it, and also of perception, would be achieved. Discussion of the distinction can be facilitated, however, by confining it to original perceptions and by attributing dimensional characteristics to visible figure. Such a figure depending on what is being viewed may be described as circular, triangular, quadrangular, and so on.

Having said that mind was an "unextended and indivisible substance," Reid inferred that "there cannot be in it any thing that resembles extension." Evidently if extension is in the mind, it follows that mind must be extended. Since Reid supposed that sensation is "in the mind" or an "impression on the mind," it would seem that sensation cannot be extended nor can it have shape. This interpretation is borne out in his discussion of pain, for he said that it would be absurd to think that the "pain of the gout resembles a square or a triangle." But since visible figure avowedly possesses dimensional attributes, in Reid's theory it cannot be an "impression on the mind." Therefore, the visible figure is not a sensation.

I feel a pain," he says, denotes a sensation. It is phenomenally subjective or a state of feeling without reference either to its cause or to an object. On the other hand, "I feel a pain in my toe" is quite different. This statement includes a reference to an object and the possible cause of the pain and defines, according to Reid, a perception. This perception thus has two aspects, a sensation and an object. One is "in the mind" and the other is obviously not since it refers to a part of the body. The object-reference of the sensation occurs when the sensation is "combined in our thought, with the cause of it, which is really in the toe." The combination is effected by an "operation of the mind" which reflects a law of our constitution; therefore, this perception is an original perception. However, the sensation in itself conveys no information as to its source in the body. The location of the source may be in the toe, in the tooth, or in any part of the body. But the innate operations of the mind determine the localization of pain in the appropriate parts of the body. Says Reid:

> How do we know the parts of our bodies affected by particular pains? Not by experience or by reasoning, but by the constitution of nature. The sensation of pain is, no doubt, in the mind, and cannot be said to have any relation, from its own nature, to any part of the body: but this sensation, by our constitution, gives a perception of some particular part of the body, whose disorder causes the uneasy sensation. If it were not so, a man who never before felt either the gout or the toothach, when he is first seized with the gout in his toe, might mistake it for the toothach.

What is true for a pain-sensation is also true for all sensations.

The three original perceptions of sight, in Reid's theory, convey some information of spatial attributes of objects. A color sensation, on the other hand, conveys none since it is presumed to be a conscious state similar to pain or pleasure. But this formulation leads to a problem. When we hurt our foot there is no doubt that pain is felt. However, in looking at an object, there is no feeling at all—we simply see it. We say, according to Reid, "we *perceive* the colour of the body, not that we feel it." He resolves the problem by supposing that the visual sensation is "indifferent" and "draws no attention" whereas the pain-sensation does.

A sensation of color, like that of pain, is merely a feeling or subjective state of consciousness. It has no resemblance to an external object, has no form, and conveys no information of its cause in the stimulation of the retina or of any object external to the mind. We may pause to consider the objection that visible figure, in being regarded as an original perception, is necessarily colored. We cannot imagine the possibility of a figure devoid of color. This objection implies that the figure is in the mind because its color is in the mind. In this case the mind is shaped. This objection, partly acknowledged by Reid, is resolved by regarding color and figure as separate entities. Visible figure, however, must still be accounted for. Reid says that the "same material [retinal] impression suggests both colour and visible figure" to the mind. According to him, the color is in the mind whereas the visible figure is "presented" to the mind or is "altogether external" to the mind. The color, however, "is always joined with it." The laws of our constitution are responsible for the double suggestion and the joining of color to figure.[2]

Reid omitted one important fact in his treatment of visible figure as an original perception. A perception, he says, is distinguished from sensation because it refers to an object. The feeling of pain in the toe is a perception because an object (the toe) has been combined by the mind with the feeling. The toe as an object also has a location. And, of course, the toe is external to the mind. But since the visible figure is the object of the original perception, it ought to have a location. It is this fact of location which Reid failed to discuss. It would seem, however, that he implicitly supposed the retina was its original phenomenal locus. According to him, "the visible figure of a body may, by mathematical reasoning, be inferred from its real figure, distance, and position, with regard to the eye." However, mathematical reasoning can only lead to inferences concerning the characteristics of retinal pictures or images on the basis of the characteristics of external objects and the laws of optics. The mathematician can infer that the sum of the angles of the image of a triangle projected by an external plane triangle exceeds 180° or that the size of the image shrinks as an object recedes from the eye, but he cannot know whether these images will produce any mental effect whatsoever. And this is still true even if he knows that the action of light causes a material impression on the retina. Those properties of the retinal image inferred by the mathematician are the very properties which Reid ascribed to the visible figure. Evidently Reid presupposed a geometric congruency of visible figure and retinal image or "retinal impression." It is in this presupposition that Reid might have assumed that the phenomenal locus of the visible figure was in the eye. We may observe that the "objects" of an original perception are presumed to have some location, as in his acceptance of the Cheselden data. But since the "objects" touching the eye do not constitute the visible figures, the mathematician could never ascertain this to be the case on the basis of reasoning, their phenomenal locus must be elsewhere and the most probable place is the retina. If this is what Reid meant, the visible figure would be external to the mind but the sensation which is joined to it would be in the mind. Thus Reid could save the assumption of an unextended mind substance although accepting visible figure as an original and extended entity. This interpretation of Reid's theory would not mean that the visible figure should ever be felt to be localized in the retina; for an innate operation of the mind such as the law of visible direction would instantaneously produce the phenomenal externalization of the figure to the outer surface of the eye.[3]

In speaking of acquired perceptions of sight, the object and its reference are quite clear. For then Reid refers to what the average person says he sees: a man, a tree, and so on, at a distance. These perceptions, however, still retain the subjective sensational component of color. Thus in calling "I see a tree" a perception, Reid is referring to one that has been acquired. The tree perceived at a distance is the object and its color the sensation.

The *Dictionary of Philosophy and Psychology* (1901) says, "The first English writer who made a serious attempt to give a precise and circumscribed meaning to the word perception is Reid. His views, so far as they are psychological and not epistemological, agree in substance with those of modern psychologists." The concepts of sensation and perception are defined thus:

> Sensation: Subjective state produced by an external stimulus without implying any awareness of an object. To have a sensation is merely to have a certain kind of feeling due to an impression on the organs of sense.
>
> Perception: To be aware of an object by means of a present sensation.

HAMILTON

Asks Hamilton, "Does Vision afford us a primary knowledge of extension?" Its meaning, he says, refers only to the bi-dimensional "figured extension" of "plane figures." The question was asked in the context of a discussion of the opinion of many philosophers who believed that "extension is not an object of sight" and who maintained that perceived extension was to be explained in terms of acts of memory or associations. Hamilton selected several of its representatives, such as Stewart and Brown, as targets of an aggressive critique.

Stewart, who wished to illustrate the general principle that the "mind can only attend to one thing at once," supposed the "eye to be fixed in a particular position, and the picture of an object to be painted on the retina." According to him, the outline of the picture consists of a series of separated points each of which constitutes a "distinct object of attention to the mind." A point so perceived is defined as a *minimum visibile*. In order to explain why the "mind does at one and the same time perceive every point in the outline of the object," he said that the mind shifts its attention from one point of the outline to the other. "These acts of attention," moreover, "are performed with such rapidity, that the effect, with respect to us, is the same as if the perception were instantaneous." He added as a further condition, the ability of the mind to remember all preceding perceived points while its attention is engaged in perceiving a particular point. "Without the faculty of memory, we could have had no perception of visible figure."

The assumption of mind as a "simple and indivisible" substance and the rejection of Reid's original laws of the mind were the two principal reasons at the basis of Brown's rejection of the perception of form as an object of sight. What he said about sensation as a secondary quality was similar to Reid's concept of sensation, but he emphasized a feature which Reid did not discuss. The mind, according to Brown, can have but one sensation at a time. To suppose two simultaneous sensations is "manifestly absurd" because, then, the mind would be complex and divisible. The "phenomena of the mind," he concluded are "obviously successive." The perception of form, in his opinion, was the result of the intimate association of the succession of muscular sensations which accompanied the touching of an object and movements of the eye with the succession of color sensations. Brown considered an objection: the shape and color are perceived as a single simultaneous unit and not one independently of the other. The theory, he said, was not invalidated because the two successions are so "blended" that an appearance of unity is perceived. Despite this appearance, however, Brown believed perception was still a compound of visual and muscular sensations. We may observe that Brown could not concede the authenticity of the appearance of simultaneity for, in his opinion, the mind could have but "one feeling" at any moment.

Hamilton observed that Brown's theory logically implied the perception of one *minimum visibile* at one moment, as explicitly stated by Stewart, since the simultaneous perception of two *minimum visibilia* would mean that the mind was extended. He advanced a number of objections to the common hypothesis which, inasmuch as they cannot be separated from his own theoretical position, will be discussed together.[4]

WHOLE AND PARTS

Says Hamilton:

> On this hypothesis, we must suppose that at every instantaneous opening of
> the eyelids, the moment sufficient for us to take in the figure of the objects
> comprehended in the sphere of vision, is subdivided into almost infinitesimal
> parts, in each of which a separate act of attention is performed. This is, of
> itself, sufficiently inconceivable.

The hypothesis, moreover, would require the "addition of an almost
infinite number of separate and consecutive acts of attention." Hamilton also included the number of associations within the scope of the
"almost infinite number." He added what he regarded to be a "self-evident" refutation of the hypothesis. Everyone supposes that the perception of color is an original perception which necessarily implies that
one color sensation can be discriminated from another color sensation.
Imagine now that one color is surrounded by another color. The contrasting colors bounding each other will meet in a "visible line" and
"thus constitute the outline of a visible figure." He concluded, "The
perception of extension, therefore, is necessarily given in the perception of colors."

According to Hamilton, "The mind in elaborating its knowledge,
proceeds by analysis, from the whole to the parts." This thesis is extensively discussed through many examples, of which we cite a few. In perceiving the face of a friend today we immediately recognize him as the
same person we saw yesterday. The immediacy of recognition excludes
its interpretation in terms of successive acts of attention directed to the
individual parts of either the perceived or remembered face. The simultaneous apprehension of the perceived and remembered wholes,
and their similarity as well, are responsible for the recognition. Indeed, knowledge of the individual parts may be relatively unimpor-
tant. Thus, we may not even know the color of the eyes or some other
facial characteristic and, yet, recognition still occurs. To attain this
kind of knowledge, a "detailed examination of its parts" is necessary
by directing our attention to them. The ordinary person cannot apprehend the difference between two sheep, and even if they were presented to him twice, "he would be unable to discriminate the one from
the other." A shepherd on the other hand "can distinguish every indi-

vidual sheep" because he can descend from the vague knowledge that makes every sheep a "repetition of the same undifferenced unit" to a "definite knowledge of qualities by which each is contrasted from its neighbor." The ordinary person, however, makes the "whole of each sheep" the object of knowledge and consequently he cannot "discriminate them from each other." A child who has been taught to say *papa* when his father is pointed to, will apply the name to other men he sees. All men at first "appear to him similar" because he reacts to the "more striking appearances of objects," but with further instruction he "studies to discriminate the objects," sees their differences, and consequently comes to apply the designating name to one object only. Perceived wholes, Hamilton concludes, are prior to the perception of the parts.

The contested hypothesis, on the other hand, presupposes a "synthetic approach," that we know the "whole through the parts" and the "parts better than the whole." It further presupposes that "we know the face of a friend through the multitude of perceptions which we have of the different points of which it is made up." The "points" composing the nose ought to be more "vivid" than the nose, and this part more vivid than the "whole countenance." Hamilton dismisses this hypothesis as incorrect and concludes, "In fact, on the doctrine of these philosophers, if the mind, as they maintain, were unable to comprehend more than one perceptible minimum at a time, the greatest of all inconceivable marvels would be, how it has contrived to realize the knowledge of wholes and masses which it has."

It is important to realize that the original perception of form so strenuously argued for by Hamilton, is only the perception of a bi-dimensional outline which corresponds to the retinal image. For the further understanding of this assumption and other features of Hamilton's theory we may consider his opinion concerning "mind" and external reference.[5]

MIND AND EXTERNAL REFERENCE

Hamilton's theory of perception is based on what he terms the principle of the "veracity of consciousness." "The possibility of all philosophy is dependent," he says, "on the truth of consciousness." The facts of consciousness are "authentic," the "authority" of consciousness is unchallengeable and it cannot be a "false witness." From this principle he inferred that a "sensation is actually felt . . . where it is felt to be." We may consider the feeling of pain in the toe for the purpose of illustrating the point Hamilton wishes to make. On the basis of the testimony of consciousness we feel pain in the toe, and as a fact of consciousness it is indubitable. This is equivalent, according to Hamilton, to asserting that the sensation of pain is localized in the toe. Other philosophers, he says, who supposed that the sensation is a "mere affection of the mind" denied this principle. They are led to this opinion by supposing that the mind, in being located in the brain, "only perceives in the head." In order to avoid attributing the "properties of extension and place" to the mind, they may further suppose its "seat to be but a point." These opinions clearly contradict the veracity principle, we do not feel the pain sensation in the head or in the brain nor do we perceive a point. In continuation with this discussion Hamilton further maintains:

> We have no right, however, to say that it is limited to any one part of the organism; for even if we admit that the nervous system is the part to which it is proximately united, still the nervous system is itself universally ramified throughout the body; and we have no more right to deny that the mind feels at the finger-points, as consciousness assures us, than to assert that it thinks exclusively in the brain.

It is "simpler and more philosophical" to suppose that the mind is "united with the nervous system in its whole extent" and that it is "really present wherever we are conscious it acts." Therefore, since pain is felt in the toe, the mind extends to the nerve endings in that member.[6]

Hamilton discussed several meanings of the word "object" in the phrase "object of perception." It may refer to the external object, but in this case it can never be perceived. It may also refer to the "organic affection" in the retina or in the brain. The supposition that the cerebral affection is the object would imply that the mind is located in the brain only. Therefore, this affection would be perceived as an affection either of the mind or in the head. However, Hamilton wishes to make the "perception . . . as different from the Self" an intrinsic property of mind in its relation to the body. From the way Hamilton has conceived the problem, his only recourse is to suppose that the retinal affection is the object of perception (with some qualification), and to further suppose the presence of mind in the retina. Thus an original perception in being retinally localized would have not only the property of "non-ego" but also the properties of extension and shape. That this is Hamilton's position may be inferred from the assertions:

> (1) Therefore the thing perceived and the percipient organ must meet in a place,—must be contiguous. The consequence of this doctrine is a complete simplification of the theory of perception and a return to a most ancient speculation on the point. (2) I would, therefore, establish as a fundamental position of the doctrine of an immediate perception, the opinion of Democritus, that all our senses are only modifications of touch; in other words, that the external object of perception is always in contact with the organ of sense.

Thus the place of contiguity of mind and body of the first statement becomes the retina in the second statement. Just as the touching of the toe produces a localized sensation there, so too the pressure of light in acting upon the retina produces the localization of the original phenomenal object in the retina. Hamilton most clearly defines the object of perception in relation to hearing. "The object of your hearing is not the vibrations of my larynx, nor the vibrations of the intervening air; but the vibrations determined thereby in the cavity of the internal ear, and in immediate contact with the auditory nerves." Should this statement be transposed to vision, the object of seeing would be in immediate contact with the optic nerves.[7]

Said Hamilton, "corporeal movement and the mental perception are simultaneous." Since "movement" refers to the organic affection at the place where a sensory organ receives stimulation, the mental perception is evidently formed in the organ itself: in the eye, ear, and so on. Since mind is necessary to perception, he presupposed that mind must extend to each of these organs so that the necessary simultaneity could be achieved. Therefore, he further presupposed not only that the retinal image is perceived but also that it is perceived in the retina. This perception, therefore, would be a bi-dimensional or a "plane" figure.

If in fact Hamilton did presuppose the object of vision to be in the retina, it is also evident that he would want this object to appear detached from the body. Incidentally, the object presumed to be in immediate contact with the retina is inverted, and therefore it should be perceived as upside down. In order to explain the natural perception of externality and the erect appearance of objects Hamilton introduced the law of visible direction which he defined as the "natural perception . . . of the direction of the rays of light." The original perception of externality, in his view, would be objects touching the eyes; the Cheselden Case is cited as confirming this opinion. It is in the discussion of this case that Hamilton, the law of visible direction being temporarily set aside, presupposed that the original localization of perception would be somewhere in the eye. He wrote:

> In the case of Cheselden—that in which the blindness previous to the recovery of sight was most perfect, and therefore the most instructive upon record—the patient, though he had little or no perception of *distance,* i.e. of the *degree of externality,* had still a perception of that externality absolutely. The objects, he said, seemed to "touch his eyes, as what he felt did his skin"; but they did not appear to him as if *in* his eyes, far less as a mere affection of the organ. . . . This natural perception of Outness, which is the foundation of our acquired knowledge of distance, seems given us in the natural perception we have of the direction of the rays of light.[8]

Moreover, in having posited the perception of the direction of light rays, Hamilton must have the mind present in the retina in order for this perception to occur. For if the mind were situated only in the brain, a possibility against which he argued, the mind would be unable to perceive the rays.

He maintained that the verification of the natural perception of outness in the Cheselden Case invalidated Berkeley's theory of perception. All other perceptions are acquired. The mode of learning as outlined by him generally was similar to what Berkeley and Reid had already said. Incidentally, Hamilton apparently contradicted his own firmly enunciated principle pertaining to the "veracity of consciousness" since no one perceives objects as touching the eyes. But here he would have followed the traditional doctrine, the eye-localization not being noticed after learning.

An important but obscure feature of Hamilton's doctrine relates to the explanation of perception in terms of innate principles of the mind. One such principle which pertains to "locomotive energy," is the ability of the mind to expend and to appreciate the degree of "mental energy" necessary to overcome an external force which impedes or resists the action of muscles. In this view, a muscular feeling, which originates in the stimulation of nerve endings in muscles, is a passive state of consciousness. On the basis of this feeling, we become aware of certain tension in the muscles but we cannot judge whether an external force is responsible for the tension. And even if we could, we would not know the magnitude of this force. The expenditure of energy, which Hamilton also termed an action of the mind, is essential to such knowledge. Moreover, he maintained that this principle was necessary for the perception of externality. Without any action of the mind whatever, the mind, being passive, would only experience sensation and not sensation localized in part of the body. By way of illustration we may consider a case study which Hamilton regarded as "remarkable." A man was paralyzed in one-half of the body but his ability to experience pain was unimpaired. When his hand was strongly and secretly squeezed the pain was so intense that he screamed. This pain, however, was "merely general"; it was not localized in any part of the body. But on recovery from the paralysis he also "recovered the power of localizing his sensations." While paralyzed he was unable to expend any energy to oppose the pressure applied to his hand, whereas the facts were different subsequent to his recovery. In one instance there was only the subjective feeling or "mere sensation" and in the other, a feeling localized in part of the body or "perception."

Although he did not consider this "rare case" to be conclusive, it may nevertheless contribute to an understanding of his theory of perception. We have already noted his assumption that mind is present in the place of the body where pain is localized. Therefore, the inability of the paralytic to localize pain in the hand seems to mean either the mind was no longer present in the hand or the ability of the mind to act had been temporarily neutralized by the paralysis. In any case Hamilton seems to have presupposed that pain would be mind-localized when mind is passive.

Hamilton discussed this case in the general context of the natural perceptions of sight, and we shall suppose that it is relevant to them. In this same context he asserted as a basic principle that "perception results from action" and as a further principle, "the only object perceived is the organ itself, as modified, or what is in contact with the organ, as resisting." We observe that the retina is the only organ of the visual sense that may be capable of resisting the action of light. By virtue of the presence of the mind in the retina, together with its ability to perceive resistance to light, the mind would perceive color and form as though extended on the retina. This perception, related to an impression of the body as in the case of pain localization, would exemplify the meaning of "non-ego." But since Hamilton wants the perceived object to appear as external to the body, another innate principle becomes necessary. In this instance, the ability of the mind to perceive the direction of light rays would be relevant. This ability would enable the mind to project the image so that it is perceived as an entity in space, detached from the self and from the body. The result of this projection would be the perception of objects touching the eye.

Hamilton never explained what he meant by the visual sense being a modification of the sense of touch. Did the action of light cause the retinal endings to move? A positive answer is indicated when he said "corporeal movement" in the organ of sense was produced by the contact of an object with the organ. And if the retinal elements are presumed to move, they could then offer resistance to the continuation of this motion. Perhaps this explains why he did not accept the supposition already common in his period that the retinal effects produced by light were electrical or chemical in nature, for the concept of touch or contact is not readily reconcilable with this supposition.[9]

MÜLLER

In his extensive discussion of the "physiology of the senses" Müller insisted that the external object could not be the object of perception because it was at some distance from the eye. However, the object produced a retinal image which, in turn, might determine another image in the brain. The image, whether retinal or cerebral, caused an "idea of sense." Therefore, he maintained that the immediate object of perception had to be an idea or image, and for this reason he said the "mind perceives images or ideas." The question arose as to whether mind perceived the image as a simultaneous extended form so that the perception would represent the relations among the different parts of the retinal image or whether the mind perceived the image as a succession of parts.

He considered in this regard the theory of Herbart and his followers, which we shall state and paraphrase from Müller's statement. Herbart, who supposed the mind to be an unextended, immaterial, and indivisible substance, regarded sensation as a mathematical point because the mind substance was "conceived only as a mathematical point." He had also endowed the mind with the ability of quickly traveling over each point of the extended cerebral image so as to explain the perception of extension. Müller stated several objections to Herbart's hypothesis and considered the possibility of circumventing them on the supposition that the mind is stationary at a particular point of the image. In his view this supposition would imply that the cerebral seat of sensation is also a mathematical point and he said, "But there is no indication in the brain of any provision for such a concentration of all sensual impressions upon a single point." Steinbuch, said Müller, revised Herbart's hypothesis and supposed that the retina was the seat of vision. However, he limited perception to the affection of a single retinal point of the image, and for the purpose of explaining the perception of extension or form he invoked the conscious contraction of the muscles of the eye so that the eye would be moved in the ways appropriate to the perceived form. According to him, perception of form was the product of acquired associations. Müller did not understand how this explanation could be reconciled with the "power which we enjoy of perceiving in a moment all parts of an impression [retinal image] occupying a considerable extent." He also raised a factual objection which in its statement contains a central point of Müller's own theory of perception. He said,

> But if we reflect, that a new-born animal gives evidence of the perception of position and form, by means of the sense of sight, in its immediately applying itself to the teats, we shall scarcely doubt the fact that, antecedently to all education, impressions of form and position or extension in space are perceived in the retina.

His doctrine of "innate" form perception applies to human vision as well as to animal vision, but the important thing to observe is the fact that he said the "impression of form is perceived in the retina" which contrasts with the implication in Herbart's hypothesis that this impression is perceived in the brain. In concluding his appraisal of the hypothesis he said:

> The most probable view, therefore, is, that the mind is present at the same time in all parts of the brain, without itself being composed of

parts, and that it recognises the extension and qualities of form and position in the impressions on the senses, by virtue of its general presence.

We may observe that Herbart's hypothesis implied that the mind, regarded as a "point," could only be at a single position at a given moment for the perception of one point of the cerebral image; whereas Müller implied that the mind is simultaneously present at every point of the image. In view of what he said concerning the perception of form in the retina, the general presence of the mind would be required in all parts of the retina. Müller discussed these issues in the "metaphysical" section toward the end of the *Physiology of the Senses,* but a similar point of view is also evident in other sections.[10]

Müller pointed out that in gazing at the blue sky we can see an "indistinct confused movement, as of points crossing each other in all directions." The paths of these points, quite short and apparently bright, represent the "visible movement of the blood." The capillaries supplying the retina with blood, being placed slightly in front of the retina, intercept light rays. Under ordinary viewing conditions, however, the contours of the capillaries and of the moving dark blood cannot be observed. Moreover, with the right viewing conditions, it is possible to see the branches of the blood vessels as well. In discussing such facts, Müller stated, "we have here a distinct demonstration of the axiom, that in vision we perceive merely certain states of the retina, and that the retina is itself the field of vision." The following question is then asked: "Where is the state of the retina perceived; in the retina itself, or in the brain?" Müller said this question could not be decisively answered because of inadequacies in the anatomical knowledge of the nervous system. For instance, the number of fibers in the optic nerve at the retina exceeds the number of fibers of this nerve at its presumed place of termination in the brain, and if this observation is confirmed in further anatomical investigation, he does not see how the cerebral image could represent all parts of the retinal image so as to explain human vision. As a provisional opinion, therefore, he says that the "state of the retina" or retinal images are "perceived in the retina itself." The fact that "nerves of the higher senses are merely prolongations of the sensorium," moreover, may make it possible for the "action of the mind" to extend to the retina. The retina evidently is to be regarded as the seat of visual sensation. Similar considerations apply to the other higher senses; for instance, "The sound itself is always seated but in one place, namely, in our ear." Müller's development of these issues is guided by an analogy to the sense of touch, where the perceived sensation seems to "occupy the seat of its production." [11]

The learning of external reference, according to Müller, begins while the child is *in utero*. There the child will have learned the "obscure conceptions of a percipient body opposed to the external world," a world which occupies space. The way in which the child opposes and resists the actions of the uterine wall impinging against its body contributes to the development of such conceptions. The child also learns a conception of self and the idea of things which are external to the self. By touching himself and the uterine wall, he learns too that he has a body different from the wall enclosing him. He gains in short the "idea of an external world as the cause of sensations." Müller summarizes this phase of learning thus:

> Though the sensations of the being actually inform him only of the states of himself, of his nerves, and of his skin, acted on by external impressions, yet, henceforth, the idea of the perception of the external cause becomes inseparably associated with the sensation of touch; and such the condition of sensation in the adult.

Müller acknowledged that it is difficult to know how a child experiences the world after birth when he can now see, and he surmised that the child will not perceive images in the retina because he does not yet know that the image of his body is distinct from the images of the new objects now in external space. The "obscure ideas" acquired prenatally together with some additional learning may make him realize that the images of things are external to himself but still part of the images of his body. This phase of learning with some accompanying evidence is described by Müller as follows:

> The images of objects are formed in the retina in one surface, just as the retina is extended in that form. They will appear to the mind as depicted on a surface, and will excite no idea of proximity or distance, or of the actual occupation of space. However soon the child may recognise the images as things exterior to itself, they still appear to it to occupy one plane, to be all at the same distance from it: it catches at the most distant, as at the nearest object,—it grasps at the moon. The boy born blind, to whom Cheselden restored sight by operation, saw all objects as

if they lay in one plane, although in him the ideas of the corporeal world obtained through the sense of touch were completely developed. It seemed to him as if the objects 'touched his eyes as what he felt did his skin'.[12]

Inasmuch as the retina is the seat of sensation and it is of small size, the original perception of image size ought to be correspondingly small. "The actual size of the field of vision depends on the extent of the retina, for only so many images can be seen at any one time as can occupy the retina at the same time; and thus considered the retina, of which the affections are perceived by the sensorium, is itself the field of vision." Müller then supposes that the "mind projects the images on the retina towards the exterior." Depending on the degree of projection, the "size of the field of vision," he says, can "appear very small or very large." But we may observe that if such action of the mind is excluded, the size of the field of vision must be very small. This is a necessary consequence of one of the "general laws" of the senses which he formulated: *"That sensations are referred from their proper seat towards the exterior, is owing, not to anything in the nature of the nerves themselves, but to the accompanying idea derived from experience."* [13]

The ideas derived through the sense of touch and movements of the body are the means for the projection of the images. These ideas become associated with the "images of objects" so that these images appear to be at some distance. Through association we also learn to perceive the size, shape, solidity, and relative distance of these images.[14]

The nature of the projection as supposed by Müller is depicted in Figure 7.1. It will be observed that the orientation of the image "projected by the agency of the mind" is the same as the orientation of the retinal image, but inverted in respect to the orientation of the object. Although the orientations of the projected image and object are inverse, Müller neither supposed erect appearance to be an acquired perception nor did he even consider it to be a problem. He asked: "whether we really see the images inverted, as they are in the retina; or erect, as in the object itself." In his answer to this query, inversion is regarded as a relational term involving the comparison of two things. He pointed out that since we perceive images only, "inversion" has no meaning. The second term of the comparison is not known to the perceiver. To be sure the study of optics proves the retinal image

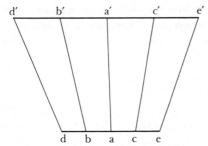

Figure 7.1. (After Müller's Figure 97.) If the retina is regarded as a plane surface, the points d through e represent points of the retinal image. The corresponding points in the projected image are represented by d' through e'. Although the light rays cross inside the eye, the orientation of the image points in the retinal image is the same as the orientation in the projected image points. Thus the image $d'-e'$ and object have reversed orientations.

to be reversed, he said, but this is of no consequence since the relative position of the images is the same as that of the external objects. Even the supposition that "we do see objects reversed" leads to no particular problem, for everything is seen reversed. The fact that the sense of touch "perceives every thing in its erect position" does not lead to the conclusion that there is a "discordant" relation between sight and touch; "even the image of our hand," continued Müller, "while used in touch, is seen inverted." Therefore in touching, say, the upper part of the object, we perceive the image of that part as being in agreement with the perceived image of the hand. He concluded, "This position in which we see objects, we call therefore the erect position." [15]

Concluding Comments

By whatever the route and however defined, Reid, Hamilton, and Müller share the common feature of accepting an original perception of form in two dimensions. Hamilton and Müller, as did Reid, presupposed some degree of resemblance between the original perception and the external object in respect to extension and other similar primary qualities. Moreover, the Cheselden data were accepted except for the feature pertaining to form; in their view the boy could discriminate the forms of objects. Hamilton attributed the boy's failure to identify objects to the inability to directly correlate the tactual names with the new perceptions.[16]

However, they neglected to account for a significant feature of the Cheselden data, namely, "objects touching the eyes." The law of visible direction which Reid and Hamilton accepted for the purpose of explaining erect vision, and which Hamilton proposed for the explanation of the natural perception of externality, is neutral in respect to the phenomenal locus of a perceived object. They could have supposed this locus to be somewhat to one side of the point where the rays intersect inside the eye, or at any distance away from the eye. Although Müller had a different conception of projection, there is a similar if not more critical a problem. For in supposing that the locus of the phenomenal object is in the retina and that the projection is the result of experience, it would have to be explained how this object apparently detaches itself from the retina. Evidently the Cheselden data dictated their choice of the cornea's outer surface; and they did not see that there was a problem for explanation, irrespective of whether the projection was regarded as original or as acquired.[17]

Reid, Hamilton, and Müller said that the localization of pain in either the real or phantom limb was original or innate. It may be asked why they did not accept a similar opinion in respect to distance perception. Thus they could have supposed the perception of a bi-dimensional form at some undefined distance "away from the eye" to be an original datum of sight. The reason that they did not do so may lie in the common assumption:

> It may be taken for a general rule that things which are produced by custom may be undone or changed by disuse or contrary custom. On the other hand, it is a strong argument that an effect is not owing to custom, but to the constitution of nature, when a contrary custom is found neither to change nor to weaken it.

This statement quoted from Reid has its parallel much later in Müller who said, "an innate property . . . never undergoes any change." The phantom limb experience presumably did not disappear even many years after surgery, said Müller, and hence the localization was innate. But the Cheselden boy at first saw things "touching the eye" and later at some distance; distance perception obviously changes and is therefore acquired.[18]

We may observe that the coextensivity of mind and body presupposed by Hamilton and Müller might imply that the mind is extended; since it is distributed throughout the nervous system, the mind ought to be regarded as extended. However, both accepted the traditional assumption of an unextended mind. Hamilton, in referring to this question, asserted that we are "ignorant" of the relationship of mind and body—his mystery of mysteries.

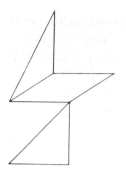

8 MILL, BAIN, LOTZE

What is it we mean, or what is it which leads us to say, that the objects we perceive are external to us, and not a part of our own thoughts? J. S. Mill, 1865

The theories of J. S. Mill, Bain, and Lotze presuppose Reid's dichotomy of sensation and perception but further presuppose, however, the absence of any original perception. Their collective position is represented in Bain's distinction of two types of consciousness—"the Object consciousness and the Subject consciousness." The first type is illustrated by the "experience or consciousness of a tree, river, a constellation" and the second type, by the "experience of a pleasure, a pain, a volition, a thought." The transition from *subject* to *object* consciousness is effected by acquired associations. Thus it is supposed that the "laws of association" can explain the perception of form. Fundamental to this approach is the assumption of an unextended mind. Although there are some important differences in their theories, as will be observed subsequently, nevertheless there is considerable overlap. Generally those aspects which give a particular theory its distinctive character will be emphasized.[1]

Mill and Bain were friends who mutually influenced each other in the development of their theories. Both regarded themselves as followers of Berkeley's theory and both interpreted the data of the Cheselden report as important evidence for this theory. Lotze, who did not acknowledge the influence of any predecessor, regarded his theory as the logical development of the assumption of an unextended mind. Interested only in understanding the "first formation of spatial ideas," he did not regard the data of resighted persons as relevant because whatever spatial knowledge had been acquired while blind, through touch and movement, might have affected their visual perceptions on restoration of sight.

J. S. MILL

Mill's theoretical outlook developed over a period of about two decades. In 1842 and 1843 the main features of Berkeley's theory of "visible objects," as qualified by the assumption of the constancy hypothesis, and Berkeley's explanation were accepted. At that time Mill accepted form as an attribute of original perception but in the further development of his theory in response to Hamilton, this attribute was questioned.

WHOLES AND PARTS

Mill examines and rejects Hamilton's "self-evident" proof that perception of shape is immediately given by sight. In order to ascertain what can be "cognised by sight alone," Mill stipulates a non-moving eye as a criterion: "If we once allow the eye to follow the direction of a line or the periphery of a figure, we have no longer merely sight, but important muscular sensations superadded." Since Hamilton ignored the criterion and the possibility of eye-movement his argument, Mill says, is not decisive. Mill then asserts his own opinion that the muscular modifications of the shape of lens and direction of the optic axis are important "in giving us our acquired perceptions of sight." And he further asserts that in the absence of any such modification, "the impression we should have of a boundary between two colours would be so vague and indistinct as to be merely rudimentary."

In granting some "rudimentary conception" it is apparent that

Mill's rejection of the Hamilton argument is not absolute. Writes Mill:

> . . . for it is evident that even without moving the eye we are capable of having two sensations of colour at once, and that the boundary which separates the colours must give some specific affection of sight, otherwise we should have no discriminative impressions capable of afterwards becoming, by association, representative of the cognitions of lines and figures which we owe to the tactual and the muscular sense.

Although the "specific affection of sight" is not defined, Mill probably means that by the immovable eye we can perceive a small segment of a boundary, this segment being straight or curved. For if this degree of perception were not granted, we should never be able to learn the perceptions of a square and circle through associations, where the external objects are correspondingly a square and a circle. The main difference between Mill and Hamilton then lies in how much of a perceived form is given by the motionless eye, for one a "part" and the other a "whole." [2]

Laws of Association

Mill believed that the laws of association, which had been formulated by others before him but which he further developed, would enable him to answer other objections raised by Hamilton concerning "wholes and parts."

Law of inseparable association. "When two phenomena have been very often experienced in conjunction, and have not, in any single instance, occurred separately either in experience or in thought, there is produced between them [an] Inseparable . . . Association." Color and form have never been perceived independently of one another. Through repetition the association between them becomes so "irresistible" that we cannot even think them to have ever been separable entities. Mill deduces another though unnamed law from the general law. He writes: "When an association has acquired this character of inseparability . . . things which we are unable to conceive apart, appear incapable of existing apart; and the belief we have in their coexistence, though really a product of experience, seems intuitive." Thus we come to regard a perceived colored form as intuitive rather than as the product of association. His point is made somewhat more concretely in another example of the "perceptions of sight which, though instantaneous and unhesitating, are not intuitive." Says Mill:

> We see, and cannot help seeing, what we have learnt to infer, even when we know that the inference is erroneous, and that the apparent perception is deceptive. We cannot help seeing the moon larger when near the horizon, though we know that she is of precisely the same size.

But the seeing of the moon larger at the horizon is not true seeing, according to Mill, since it represents neither an intuitive nor an original perception. "What we see," he says, "is a very minute fragment of what we think we see." [3]

The law of inseparable association and its consequence are important to Mill in overcoming Hamilton's objections to the doctrine of an acquired form percept. For instance, Hamilton concluded from his inability to conceive of color dissociated from form that the perception of form was an original perception. Mill concedes the inability, explains it as the consequence of associations, and denies the conclusion. Hamilton is correct in believing form to be currently intuitive, but incorrect in supposing it to be an original intuition.

Law of obliviscence. "When a number of ideas suggest one another by association with such certainty and rapidity as to coalesce together in a group, all those members of the group which remain long without being specially attended to, have a tendency to drop out of consciousness. Our consciousness of them becomes more and more faint and evanescent, until no effort of attention can recall it into distinctness, or at last recall it at all." [4]

The law may account for the inability to recover the original "parts" in present consciousness but it is clearly insufficient, for it does not explain why a "whole" is perceived. For this reason another law is necessary.

Law of attention. "We attend only to that which, either on its own or on some other account, interests us. In consequence, what interests us only momentarily we only attend to momentarily; and do not go on attending to it, when that, for the sake of which alone it interested us, has been attained."

Mill regards this law as decisive in invalidating Hamilton's thesis that wholes precede parts. The details of the face are of no importance in their own right except to serve as "signs" that it is the face of a friend we see. In having served this function we fail to notice them, since the percept of the face, the object of interest, is paramount. In confirmation he cites the case of reading and the apprehension of meaning. The letters and syllables composing words "must have been present to us for at least a passing moment" and yet later we usually "retain no impression" of them. Our attention is directed to meaning rather than to the parts making up the words. This same example also illustrates the fact that "our knowledge begins with the parts, and not with the whole." We first attended to letters and syllables before learning the meanings of words and sentences; after learning has been accomplished we no longer attend to parts. For such reasons Mill says, "In our perceptions of objects, it is generally the wholes, and the wholes alone, that interests us." [5]

Law of psychological chemistry. The laws of association thus far described by Mill are adjunctive—a sensation or idea joined or linked to some other sensation or idea. These laws merely inform us that the linkage is inseparable, specifying the conditions determining which "idea" is remembered or attended. The two sensations linked associationally, however, retain their individual identity. The concept of adjunctivity of association implies several basic problems which we shall first consider in reference to Berkeley's theory because the law of "psychological chemistry," which was introduced to resolve them, represents an important revision of this theory.

In Berkeley's theory the "visible" and "tangible" ideas which compose an acquired perception are "confused." However, the confusion in effect would mean that seeing and touching cannot be discriminated. Nevertheless we may affirm a certainty in our ability to perform this discrimination which is equal to our certainty in distinguishing seeing from hearing. When we see a color we don't believe we hear it. Our consciousness in touching a table with eyes closed is surely different from that of looking at the table without touching it. But granting the confusion of visible and tangible ideas for the sake of argument, another problem arises. The developed visual consciousness such as seeing an object at a distance would be delusive, for it fails to disclose the tangible or tactual idea as its most distinctive component. Further, an acquired perception would not be authentically visual. The "visible object" remains invariable as one term of an acquired connection which serves as a sign in suggesting the tangible idea, but this idea is nonvisual. If the viewer could but recover the original appearance while observing the horizontal moon, he would say: "I see the moon's size to be the same as that which I should see were I to observe it in its zenith position." This appearance although not actually recoverable in the present or developed consciousness would be authentic. Another problem inherent in Berkeley's theory concerns the origin of the spatial characteristics of an acquired perception. Since the "visible" and "tangible" ideas do not possess these characteristics, the acquired connections apparently could not lead to their emergence. For instance, Berkeley spoke of the "enlarged appearance" of the horizontal moon. This appearance is neither a visible idea nor a tangible idea, hence the theory cannot account for it.

We may consider Mill's explanation of perceived form in terms of the association between visual sensations and the muscular sensations of eye-movement. Each set of sensations is successive, yet we apparently perceive some figure as a simultaneous whole. Neither set contains the representation of perceived form, whence the origin of this form? These and other issues are implicit when Mill, in discussing the law of inseparable association, writes: "The ideas of all the successive tactual and muscular feelings which accompany the passage of the hand over the whole of the coloured surface, are made to flash in the mind at once: and impressions which were successive in sensation become coexistent in thought." [6] We may observe that the law might explain the coexistence of the ideas of one visual sensation and one muscular sensation but it could not explain the simultaneous coexistence of more than one pair of such ideas.

Moreover, it is evident that we are not conscious of the "flash" of muscular feelings or their ideas. A form, no matter how closely it is attended, provides no evidence of its muscular origin. But if this absence is to be explained in accordance with the law of attention, we ought not to notice the color sensation either. For a color sensation as such is said to be of no interest. How then do we have the distinct perception of form? The way out from these and other difficulties lies in the law of psychological or "mental" chemistry. This law along with an illustrative example is stated thus:

When many impressions or ideas are operating in the mind together, there sometimes takes place a process of a similar kind to chemical combination. When impressions have been so often experienced in conjunction that each of them calls up readily and instantaneously the ideas of the whole group, those ideas sometimes melt and coalesce into one another, and appear not several ideas, but one, in the same manner as, when the seven prismatic colours are presented to the eye in rapid succession the sensation produced is that of white.[7]

Let us consider first the example of the prismatic colors. A wheel has seven segments; one is red, another green, and so on. When rapidly rotated the colors on the wheel produce seven sensations. These sensations by virtue of the postulated law "fuse" psychically and generate a new sensation, namely, that of white. We are conscious of the new sensation only, for the components of the underlying sensations disappear in the final product. Similarly the muscular sensations produced by tracking movements of the eye so coalesce with color sensations as to lead to a new product. The resulting perceived form is a simultaneous unity, of which the component sensations can never be uncovered in consciousness. It is for such reasons that Mill says that the percept is "generated" rather than "composed" by the sensations. For if it were composed, the previously stated laws might lead to the prediction of its decomposition into components. In respect to the moon illusion, the fusion of sensation and inference would determine a single final fact of consciousness. Thus Mill may say we cannot help but see it as of a larger size.[8]

THE PSYCHOLOGICAL METHOD

Inasmuch as Mill regarded the "chemistry" law as consistent with Hamilton's principle of the "veracity of consciousness," this principle alone could not be decisive in the determination of what is original or acquired in perception. However, the neutralization of this principle in this way did not appear sufficient to Mill, for an important segment of philosophical opinion espoused it in criticism of empiristic theory just as Hamilton had done. Believing that its complete inadequacy had to be revealed in many different ways, Mill introduced the distinction between the "psychological" and "introspective" methods toward this end. He regarded the "psychological method," the one favored by him, as the method of science. The adherents of the veracity principle of consciousness, he said, adopted the "introspective method."

A proponent of the introspective method commences with some fact of consciousness and, as it were, merely reads off its explanation as contained in the fact itself, disregarding its history. We perceive color and extension as unitary, and the book we perceive has a thing-like or objective status quite different from a self-referred feeling such as joy. These facts of consciousness are then interpreted to be original aspects of visual consciousness because, on further introspective investigation, the introspectionist finds no evidence of one "element" followed by another "element" nor evidence of any association. The psychological method, on the other hand, Mill insists assures us that these very same facts may be explained by the laws of association when the history of their formation is examined. The introspectionist already agrees that such percepts as distance and solidity are acquired in experience. But here he could have also asserted his previous opinion, inasmuch as these percepts have the same immediacy as do the others. Since he does not do so, Mill points out, he is exposed to the charge of inconsistency.

The introspectionist, according to Mill, fails to recognize that the present consciousness is acquired or "artificial." Only the original state of consciousness, therefore, can be regarded as "authentic." Although believing that the determination of the authentic state cannot be obtained from the present state, Mill does not doubt the veracity of consciousness as long as we delimit our description. Thus he writes, "It is true that I cannot doubt my present impression: I cannot doubt that when I perceive colour or weight, I perceive them as in an object. Neither can I doubt that when I look at two fields, I perceive which of them is farthest off." What can be doubted is the inference drawn in respect to original consciousness. He then goes on to point out that the "first impressions in the infant" would constitute the "genuine testimony of Consciousness." Inasmuch as this "experiment" cannot be performed, he adds, the nature of the infant's consciousness can only be surmised. Nevertheless, we may form a probable estimate of its nature by studying those mental facts which everyone agrees are not original but which also appear to be intuitive. In these instances the "original elements of the mind" are already known, the laws of association can be invoked, and the present mental facts are thus explained. But when there is disagreement, Mill urges us to adopt that hypothesis of original consciousness which allows the same laws to be the principles of explanation for the admittedly disputed facts. This more parsimonious and more consistent procedure defines the "psychological method." To be sure the success of this method hinges on the consent accorded the hypothesis advanced concerning the content of original consciousness. Nevertheless, this method "must be examined and disproved" before adopting the hypothesis recommended by Hamilton. This is the line of reasoning at the basis of Mill's ardent defense of the hypothesis that the original or first consciousness is subjective consciousness.[9]

The Cheselden Case and the case of the paralytic cited by Hamilton seemed to be the important evidence at the basis of Mill's hypothesis.

Mill opposes Hamilton's interpretation of the first case as constituting a refutation of Berkeley's theory and evidence for the natural perception of externality. According to Mill, the boy "concluded" that objects touched his eyes, not that he perceived them there. In further discussion he presupposes that the boy's new perceptions were subjective or mind-localized. He quotes the case of the paralytic after Hamilton and re-interprets it as evidence for the acquisition of pain-localization through associations. Apparently before the associations have been acquired, pain also would be mind-localized.[10]

BAIN

The general theoretical position of Bain was identical to Mill's except for a different attitude toward the law of psychological chemistry. Bain had provided empiristic explanations of form, single vision, stereopsis, solidity, size, distance, external reference and erect appearance. Sensations of body movement were crucial: form and magnitude result from ocular sweeps and also the touching of objects; erect appearance is the consequence of the eye's up or down motion. Although processes of reasoning or judging were often interwoven in these explanations, Bain's exclusive emphasis resided in the association laws and "muscular consciousness." Bain also had explained perceptions from a physiological standpoint, the aspect of his theory which will be stressed in our account, but Mill minimized this aspect of Bain's theory although agreeing with the value of physiological investigation in principle.

We shall select two examples of acquired perceptions in order to illustrate the general features of Bain's approach.

Form. When the "eye scans the successive parts" of a figure, the motion of the eye is believed to correspond to the objective form. Says Bain, ". . . by a horizontal sweep, we take in a horizontal line; by a circular sweep, we derive the muscular impression of a circle; by a sudden change of direction, we are cognizant of an angle." The ocular motion is also required for the perception of small figures, for instance, in looking at a circle "one-tenth inch in diameter." In this case, however, Bain supposed that the learning of the forms of larger objects occurred first, the appropriate motions then being transferred to the small figures which in themselves do not "demand an extensive ocular sweep." [11]

Size constancy. Bain's explanation of the "perception of real magnitude" supposes the previous learning of perceived distance by means of "locomotive sensations," and their subsequent association with "convergence sensations." A particular "inclination of the optic axes" thus comes to denote one rather than another distance. It further supposes the previous learning of "retinal magnitude" through ocular motion. ("Retinal magnitude" is synonymous with "visible magnitude.") At this stage the viewer would merely see an object expanding or shrinking in size as its distance varies. Another type of learning is therefore essential, one which Bain terms the "muscular appreciation" of the size of an object. He supposes a man of a height of six feet to be moving toward or away from the viewer. When approaching, the increase in retinal magnitude is accompanied by a corresponding increase in the angle of the optic axes; when receding, the decrease in one is proportional to the decrease in the other. In normal viewing conditions this covariation is always present. And for this reason, says Bain, "the concurrence of these two conditions always suggests . . . the same muscular appreciation." The sameness of this "appreciation" is equivalent to the "perception of the same size."

The inclination of the axes is essential, for if the retinal magnitude directly suggested the same muscular size the known facts of size perception could not be accounted for. We may consider a man and a midget identical except for size, where the midget is near and the man proportionately more distant. Although the retinal magnitudes are the same, the man looks larger than the midget.[12]

Bain evidently supposed that the terms of an association are linked adjunctively or sequentially, as in his explanation of form perception. In an extensive discussion of the laws of association, the notion of "succession" or "coherence" is conspicuous. For instance, Bain's law of contiguity refers to various sensations, feelings, and actions which "tend to grow together, or cohere." "Cohere" has the present dictionary meaning of one thing firmly stuck to another thing, and its meaning remains the same on substituting sensation or even idea for "thing." Therefore, the associated contents, in thus cohering, still retain the same identity as they had before the formation of the association. This type of association was often regarded at that time as "mechanical" in contrast to one that is "chemical." Obviously, then, there is no room for the "chemistry" law in Bain's system and, in fact, this law is nowhere stated. Bain's conception of association is a necessary consequence of his psychophysiology.

LAW OF CONCOMITANT VARIATION

Empiristic explanations of acquired perceptions from the time of Locke and Berkeley were "psychological." Although there had been much discussion of the way in which the "mind" or the "intellect" formed associations and perceptions, no attempt was made to relate them to the physiology and anatomy of the brain. Moreover, the psychophysical postulate as stated by Descartes or Malebranche was ignored. Bain was the first empirist to consider the facts of perception from a physiological standpoint and to provide physiological explanations of them.

Bain's law of "concomitant variation" asserts a one-to-one correlation between mental events and physical states of the brain. This law, he says, is of general validity and applies to the original as well as the acquired states of consciousness. "Mental science" is said to reveal that the acquired states of consciousness consist of a large number of complex associations. In accordance with the law, each association is believed to have a corresponding "connection" or "track" in the brain. Of the several statements of the law, the one concerning the "mechanism of retention" is most appropriate to our purpose. Says Bain, "For every act of memory, every exercise of bodily aptitude, every habit, recollection, train of ideas, there is a specific grouping, or co-ordination, of sensations and movements, by virtue of specific growths in the cell junctions." Since Bain regards all perceptions as learned, they necessarily exemplify the mechanism of retention. Thus every "visible form" is said to have a distinct representation in the brain paths or its "own track in that labyrinth of fibres and corpuscles called the brain." We turn to Bain's conception of the formation of the tracks.

The optic nerve is a sensory or afferent nerve consisting of a very large number of fibers, at least "100,000," each insulated from the other and each terminating in a cell in the brain. Motor or efferent nerves have a similar composition of insulated fibers. The fibers of a particular motor nerve, such as one controlling motions of the ocular muscles, each originate in a brain cell and terminate in a muscle. The brain, by means of a myriad of cross connections between the clusters of sensory and motor cells, serves to coordinate the actions of the two types of nerves. The incoming afferent currents are re-routed in the brain to an outgoing motor nerve which, on arriving in a muscle group, cause a variety of movements. A sensory cell joined to a motor cell by fiber defines a "connection" or "track," the transit of current along this path defining a "circuit of action." Insulation of the fibers is essential for the independent conduction of currents along given circuits. For if the insulation were absent, the currents in adjoining fibers would fuse, and the possibility for securing consistent information of the world, and acting in a consistent manner in relation to the world, would be out of the question. The nervous system and brain can be considered as similar to a "telegraph system": the fibers correspond to the wires along which electric currents flow, and the brain corresponds to the central station in which interconnections are established. A message at the input end is converted into electric currents which pass along to the central station where they are appropriately shunted by means of relays so that at the output end they are again reconverted into a message at some given destination. In this scheme the path of wires between input and output ends is fixed, for otherwise a message would not arrive at its correct destination. "Just as," says Bain in further explanation, "by means of the distribution of post-offices and lines of road, a letter from any village in Europe can be speedily sent to any other village." The action of the nerve network is presumed to be similar.

The cross connections in the brain, says Bain, are either inborn or acquired. For simplicity of discussion we choose a single fiber in the optic nerve and a single fiber in the efferent nerve to the muscles of the eye, and their corresponding sensory and motor cells in the brain. Bain supposes that the two cells are close to each other in a common brain center. If there is a pre-fixed connection between them the circuit is complete and the current, of course, flows uninterruptedly. This closed circuit of action defines a reflex. But when the pre-fixed connection is absent the cells may be joined by a "structural growth." The cells so joined represent an "acquired track." To explain the "growth" Bain supposes that an incoming current at the common center induces an outgoing current in the motor fiber which, to some extent, diminishes the resistance in the brain tissue between the cells. Through further current inductions the resistance is so reduced that current directly flows from one cell to another. The path which is formed defines "structural growth" or an acquired connection. A similar explanation applies to the formation of paths between clusters of sensory and motor cells. With many repetitions the current moves along the new path with reflex-like automaticity.

Before the connections are established the mental effect can only be the concomitant of the currents flowing into the sensory cells. In this instance the effect is merely an "optical or visual feeling"; it has no form. But when the sensory and motor cells have been united by "growths," the currents can flow from one type of cell to the other. The corresponding mental effect is now a visible form. According to this conception, therefore, the form is a "compound" of optical and muscular feelings. Moreover, since the patterns of ocular motion correspond to unique "tracks," every perceived form will have its distinct counterpart in the brain. And the same is true for "every letter of the alphabet." The same physiological model presumably applies in the explanation of the perceptions of distance and size. Bain does not supply any detail of their acquisition, and he refers to the associations between sensations or the associations between sensations and ideas in a general way. In any case the law of concomitant variation would include in its scope every difference in perceived distance and size.

It is important to realize that Bain regards the "muscular consciousness" as the "indispensable element" of any percept; for instance, "a circle is a series of ocular movements." This conclusion also applies to visual imagery as well as to any other fact of "mental life." Bain does not of course mean that the movements are executed with the same vigor or the same degree as existed in childhood when the associations were acquired. Nevertheless a "muscular trace" of some sort is always presumed to exist.

In an experiment on after-images, to which Bain refers, we continue to have an impression even though our eyes are turned away from the original stimulus. Since the "incoming currents" persist for some time, the impression continues. But the currents are reduced in intensity, therefore the after-image is somewhat fainter than the original impression. Similarly, there is a "continuing impression of a feebler kind" when the sound of a bell stimulating the ear ceases. The feebler impressions in these instances are the immediate after-effects of stimulation. However, Bain also maintains that the explanation is similar for those "impressions *reproduced* by mental causes alone." The wish to recall the physical appearance of a person met the previous week, a mental cause, leads to the reproduction of the original impression. The recalled impression, which Bain also calls idea, although similar to the former impression is a fainter copy of it. The wish to recall the original impression, he says, re-induces the same currents in the brain. But since the revived currents are not "equal in energy to those of direct stimulation at first hand," the mental image is correspondingly weaker. After having cited further evidence of this kind, Bain speculates as to what the "cerebral seat of those renewed impressions" might be. He says,

> What is the manner of occupation of the brain with a resuscitated feeling of resistance, a smell, or a sound? There is only one answer that seems admissible. *The renewed feeling occupies the very same parts, and in the same manner, as the original feeling, and no other parts, nor in any other assignable manner.*

The cerebral seat to which Bain refers is the very same as the set of sensori-motor paths through which currents pass on direct stimulation. A "mental force" causes the revival of those same currents, though reduced in intensity. A remembered impression, in being the counterpart of a former impression, reproduces the compound of optical and muscular feelings.[13] The equivalency of the two impressions is brought out by Bain in a reply to a critic:

> Naked outlines, as the diagrams of Euclid and the alphabetical characters, are to say the least of it, three parts muscular and one part optical; their retention is supposed to depend upon the adhesive property of the ocular muscles and their nerve centres, and not upon purely optical circles. The memory of a visible form, as the rainbow, contains the consciousness of a muscular sweep; the windings of a river, which, is in actual view, have to be followed by movements of the eyes, are remembered

as ideal movements. Now, although everyone may not acquiesce in this mode of representing vision, yet the very existence of such a theory should have restrained Dr. Bastian from putting forward sight as the unquestioned type of *passive* sensations.[14]

In the following passage Bain anticipates and answers an objection to the doctrine of renewed impressions:

> To this doctrine it may be objected, that the loss of eyesight would be the loss of memory of visible things; that Milton's imagination must have been destroyed when he became blind. The answer is, that the inner circles of the brain must ever be the chief part of the agency both in sensations and in ideas. The destruction of the organ of sense, while rendering sensation impossible, can be but a small check upon the inward activity; it cuts off merely the extremity of the course described by the nerve currents. Moreover, the decay of the optic sensibility does not impair the activity of the *muscles* of the eye, wherein are embodied the perceptions of visible motion, form, extension, etc., which are one half, and not the least important half, of the picture.[15]

Obviously muscular activity is presumed to be the essential factor in visual imagery and perception since optical sensations have no form. Therefore, should we suppose the opposite situation, the optic nerve intact and the ocular muscles destroyed, there could neither be imagery nor perception.

Finally the law of psychological chemistry and its exclusion in Bain's theory may be considered. Mill had maintained that the fusion was psychic, "organic fusion" was rejected by him in discussing the example of prismatic colors. However, psychic fusion contradicts the law of concomitant variation. On the other hand, if organic fusion were supposed, Bain's theory could not account for it, for the tracks in the brain, however complicated, were regarded as always sensori-motor. Further, in accordance with the law of concomitant variation, as Bain indicated, representations of the sensory and motor components in consciousness are necessitated. Thus his failure to appeal to psychological chemistry is consistent with his over-all theory. For Bain, therefore, "object consciousness" is muscular consciousness.

Bain failed to note the necessary implication of his theory that consciousness is delusory, inasmuch as there is no awareness of the muscular consciousness which he believed was the critical component of a visual percept. Moreover, his theory could not in principle account for any visual fact or the transformation of qualitative data to perception.[16]

LOTZE

Lotze, unlike Mill and Bain, attributed various innate abilities to the soul or mind such as the "tendency to form an intuition of space." These admittedly unexplainable capacities had to be postulated, according to Lotze, inasmuch as series of qualitative states could not directly give rise to the idea of space. But this did not imply an original perception of extension, for otherwise the assumption of the mind as an unextended and "supersensible essence" would be contradicted. He provided an example and a metaphor for the purpose of clarifying the relation of mind to body and the fundamental nature of the "problem of space."

Chord example. Says Lotze, "Many impressions exist conjointly in the soul, although not spatially side by side with one another; but they are merely together in the same way as the synchronous tones of a chord; that is to say, qualitatively different, but not side by side with, above or below, one another." When two keys at the opposite ends of a piano are struck simultaneously the listener may hear two sounds, but he does not hear one sound as though it were to the left or above the other sound. Precisely the same considerations would apply to vision when the retina is stimulated by some external object. The mind may receive and perceive two color impressions, but they are not perceived in any spatial relation. Moreover, the color impressions do not convey any information in respect to the location of the luminous points in space which, upon stimulating the retina, produce them.

Lens model. A lens collects the rays of light reflected from an object, and brings them to a point of focus or convergence beyond which the rays diverge. The geometrical relationships among the points of the object are preserved along all sections of the converging and diverging rays. But at the focal point itself the geometrical relationship is completely lost. Figure 8.1 schematically represents this situation; A and B are points in the external object, F is the focal point, A' and B' are the image points. The spatial relation of the points on the object is preserved in the spatial relation of the image points although this rela-

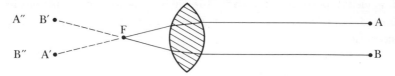

FIGURE 8.1

tion is lost when the rays unite into a single point at F. In this metaphor the two convergent rays represent nervous excitations or processes which "pass over into the soul" at the place F in the brain.
When the nervous excitations originate in the stimulation of two
points of the retina, their spatial separation disappears at F. Now
should $A''B''$ (or $B'A'$) represent an original perceived "spatial
image," the soul would be an extended substance. Since this hypothesis
is not allowable, the soul is apparently confined to an "indivisible
point" or the "image of a point." Lotze expresses some reservation
about this conception of the soul since the "point" may be construed
in spatial terms. Barring this reservation, the lens model, according to
him, is useful for understanding the "problem confronting the soul"
and the way in which spatial percepts are acquired.[17]

When some object stimulates the retina a large number of nervous
excitations are simultaneously aroused which, upon converging to the
same "point," enable the soul to have a corresponding number of color
sensations. These sensations or impressions "exist in the soul in a completely non-spatial way and are distinguished simply by their qualitative content, just as the simultaneous notes of a chord are heard apart
from one another, and yet not side by side with another, in space."
The soul's problem according to Lotze is this:

> From this non-spatial material the soul has to re-create entirely afresh the
> spatial image that has disappeared; and in order to do this it must be
> able to assign to each single impression the position it is to take up in
> this image relatively to the rest and side by side with them.

The re-created spatial image is a two-dimensional field of vision which
has an orderly arrangement of impressions which correspond to the arrangement of the points in the external object. This spatial image is
represented in Figure 8.1 by $A''B''$. The fact that its orientation is the

same as that of the external object results from an up and down motion of the eye, and for this reason $B'A'$ is not designated as the representative of the spatial image.[18]

THE PROBLEM AND SOLUTION

Lotze attributed the inborn power to reconstruct a spatial image to the soul but, in his view, this power was insufficient for the orderly allocation of impressions. Each of these impressions must have some distinctive sign that conveys to the soul its location in the field of vision. Inasmuch as these signs are not yet available, the soul does not possess the necessary data for the exercise of its inborn power. The following metaphor, adapted from Lotze, may clarify the problem. A clerk at the main post office is required to sort out a pile of letters into a number of mail sacks, each sack bearing the name of the city for which the letters to be placed therein are destined. His task is simple, for he merely notes the name of the city on the envelope and then places it in the sack with the same tag. But if no letter has the name of a city, the task is impossible. However well he understands the instructions for sorting, he cannot execute them. If the pile of letters is regarded as corresponding to the qualitative content at the "indivisible point," the soul is in a similar predicament.[19]

"Local signs" provide the means for the elicitation of the soul's innate ability to refer visual impressions to their distinctive places in the field of vision. Since each visual impression comes to be associated with a "sign" peculiar to it, the soul reconstructs the spatial image that had been lost when the visual impressions originally entered consciousness.

The muscles controlling the disposition of the eye enable the imaging of an external luminous source on the "yellow spot." Irrespective of the original place of retinal stimulation away from the yellow spot, the reflexive or automatic motion of the eye is such that the stimulation is received on that very spot. The excursion of the eye is presumed to be correlated with a feeling of movement unique to it. Such a feeling of movement, subsequent to the formation of associations, defines the local sign for the particular stimulated retinal point. Lotze says that automatic motion of the eye in various directions and in various degrees of magnitude guarantees an exact correspondence between every stimulated retinal point and a feeling of movement. The theory of local signs can be best clarified and further elaborated in terms of an example and a diagram (Figure 8.2).

The eye is initially in the resting state as indicated in the diagram. The introduction of the luminous point L, which stimulates retinal point a away from the yellow spot Y, causes the soul to receive a visible impression or color sensation. The eye now rotates reflexly so as to bring Y to the position where it can be stimulated; corresponding to this excursion, the soul experiences a sensation of movement. If we suppose that the eye has returned to its resting state, the automatic motion of the eye comes into operation, causing the yellow spot to receive the stimulation again. This cycle is repeated many times. During a particular excursion every retinal point in the arc of rotation aY receives stimulation and, as a consequence, the soul receives a series of visible impressions. "Now while the eye is passing through the arc," writes Lotze, "the soul receives at each instant a feeling of its momentary position." Thus there are two series of coordinated successive states of qualitative content: visible impressions and feelings of position.

When the eye is in the resting state, A denotes the first feeling of position in the series which corresponds to the retinal point a. During the repeated excursions of the eye, A becomes associated with all subsequent feelings of position so that when the eye is in the resting state, it "reproduces in memory the entire series." In this instance, A is the local sign connected with a. Inasmuch as the eye need no longer move

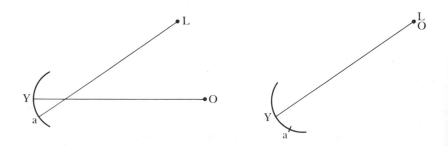

FIGURE 8.2. In the left hand figure, YO represents the optic axis and the position of the resting state of the eye before it turns upon the introduction of the luminous source L. In the right hand figure, the eye has reflexly rotated through an arc measured by aY, bringing the yellow spot into position to receive the stimulation; one end of the optic axis now coincides with L. See text for further discussion.

after the formation of the association, the "sign" is defined as a "feeling of movement." The soul has thus far achieved the location of a single visible impression in the field of vision. And if we regard Figure 8.2 as either a side or top view, we observe that motion of the eye is responsible for the assignment of the impression to the upper or left part of the field. Now if L is eliminated and another luminous source introduced, another local sign is joined to the particular retinal point which is stimulated. When the two sources are presented simultaneously, the soul perceives two spatially separated visible impressions. After all other local signs have been acquired, we are enabled to perceive forms such as a triangle, circle, and so on. We should observe that the re-created spatial image is necessarily bi-dimensional, for the motion of the source L along the same line La does not change the spot of the retina receiving the stimulation; the local sign, therefore, is constant.

Lotze explains the elicitation of feelings of movement when the retina of the completely stationary eye receives simultaneous stimulation as follows. The stimulation of two points on opposite sides of the optic axis and equidistant from the axis elicit two feelings of movement which are of the same magnitude but opposite in direction. However, these feelings do not cancel each other out. A "tension" is created in the muscles of the eye which corresponds to the intensity of the feelings of movement. If the two points are more widely separated, there is a commensurate increase in the tension. The degree of tension signifies the magnitude of the spatial separation of the two points. Modifying one of Lotze's examples, it is analogous to two men tugging at opposite ends of a rope with the same force. Though there is tension in the rope, all is stationary. Moreover, if they increase their force proportionately, there is only an increase in the tension.[20]

The substance of Lotze's theory may be summarized thus: the qualitative content of visible impressions, originally represented as an "indivisible point," undergoes re-expansion in the spatial image by means of the qualitative content of local signs in conjunction with the innate abilities of the soul.

After outlining the theory of local signs, Lotze expressed some reservation and doubt concerning its validity but also maintained that in some way it must be correct. He said,

> I should be very prejudiced if I felt no alarm at the artificiality of these ideas. But my intention was not to recommend the hypothesis at all costs,

but honestly to recount all the presuppositions it involves; and, further, I do not know that it is possible to reach the end we aim at in any simpler way, or that the artificiality lies anywhere but in the facts themselves. The fact itself is strange enough—and it cannot be got rid of—that we can see an unnumbered mass of different-coloured points at once, and can distinguish them. . . . The only question, therefore, is whether internal experience witnesses to the truth of our hypothesis, or whether any other source of knowledge opposes to it objections which are insuperable.[21]

EXTERNAL REFERENCE

The outward projection of the "total internal image" must be learned, according to Lotze, because the soul has "no original tendency" to project the image. After observing that an adequate explanation of the acquired projection is impossible, he suggests the importance of the movements in closing and opening the eye. The disappearance and reappearance of the perceived image causes us to "naturally associate" the image with the eye so that the "visible world is *in front* before our eyes." Moreover, by lateral movements of the eye or by motion of the body about its vertical axis, we perceive the succession of images as lying in front. Although in this motion the retinal images shift across the retina, we do not perceive objects in motion because we are aware of the feelings of movement of either the eye or the body. The feelings of such movements make us think that the objects in the world are immovable and, as a consequence, the images we project are not perceived as though in motion. In such ways we arrive at the "ordinary perception of the spherical space that surrounds us on all sides." This space, however, is only one of "superficial extension." Through touch and movement the "third spatial direction" is learned. The surface comprising the projection of the visible impressions apparently represents the retinal surface turned outward. For when Lotze expresses himself with some degree of definiteness, he supposes that the impressions are at first localized on the retinal surface.[22]

CONCLUDING COMMENTS

Hamilton's objection to the assumption of the initial perception of but one *minimum visibile,* which required an "almost infinite number of associations" for the perception of the human face alone, was not answered by Mill in his protracted reply to Hamilton although he had quoted this objection in his defense of the doctrines of those criticized by Hamilton. When Mill explained the "interest" conferred on the whole face and the inattention to its parts in terms of the association laws, he accepted the perception of the whole as a given in this phase of the argument but he never did show how this percept might arise through the association of successive parts. This is an instance of what Hamilton once called "begging the question" in still another argument, one which we did not cite, in criticism of the theories of his predecessors. Those who in principle denied an original perception of extension, he said, still presupposed extension in the very explanation of its purported origin in experience. Mill's "rudimentary conception" is another example of this kind, since apparently the original perception of some extension was conceded. Lotze's theory is based on the artificial assumption that the local signs are learned individually. However, the retina is stimulated simultaneously by many luminous points rather than by merely one. To suppose that the consistent excursion of the eye between the yellow spot and each retinal point can develop in these circumstances so that each point acquires its own characteristic sign represents another example of "begging the question."

Apparently Mill and Bain did not realize the validity of Hamilton's argument pertaining to the number of associations. Their theory supposed that patterned eye-movements corresponding to the objective shape were essential to the development of perceived form. Yet when we consider the large number of discriminations that we make among the members of the class of triangles, quadrilaterals, pentagons, and closed curves, their learning would seem to involve the almost infinite number of associations that Hamilton suggested in considering the perception of the human face. A similar point applies to Lotze, although his theory did not suppose patterned eye-movements because the motion of the eye merely would serve to bring the image of the luminous source to the yellow spot. Since the number of acquired local signs corresponds to the number of retinal points, the number of associations is already quite large. Its magnitude is increased further because each local sign represents the associations of the initial feeling of position together with the intermediate feelings of position for a particular excursion of the eye. Furthermore, Lotze, in referring to an experiment in the momentary illumination of an electric spark, conceded the perception of an extended differentiated surface. However, this implies a near instantaneous summation of a large number of local signs (feelings of movement), each with its individual vector, for the soul's appreciation of the given tension in the stationary eye for determining the particular momentary perception. Finally, Mill, Bain, and Lotze did not realize that their theories, when concretely stated in relation to the development of perceived form and extension, implied that only one *minimum visibile* would originally be perceived at a given moment. For if two *minimum visibilia* were simultaneously perceived when two luminous sources stimulated the retina, the perceived interval would represent an original perception of extension.[23]

However successful the "chemistry" law may have been in resolving the problems in answer to Hamilton, it introduced other problems. From the standpoint of present consciousness, there is no awareness of the individual sensations the law presupposed for its operation. For instance, we see only whiteness when the color wheel spins; the sensations of the seven prismatic colors, although "in the mind," are thus presumed to remain unnoticed. In momentary illumination we see a form as a whole although the time interval is too short to permit the ocular tracking of the outline. Thus there is the problem of explaining the perceived form since at least one ingredient essential to the operation of the law is missing (muscular feelings). Although Lotze had explained the simultaneity of perception in momentary illumination, the concept of unnoticed sensation is an essential feature of the theory. Lotze said that visual impressions and feeling of movements act as "stimuli" to the soul which enable the innate principle to be called forth. This conception, however, implies that the "stimuli" remain unnoticed in the developed perception.[24]

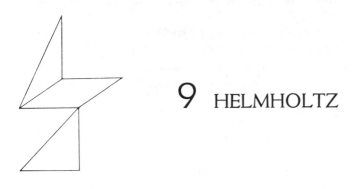

9 HELMHOLTZ

The nativistic theory introduces an unnecessary hypothesis.
Helmholtz, 1867

Helmholtz, who coined the empirism-nativism dichotomy for the purpose of describing what he regarded as the two main and controversial theories of perception, developed his empiristic theory in contrast to and in opposition to nativistic theory. He stated many objections to nativistic theory which, he said, presupposed that perceptions were innate, to be explained in terms of "pre-established mechanism" or inborn anatomical connections, and which was favored by many German physiologists. Nativists advanced dubious or unwarranted hypotheses concerning the relationship of perception to organic structures. One physiologist claimed that the "mind" could perceive the elements and spatial dimensions of the retina; another explained the erect appearance of objects in terms of an "erect image" formed in the brain through the inversion of fibers from the retina to the brain. Many physiologists supposed an orderly arrangement of fibers from the retinas to the brain for the purpose of explaining the localization of sensation in the visual field and single vision. Such hypotheses were either "fantastic" or not supported in evidence. Moreover, a given nativistic theory was either internally inconsistent or inconsistent with some other nativistic theory. All nativists were inconsistent in the sense that they appealed to "experience" or "training" in order to explain some perceptual facts. Finally, "nativistic theory . . . cuts short any investigation relative to the origin of perceptions since it considers them as original or innate."

On the other hand, empiristic theory was free of these difficulties since its starting point was the unquestionable importance of "psychic operations" in the explanation of those mental phenomena which would not include perception. The explication of these operations would be rather difficult in reference to perception, but their "laws" nevertheless were already familiar to us through the "facts of everyday experience." After further developing this line of thought, Helmholtz concluded that the doctrine of the "association of ideas" provided the framework for understanding the effects of psychic operations in perception, and for unifying the known facts of perception consistently in terms of a single theory. Moreover, reliance on the laws pertaining to the association of ideas would obviate the necessity for supposing anatomical and physiological hypotheses "invented *ad hoc*" for explaining particular facts.

The psychic operations or activities presupposed by Helmholtz for explaining the development of visual perceptions include judgment, expectation, and reasoning, these being regarded as "unconscious" and "obligatory." He did not, however, consider the association laws to be known to that degree which would permit their application to the delineation of the specific details in the formation of a percept in any decisive fashion. In his view the empiristic hypothesis gains in scientific plausibility relative to the weaknesses in the nativistic hypothesis. However, Helmholtz makes it clear that the status of the empiristic hypothesis is to be regarded as provisional. His attitude toward the two rival hypotheses is succinctly stated in the concluding paragraph of his monumental three-volume work on physiological optics:

> However, I know in a formal way that the questions we have discussed here have not yet been completely resolved. I chose my point of view because of the simplicity of the explanations that can be deduced from it. Moreover, I have also been further guided by certain considerations of

method; in effect, it seems to me always preferable to establish the explanations of natural events in terms of the fewest and firmest possible assumptions. But I must also say that the more I learned to control my attention and the movements of my eyes in the course of these investigations which have absorbed a good part of my life, the less admissible it seemed to me that the principal facts in this field could be explained through the action of pre-existing nervous mechanism.[1]

SENSATION

Contemporaries of Helmholtz regarded his theory as being derived from Berkeley's theory. For instance, Sully, in a review of theories of visual perception in Germany in 1878, said, "Helmholtz explains the visual perception of distance (monocular and binocular) much after the manner of English associationists." J. S. Mill and Bain were the associationists to whom he referred in this article. A few years later Sully wrote, "This view of seeing [Berkeley's] as having reference to touch has, in the main, been developed by English psychologists, though it has received important support from German psychologists and physiologists, among whom the name of Helmholtz deserves particular mention." [2]

Actually Helmholtz did not specify the characteristics of visual sensation so that a direct link between his theory and the theories of the English associationists could be established. However, his adherence to the doctrine of nonspatial content as set forth by Mill and Bain, and also Lotze, may be surmised. Thus a cursory comparison of the second and third volumes on physiological optics entitled *Theory of Light Sensations* and *Theory of Visual Perceptions* would indicate that "spatial relations" are allocated to the latter rather than to the former volume. This division is even more conspicuous in his popular summary of the main theoretical issues of these volumes in *Recent Progress in the Theory of Vision*. More important, however, is the alternative implicit in his objection to the nativistic assumption that excitations of adjacent portions of the retina when conducted to the brain would directly cause spatially separated sensations rather than a single uniform sensation.

Helmholtz gives examples of perception in which the stimulation of different nerves is not accompanied by the "perception of spatial separation." For instance, he points out that the existence of three distinct receptors which would respond to the same number of components of light radiation is a reasonable assumption; nevertheless, the color sensations arising from the stimulation of the three receptors are not separated. Similarly, sounds may be perceived as nonspatial though the impressions corresponding to them affect different nerves. Helmholtz concludes that the local separation of excitations on the retina or in their conduction along different nerves is not sufficient for the perceived spatial separation of sensations. "Something else," he says, would have to be "added" to sensations in order to produce the perception of spatial separation. This "something else" is the hypothesis of "local signs" proposed by Lotze. Although regarding the attempt to define the nature of local signs as "premature," Helmholtz believes that their existence cannot be doubted.

However, the failure to define what local signs might be and to describe how they might be acquired, makes Helmholtz's theory less concrete than Lotze's. In any case the motion of the eye is regarded as essential to the spatial separation of sensations, and in the acquisition of the perceptions of form and visual direction. Apparently, then, before the acquisition of local signs there would be no perception of separation, form, and direction. Furthermore, the assumption that color sensations are not originally separated spatially, as in the analogy of sounds, would imply the denial of a sensation of form. The content of visual sensation, in other words, would be merely qualitative. It is important to mention, however, that Helmholtz nowhere explicitly stated that form was not an attribute of sensation. Indeed his discussion of the acquisition of perceptions presupposed a form sensation or equivalently, a "visual field" or "field of vision." [3]

The "visual field," which Helmholtz defined in relation to monocular viewing, is a spherical surface representing the "retina itself with all its images and special characteristics projected outside." The apparent images on this surface, referred to by him as "visual images," not only possess form but are also spatially separated one from the other. Moreover, they have a curvature corresponding to the surface but when sufficiently small they are "flat." These images do not necessarily represent our perceptions, for in looking at objects we may see them extended in the third dimension. Such perceptions are referred to as "perceptual images."

When Helmholtz takes up the question of the acquisition of the third dimension, he supposes the existence of the flat visual image as a necessary condition for the formation of the perceptual image. This apparent contradiction to the assumption of sensation as a qualitative state, we believe, is resolvable in two ways. Muscular feelings derived from various motions of the eye give the visual image its shape, and the feelings derived from the motion of the head or interposition of the hand between the eye and a luminous source lead to its exteriorization in the visual field. These factors, indicated by Helmholtz in respect to the formation of the visual surface and its images, are not delineated in detail. In any case, however the forms of the visual images have been acquired, these can then be utilized as givens for the purpose of explaining the perception of the third dimension. However, this resolution is not quite satisfactory since Helmholtz regards the visual image as a sensation in other contexts, as in the discussion of the binocular perception of the third dimension, and of relief or solidity.

In contrasting the relative merits of the nativistic and empiristic theories, Helmholtz says the nativist explained the relief of the monocularly derived perceptual image in terms of learning, and he acknowledges that the bi-dimensional characteristics of the visual field could be explained adequately either by the empirist or by the nativist. At this point Helmholtz decides to accept the nativistic position for the purpose of emphasizing the central issue which affords the effective basis for decision between the two rival theories. When looking at an actually solid object with two eyes we see one object in its three dimensions. In other words, the perceptual image is single and "solid." The nativist maintained that this perceptual image was of innate origin and he proposed to account for it in terms of inborn anatomical structures. Helmholtz points out that this argument presupposes the anatomical unification of two retinal images in the brain. Although not agreeing with the correctness of this supposition, he decides to accept it anyway so that he can show that the solidity of the perceptual image is not explained. The crux of his argument is contained in the following passage:

> Each of our eyes projects a flat image on its own retina. However we may suppose the conducting nerves to be arranged, the two retinal images united in the brain must always be represented by a flat image. But in place of the flat retinal images we find in our perception a corporeal image extended in three dimensions.

In effect, in terms of his very own assumptions the nativist ends up with a flat cerebral image and not with the cerebral image that ought to be the anatomical correlate of an innate three-dimensional perceptual or corporeal image. He really should adopt the position of the empirist. He already did so for monocular viewing, the flat brain image being supposed, and he should do the same for binocular viewing. Irrespective of the mode of viewing and of anatomical considerations, the psychic counterpart of events in the brain is a bi-dimensional visual image. In having thus developed what he considers to be an important weakness in the nativistic position, Helmholtz can afford the concession of a form sensation though in other contexts he implies otherwise. The same line of argument is apparent when he supposes in the above quotation that the two retinal images are combined in the brain through organic arrangements, thus implying the acceptance of an innate fusion of the two visual fields. But this he does only for the purpose of refuting the nativistic position in respect to the third dimension, for his actual opinion is that the "fusion" into a single visual field results from "psychical action." [4]

TWO ASSUMPTIONS

Of the many assumptions which helped influence Helmholtz's theory of sensation and perception, the assumptions of the "constancy hypothesis" and "modification rule" only will be considered because their discussion facilitates an understanding of Helmholtz's approach to evidence.

Constancy Hypothesis

Generally, Helmholtz supposed that the dimensional characteristics of the visual image were similar to the dimensional characteristics of the retinal image, as in his definition of the visual field. Further, he considered the possibility that the brain image might be three-dimensional because the brain has "three dimensions" but rejected it as improbable and unnecessary. Nevertheless, this is an interesting conjecture, for if the tri-dimensional brain image were postulated, perceptual solidity would represent an innate perception. In dismissing this possibility, he maintained that the hand in conforming to the shape of an object would be sufficient for producing the "idea" of the third dimension. [5]

Helmholtz's psychophysiology is similar to Bain's. For instance, the anatomy and action of the nervous system is "compared with telegraph wires traversing a country." Helmholtz differed from Bain in that he did not relate the explanation of the development of perception to brain mechanisms, nor did he refer to the psychophysical postulate such as the "law of concomitant variation" in his interpretation of perception. However, Helmholtz stipulated an important assumption, generally known in his time as the "law of isolated conduction"—also implicit in Bain's theory—which is related to the telegraph analogy and which also clarifies the meaning of the constancy hypothesis. In referring to the importance of cones in effecting spatial discriminations, he says:

> We may allow that each of them has its nervous fiber which, through the mediation of the optic nerve, extends to the brain in isolation in order to conduct there the impression it receives, so that the state of excitation of each of these cones may give rise to one isolated sensation.

This law, the basis of Helmholtz's definition of visual sensation, asserts a fixed or constant relationship between retinal excitation and its psychic concomitant. Furthermore, whenever an object is viewed so as to project the same retinal image, the object will always produce the same sensation, providing the state of the retina is unchanged. The qualification is necessary because the state of the retina may be different as the result of previous stimulation. For instance, when a red surface is looked at for some time and the eyes then turned to a gray patch, the patch will appear greenish rather than gray. The receptors on the retina most sensitive to red illumination become fatigued as a consequence of the previous stimulation and thus do not readily respond when the gray patch is viewed. Instead the still-fresh green receptors respond, the patch thus looking green. In this instance, however, the relationship between excitation and sensation remains the same. The law of isolated conduction, as we shall subsequently observe, is important in Helmholtz's explanation of simultaneous color contrast.[6]

Modification Rule

A visual perception (or perceptual image) has a twofold meaning in Helmholtz's theory. On the one hand, it is a neutral category referring to a present state of consciousness without any commitment to its interpretation in terms of past experience. It is for this reason that the wide range of facts brought together in his text on physiological optics make it a useful reference source a century after its publication. On the other hand, when Helmholtz considers the question of origin, it has the meaning of an acquired perception. In this definition the perceptual image represents the product of the effects of past and present stimulation. The traces of the past effects are generically referred to as memory images, and they include not only visual images but also the effects of movements of the eyes and other parts of the body. The unification of all such past images through the laws of association defines "idea." Perception, in other words, is the combination of idea and present sensation.

Having observed that the ideational and sensational components in a present perception cannot be distinguished by the perceiver, Helmholtz points out that a perceptual image is as direct and vivid as any sensational quality. The third dimension of the binocular "solid image," for instance, seems to be as obligatory and immediate as the other two dimensions. The nativist, he says, appealed to this very fact in rejecting empiristic theory. However, he does not regard this argument as decisive since the nativist accepted many perceptual facts, such as the third dimension perceived in monocular viewing, as the products of experience, facts which nevertheless possess the same directness and vividness as those other percepts presumably of innate origin. Although the nativist was exposed to the charge of inconsistency, alone a sufficient reason for rejecting his position, Helmholtz proposes to clinch his argument with a positive criterion or "rule."

The present sensation is a direct concomitant of physiological events and, as already observed in the discussion of the law of isolated conduction, is a fixed function of the stimulation received from the same object, providing the objective conditions and state of the retina are the same. Now if it be supposed for the sake of argument that a perceptual image is composed only of sensational elements, it ought not be changed either by an "act of the understanding" or by factors of experience. Therefore, any feature of the image which can be altered, cannot be of sensational origin. This reasoning is at the basis of the rule: "Whatever, therefore, can be overcome by factors of experience, we must consider as being itself the product of experience and training." The observance of this rule will show that nearly all space perceptions result from "experience and training."

Thus the modification of a percept, as some experiments demonstrated, would implicate "idea" or "memory" as a causal factor. In its most general application the rule also included those changes in percept which would result from acts of judgment. It by no means followed, according to Helmholtz, that the failure to alter a percept would imply that present sensation is its sole cause. For an "idea" could be so strong as the result of practice that it would not be overcome either by judgment or further experience.[7]

ACQUISITION OF PERCEPTIONS

Generally the empiristic theory before Helmholtz stressed the acquisition of the spatial attributes of percepts but he increased the scope of the theory by providing evidence which, in his view, showed that the perception of sensible qualities such as color might be the product of experience in certain circumstances. The evidence and its interpretation is given in the second volume of his work on physiological optics (*Theory of Light Sensations*). Subsequent to the discussion of this evidence, other evidence pertaining to the acquisition of "space perception," a topic of the third volume, will be considered.

Simultaneous Color Contrast

When a gray patch is placed on a colored background and then covered with fine white tissue paper so that its border coincides with the border of the background, the patch is perceived as having a hue which is complementary to that of the ground. For instance, the gray patch in these circumstances has a pink-red color when the ground is green. Helmholtz said that the induced complementary hue, rather than being an "act of sensation," is the result of "acts of unconscious or involuntary judgment" acquired in experience. The green background on being viewed through the tissue paper makes us see the tissue itself as greenish. We judge the white expanse, behind which lies the gray patch, as greenish but we also observe that it is white. Moreover, he says, we consider the patch as an "object" seen through a greenish veil. In order to explain the observed whiteness of the small expanse the hue of the gray patch would have to be pink-red because this hue when combined with the judged green gives white. That is to say, two colors would be substituted for the small white expanse, the greenish and pink-red hues. This judged green is "seen" as a continuation of the green of the tissue and the pink-red is attributed to the patch. According to Helmholtz, we are only conscious of the complementary pink-red. The judged green, the observed small white expanse, the seeing of the gray as an object behind the greenish veil, and so on, represent "unconscious acts." But since we are only immediately conscious of the induced color we may erroneously suppose this color to be a direct sensation although, according to him, it is a "deception of judgment." He reports the result of an experiment, in which he drew a black outline corresponding to the contour of the patch on the white tissue, as constituting a verification of the psychological explanation. The black-outlined white expanse, he said, now appears white although surrounded by the green colored tissue. We regard the white expanse as the "object" because the border interrupts the continuity of the surface; when the border is eliminated, the gray patch is again perceived as the object and the induced pink-red reappears. Since the retinal stimulation from the small white expanse was constant, the change in appearance in his view was the result of "psychic factors."

Helmholtz cites the following observation and interpretation for the purpose of clarifying some of the points in the above explanation. When an actually pink-red object is viewed through a green glass and perceived as lying behind it, it is seen as white because the objective color combines with the color of the glass to produce the white light stimulating the retina. The above explanation, as it were, reverses the steps; the unconsciously seen small white expanse is decomposed in the imagination into greenish color which is unconsciously perceived as a continuation of the surrounding greenish tissue and the consciously perceived pink-red complementary color which is attributed to the patch. Moreover, the perceived whiteness of the actually pink-red object is an "illusion" because it does not correctly represent the objective color, but it is not an "illusion of judgment" because stimulation of the retina by white light corresponds to it. On the other hand, the induced color is an illusion of judgment because there is no corresponding red light stimulating the retina.

Helmholtz realized that his explanation of contrast phenomena would seem unusual, for he asked those readers who might be surprised that a "psychic function can cause us to see a color in the visual field where it does not exist" to suspend their judgment until they had studied the many and similar observations in the volume on space perception. The importance of his explanation lies in the fact that it contradicted the popular view held by many physiologists that induced color was a sensation. In showing that it could be the result of an illusory judgment, the empiristic explanation of spatial perceptions became more plausible.[8]

The physiological explanation to which Helmholtz took exception may be stated in a summary fashion as follows. The green light of the ground activates a process in the retinal receptors receiving stimulation such that the sensation to which it gives rise is that of a green color. At the same time the opposite or red process develops in the same retinal area but does not express itself in sensation because of the continued stimulation by the green light. However, this new process irradiates by means of lateral connections into adjoining retinal areas such as the portion receiving stimulation from the small white expanse. Since this portion does not receive stimulation from the green light, the irradiated process gives rise to the complementary pink-red color. The processes and interconnections presupposed in this explanation were completely hypothetical. In any case, it contradicted the law of isolated conduction since the psychic effect of circumscribed retinal stimulation was held to be contingent on the stimulation received by other parts of the retina. Helmholtz cited many experimental observations which in his view invalidated the explanation. But even on theoretical grounds he would have opposed the explanation because it introduced physiological hypotheses which had not been verified.[9]

Space Perceptions

Having discussed the formation and projection of images on the visual field, Helmholtz points out that they are two-dimensional. He then sets forth several conditions for obtaining a "complete knowledge of the actual distribution of objects in space." Thus the distance from the eye along the line of sight for each of the points "we see" and the "apparent size," the size corresponding to the size of the retinal image, must be known. After further discussion along this line he turns to evidence.

Size-distance relationship. According to Helmholtz, this relationship is learned through extensive experience. In substantiation he recalls an incident from his childhood when he saw people standing on the platform of a church tower in Potsdam. In supposing them to be "puppets" he asked his mother to get them for him, which he thought she could do by extending her arm. He explains his recollection of the incident because through this "error" he learned that "perspective makes objects look smaller." Evidently the people must have been perceived as being relatively close to him and, for this reason, he asked his mother to reach for them. But after acquiring the idea of distance they would look both larger and more distant, and he would no longer suppose that they could be reached through extension of the arm. We may observe that Helmholtz's recollection and interpretation of it may be regarded as an example of the learning of size constancy.[10]

Windmill illusion. When a windmill is observed at twilight from a distance, the mill and vanes are seen in silhouette. We shall suppose that the windmill is viewed obliquely from a frontal position and that the actual motion of the vanes to the right of the axis of rotation is in an up direction. It is said that the observer sees the vanes to the right of the axis sometimes moving up and sometimes moving down. This phenomenal reversal in motion is sometimes referred to as the "windmill illusion." The illusory motion, according to Helmholtz, is correlated with phenomenal perspective reversals. At first the observer sees the windmill as though he were looking at it from the front; the mill seems to be behind the plane of the moving vanes, and the right edge of the vanes seems to be more distant than the mill's axis. Corresponding to this perceived perspective, the observer sees the vanes moving up. On the other hand, he sees the windmill as though looking at it from behind, the right edge of the vanes now appearing closer than the axis. In this instance, he sees the vanes to the right of the axis moving down. The phenomenal perspective reversals are sudden, and typically spontaneous. Since the windmill is seen only in outline the observer cannot judge the relative distance of its parts, nor does he know whether he is looking at it from in front or behind. Thus the "image" he receives from the windmill can be interpreted in two ways, each "interpretation" corresponding to a phenomenal perspective. And depending on the interpretation, he sees either an up or a down motion. Although the choice of one or the other interpretation is usually involuntary, the observer can "voluntarily elicit the change by vividly

FIGURE 9.1. The vanes of the windmill to the right of the axis of rotation are always moving in an upward direction. The observer, according to Helmholtz, sees this motion alternating with a perceived downward motion of the vanes on the same side of the axis of rotation. The right side of the plane of motion of the vanes may be perceived as more distant or closer than the left side. Corresponding to the apparent shift in the plane of the motion, the observer sees the right side of the vanes moving up or down. The fact that the mill may be seen as though behind or in front of the apparent plane of the vanes is evident in the inspection of the photograph. (The photograph, which is of a model windmill, is by S. Ferris.)

picturing to himself the conditions which would give rise to the opposite motion." Because of the historical and contemporary interest in the windmill illusion, another and probably the first scientific analysis of it by R. Smith—to whose work on optics Helmholtz often refers—is given in Figure 9.2.[11]

Conversion of relief. When a plaster impression of a medal is looked at under the right conditions, it will appear in relief as though the medal itself were being viewed. This "conversion of relief" can be

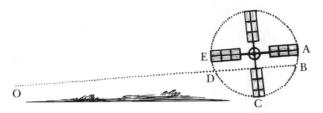

FIGURE 9.2. Smith (1738) brought together and explained several "fallacies in vision." A fallacy of relevance in understanding his explanation of the perceived motion of the windmill concerns the phenomenon of perspective reversal but he expressed it in relation to the perception of the "oblique situation" of a row of lamps in entering a street at night. Although the lamp at the right end of the row was actually the one closest to the "spectator," he sometimes perceived this lamp as more distant than the lamp at the left end. The "imagination" was held to be an important factor in the perception of oblique situation. He then continued,

> Hence we sometimes mistake the position of a weather-cock or a flag; and by taking the nearest end of the sail of a wind-mill for the remotest, we sometimes mistake the course of its circular motion. For if a spectator at O, situated nearly in the plane of the sails produced, imagines the farthest end A of a sail AE to be the nearest, and the real motion of the sails be in the order of the $A B C D E$; when A is moved to B and the line BO is drawn, cutting the circle $ABCDE$ in D; since he first imagined the end A to be at E, he will not now conceive it at B but at D; so will imagine the course of the motion to be from E to D; which is contrary to the real motion from A to B. The uncertainty we sometimes find in the course of the motion of a branch or hoop of lighted candles, turned around at a distance, is owing to the same cause . . . .

Smith concluded this paragraph by citing several examples of conversion of relief.[12]

altered by changing the direction of light so that the matrix is correctly perceived as an intaglio. With conditions constant the two percepts may reverse spontaneously. Viewing the concave side of a theatrical mask from an appropriate distance will also produce the perception of a face in relief, though in this instance spontaneous reversal is difficult if not impossible to achieve. In this context Helmholtz also cites the perceived relief and its reversibility of perspective drawings, such as the Necker Cube, and the fluctuating perspective interpretations of the windmill. In his opinion the "idea" of the third dimension of the external object and also knowledge of the direction of illumination falling across it are responsible for some of these reversible relief effects. The imaging of one or another object, as in the case of perspective drawings, would cause the perception to change so as to agree with the image. Finally eye-movements are considered as another major factor in changing the perceptions of drawings. For instance, the successive fixations of the two inner vertices of the Necker Cube facilitate changes of "interpretation." Necker, to whom Helmholtz refers, said that on fixating one vertex the eye automatically adjusted so that distinct vision could be obtained. This vertex was seen nearer whereas the other vertices, being seen indistinctly, were seen more distant. When the other vertex was fixated, this was seen more distinctly and closer. Eye-movements, said Helmholtz, also contribute to the fluctuating interpretations of the windmill in some circumstances.[13]

According to Helmholtz, these monocularly derived perceptions of the third dimension and size illustrate the importance of the "association of ideas." Some of the details of the acquisition of perceptions are provided in the discussion of binocularly perceived depth, and in the context of his opposition to nativistic theory. He raises the question:

> How is it possible that two different perspective and plane retinal images, two images consisting of two dimensions, can unite in a corporeal perceptual image, an image of three dimensions?

His answer is related to a hypothetical description of an infant and to his own experience in viewing pictures through a stereoscope. It is obvious that this explanation is intended to be suggestive only, for he says that a "complete explanation of the psychical activities" cannot as yet be given. The explanation, summarized and partly paraphrased, is as follows. The child at first plays with his hands and does not yet know how to direct either his eyes or his hands to a colored object that attracts his attention. Somewhat later he seizes a toy and turns it in all directions. He looks at it from different points of view and feels and licks it in all its parts. After a few weeks of this activity he learns to recognize the different visual images as belonging to the same object. All these visual images taken together at the same time represent to the child his visual idea of the spatial form of the toy. In this process the child acquires the perceptual image of a three-dimensional object. In additional learning the child acquires the conception of a three-dimensional object, one which represents the association of all the perceptual images that were gained when the object was viewed from different positions. Moreover, during the course of this learning the child acquires the idea that there is but a single object before him. After a while the child merely perceives a single three-dimensional object without any awareness of the mental activity which accompanies the perception. In viewing complex stereoscopic pictures such as that representing a crystalline form, Helmholtz notes that at first it was difficult for him to unite the two images. He then tried to fuse them by directing the motion of his eyes to two corresponding points. Although temporarily uniting them, he could not maintain the fusion since he did not yet know the meaning of the images. But in tracking different lines in the figure he suddenly comprehended the three-dimensional form that was represented. From that point on Helmholtz perceived a unified corporeal form without any dissociation of the two images.[14]

Other Evidence

We have deferred two other sources of evidence which Helmholtz cited as supporting his theory because they raise certain problems of interpretation. He says that a child of three months of age cannot direct his hands to exterior objects, and maintains that experience is necessary for him to learn the correspondence between the motions of his hands and eyes in reaching to and seeing the same object. The adult, moreover, requires constant experience for preserving the exactitude of this relation. In substantiation Helmholtz reports the results of an experiment in which he placed two prisms before his eyes so that objects were phenomenally displaced to the left. Having observed an object within reach he closed his eyes and tried to touch it, and he found that his hand passed to the left of the object. With eyes now open he followed the motion of his hand in reaching for and touching the object in a number of trials. When he again closed his eyes he had no difficulty in touching the object correctly. The prisms had disrupted the previous harmonious correspondence between visual and tactual perceptions and another correspondence was established. He interprets these results as proving that the "visual perception" can be rectified by touch or that we can "learn to see correctly through the prisms."

Although this interpretation suggests an alteration in phenomenal direction from left to right, the perceived direction now coinciding with the actual direction, Helmholtz seems to be referring to an alteration in the judgment of the position of the object. When he first looked through the prisms and again after the few trials of seeing and touching, the object continued to appear displaced to the left. He learned to adjust the motion of his hand to this constant phenomenal displacement in direction. But we may observe that the previous examples of acquired perceptions concerned phenomenal alterations or changes in appearance. The pink-red of the gray patch in the color experiment is different from the gray that would be perceived when the patch is viewed on a white ground; things may at first look small and then large as in the recollection of the Potsdam incident, and so on. Thus the phrase "learning to see" has a double meaning.[15]

Evidence of the resighted. After an extensive discussion of eye-movements in the formation of the monocular visual field, and before discussing depth perception, Helmholtz quotes the case of Cheselden's patient and another case almost verbatim as important in the "understanding of visual phenomena." His principal interest in citing and discussing them concerns their ability to "distinguish forms."

He points out that Cheselden's patient was not totally blind and that he might have learned to direct his eyes to objects and to judge their position. Thus to some degree, though quite imperfect and inexact, "localization in the visual field" might have developed. Apparently, then, what the boy perceived subsequent to the operation could not completely decide the issue as to what was originally given by the sense of sight. Quite possibly for this reason Helmholtz does not discuss "objects touching the eyes" and other aspects of the report. But he must have taken for granted the boy's inability to distinguish forms for he concludes his brief discussion by observing that the "influence of training in the production of visual perceptions is quite obvious." The second report, the Wardrop Case of 1826, concerns a woman whose blindness was almost total before restoration of sight to one eye at the age of 46 (see Appendix B). Helmholtz's quotation of the case begins with the events on the seventeenth of February with her return home after the operation and continues through the end of the report, having previously summarized the nonquoted portion. His major interpretations of this case and other related observations of interest are stated in the following extract.

One must note that, already several days before the last operation, the patient tried to see her hands, although she had not yet completely recovered her sight; in this way, she could very well have learned to recognize them in the visual field and to follow their movements with her eyes. Moreover, before that she could have learned to direct her eyes to the sun, thus partly acquiring the ability to direct her attention and to recognize vaguely the source of light which stimulated her eye. The optical images formed in her retina seem to have been rather good, since she was able to distinguish the numbers and hands of a watch, a rental sign on a window located on the opposite side of the street, and, while going by in a carriage, wax-candles and jewelry in shopwindows. The first objects she learned to recognize were either in motion, such as persons, or those conspicuous in color, like reddish colored doors, an orange, garments of a woman. It is, moreover, likewise remarkable how new-born infants most rapidly learn to distinguish and to follow with their eyes persons and their faces rather than other objects. Persons naturally attract greater interest than other objects and are above all discriminated from them in the visual field by the nature of their movements. Through these movements they are characterized as a coherent whole, and the face, in the form of a reddish white patch with its two gleaming eyes, is surely a part of this whole which must be easily recognizable even when one hasn't seen it very often.[16]

We may observe that Helmholtz here concerns himself with the question of learning to recognize rather than the question of what is immediately given in the woman's perceptions of things, or how things look to her, and their possible development through training. Indeed he supposes that those appearances pertaining to spatial characteristics such as size, form, position, and lateral motion of objects are as immediate and directly given as color. And this assumption is especially evident in the description of the new-born baby's reaction to the face. That recognition is Helmholtz's primary interest in the Wardrop data is apparent in his continued discussion of it. Thus he takes up the question of the woman's form discriminations eighteen days after the operation and explains them in reference to eye-movements. When the eye follows the perimeters of a circle and square, he says, the ability to distinguish these simple forms may be readily acquired. Through similar excursions of the eye she may have learned to distinguish a rectilinear contour from a curved one, and to identify an angle. He continues, "One may explain in the same way the fact that she recognized his nose as a protrusion in the reddish patch which framed the face of her brother in her visual field." [17]

In concluding his evaluation of the Wardrop Case, Helmholtz observes that some revision in his "theory of local signs" is necessary because of the "rapidity with which the patient learned to see some things." Apparently, the concept of "learning to see" has the meaning, at least in the context of this case, of learning to name, identify, or to recognize things; rather than the meaning of the change in the appearance of things that might occur as the result of training or experience. [18]

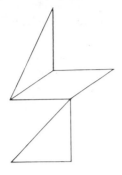

10 SUMMARY

We perceive only while we act.   Whewell, 1840

We hold unequivocally that perception without motor consciousness is impossible.   Ladd, 1898

Although the development of empiristic theory beginning with Locke has been represented by a relatively small sample, all other exponents of the theory through the end of the nineteenth century can be coordinated with this sample. Thus theorists toward the end of the century who denied the sensation of form, advocated the theories of Mill, Bain, or Lotze; whereas those who affirmed an original perception of form, adopted the doctrines of Reid, Hamilton, or Müller. The fact that some of these theorists deviated to some degree from their respective prototypes is not theoretically significant since the basic assumptions were the same. Furthermore, these prototypes can be coordinated with the two concepts of "visible objects" which Berkeley had expressed, hence they can be regarded as variations of Berkeley's theory.

The significant feature of Berkeley's theory which was adopted by all empirists was the rejection of the perception of distance as an original datum of sight. They maintained that effects of touch, the movements of the eyes and the movement of the whole body were the means for the acquisition of perceived distance. That this phase of Berkeley's theory had achieved a nearly universal acceptance is indicated in a historical survey of theories of space perception by William James in 1890. He noted that only four theorists before him (Panum, Abbott, Stumpf, and Hering) had in any way defined distance as an attribute of visual sensation. Apparently the central issue of the empiristic-nativistic controversy in the nineteenth century concerned form rather than distance. Ribot, who reviewed theories of perception from this standpoint in 1886, stated it thus: "What is the peculiar object of sight? This very simple question sums up the debate. If we reply: Color, we are empirists. If we rely: Colored extension, we cast our lot with the nativists." "Colored extension" refers to bi-dimensional extension and form since only a few nativists supposed that the perception of solidity was an original perception. Thus Locke, having supposed that the original perception of a globe is a flat circle, can be regarded as a nativist. And insofar as Berkeley presupposed this assumption in his discussion of the perception of distance and magnitude, he too can be regarded as a nativist. But when he repudiated the Locke assumption, disavowing the original perception of form, he can be regarded as an empirist.[1]

A few of the assumptions and issues will be stated mainly as they appeared to theorists in approximately the last quarter of the nineteenth century; those theorists who have been discussed in previous chapters will be excluded. Furthermore, the evidence that was regarded as a decisive confirmation of empiristic theory will be summarized.

THE CONSTANCY HYPOTHESIS

The common theoretical justification that was given for the original nonperceivability of distance was the *Molyneux Premise,* for which Berkeley was cited as having made an important contribution to a theory of vision. Also it was generally believed that the spatial attributes of size and form of original perception corresponded to the spatial attributes of the retinal image. Said Wundt in 1896 in respect to a child during his first year: "The perception of size, of distance, and of various three-dimensional figures, remains for a long time very imperfect. Especially, distant objects are all thought to be near at hand, so that they appear relatively small to the child." Inasmuch as it was thought that shape constancy was learned, the form of the original perception would conform to the perspective changes of the retinal image. Clifford (1873), having developed the idea that the "imagination" can "fill in" so as to correct the deficiencies of original perception, said: "I sometimes imagine that I see two lines in a position which I call parallel. Parallelism is impossible on the curved pictures of my retina; so this is part of the filling in. Now whenever I imagine that I see a quadrilateral figure whose opposite sides are parallel, I always fill them in so that the opposite sides are also *equal*. This equality is also a part of the filling in, and relates to possible perceptions other than the one immediately present."

Furthermore, the usual opinion was that original perception was bi-dimensional. For instance, Porter, whose text of 1868 was widely used in American universities until superseded by the texts of James of 1890 and 1892, said: "The object of vision is, however, an extended superficies only. By vision only, a sphere is perceived simply as a delicately-shaded circular disc. A cube is a flat surface with abruptly-shaded portions, bounded by converging lines."

The composition of original perception as a mosaic of sensations was another feature of the constancy hypothesis which, although usually implicit, was sometimes made explicit. Each stimulated retinal element or small area of elements, it was presupposed, would yield a sensation (or *minimum visibile*) independent of any other sensation. At the basis of this notion was the "law of isolated conduction," a law that was related to widely accepted analogies concerning the nervous system and its functioning. Thus Pearson regarded the brain as a "central telephone exchange," and Clifford referred to it as a "telegraph system." Says Clifford:

> . . . it can be made out distinctly that I could not possibly see either the surface of a thing, or a motion, as continuous; for the sensitive portion of my retina, which receives impressions, is not itself a continuous surface, but consists of an enormously large but still finite number of nerve filaments distributed in a sort of net-work. And the messages that go along my nerves do not consist in any continuous action, but in a series of distinct waves succeeding one another at very small but still finite intervals. All I can possibly have seen therefore at any moment is a picture made

of a very large number of very small patches, exceedingly near to one another, but not actually touching. . . . Let us now put shortly together what we have said about this sensation of sight. I shall use the word mosaic to represent a few disconnected patches which a painter might put down with a view of remembering a scene he had no time to sketch. . . . The utmost I can really see is a panorama painted in mosaic. . . .[2]

EXTERNAL REFERENCE

In a discussion of the problems of pain localization and the "outness" of color in 1871, Huxley noted that a "state of consciousness" called "pain" arises when the finger is pricked and that another state of consciousness accompanies the pain so that the pain is felt in the finger. "I am just as certain that the pain is in my finger," he said, "as I am that I have it at all." He was as certain that the pain could not be in the finger or anywhere near the finger because the "seat of consciousness" may be two feet away. An unlearned "act of the mind" would be responsible for the "*extradition* of that consciousness, which has its seat in the brain, to a definite point of the body." When the problem of the externalization of visual sensation is taken up, the process of extradition is regarded as more complete than the extradition of pain. The discussion of extradition is in the context of evaluating Berkeley's theory of sensation, which, Huxley said, supposes that "colours do not appear to be at any distance from us." Huxley differed from this opinion thus,

> I have made endless experiments on this point, and by no effort of the imagination can I persuade myself, when looking at a colour, that the colour is in my mind, and not at a "distance off," though of course I know perfectly well, as a matter of reason, that colour is subjective. . . . In fact, it appears to me that it is the special peculiarity of visual sensations, that they invariably give rise to the idea of remoteness, and that Berkeley's dictum ought to be reversed. For I think that any one who interrogates his consciousness carefully will find that "every proper visual idea" appears to be without the mind and at a distance off.[3]

Evidently Huxley interpreted Berkeley's theory to imply that color is mind-localized. However, in contradicting the theory he invoked innate acts of extradition, and if these were excluded his position would be identical with Berkeley's.

Of all empirists, Taine (1869) has the longest and most detailed discussion of the localization and projection of sensations, which he interprets from the standpoints of physiology, psychology, and philosophy. His theoretical position is identical with Huxley's except for the explanation of localization and projection in terms of "localizing judgments" based on the "sensation of contact." Generally he supposes that the sense of touch determines the "sensation of contact" which in association with color or some other sensation causes the sensation to be "situated" at the place that has been touched. In his view, sensory stimulation when transmitted to the brain would produce mind-localized sensation, or sensation that would be experienced in the brain if the brain were accessible to touch. "In the first place, we see that this judgment must invariably be false; for the touch can never arrive at the sensory centres, to check or modify the commenced sensation; the sensory centres are in the box of the cranium in a place our hands cannot reach." The first "localizing judgment," he says, will cause a sensation to be placed at the extremity of nerves or, more exactly, in its proximity. "The touch cannot reach the exact spot. The finger cannot reach the retina at the back of the eye, nor the pituitary membrane at the inner part of the nose, nor the acoustic nerve in the labyrinth of the ear, nor, in general, any nervous periphery." However, the finger can touch the outer appendages such as the "eyeball" and this is where sensations are first localized. In verification of the theory Taine cites the cases of the resighted who immediately upon seeing "situate their new sensations at the surface of the eyeball, and not at the back of the orbit." The muscular sensation of opening and closing the eyelids would be another factor contributing to the corneal localization of visual sensation. The referral of sensation to objects comes about as the result of another "localizing judgment." Says Taine:

> All our sensations of color are thus projected out of our body, and clothe more or less distant objects, furniture, walls, houses, trees, the sky, and the rest. This is why, when we afterwards reflect on them, we cease to attribute them to ourselves; they are alienated and detached from us, so far as to appear different from us. . . . In fact, as far as we are concerned, this operation is but a means: we pay no attention to it; the color and the object denoted by the color are what alone interest us. Consequently, we forget or omit to observe the intermediate steps by which we localize our sensation; they are to us as though they did not exist; and we there-

upon consider that we directly perceive the color and colored object as situated at a certain distance off.

The fact that empirists referred to Taine's opinions without dissent gives us some idea as to how they understood the problem and its resolution. Generally, it was supposed that the exteriorization of color sensation as well as the localization of pain were acquired as the product of associations.[4]

NATURE OF THE MIND

A visual perception in Berkeley's theory represents an adjunctive association between visual and tactual elements or, alternatively, it is composed of a visual (sensational) consciousness and a tactual consciousness. In later development of the theory, as in Bain, the concomitants of visual and tactual elements in the anatomy and functioning of the nervous system were specified. The outgoing or efferent currents flowing into the motor centers and the faint revived sensations they occasion subsequent to the formation of connections were thought to be the physiological basis for seeing objects, distances, and so on. But since Bain supposed that the incoming sensations, for which the currents to the sensory centers are responsible, are ignored and not present in consciousness, the acquired consciousness would be muscular both in its origin and in its present constitution. His theory also required that the path of incoming and outgoing currents be intact for an acquired state of consciousness to arise. If the connection were broken at the motor center, the state of consciousness, as we know it to be, would be impossible. A hypothetical individual whose anatomical paths were so severed would be reduced to Berkeley's "unbodied spirit," and this "spirit" would be unable to see, hear, think, or remember. It was for reasons such as these that the concept of consciousness as "muscular" or "tactual" was widely adopted and became known as the "sensori-motor theory of consciousness."

This theory, which supposes a visual perception is a "complex" or "compound" state consisting of visual sensation and the revived idea or faint sensation of motor action, implies that consciouness is delusory. Taine, whose theory is similar to Bain's theory, regarded perception as a "compound" or as an "agglutination" of sensations; and like

Bain, "mental chemistry" was not included in the description of perception. The projection of color sensations on objects as a compound would include the following: the localization of sensation on the surface of the eyeball, the faint revival of the sensation of contact which led to this localization, the faint revival of the sensations of the motor action in walking to, reaching for, and touching objects. The revival of the latter type of sensation would be the basis for the "direct perception of the color and colored object situated at a certain distance off" since without it, we should experience the color sensation as eye-localized. As a direct consequence of his theory, consciousness is a delusion because that so-called direct perception which we believe is only visual, is actually the faint revival of muscular sensations. The fact that Taine often referred to the projection of color sensation as an "illusion" suggests his recognition and acceptance of the implication we have attributed to his theory. The followers of Berkeley's theory, however, most often failed to recognize this implication. John Dewey is a noteworthy example of a philosopher who, in having described the theory in traditional terms (1886), did not realize that the developed visual consciousness would have to be regarded as delusory.[5]

Höffding (1891), who also accepted the sensory-motor theory, recognized these and other problems and he saw that some revision was necessary. His theory of perception, he said, was the same as Berkeley's. Having developed the theory in terms of adjunctive associations between sensational and motor elements, he observed the special problem arising in the perception of form on the basis of the assumption that the associated contents consist of two successive series of qualitative sensations. After some discussion of Lotze's theory of local signs he said, "But there still remains an unexplained residue, for the psychological product has a property not possessed by the elements out of which it has arisen, that very property which gives rise to the problem, namely the extensive form." In observing that the "general laws of association" and the assumption of an "intuition of space" are both inadequate for resolving this problem, he continued, "A transformation must therefore be admitted, a psychical synthesis, analogous to the chemical synthesis, out of which arise compound substances with properties not possessed by the elements." Apparently some principle equivalent to the law of psychological chemistry is essential for explaining the new property of spatiality, the simultaneity of a percept, and the nonawareness of the original sensations. Although Höffding did not apply his concept of synthesizing principle to the explanation of the convex appearance of a globe, it seems probable that he would have said that this appearance arises from the psychic fusion of a bi-dimensional visual field and motor sensations. Thus the new property of the psychological product would not be contained in either component and, furthermore, there would not be any awareness of the components and their properties.

A few pages later, however, Höffding apparently implied a contradictory opinion: "We have seen that the percept is always complex, since in it fresh sensations blend immediately with memories." For if the percept of extensive form or convex appearance represents a new property, the percept would be unitary and not complex. This apparent contradiction may be resolved in reference to his belief that "psychical synthesis" originates in the "constructive power of consciousness." The "mind" at first would apprehend the associated visual and motor elements and then, by virtue of its constructive power, synthesize the elements so as to produce the new property. When Höffding said the percept is complex he must have been referring not to its present status in consciousness but rather to the operations of the mind which led to its formation.[6]

The principle of "mental chemistry," however, had an unsettled character among the followers of Berkeley's theory in Höffding's period. For instance, Sully in 1886 did not resort to this principle in his theory of perception, which he said followed the "main lines" of Berkeley's theory. In exemplifying the influence of memory on perception, he said, "In seeing a globe . . . we are reproducing tactile experiences." Sully had previously said that if it were not for tactile experiences the globe would look flat. Since the reproduced tactile experiences are regarded as faint revivals of the previous tactile experiences, the present perception of the globe would represent the adjunctive association of the flat appearance and the reproduced tactile experiences. In 1892, still following the "main lines" of Berkeley's theory, he came to accept "mental chemistry" much in the same way as expressed by Höffding. However, he often reverted to his previous position as exemplified in the quotation.[7]

The assumption of an unextended mind which was influential in the development of perceptual theory and the empiristic approach continued to agitate philosophers and scientists in Höffding's period. However, the constancy hypothesis was the more important assumption. Those who maintained a noncommittal attitude as to the nature of mind and those, few in number, who regarded mind as extended, presupposed the constancy hypothesis and adopted the main features of Berkeleyan theory. The acceptance of this assumption is particularly evident in the widely quoted *Molyneux Premise,* and in the assumption that the original perception of form is bi-dimensional. The denial of a form-sensation, however, did not represent a necessary departure from the constancy hypothesis. For instance, those who followed Lotze's theory supposed, as Lotze did, that stimulation of a particular retinal element would give rise to the same sensation. This is a logical necessity to make the theory of local signs workable but, in any case, it is also based on the law of isolated conduction. The difference between Lotze and those who supposed an original bi-dimensional visual form lies in the fact that for him each sensation of the mosaic of sensations is apprehended successively, whereas for the others, the sensations are apprehended simultaneously.[8]

Definition of Perception

Definitions have always varied considerably but toward the end of the nineteenth century the variation was even greater. The development of a new philosophical terminology, arguments among philosophers over various problems, and criticism of traditional theories were mainly responsible for the failure to arrive at a uniform definition. The definition proposed by Sully in 1884, which he repeated in other works before and afterward, seemed acceptable and was widely cited. In his view the mind is "passive" in sensation but "active" in perception.

> Perception is a complex mental act or process, involving presentative and representative elements. More particularly, perception is that process by which the mind, after discriminating and identifying a sense-impression (simple or complex), supplements it by an accompaniment or escort of revived sensations, the whole aggregate of actual and revived sensations being solidified or 'integrated' into the form of a percept, that is, an apparently immediate apprehension or cognition of an object now present in a particular locality or region of space.[9]

The Evidence

Observations of infants and the data of the resighted constituted the main types of evidence which were cited in proof of Berkeleyan theory.

In 1892 Sully summarized some of the "facts [which] seem to show conclusively that particular space-intuitions . . . have to be acquired." Summarizing these facts still further, he pointed out that the infant must learn to fixate an object, to blink his eyes, to move his eyes in various directions, to track a moving object, and to extend his arm straight out toward an object. This type of learning, which would be gradual, establishes the "proposition that the child only begins to attain to complete vision and to co-ordinate sight and touch towards the end of the first half-year." The rapidity of this learning, he says, suggests the importance of "inherited arrangements" as a contributory factor. Dewey cited the following observation as evidence for Berkeley's theory: "The child grasping for the moon, and crying because he cannot get it, illustrate the defective nature of visual space perception, when not associated with muscular sensations." Observations and "facts" of this kind were widely cited in the period. Helmholtz's recollection of his experience as a child in Potsdam was also quoted as evidence, although not very frequently.[10]

The citation of the prestigious Cheselden report as the important source of evidence for empiristic theory continued into the period under discussion. For instance, Saisset, in an article in an encyclopedia of 1875, said, "Rigorous experiments establish that originally all exterior objects are given to us by sight as though extended on a unique surface perpendicular to a visual ray, and in some way tangent to the orbit of the eye." After referring to the necessity of extensive training for the infant's learning to see everything in the "same plane," he continued, "This curious fact has been put beyond all dispute by the celebrated experiment of Cheselden." However, many other cases, besides the Wardrop case, which were cited as supporting some phase of Berkeleyan theory had accumulated by 1900. The patients of Franz and Nunneley were two such cases. In respect to the postoperative vision of the patients, portions of one report will be excerpted and the other report will be quoted fully because of its brevity. The two patients, before the operation, could see and recognize colors in bright light; but because of the nature of the opacities in their lenses they could not perceive objects. Franz's patient was totally blind in the right eye, which was inoperable.

Franz's Case (1841)

Franz restored vision in the left eye of a boy of eighteen. Immediately after the operation he attempted a few experiments but he had to terminate them because of the "pain which light produced in the eye." Both eyes were closed with strips of court-plaster for forty-eight hours.

> On opening the eye for the first time on the third day after the operation, I asked the patient what he could see; he answered that he saw an extensive field of light, in which everything appeared dull, confused, and in motion. He could not distinguish objects. The pain produced by the light forced him to close the eye immediately. Two days afterwards, the eye, which had been kept closed by means of court-plaster, was again opened. He now described what he saw as a number of opaque watery spheres, which moved with the movements of the eye, but, when the eye was at rest, remained stationary, and then partially covered each other.

Franz waited until the pain subsided so that he could perform a series of experiments; he did not say how long this took, nor did he say whether the eye had been covered. The second experiment dealt with recognition of outline figures drawn on paper: "The outline in black of a square, six inches in diameter, within which a circle had been drawn, and within the latter a triangle, was, after careful examination, recognized and correctly described by him. . . . A line consisting of angles, or in other words, a zigzag, and a spiral line, both drawn on a sheet of paper, he observed to be different, but could not describe them otherwise than by imitating their forms with his finger in the air. He said he had no idea of these figures."

The next experiment was concerned with the recognition of solid objects:

> At the distance of three feet and on a level with the eye, a solid *cube* and a *sphere*, each of four inches in diameter, were placed before him. Allowing him to move the head in a lateral direction no farther than was necessary to compensate the point of view of the right amaurotic eye, I . . .

requested him to state decidedly what he observed. After attentively examining these bodies, he said he saw a *quadrangular* and a *circular* figure, and after some consideration he pronounced the one a *square* and the other a *disc*. His eye being then closed, the cube was taken away, and a disc of equal size substituted and placed next to the sphere. On again opening his eye, he observed no difference in these objects, but regarded them as both discs. . . . A pyramid, placed before him with one of its sides towards his eye, he saw as a plane triangle. . . . On the conclusion of these experiments, I asked him to describe the sensations the objects had produced, whereupon he said that immediately on opening his eye, he had discovered a difference in the two objects, the cube and the sphere, placed before him, and perceived that they were not drawings, but that he had not been able to form from them the idea of a square and a disc, until he perceived a sensation of what he saw in the points of his fingers, as if he really touched the objects. When I gave the three bodies (the sphere, cube, and pyramid) into his hand, he was much surprised that he had not recognized them as such by sight, as he was well acquainted with these solid mathematical figures by his touch.

Franz continues:

When the patient first acquired the faculty of sight, all objects appeared to him so near that he was sometimes afraid of coming in contact with them, though they were in reality at a great distance from him. . . . If he wished to form an estimate of the distance of objects from his own person, or of two objects from each other, without moving from his place, he examined the objects from different points of view by turning his head to the right and to the left. . . . All objects appeared to him perfectly flat; thus, although he very well knew by his touch that the nose was prominent, and the eyes sunk deeper in the head, he saw the human face only as a plane.

There are two discrepancies in this report which Franz did not note. In continuation of the above he said: "The human face pleased him more than any other object presented to his view; the eyes he thought most beautiful, especially when in motion; the nose disagreeable, on account of its form and great prominence; the movement of the lower jaw in eating he considered very ugly." Since "prominence" refers to the third dimension, it would appear that the boy did not see the face as flat. In a comment of one of the experiments he undertook, Franz said: "On being questioned with respect to reflected light, he said that he was always obliged to bear in mind, that the looking-glass was fastened to the wall, in order to correct his idea of the apparent situation of objects behind the glass." Thus the objects perceived by reflection appeared to be somewhat behind the surface of the mirror, which suggests that the boy perceived relative distance. However, these two percepts may not be descriptive of the boy's perceptions when the boy first acquired the faculty of sight. However, the perception of the "extensive field of light" and the "opaque watery spheres," having occurred so early in the boy's postoperative experience, suggest an original perception not only of extension but also of three-dimensional figures. The "opaque watery spheres" which he described represent the effects of particles in his eye; obviously such particles cannot be touched. Franz was interested in securing an answer to the Molyneux problem, therefore, it might have been unnecessary for him to refer to such percepts and to the discrepancies. Of further interest is the report that the boy could see the forms of figures drawn on paper, figures that cannot be touched.

Nunneley's Case (1858)

Nunneley had ascertained the fact that a boy of nine could recognize a sphere and a globe tactually before the operation. After restoring sight to both eyes, he said:

> After keeping him in a dark room for a few days, until the opaque particles of lenses were nearly absorbed, and the eyes clear, the same objects, which had been kept carefully from him, were again presented to his notice. He could at once perceive a difference in their shapes; though he could not in the least say which was the cube, and which the sphere, he saw they were not of the same figure. It was not until they had many times been placed in his hands, that he learnt to distinguish by the eye the one which he had just had in his hands, from the other placed beside it. He gradually became more correct in his perception, but it was only after several days that he could or would tell by the eyes alone, which was the sphere and which the cube; when asked, he always, before answering, wished to take both into his hands; even when this was allowed, when immediately afterwards the objects were placed before the eyes, he was not certain of the figure. Of distance he had not the least conception. He said everything touched his eyes, and walked most carefully about, with his hands held out before him, to prevent things hurting his eyes by

touching them. Great care was requisite to prevent him falling over objects, or walking against them. Improvement gradually went on, and his subsequent sight was and now is, comparatively perfect.

The Franz case was regarded as favorable to the Berkeleyan theory because the report said that the boy saw all objects flat. Franz was silent as to whether objects touched the boy's eye. On the other hand, the Nunneley case also was regarded as favorable to the theory because the boy said "everything touched his eyes" but the report fails to state whether he saw things as flat. Evidently, there are inconsistencies in the citation and interpretation of the evidence.[11]

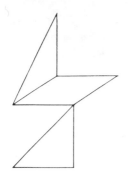

11 CONDILLAC, BAILEY, AND REACTIONS

But philosophers in order to explain the phenomena of vision have supposed that we form certain judgments of which we cannot experience any consciousness. Condillac, 1746

If the theory of Berkeley should consequently fall, its general reception by philosophers heretofore must be considered as one of the most extraordinary circumstances to be found in the annals of speculative philosophy. Bailey, 1842

The first business of the philosopher is to ascertain facts before he devises theories to account for them. Abbott, 1864

It is no doubt common for scientific men to discredit new facts, for no other reason than that they do not fit with theories that have been raised on too narrow foundations; but when they do this they are only geologists, or psychologists—they are not philosophers. Spalding, 1873

CONDILLAC

In the *Origin of Human Knowledge* of 1746 Condillac had a short single chapter which was apparently the first critique and rejection of the empiristic theory advocated by Locke and Berkeley. His immediate aim was to rebut Voltaire's exposition and support of them in 1738. We have already noted one reason for his rejection of their theory. We have also noted his opinion that the spatial aspects of perceptions are not learned, and his later retraction of this opinion. Despite the brevity of the critique and its repudiation in 1754, it nevertheless stated and anticipated many of the important ideas of later criticism. The "metaphysical" reason for the critique was to affirm the general criterion or "law" that we ought to posit in respect to consciousness only "what every man may, with the least reflection, perceive within himself." Condillac observed that although Locke and Berkeley themselves generally supposed this very law, their theory of perception was in contradiction to it. The critique is directed to the perception of the globe, the Molyneux problem—the relevant sections of Locke's *Essay* being quoted *in extenso*—and also to the Cheselden data.

Condillac stated that Locke's entire reasoning was based on the true supposition that the "image traced out in the eye at sight of the globe is only a flat circle, variously colored and shadowed." But Locke also supposed "without proof" that the resulting mental impression "gives us only the perception of this circle." Condillac, invoking the general criterion, regarded this particular supposition as "false": "For my part when I look at a globe, I see something other than a flat circle." We may observe that he was calling attention to Locke's acceptance of the constancy hypothesis, which he also deemed to be false by referring to his own conscious experience. In examining other assumptions at the basis of Locke's explanation, he proposed further arguments in refutation. He pointed out that on the assumption that the ideas of touch have been joined to visual sensation, "we would never confuse them with it, as Locke supposes."

Condillac accepted in principle the typical supposition that so many judgments pass through the mind that we might forget them a "moment" afterward but he observed that when they are "the object of our reflection, our consciousness of them would be so vivid that we should no longer be able to call them into question." Clearly he is referring to the fact that we cannot make ourselves conscious of the original perception of the flat circle, its alteration by the judgment, and the tactual "idea of convexity," regardless of the degree of attention we direct to this possibility. And for this reason he asserted that this argument alone sufficed to "destroy Locke's opinion." Furthermore, Locke presupposed knowledge of the "images convex bodies produce in us," but the great majority of men do not have this knowledge and yet "they see these figures as well as philosophers." Finally, Condillac generalized Locke's discussion of the perception of figures so as to include the "ideas of distance, situation, magnitude and extension" because these ideas "which the sight of a field cause in us, are all to be found in miniature in the perception of the different parts of the globe." To exemplify this meaning he paraphrased the quotation from Locke pertaining to the globe so as to refer to these ideas. For instance, Locke ought to say: "When we look at a vast field, it is certain that the idea which is imprinted in our mind by this prospect, represents a flat surface, variously shadowed and colored, with different degrees of light impressed in our eyes." Condillac then continued, pointing out that the judged ideas of distance, situation, and so on, were presumed to be joined to and confused with visual sensation. He said that although Locke himself did not draw these consequences, Berkeley did— Berkeley's opinion being sanctioned by the "celebrated Voltaire." It is obvious that Condillac considers the critique of Locke to apply also to Berkeley.

Furthermore, in referring to the halving in size of the retinal image of a man when his distance is doubled, he said that according to Berkeley's theory, the man at first would be seen as of half his real size but when the "idea" of his actual size has been acquired through experience, "we see him as almost of the same size." In one of his more interesting comments on what he regarded as Berkeley's explanation of size constancy, he said, "I confess there is something which I could not corroborate in my own experience. Could a first perception be eclipsed so quickly, and a judgment replacing it so suddenly that we could not notice the transition from one to the other, even when our entire attention be given to it?" Evidently Condillac interpreted Berkeley's theory as being similar to Locke's in respect to the suppositions of the original perception of a flat suface, the failure to notice the flat surface when replaced by judgment, and the transition itself. And further, the

theory was to be rejected on the grounds that we could not make ourselves conscious of these events. Although not made explicit by him,
he was also rejecting for the same reason, the supposition that the idea
derived through touch is equivalent to the acquired perception.

Condillac considered the implication of the assumption that only
light and colors are originally perceived, which as we have already observed he would regard as a "mathematical point." To rebut this conception he again referred to the "law" and wrote, "I look before me,
above, below, to the right, to the left: I see a light spread in every
direction, and several colors which certainly are not concentrated in a
point. . . . I find there, independently of any judgment, without the
aid of other senses, the idea of extension with all its dimensions." A
man born blind who recovers sight, he asserted, would also perceive an
extension in its three dimensions. He acknowledged, however, that the
Cheselden "experiment," of which he quotes Voltaire's paraphrased extract, apparently contradicted his opinion. However, he offered a "few
reflections" which might sufficiently "explain this experiment." In this
explanation he resolved the apparent contradiction by questioning the
validity of the Cheselden data.

Condillac describes and explains the "whole mechanism of the
eye," and he points out that perfect harmonious cooperation of many
muscles is essential for the formation of a distinct retinal image. Defects in the action of muscles may cause the image to be confused and
even erect so that objects "will appear to us confused and inverted."
The proper functioning of the mechanism requires not only the absence of defects but also "long exercise." Through such exercise, the
muscles, upon stimulation of the retina, respond with a "quickness
which is impossible to believe." Condillac is here describing the normal eye, and observes that the case is somewhat different for the Cheselden boy. During the period of blindness for "14 years" the mechanism
of his eye had become "stiff" and "immovable" through disuse. On immediate recovery of sight, therefore, his retinal image was confused,
and similarly his perception. But after practice the muscles of the eye
became flexible and their action coordinated, and this enabled him to
see objects quite differently then he did at first. Moreover, the fact that
the boy "groped for two months" did not prove the sense of touch
was necessary for the perceptions that developed in this period. The
touching of objects might have given him the occasion for further exercise of the sense of sight, by which Condillac meant that the eye in

following or looking at some object that has been touched acquired greater flexibility of action. He expressed the further opinion that the boy would have "obtained the same ideas by sight," though certainly more slowly, even if he did not use his hands "every time he opened his eyes to light."

In brief, Condillac accounts for the boy's perceptions immediately following the operation in terms of impairment to optical structures resulting from the long period of light deprivation. The subsequent improvement is the result of recovery from that impairment by virtue of exercise of the optical apparatus. Finally, he regards the interpretation accorded the Cheselden data as corroborating the theory of Locke and Berkeley to be the result of "prejudice" by its adherents and, for this reason, they fail to realize that the boy's "defective manner" of perceiving objects immediately after the operation could be explained in some other way. We may observe that Condillac called attention to the important possibility—probably the first to have done so—that optical damage and recovery therefrom were sufficient to account for the Cheselden data. He surely would have asserted this opinion even more strongly if he had but known that the boy's vision was monocular for about a year and not binocular as Voltaire had suggested, and that the single eye had no lens.[1]

Condillac's rejection of the constancy hypothesis in reference to the "law of consciousness" is the most significant theoretical point raised in the critique. The rejection of the hypothesis would make it unnecessary to suppose unnoticed sensations, judgments, and transitions. The perception of convexity and other percepts would be nondecomposable facts of consciousness directly arising from the propagation of the effects of sensory stimulation to the brain.

Having set forth a number of objections to the theory of Locke and Berkeley, which seemed so decisive to Condillac in 1746 and which would be so regarded from the perspective of the present day, the subsequent retraction of the critique and unreserved adoption of Berkeley's theory in 1754 was indeed surprising. The very same objections are applicable to his revised theory, a fact which Condillac fails to note. In the eight intervening years there had been no change in the nature of the evidence, the Cheselden data still being the only evidence. But in 1754 Condillac cites this case as confirmatory of his empiristic approach without indicating his previous reservation in respect to the possibility of ocular damage. Furthermore, the boy is presumed to have been perfectly resighted. Nevertheless he must have had some qualms for he points out an internal contradiction in the Cheselden report which, however, he explains away. He offers a series of experimental suggestions for ascertaining more precisely what a resighted man will see and the contributory importance of the sense of touch. In any case the data are interpreted as decisive, and indeed constitute the experimental justification for the new theory.[2]

The merit in the critique generally was neglected in subsequent theories of perception. Condillac himself might have been responsible for his own neglect by his retraction and conversion to the opposite point of view which Berkeley's theory represents. Moreover, a critic undermines the value of his criticism by rejecting it as a "prejudice." This consideration alone might make it unlikely for others to assess the merit of the critic's earlier but rejected work, especially when the vigorously expounded new position is in agreement with the prevailing opinion.[3]

BAILEY

The next significant critique of Berkeley's theory was set forth by Bailey in his work of 1842, *A Review of Berkeley's Theory of Vision, Designed to Show the Unsoundness of that Celebrated Speculation,* and in a monograph the year following. The critique although mainly concerned with Berkeley's *Essay,* also was intended to apply to its many exponents in Great Britain and the continent, whom Bailey often cited to illustrate his arguments. Moreover, he recorded the dissent of Condillac and its unreserved retraction, but otherwise failed to refer to it. In a number of publications in the following decade, Bailey undertook an extensive analysis of the Berkeleyan theory and other philosophical theories of perception.

His own approach to perception, already explicit in 1842, supposed that the basic percepts thus far discussed were "intuitive" or innate. He indicated that at first he was inclined to accept the validity of Berkeley's theory in a general way but when he later examined the doctrine of the "Association of Ideas" in detail, he became convinced of its "erroneousness." His comprehensive examination of associationism may alone suffice to establish his asserted claim to originality.

Moreover, in probably being the first even to ask whether the laws of association could, in fact, explain the requisite steps in the acquisition of perceptions, he called attention to a problem that had been previously neglected. According to Bailey, the associations required in the Berkeleyan theory could not be the basis for perception since no explanation of their formation was possible. Moreover, in his opinion the mere inconsistency of the theory with the "facts of consciousness" sufficed for its invalidation. Of course, this had been the central point of the critique by Condillac (his "law") and, for this reason, Bailey's critique shared many significant similarities with it.

Bailey's evaluation of the Berkeleyan theory will be subdivided into a "critique" and the statement of his own "theory." Further criticisms will be included in the section on "theory" because of their general significance.

THE CRITIQUE

Berkeley's theory presupposes the doctrine of the association of ideas which was expressed in a variety of terms such as "connection," "suggestion," "custom" or "experience," "sign and thing signified." Two widely accepted principles of association dominate Bailey's discussion of associative processes in their relation to visual learning. (1) *Sensations or ideas must be discriminable before they can be linked associatively.* The principle means that a set of visual sensations and a set of muscular sensations, whether derived from touch or locomotion, must each be discriminable if linkages are to develop between them. Suppose words and meanings to be substituted for the two sets, where the requirement is the association of one meaning to one word. Obviously the words must be discriminable one from the other, and likewise for the meanings. If two words "look alike" a unique meaning for each cannot be learned, and conversely, if two meanings are identical a unique word for each cannot be assigned. (2) *An idea is a copy of a sensation.* Its meaning has already been discussed, the proposition being evident when idea is regarded as a faint revival of sensation. Accordingly, visual and tactual ideas are presumably counterparts of their respective sensations. Sometimes Bailey states this principle in a form where "conception" is substituted for "idea" and "perception" for "sensation," but the change in terminology is not critical. He points out that if any dimensional attribute is absent in visual sensation, it necessarily must be absent in the visual idea corresponding to it.[4]

Bailey observes that Berkeley's theory asserts that a visual perception represents the idea or sensation of muscular action and that a visible sign suggests the feeling of touch or locomotion. But since the sign is ignored he concludes that the idea of touch or locomotion ought to be paramount in consciousness when looking at objects. He then writes, "Yet, for my own part, on appealing to my consciousness, I can discover no such suggestions. I see various objects around me in the room where I am writing; I see the table and floor extending in a direction from my eye, but I am not conscious of any conception of tangible spaces." Bailey, of course, means that there is no awareness of any tactual ideas in the visual perception of outness, distance, size, form, and solidity. He regarded this "appeal to consciousness" as decisively invalidating Berkeley's theory and, moreover, he concluded that the nature of associations supposed by it could not in fact explain what he sees. Nevertheless he decides to examine this conclusion using only the above two principles. After this examination he finds that these principles are violated and he draws the further conclusion that the associations presupposed by Berkeley's theory in fact can never develop. We shall give several examples of Bailey's line of reasoning.

On the Formation of Associations

External reference or "outness." Bailey points out that Berkeley's theory supposes visual sensation to be "merely an internal feeling" or mind-localized. Thus before any learning, the infant feels objects as though mind-localized, but by reaching out for objects he obtains the ideas derived from the sensations of the movement of the arm and hand which ultimately become linked to visual sensation so that he apparently comes to perceive objects as in space. For expository convenience we may denote the visual sensation by V and the group of muscular sensations or ideas by T. But no matter how often the sequence $V–T$ is practiced, the very same sequence always prevails. Therefore, adults ought to be conscious of this sequence. However, in Berkeley's theory V is presumed to drop out of consciousness and this explains why adults are not conscious of objects as a subjective event. But this in turn introduces another problem. If T is the determining factor of the perception, we ought to be conscious of it. However, we are not in fact conscious of T, hence associations cannot account for external reference.

Let us now return to the V term of the sequence. Is Berkeley entitled to say that it is ignored? Bailey thinks not. For a sign to denote something else, the sign itself must be noticed. He observes, however, that Berkeley advanced the linguistic metaphor for explaining why the visible sign is not noticed when some connection is frequently practiced. Bailey now declares the metaphor to be inappropriate. Although in reading we usually do not have any distinct awareness of the words themselves, he says, nevertheless if the reading pace is slowed it is certain that we will notice them. Therefore, awareness of V ought to be possible, but this never happens no matter how intently we try to detect its presence.

Suppose we leave V as the completely ignored item and reinstate T as the item of which we are supposedly aware. Bailey acknowledges the implication that the consciousness itself of seeing objects at a distance would be a delusion, and he attempts to recast Berkeley's theory so as to avoid this implication. Thus no matter how many repetitions of V and T may be supposed, the former "will invariably suggest" the latter. Therefore in perceiving distance so vividly that we think we see it, "we should have a tendency to believe that we actually felt it with the touch." But since we have no such belief of touching while perceiving visually, Berkeley's theory demands a "conversion" or "transmutation" of the muscular feeling into a visual idea or perception. However, the supposition that T is transformed or transmuted into a visual idea by virtue of its linkage to V would be "absurd" because an idea remains in the same modality as the sensation it copies. There is no way in which an idea of one sense can cross over, so to speak, and become an idea of another sense. And should one suppose this possibility for the sake of argument the following consequence would ensue. "As well it might be contended," says Bailey, "that the sight of a rose would convert the fragrance which we perceived at the same time into a visible quality. . . ." In other words we should believe we *see* the scent instead of merely smelling it. But if the possibility of transmutation is retracted, the theory must return to the alternative that T itself is experienced and the implication that consciousness is delusory. Thus Berkeley's theory has two difficulties by either admitting a process of transformation or by denying it.[5]

There is still another alternative to consider, namely, that the transformation occurs within the visual modality itself. The second principle, however, is sufficient to exclude this possibility. Since visual sensation does not directly convey the attribute of external reference, no idea of it can have or ever come to have this attribute.[6]

The final outcome of this line of reasoning is that associationism is completely inadequate to account for the acquisition of external reference. It is important to observe in this connection that Bailey is writing in the period before the concept of "mental chemistry" was invoked. However, we shall later observe that this concept does not have the explanatory significance attributed to it. Moreover, we wish to point out that Bailey regarded his analysis as also applying to the premise that objects are originally felt "in" or as "touching" the eyes, and other perceptual facts.

Solidity. Let us suppose, as does Bailey, a man born blind whose sight is perfectly restored to both eyes. In other words it is assumed that his eyes function as ours do: an image can be brought into clear focus on the retina and the muscles suffer no impairment whatever. In discussing this hypothetical man's immediate vision on gaining sight in the context of perceived relative distance and solidity, Bailey supposes for the sake of argument that the man will originally see a variety of colors disposed in a plane at some apparent but unspecified distance from his eyes. However, if we let V represent the perceived plane and T the idea of tactual or locomotive distance and solidity, the analysis and conclusion drawn in the above discussion of external reference are applicable here too.

In turning to the then-recent discoveries of Wheatstone, Bailey observes, as in fact Wheatstone already had pointed out, that a solid object projects slightly different retinal images whereas a drawing of it projects two identical images. Berkeley's theory, according to him, would predict that the perfectly resighted man will at first see the object and drawing as "plane figures." Now if the experiment is tried of having him look at and touch the solid object and its drawing, Bailey argues that the necessary associations that would explain the perception of relief in one instance and the perception of flatness in the other could not be acquired. Since the "visible appearances" are the same and the tactual ideas different, a specific appearance could not suggest the idea appropriate to the particular perception. He recognizes that the pair of images projected by the solid is different from the pair projected by the planar representation, but he points out that such differences could not be the basis for discriminating one appearance from the other because they are "imperceptible" and thus "incapable of forming links in any association."

After supplying further arguments he concludes, "Thus if the projection of two different perspective figures on the two retinae did not originally engender the impression of an object of three dimensions, no process of association could possibly enable it to produce that effect." In his opinion the Wheatstone discoveries provide an experimental invalidation of Berkeley's theory and prove the "perception of the three dimensions of space to be a simple and direct function of sight. . . ." Although the inadequacy of the theory of associations sufficiently establishes this conclusion, he also believes the conclusion is strengthened by the ambiguity of the *Molyneux Premise*. After an extensive analysis of the geometric portion of the premise, he concludes that Berkeley and others ought to maintain that the retinal impression is a two-dimensional expanse as Locke had supposed rather than a "point." Moreover, he objects to the supposition of a bi-dimensional "mental effect" on the grounds that this is a "gratuitous assumption" determined by *"a priori reasoning."* On the other hand, he believes that it is quite possible for the retinal impression, on being transmitted to the brain, to be correlated with the "intuitive perception" of three dimensions. In any case, "Whether the mental effect does or does not comprise such a perception, is a question of fact which can be determined only by an appeal to evidence." [7]

On Evidence

Although regarding the "appeal to consciousness" as an evidential refutation of the Berkeleyan theory, Bailey turns to an examination of infants, animals, and the resighted as three other types of evidence.

Infants. He points out that Berkeley's theory supposes the sense of touch to educate the sense of sight in infancy and yet no test of the theory in relation to what actually occurs in that period is undertaken by its proponents. When he himself examines the available evidence he finds that the theory is contradicted. He quotes observations of physiologists which indicate that the sense of touch develops much later than that of sight. At the beginning of the second month, the infant "spontaneously directs his eyes toward objects," and long before the age of six months when the child can start to properly use his hands he is "sensible of the smiles of his mother or nurse; he shows an interest in the human face, which manifestly implies that he perceives objects by his sight to be at some distance from him." Thus judging on the basis of his reactions, the infant perceives the human face as a distinct spatial entity without the assistance of touch. The child does not show the same interest in the mother's neck or other objects in its immediate surrounding. Moreover he can discriminate a smiling mother's face in contrast with a nonsmiling one. Clearly, the perceived distinction of the face in two conditions could not have been acquired tactually. His responses do not justify the belief that he perceives things as though touching the eyes or internal feelings. "It would be a monstrous supposition that during these four or five months . . . antecedently to any assistance from touch, he should have an impression that they were all equally near or equally remote." Moreover, Bailey is convinced that the infant perceives relative distances because he can proportion his movements, though inaccurately, to the actual distances of objects. In the further development of the sense of touch the child can respond accurately in touching what he sees. "In these attempts," he adds, "he is obviously learning how to adjust his muscular efforts to visible distances." Bailey continues, "Here is no process of learning to see with precision by the help of touch, but one of learning to touch with precision by the help of sight." After further discussion of the child accurately reaching for objects to the left or to the right and accurately grasping objects according to their magnitude, he supposes that the relation of sight and touch is opposite to what "Berkeley's theory requires it to be." He concludes the chapter on infants by observing, "visual perceptions of distance precede and are implied in the effort to adjust the action of the muscles so as to reach visible objects." Evidently in his opinion we learn to act through perception rather than learn to see through action.

Clearly his discussion of infants can be related to the first of the two principles of association. The young child discriminates visual sensations but he cannot yet discriminate muscular sensations. Hence associations cannot explain the development of visual perception in the child.[8]

Animals. The examination of the evidence of the behaviors of those lower animals born or hatched in a relatively mature state, he says, decisively refute the Berkeleyan theory. In acknowledging that we really cannot know what an animal experiences or sees, judgment on the basis of movements in relation to objects only being possible, Bailey cites already well-known data gathered by naturalists and others. When the egg of an alligator in sand was broken open, the emerging animal was "perfect in its motions and passions" and immediately headed for the water. An attempt was made to hinder it whereupon "it assumed a threatening aspect and bit the stick presented to it." A chick snapped at a fly while shell was still stuck to its tail. An ape, while still "hanging to the breasts of its mother during the first days of its existence," attentively examined objects "without touching them." Subsequently, "from its first movements it shows a very exact *coup d'oeil* every time it has occasion to leap, or to seize hold of anything." These and other similar observations Bailey concludes, are "positive proof that a perception of degrees of distance is immediately possessed at birth through the unassisted organs of vision." He also points out that there is a natural correlation between the visual perception of distance and the action and muscular effort in reaching or leaping to objects. He scoffs at the idea that a bird of prey "learns distances by the touch," for an eagle can distinguish its prey from a considerable distance and then "rush upon it with the velocity of an arrow."

He believes that the "direct and intuitive perception of distance" demonstrated by these animals probably applies to human vision as well, the organs of sight being essentially the same, but admits that infants immediately after birth do not exhibit the same "perfect perception of distance." However, he does not regard this fact as constituting a sufficient reason for rejecting an inference from animal to human vision. The senses in infants are "organically immature" whereas an animal may be "almost instantly endowed with the use of his senses, muscles, nerves, and brain." A "gradual growth" of the human senses is necessary before they can arrive at their complete state of development and maturity. He alludes to the fact that the focusing mechanism of the eye is inadequate at birth and as a consequence even the "perception of colour and figure" may be defective. The infant may not even be able to perceive distance very well for this reason. When maturation is complete, however, the infant can perceive color, figure, and distance. Therefore, "the imperfection in the action or functions of any of these organs at birth, or while they are in a state of progression, is no proof that the function is not natural to the organ, and would not be performed independently of experience." The senses of taste and smell also may be defective at birth, he adds, but no one would suppose that we learn to taste and to smell because tasting and smelling appear somewhat later.[9]

The data from lower animals, in Bailey's opinion, challenge Berkeley's theory at its most central point. The theory rests on "one solitary reason of an *a priori* character." The reason, the *Molyneux Premise,* was at the basis of J. S. Mill's assertion that a "direct and intuitive perception of distance" was an "organic impossibility." A line turned endwise projects but a single point on the retina. This is the geometric portion of the premise. It is then inferred that distance necessarily cannot be perceived by sight, or that distance is invisible. Bailey points out that the geometric portion applies to both human and animal eye alike. Since the young of lower animals can perceive distance, the conclusion of the premise is unjustified. And furthermore, he says, Berkeley's theory is refuted because it presupposes the necessity of the conclusion. Although Bailey generalizes from animal to human perception on the basis of the structural similarity of the eye, he does not feel called upon to urge that every human percept is intuitive. In his opinion, investigation rather than appeal to an *a priori* postulate is necessary for establishing the facts.[10]

In an early period some followers of Berkeleyan theory maintained that lower animals had to learn to see in the same way as did humans. But when the data became fully known those who accepted its validity no longer supposed that these animals had to learn to see. However, it was believed that Berkeley's theory was in no way impaired by this concession, for it was supposed that associations in animals are "instinctive" whereas in humans they are acquired. It is important to observe that this distinction does not question *Molyneux's Premise.* Since the connections between visible signs and the ideas derived from muscular sensations are presumed to be acquired by humans but instinctive for animals, the premise underlies both types of associations. When Bailey asserts that the perception of distance in animals is "direct or intuitive" he excludes any associational linkage as a component of that perception. For this reason he claims the case of animals falsifies the premise and, as a consequence, Berkeley's theory is refuted.

Bailey's argument was challenged by J. S. Mill who, in acknowledging that the animal evidence was "the most serious difficulty the theory of Berkeley has to encounter," claimed that the hypothesis of an "instinctive interpretation of signs" could void the charge of refutation. He cited "degrees of brightness and visible magnitude" as two signs that might instinctively suggest the distance of objects to the animal.[11] Presumably, as an object recedes from the animal its visible appearance becomes less bright and smaller, thus enabling the animal to instinctively infer the increasing distance of the object. Bailey counters Mill's hypothesis: "To interpret a sign of distance, as of anything else, you must first know the thing indicated. Distance, according to Berkeley, is exclusively a tangible thing. The instinctive interpretation of its signs would therefore imply the mental conception of a tangible object, which by the hypothesis had never been felt; 'a copy,' as metaphysicians call it, of a tactual sensation never experienced." [12]

Bailey here implies that Mill's hypothesis requires an animal to have an innate knowledge of objects or innate tactual ideas. Thus an animal is called upon to make instinctive comparisons in the appearances of the same object at different distances and to infer from these comparisons, again instinctively, the different distances of that object. In short, the animal must possess some notion of the identity of an object even though it produces a variable visible appearance. When an object recedes from the animal, its retinal image shrinks. In order to properly interpret the shrinking appearance as a sign of increasing distance, the animal must know that an object of the same size is responsible for the change in appearance. If it did not possess this knowledge, the shrinking appearance might merely denote an object actually shrinking in size when remaining at the same unspecified distance. Mill must have had some reservation in his commitment to the hypothesis he proposed, for in further discussion of animal evidence he admits he was "unable to solve" the question raised by Bailey's rejection of the *Molyneux Premise*. But whatever the doubt he entertained in the interpretation of animal data, he thought the Cheselden case strongly established the position that man must learn to see. Brown, who advanced a similar argument before Mill, conceded that young animals do not have to "learn to see," explained their perceptions in terms of "instinctive suggestion," and he even allowed that there is no "physical impossibility" of a "similar original suggestion" in man. The issue, Brown said, is to be resolved by experiment and observation. But that man must "truly learn to see" has been in fact "demonstrated by experiment," such as the Cheselden case.[13]

The Cheselden case. One basic question Bailey raises concerns the sense in which the Cheselden data constitute a confirmation of Berkeley's theory. In one approach he accepts the data at face value but finds that the theory is contradicted anyway. Berkeley predicted that a resighted man at first would see or think objects to be "in his eye or in his mind." But in saying that things touched his eyes, the boy is "clearly stating that visible objects appeared *external*" to his mind and even to his body. Bailey merely states this possibility to show that another interpretation of the data is feasible for he basically rejects its admissibility as scientific evidence. Thus he says, "The narrative of Cheselden, which has been so celebrated and thought to be conclusive, appears to me, I confess, exceedingly loose, meagre, and unsatisfactory." The report is so vague that it is difficult to know exactly what it is supposed to prove. Then too it is difficult to ascertain what the boy actually saw because the narration generally represents the words and interpretation of the author. But the general acceptance of the data, in Bailey's view, justifies a detailed scrutiny.

In asking whether the data confirm the Berkeleyan thesis that "objects are not originally perceived to be at different distances," Bailey finds that the supportive evidence rests on the ambiguity of a critical phrase. The report says that the boy on first seeing "was so far from making any judgments about distances, that he thought all objects whatever touched his eyes. . . ." He points out that a judgment about distance is quite different from a perception of distance. Suppose the boy had been shown two objects at different distances and the surgeon had asked for a comparative estimate in terms of feet or number of paces. Obviously the boy would be unable to estimate the distances even if he perceived the objects to be at different distances. As a consequence he might very well have told the surgeon that he could not make any "judgments about distances," subsequently to be misinterpreted as meaning that he did not perceive relative distances visually. Bailey interprets the boy's comment "touching the eyes" in a similar way. He points out, as before, that the boy can't tell how far away an object is from him in terms of number of feet or some other measure. Moreover, while blind, he experienced an actual contact between his body and the objects he touched. On recovery of sight "he might naturally think in the first flush of novelty," says Bailey, "that the objects of the new sense were perceived in some analogous way." Since the "analogical language" of touch is the only one available to him for the purpose of communication, the boy says "all objects touched his eyes . . . as what he felt, did his skin."

Bailey supposes that the boy saw his cat and dog as having different forms but could not transfer the appropriate names he had learned through the sense of touch. For their correct naming on the basis of sight alone, previous experience in correlating visual and tactual data was necessary. Thus when Cheselden says that the boy "knew not the shape of anything," he could have been referring to naming objects rather than visually discriminating them. Bailey further contends that the "learning to see forms" through the sense of touch is, in fact, impossible and that its only meaning pertains to learning to judge or to label. For if the boy could not visually discriminate shapes, it would have been impossible for him to connect different tactual ideas to them so as to enable the subsequent development of distinct visual forms. He considers the points at issue to be the same as in learning the associations between colors and smells where, obviously, the role of touch is excluded. As a hypothetical example, he supposes the boy had to learn to associate the colors and fragrances of two essences, their scents already being familiar to him. He then says, "After he had taken up the bottle containing the blue essence, looked at it and snuffed its perfume, he might set down with the appropriate exclamation. 'So I shall know this essence another time.' This would be just as much learning to see colours by the smell as the other would be learning to see forms and distances by touch; that is to say, not at all."

In another approach to the Cheselden data, Bailey observes there is no necessary confirmation of Berkeley's theory even if the seeing of objects at "one uniform distance" were unquestionably proved. The previous discussion supposes the boy to have regained his sight perfectly but it is quite possible that the "unnatural circumstances" of being blind might have led to a "disorder and irregularity of function in some part of the visual apparatus including the brain." In having regained his sight imperfectly he might very well have seen things at one distance. But this does not entitle us to generalize as to what the "natural impression" might be when the sense of sight develops normally. He points out that we would not judge the action of a normal limb on the basis of the action of a limb bound from birth and later untied.

Finally he observes, in supposing the data to pertain to vision, that there is no evidence that the boy's later perceptions were acquired through the sense of touch. He therefore proposes the following hypothesis which in his view might plausibly account for visual learning:

Admitting, for the sake of argument, that when he began to see, all objects appeared to him in the same plane; what is there to show that the various figures depicted on this surface did not separate themselves by degrees into discernibly solid bodies, assuming greater or smaller distances, as he continued to look at them, without any aid from his other senses; just as a combination of various sounds poured at once on the ear, although heard at first as one confused noise, would gradually separate as we continued to listen, into elements audibly distinct?

We may observe that his re-interpretations, if only plausible, remove the Cheselden case as the "conclusive" or "uncontestable" evidential support of the Berkeleyan theory. By 1842 other similar cases, such as that of Wardrop, were cited though to a lesser degree in support of this theory. Bailey also examined them and arrived at conclusions similar to those in his discussion of the Cheselden data.[14]

THE THEORY

We may briefly observe that Bailey regards the perception of distance and other perceptual facts to be "intuitive." When he asserts that "seeing distances is a *natural function of the organ of vision,*" it is apparent that he subscribes to the innate point of view. We may further observe that there is no implication that such percepts be immediately present at birth, for the importance of maturational processes is acknowledged.

His approach to perception is based on the elaboration of the distinction between physical and mental events. He traces the chain of "material operations" beginning with the stimulation of a sensory organ, the organic effects of that stimulation in the nerves, and their transmission to some place in the brain. The states of the brain determine "states of consciousness," which he designates as the "perception of external objects." Although to be discussed subsequently, it is to be observed that the mental event resulting from the chain of physical operations is called "perception" rather than "sensation." He supposes the mental effects to have their correlated antecedent conditions in the brain in accordance with the psychophysical postulate but nevertheless asserts that their production is "unknowable" on the grounds that the two classes of events are totally different. In perceiving, there is never any awareness of the physical conditions in the brain irrespective of whether their nature is conceived as motion, or as chemical and electrical action. The only way in which we can secure information concerning "mental states" is from a "percipient" or through self-observation. For instance, to know what the mental effect is when the retina is accidentally touched with a needle, as sometimes happens in operations for cataracts, the patient's report is essential. In this case we learn that he is conscious only of light and color and not pain. Therefore, physiological investigation alone is irrelevant to understanding and predicting the "phenomena of consciousness." And this is still true no matter how perfectly the material conditions are understood. For such reasons he asserts:

> You may trace the course of light from the object to the organ, you may follow its refractions by the lens of the eye, you may detect the picture on the retina, you may explore the connection of the optic nerves with the brain; but you do not by all these discoveries, valuable as they are, alter in the slightest degree the resulting state of consciousness denominated seeing the object.

Bailey reproaches Berkeley for having failed to strictly observe the distinction between physical and mental events although, he says, Berkeley accepted this distinction. He points out that on the basis of knowledge of the stimulation of the retina Berkeley supposed the concomitant sensation to be either an internal feeling or the perception of colors in a plane. Bailey stresses two criteria in his extensive discussion of the distinction. Mental and physical facts ought always be kept distinct in any investigation, not mixing or confusing one type with the other, and no statement pertaining to consciousness ought to be advanced which is not verifiable in the observation of consciousness itself.

In accordance with the distinction, Bailey supposes that "all facts of human science" are either "physical" or "mental." His own interest is the science dealing with the "facts of consciousness" and defined by him as the "philosophy of the human mind," which he regards as a special province of knowledge as important as any other science. In proposing a classification of the phenomena of consciousness, a first step in inferring general laws, the definitions of sensation and perception are of immediate interest. Sensation is a "sensitive affection" felt to be or localized in parts of the body. "Bodily sensations," he says, "are such as are really felt to be in some part of the body." Perception, which he includes in the intellectual operations, is defined thus: "Through the organs of sense, we perceive objects to be external and different from ourselves, the percipient beings. We touch, see, hear, taste, and smell outward things." Depending on the antecedent conditions in the nerves and brain, the immediate mental effect is sensation or perception. Since either mental effect is not preceded by any other mental state denoted by internal feeling, visual sensation, or idea, it is regarded as intuitive, original, or direct. We may set forth in summary fashion those conclusions emphasized by Bailey in his discussion of visual perception.[15]

1. A percept is a "simple" or "indivisible whole" and not a "compound." In looking at a cube, the "three dimensions of space" along with its color are perceived as a unity. Its color and dimensions are not separable entities to be brought together by associative processes. Furthermore, it is not analyzable or decomposable into sensation and idea or inference.[16]

2. A percept is a primary fact of consciousness. Knowledge of material operations or physical causes does not affect its status as a fact of consciousness. Its entire content, so to speak, is given in the very consciousness of it. He clarifies his meaning by saying, "Perceiving must be considered as a primary state of consciousness in the same way as pain or hunger or fear or joy, the causes of which you ascertain, but the nature of which no knowledge can alter and no explanation elucidate." [17]

3. The "mind is passive in perception." When the ear is stimulated by a certain type of vibration a sound is heard, and when the retina is stimulated by another type of vibration a color is seen. The states of consciousness resulting from stimulation of the nerves depend only on the "respective constitutions of the nerves." The retina he says is as impassive to sound vibrations as the ear is to rays of light, but more importantly he asserts that the mind does not "determine or even modify the result." The only action required is that of directing the "organs of sense" to objects. From that point on the chain of material operations commencing with the stimulation of the retina "produce in us states of consciousness termed the perception of objects and their qualities." Any activity of the mind as a determinant of perception, such as projection, comparison, or synthesis, is denied.[18]

4. A percept affords us a direct knowledge of objects and their

characteristics. Other theories had advanced a similar thesis, but the difference lies in the original nature of the percept in Bailey's theory, and its acquired character in other theories. If "sensation" is substituted for "percept," sensation providing direct knowledge, the distinction is clear. A sensation in other theories would provide little or no information of external objects, where as for Bailey it gives us information of all the basic spatial attributes of objects. Bailey indicates that he could have as well used "sensation" for "perception" in describing what is originally given by the sense of sight. But since "perception" already had the meaning in philosophy of referring to the cognizance of objects, he thought this was the better term to use.[19]

The systematic study of the facts of consciousness is said to make it possible to detect and eliminate errors in theories of perception. Bailey observes that a number of common errors originate in the failure to maintain the distinction between mental and physical events and in the postulation of nonverifiable psychic entities and operations. He strongly characterizes these errors as "fictitious or imaginary transactions" and he cites many examples in the writings of philosophers and scientists. In selecting and illustrating several of them, we may observe that one type of error implies the other. For instance, an error arising from knowledge of material operations not only implies the confusion of mental and physical events but also "imaginary mental events."

In the discussion of the Locke assumption of a sensation of flatness and of the *Molyneux Premise,* Bailey points out that knowledge of the characteristics of the retinal impression (a physical event) is unwittingly allowed to dictate the nature of the concomitant mental effect. This is similar to asserting that pain ought to be felt, rather than color perceived, when the retina is touched with a needle. But since mental and physical events are distinctly different and since knowledge of the concomitant mental effect can only be gained from states of consciousness, Bailey argues that it is possible for a perception to be that of a three-dimensional surface notwithstanding the bi-dimensionality of the retinal impression. Moreover, the sensation of flatness, he says, is "fictitious" since the "appeal to consciousness" fails to disclose any evidence for it.

Bailey considers the hypothesis of Hobbes, who said that "color is in the mind or inheres in the mind" because the "motion" from the retina is conveyed to the brain. This hypothesis, according to Bailey, implies that the "mind is colored or . . . that we are conscious of an internal colour (green for example), as we are conscious of an emotion like joy or grief." The problem then arises as to how color comes to be "spread over objects." Apparently Hobbes supposed that since the antecedent physical condition is in the brain, color cannot be perceived as external. He also supposed that the motion is perceived but this is impossible since it is a "physical event." In this regard he discusses in greater detail the opinion of the eighteenth-century mathematician and philosopher D'Alembert who, supposing color to be a modification of the mind and its referral to a material substance to be explained through a "habit acquired in infancy," remarked:

> . . . and nothing is perhaps more extraordinary in the operations of the mind than to see it *transport its sensations out of itself and spread them, so to speak, over a substance to which they cannot belong.*

In observing that Stewart later favorably cited D'Alembert's opinion, Bailey declares that "every step implied" in this explanation is "fictitious." We are not conscious of color as an "internal feeling" nor are we conscious of those operations which lead to its externalization. "What," he asks, "causes us to spread *green* over the growing wheat, and *red* over the poppy which intrudes amongst it?" Thus even if the explanation were accepted for the sake of argument, the mind could not direct and distribute the red and green in those precise ways as required in the perception of the wheat and poppy.[20]

In another example Bailey takes up the psychological explanation of binocular solidity proposed by his contemporary Whewell, who supposed that we can "contemplate" the two retinal impressions separately and alternately, and further supposed a "higher perceptive faculty" which can recognize their similarity or dissimilarity. Whewell said this faculty "can not only unite two impressions and recognise them as belonging to one object in virtue of their coincidence, but it can also unite and identify them, even when they do not exactly coincide." Moreover, this faculty can also decide "whether or not the two ocular images can be pictures of the same solid object" and "correct and adjust their small difference" when this is necessary. Whewell concluded, "This faculty operates as if it had the power of calling before it all possible solid figures, and of ascertaining by trial whether any of those will at the same time fit both the outlines which are given by the sense." Bailey objects to this explanation by noting that we neither see the retinal images nor are we conscious of them, this alone making it impossible for the visual faculty to infer any "third form." Moreover, we are "unaware" of any process or operation presupposed in this explanation. After adverting to the confusion of mental and physical facts, Bailey concludes the explanation was meaningless.[21]

Bailey applies a similar analysis to "visible sign" and "tactual idea" and the confusion of one for the other, and also the law of projection, and rejects them for the same reasons. This phase of the critique, when considered in relation to the preceding critique of the formation of associations and citation of evidence, is in complete contradiction with Berkeley's theory and other theories derived from it.

We may observe that the constancy hypothesis and its implications are explicitly repudiated by him, thus reinstating an important but previously neglected point in Condillac's critique. The important affirmative conclusion in Bailey's critique and theory is that a visual perception is to be regarded as an integral fact of consciousness. This conclusion was the logical implication of Condillac's critique, but Bailey made it explicit.[22]

REACTIONS

In 1842 J. S. Mill replied to Bailey's critique of the Berkeleyan theory of vision. Believing a doctrine generally "supposed to be out of the reach of doubt" had been challenged, he declared: "If the doctrine be false, there must be something radically wrong in the received modes of studying mental phenomena." After rebutting the arguments and evidence cited by Bailey he concluded that Berkeley's theory was "to all appearance unshakable." In his own reply in the following year Bailey reiterated the main points of his critique, to be shortly followed by a brief rejoinder by Mill. After considering their main arguments, we shall take up the positive reactions of Abbott and Spalding.

MILL

In a previous chapter we referred to Mill's earlier theory of perception which we did not discuss except to point out that it followed Berkeley's characterization of visible objects as qualified by the assumption of the constancy hypothesis. Thus in this early theory Mill maintains that the only "colored appearances" directly given by the sense of sight are those having some representation in the retina. He says, "We can *see* nothing except in so far as it is represented on our retina; and things which represented on our retina exactly alike will be seen alike." Thus if two stars are imaged on the retina we see them as well as the interval between them. But when one star is behind the other, the interval between them has no representation on the retina and as a consequence we do not see that distance. Moreover, the "interval between an object and our eye" cannot be seen because there is no representation of that distance in the retina. These statements are justified by appeal to the *Molyneux Premise*. He points out as a direct inference from this premise that the colored appearances, also referred to as sensations or signs, are bi-dimensional. Generally, he follows Berkeley's conception of the adjunctive connection between appearances and ideas derived from the sense of touch and other features of Berkeley's associationism but stresses, however, the rapidity of "inferences" or "reasoning" from *sign* to the *thing signified*. Mill's most important deviation from Berkeley's theory concerns the phenomenal locus of visible objects. In Section 41 Berkeley had asserted, in respect to the hypothetically resighted man, that "all objects would seem to be in his eye, or rather in his mind." In having cited this section, Mill says:

> It would be a more correct version, however, of the theory, to say that such a person would at first have no conception of *in* or *out;* and would only be conscious of colors, but not of objects. When, by his sense of touch, he became acquainted with objects, and had time to associate mentally the objects he touched with the colors he saw, then, and not till then, would he begin to see objects.

In further discussion, the absence of any such "conception" by the hypothetical man apparently has the meaning that colors are at first experienced as "internal feelings," since he accepts Bailey's description of Berkeley's theory.

Bailey had argued that the absence of any awareness of tactual ideas was a sufficient refutation of Berkeley's theory. Mill's rebuttal of this objection is rather intricate, and to simplify it we shall refer to the notation of *V* (representing the visible appearance, sensation, or sign) and *T* (representing the tactual idea). Mill partly concedes the validity of Bailey's argument for he asserts that T may be recalled with "great difficulty" and that it is "peculiarly vague and shadowy." This is so because we are not in the "habit of attending" to T. He explains this habit in terms of the "laws of association," namely, when V and T are "often exercised" both become "much less acute" in "our consciousness." The argument, however, leads to another problem as Bailey pointed out later. When we look at some object, such as a globe, its convex appearance is as firm and distinct as its hue. Apparently dissatisfied himself with this argument Mill takes up another, one which represents a deviation from Berkeley's conception of the relation between V and T. He proposes the possibility that the frequency of exercise and other principles of association cause T to suggest V, such that T drops out of consciousness. This argument, however, implies a consciousness of V or, concretely, implies that we should be aware of the flat appearance of the globe. In possible recognition of this difficulty Mill offers another resolution and says:

> In our own experience, we should say, that, when we look at an object to judge of its distance from us, the idea suggested is commonly that of the length of time, or the quantity of motion, which would be requisite for reaching to the object if near to us, or walking up to it if at a distance.

In other words instead of being aware of V or T we are presumably aware of another factor, such as the amount of time or motion. We may observe that this argument is not persuasive, since we are not aware of such factors when we perceive the globe as having a convex appearance. This discussion is, of course, related to the problem of whether visual consciousness is delusory. On the one hand, Mill maintains that Berkeley's theory does not require the transmutation of T into a "perception of sight" and on the other, that "no touching or handling will ever make us *see* any thing more" than a "party-colored plane." He then goes on to say that the third dimension represents an "instantaneous act of judgment" superadded to the colored appearance as the result of experience. Clearly the judgment is supposed to be nontactual but he fails to explain how the "intellect" is able to form this judgment from tactual data. Mill did not invoke the concept of "mental chemistry" in his critique of Bailey, although it was available to him at the time.

When he considers the evidence pertaining to infants, animals, and the Cheselden case, Mill observes no contradiction to the Berkeleyan theory. To be sure, he says, the infant does not have the necessary muscular ability and thus cannot reach for objects; but objects, he maintains, are constantly touching him. The animal data can be interpreted in terms of an "instinctive association of signs" or perhaps in terms of another sensory modality since there is no proof the animals are guided to objects on the basis of sight. He concedes, however, that if both interpretations were incorrect, Berkeley's theory would be refuted. He partly accepts Bailey's explanation as to why the boy said objects touched his eyes but does not find this explanation to be complete. If the boy saw some objects as more distant than others he would not have said that "all objects seemed to touch his eyes." In Mill's view this "seems to prove completely that we are at first incapable of seeing things at unequal distances." He cites that portion of the case which concerns the boy's responses to forms, such as the cat and dog, and concludes that the "process of learning to see" shapes by means of touch is "graphically described." But in the discussion of this evidence Mill omits many relevant details. For instance, in reference to the Cheselden data, he ignores the possibility of impairment and the possible relevancy of the distinction between seeing and judging.

The final and perhaps most central point raised by Mill concerns the conceptual status of perception and sensation. He writes:

> Thus it is, that, from using the obscure word "perception" instead of the intelligible words "sensation" and "judgment" or "inference," our author leaves his antagonist unanswered, and triumphs over a shadow. It is true that Berkeley and Berkeley's adherents have set him the example of this misleading phraseology; but Mr. Bailey lives in a more accurate age, and should use language more accurately.

We may at first observe that Mill's preferred phraseology cannot merely represent a choice of words in the English language to be used to denote certain meanings. For if that were the case the word "sensation" could be defined so as to include the three-dimensional aspect of a colored appearance and Mill would then be in agreement with Bailey, the latter preferring the English word "perception" to denote this meaning. Therefore, Mill is asking that the bi-dimensional aspect of a colored appearance be accepted as a primary fact of consciousness and the tri-dimensional aspect as a secondary fact of consciousness. On the other hand, Bailey contends that a tri-dimensional aspect of the appearance is the primary fact of consciousness.[23]

In our opinion the attitude toward the *Molyneux Premise* is the basic issue dividing Mill and Bailey. Mill's acceptance of this premise is axiomatic, for in the rejoinder Mill asserts that the premise suffices to refute any theory supposing that "distance from the eye can be directly seen." Apparently, the power of this premise in Mill's thinking was such that its contestability was inconceivable. Indeed it is the prior acceptance of this very premise which determines his interpretation of data and his distinction between perception and sensation. Bailey, on the other hand, regards it as having a status contingent on evidence and the facts of consciousness. In supposing the rejection of the premise to be plausible, he is led to evaluate the evidence quite differently and also to reject the notion of sensation as proposed by Mill. But when we consider the distinction between mental and physical events, the problems raised in respect to the formation of associations, and Mill's neglect to respond to key issues, it would seem that Bailey has at least deprived the Berkeleyan theory of its alleged conclusiveness.

ABBOTT

The next extensive critique of Berkeley after Bailey's was undertaken by Abbott in his 1864 work, *Sight and Touch: An Attempt to Disprove the Received (or Berkeleian) Theory of Vision*. His interest in embarking on an investigation, unusual for a philosopher in respect to detail in physiological optics, was motivated by his realization that in Berkeleyan theory, consciousness would be "delusive." Should this be proved, says Abbott, "there is an end to all appeals to its authority." Thus his investigation represents an attempt to "vindicate the genuineness of consciousness." In acknowledging his debt to Bailey, we find many similarities: the appeal to consciousness, the impossibility of the formation of associations, an examination of cases of the resighted, and discussion of evidence from infants and animals. In contrast to Bailey, however, he enters into an extensive appraisal of Berkeleyan theory in relation to optics and a wide range of perceptual facts. Abbott's principal contemporary protagonists were Mill and Bain, the main writings of the former in 1864 being the review of Bailey's critique and rejoinder, and the review of Bain's "The Senses and the Intellect." Of the many points of interest developed by Abbott we shall only indicate the way he proposed to prove that the "assumed association of visual and tactual sensations does not exist and is even impossible."

He observes that degree of faintness is an important visible sign for the perception or judgment of distance in the Berkeleyan theory. Before learning, only the difference in the degree of faintness of two objects at different relative distances is perceived. But in walking to them, associations between the amount of locomotive feeling or quantity of motion and the difference in visible appearance are established. With practice an appearance suggests the locomotive feeling correlated to it so that no actual walk to the object is necessary. Abbott advances the following reason to prove the impossibility of formation of such an association. The individual experiences a series of changing appearances from dim to bright when walking to an object. But if we now suppose that the amount of locomotive feeling produces a distinctive awareness corresponding to the length of walk, it would become associated with the last or bright appearance in the series. Since the wrong sign is being connected with the amount of locomotive effort, the individual when returned to the starting position can never utilize faintness as the sign of distance because it cannot be connected with the requisite degree of effort. Abbott concludes, "The association required, therefore, cannot take place, for the simple reason that the ideas to be associated cannot co-exist. We cannot at one and the same moment be looking at an object five, ten, fifty yards off, and be achieving our last step towards it." His argument may be applied to other signs. For instance, consider the opinion of the period that the somewhat rounded contours of a distant tower signify its great apparent distance. Its significance could not possibly be learned since by the time the individual has walked up to the tower, it appears square-like. This rather than the appearance of rounded contours ought to become connected to the amount of exertion.

Abbott's argument was opposed by Fraser in a review of Abbott's book, with Abbott replying over a decade later. Fraser objected to the argument because Abbott neglected to mention that the "journey" can be "performed in the reverse order—away from the tangible object." Thus it may be true that the object appears bright after the individual has walked up to it but it may be supposed that he also walks backward away from the object to his original starting point so that the object again appears faint. The sign of faintness therefore could become connected with the right amount of locomotive feeling, a possibility overlooked by Abbott. This objection, however, cannot be taken very seriously since the backward locomotion, if it does occur, is rare. Fraser's second objection was more important. He said, "we are early provided with the visible signs which measure short, real distances, and we gradually apply these to other and longer ones, so that, without any special experience in each case, we are able to judge, approximately at least, from the sign alone, in a very large number of new cases." The significance of faintness as a sign, for instance, may be learned in the movement of an object held in the hand to or away from the eye or in walking to objects which are close. In having learned that change in the degree of faintness is correlated with the motion of the body in these short distances, generalization to more distant and perhaps inaccessible objects is possible. But this explanation in part begs the question, for the ability to generalize from a familiar to a "new" case is not learned. In any case the details underlying generalization should be stated if this mechanism is to be properly evaluated, and this Fraser did not do. If we choose the other example, the one pertaining to the tower, generalization from shorter distances is inapplicable since the rounding of the contour is only apparent for long distances. In this case, therefore, Abbott's argument retains its force.[24]

In another argument Abbott points out that we cannot discriminate either the "locomotive feelings" or the "tactual sensations" which supposedly explain the perception of either distance or of size. We can perceive an object 25 feet away to be at a different distance from one 25.5 feet away. But if we were to walk these two distances with eyes closed we would be unable to distinguish any difference in the amount of locomotive feeling or quantity of motion. Again with eyes closed, we cannot discriminate very slight differences in size or shape of objects through tactual manipulation. In looking at the objects, however, we "instantaneously" perceive differences in size and shape. Since one term in the supposed association is missing, the perception of distance, size, or shape cannot be explained by the association of sight and touch. Finally he observes, in respect to Mill's hypothesis of "instinctive interpretation of signs," that most animals "have no special organ of touch." Thus it is impossible for them even to have the instinctive idea of magnitude that could be suggested by a sign.[25]

SPALDING

The supporters of the "Berkeleian Theory of Vision," according to Spalding, were content in "arguing against the probability of instinctive knowledge" instead of submitting the issue "to the test of observation and experiment." By "instinctive knowledge" he was referring to what had been previously called innate or intuitive perception. Beginning with Bailey and Mill a controversy developed concerning the interpretation and validity of animal evidence, Abbott subsequently taking the side of the former and Bain that of the latter. It was thought that the behaviors of the animals might be explained in reference to some other sensory modality such as hearing and smell, or that the experience they acquired within four or five hours of birth might account for perceptions ordinarily presumed to be intuitive. With this as his background, Spalding undertook a series of experiments in 1873 which at the present time are regarded as establishing comparative psychology as a science. He chose chickens as the subjects most appropriate for testing because they hatch in a relatively mature state. But since they are not generally ready for visual tests until the age of one to three days he placed a hood over their heads on their emergence from the shell so as to keep them in total darkness until the time for testing. He then observed their behavior in relation to a variety of objects immediately after unhooding them.

In one experiment he reported that within fifteen minutes of being unhooded the chicks accurately pecked at insects and specks smaller than the dot of an *i*, followed the various motions of his hand, but did not respond to objects beyond their reach. He reported other experiments which, although concerned with hearing, are relevant in understanding the visually guided behavior of chickens. When a hen and her chicks were concealed in a box ten feet away from a chick that had been unhooded, the chick "uniformly set off straight for the box in answer to the call of the hen" from "every possible position." And in varying the experiment for the purpose of ascertaining the effect of the hen's call on chicks which remained hooded, they also correctly responded to the direction of the call. But this time on approaching the mother they collided against all objects in their path. The accuracy of the previous subjects in response to the call, therefore, was also guided by the sense of sight. In still another experiment he made the chicks deaf by placing gum in their ears and also hooded them upon their emergence from the shell. Upon being unhooded but remaining deaf, they also responded accurately not only in their avoidance of objects but also in the straight line path taken to reach the unconcealed hen. The hearing of sounds therefore was not essential to their accurate behavior in responding to objects. He concluded that the results were "decisive against the theory that the perceptions of distance and direction by the eye are the result of experience, of associations formed in the history of each individual life." In still another experiment chicks whose ears had been gummed but never hooded and later allowed to hear, accurately responded to the direction of the call of a concealed hen. He drew a conclusion concerning "space perceptions of the ear" which was similar to his conclusion concerning visual perceptions.[26]

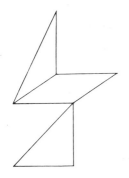

12 WILLIAM JAMES: THE "HAMLET" OF PERCEPTUAL THEORISTS

When, then, we talk of 'psychology as a natural science,' we must not assume that that means a sort of psychology that stands at last on solid ground. It means just the reverse; it means a psychology particularly fragile, and into which the waters of metaphysical criticism leak at every joint, a psychology all of whose elementary assumptions and data must be reconsidered in wider connections and translated into other terms. James, 1892

In the *Principles of Psychology* (1890) and other related works James vehemently argued against those who had supposed "sensation" was nonspatial and who then proposed to explain perception in terms of associations and special activities of the mind. In his view, a "space-sensation" had to be posited, for otherwise the spatial consciousness of the adult could not be explained. The fact that he countervailed the traditional opinion in relation to numerous experiments and the further fact that he asserted his own as emphatically as he did, made his work especially cogent even though influenced by several predecessors.

James traces the origin of the empiristic approach to Berkeley's theory, which he regards as "excessively vague" though not to the discredit of Berkeley since he was the breaker of new ground. This theory, in presupposing the *Molyneux Premise,* implies that the original perception of the world is "flat" and, furthermore, he observes that the acquired perception of distance is presumed to be a "tactile form of consciousness." The theory is rejected because he fails to detect any tactile element in his perception of the third dimension and he concludes that this dimension is a genuine fact of consciousness since it is as visually direct as the other two dimensions. The "English Associationists" who followed Berkeley, James points out, not only failed to clarify his theory but they confused it further by denying any dimension to visual sensation. In order to resolve the problem of explaining the origin of space without having supposed any original spatial content whatever, they introduced "mental chemistry" and other intellectual operations such as reasoning. These operations and their results were not only "vague" but in contradiction to their basic premise. As exponents of sensationalism they proposed to explain all contents of consciousness in terms of direct or present sensation and recalled sensation, the latter sensation being regarded as a reproduction or copy of the former. Both types of sensation represented the effects of present or past sensory stimulation. Since by hypothesis a direct sensation did not have a dimensional attribute, neither could its copy. Moreover, when the associationist invoked the principle of mental chemistry the basic premise was contradicted because the spatial product did not characterize sensation.

James's own theoretical position follows sensationalism when corrected to include "space sensation" as an original fact of consciousness and, also, as we shall observe shortly, when revised to accommodate acceptance of the psychophysical postulate.[1]

The psychologist, according to James, should study the anatomy and functioning of the brain, becoming somewhat of a "nerve physiologist," as well as the traditional "states of consciousness." Moreover, he should accept as a "working hypothesis" the thesis that brain activity causes conscious states and, in accordance with this thesis, he should frame explanations in physiological terms. The consistent development of this hypothesis presupposes the psychophysical postulate as a "law of nature." The postulate is stated thus:

> . . . however numerous and delicately differentiated the train of ideas may be, the train of brain-events that runs alongside of it must in both

respects be exactly its match, and we must postulate a neural machinery that offers a living counterpart for every shading, however fine, of the history of its owner's mind. Whatever degree of complication the latter may reach, the complication of the machinery must be quite as extreme, otherwise we should have to admit that there may be mental events to which no brain-events correspond.[2]

States of consciousness such as color-sensation, size perception, attention, inattention, reasoning, remembering, and purpose must have their distinctive counterparts in brain processes. An explanation, moreover, must be physiological since otherwise the existence of a mental event which does not have its correspondent in a brain event is supposed. Accordingly, James develops physiological explanations for these and other states of consciousness as well as the transition from one state of consciousness to another. Thus he explains habits and the laws of the association of ideas in terms of "organized brain-paths."

The psychophysical postulate had of course been employed as a hypothesis by physiological psychologists, but James differs from them by his detailed application of it to a large number of mental facts. In developing his physiological explanations James realized he was speculating, for his stated goal was to show that explanation in terms of "neural machinery" was conceivable. In any case his belief that all explanations of conscious states ought to be conceived in relation to physiological processes served as one important criterion in his critique of theories of perception and in the formulation of his own theory.

The way in which "consciousness" was to be interpreted was another criterion which James stressed. The data of consciousness as "they are concretely given to us" should be the starting point of a scientific study of the mind. These data, which in respect to visual perception comprise what we see in looking at objects, are not decomposable into aggregates either of sensations or of sensations and ideas, for there is no evidence of such components in consciousness. "Consciousness," he says, "does not appear to itself chopped up in bits." In his view then a percept represents a unitary fact of consciousness. In accordance with the psychophysical postulate a similar fact characterizes the brain correlate. Thus James says: "The consciousness, which is itself an integral thing not made of parts, 'corresponds' to the entire activity of the brain, whatever that may be, at the moment." We may consider in this regard his discussion of the seeing of yellow. When the retina is stimulated by a particular wave length at one time and by another wave length on a subsequent occasion, the excitation effects in the brain are different and the corresponding sensations are "red" and "green." But when the retina is simultaneously stimulated by these two wave lengths, we are conscious of seeing yellow. Since this conscious state is not decomposable, the excitation effects in the brain have fused into a single effect as its correlate. On the other hand, to suppose that the excitations arouse the sensations of red and green which are fused psychically would imply that the "yellow" is decomposable into the elementary underlying sensational components. This conception, however, is incorrect since there is no trace of either sensation in the perceived yellow.[3]

James contrasts his position, the "analytic method," with the prevailing "synthetic method" which supposes that the "higher states of mind" have evolved from the association, integration, or fusion of atomic states of mind such as the "simple ideas of sensation." Although this method may be didactically advantageous, "it commits one beforehand to the very questionable theory that our higher states of consciousness are compounds of units." On the other hand, we should begin with states of consciousness as they are immediately known to us and then proceed to analyze them. Analysis of such states may then reveal the elementary parts, if they in fact exist, presupposed by the synthetic method. According to James, the advantage of the analytic method lies in the absence of any initial commitment as to what consciousness ought to be.

As proponents of the synthetic method James includes the "spiritualists" and "associationists," their common basic premise being that the raw data of the senses are spaceless. Spiritualists such as Lotze posit a special mind substance which, operating upon these data by virtue of inherent laws, evolves space percepts. Associationists such as J. S. Mill explain perceptual space in reference to the associations of ideas while presumably rejecting the spiritualist's position; but James finds that he unwittingly supposes a mind substance, since he introduces "super-sensational" entities such as mental chemistry. When their proposed explanations are examined, says James, they are "unintelligible" or "mythological." Thus he cites Schopenhauer as a "spiritualist" clearly expressing a "Kantian" approach and (according to James) supposing the "Understanding" to possess spatial intuitions "antecedently to all experience" and the ability to construct or synthesize percepts. The "Intellect" can re-invert the flat visual image, give it a third dimension, and project it into space. Says James in reference to Schopenhauer:

> I call this view mythological, because I am conscious of no such Kantian machine-shop in my mind, and feel no call to disparage the powers of poor sensation in this merciless way. I have no introspective experience of mentally producing or creating space. My space-intuitions occur not in two times but once. There is not one moment of passive inextensive sensation, succeeded by another of active extensive perception, but the form I see is as immediately felt as the color which fills it out.

The appeal to consciousness so vividly described in the rejection of Schopenhauer is also intended to apply to the associationist. We shall exemplify the spirit of the above quotation and other ideas of James's in reference to his interpretation of Helmholtz, whom he classifies as a follower of English associationism.[4]

In a discussion of the "eccentric projection of sensations" James regards Helmholtz, and others, as maintaining that sensations "at first appear to us as subjective or internal" to be projected to parts of the body or to the space external to the body by means of mental acts. On the contrary, says James, he perceives a thing to be extended and external and he experiences pain in some part of the body without even being able to imagine their supposed inward localization. In his view the theory of eccentric projection mistakenly supposes that the "bodily processes which cause a sensation must also be its seat." James's first argument pertains to his introspective experience, and the second to the confusion of phenomenal and physical facts so that one fact is thought to be coterminous with the other. Thus the physical fact that excitations are conducted to the brain and there have sensation as a psychic concomitant, led to the supposition that sensation is at first experienced internally or even inside the body. Helmholtz's "intellectualistic" or psychological interpretation of color contrast is rejected because of its introspective unverifiability. According to James, "the explanation is physiological, not psychological." Experiments, he says, have "definitely proved" the validity of a physiological explanation; Helmholtz's observation of the disappearance of the induced color when a black outline is traced on the tissue was not correct because others had observed the color. The physiological hypothesis accepted by James is similar to the one outlined in the chapter on Helmholtz; the lateral irradiation of the process, however, can take place in the retina or anywhere in the pathways from the retina to the brain. The "nerve process" corresponding to the gray patch is modified by the nerve processes corresponding to the ground. The patch excites a "new nerve process" when it is inserted between the tissue and the colored background, the process being the immediate neural correlate of the pink-red color. In relation to this physiological approach he disputes Helmholtz's modification rule which, he says, "has obtained . . . an almost deplorable celebrity." He points out that Helmholtz had supposed the patch would arouse the same process in the brain irrespective of variation in adjacent processes, and for this reason he explained the induced color in terms of "mental suggestion" or "unconscious inference." This rule, James insists, is falsified on factual grounds. The induced color is a "genuine new sensation" not explainable in terms of experience or judgment.

James quotes a lengthy passage from Helmholtz in which Helmholtz gave examples of the compound nature of perception and its analysis into component sensations. For instance, the sensations derived from the two perspective views of a solid object would fuse into a synthetic "third perception" totally different from the perception of either "flat perspective view," as could be verified by alternately opening and closing the eyes. According to James, this explanation supposes the sensations included in the synthetic perception must be "unconscious states," for there is no introspective evidence of their existence when the object is viewed simultaneously with both eyes. It also "unintelligibly" supposes that a "mental fact" can be in two phases at the same time, one phase referring to the consciousness of a single three-dimensional object and the other to the two unconscious sensations. He points out what he regards as a confusion in Helmholtz's reasoning, namely, that the "organic conditions" which include the retinal impressions and their correlated effects in the brain remain the same whether in viewing separately with one eye or in viewing simultaneously with both eyes. Knowledge of what the sensation is in monocular viewing then led Helmholtz to conclude that this same sensation was present though no longer conscious in the other viewing. This error exemplifies what James terms the "psychologist's fallacy"; the knowledge of the psychologist of some objective fact makes him suppose that this same fact determines the same mental consequence irrespective of other co-present facts. Thus, in monocular viewing the psychologist knows the mental result of the retinal impression which is considered as an objective fact. Since this same objective fact prevails in binocular viewing, he supposes the mental effect to be the same. Having permitted himself to be guided by a hypothetical statement concerning sensation, he is led to an incorrect characterization of consciousness. Instead, says James, our investigation ought to begin with conscious states as actually experienced in relation to a specific situation without any supposition as to its nature. We should then find that the mental fact is merely that of perceiving one solid object, unconscious sensations and their fusion being redundant. Therefore, in his view, the organic conditions are different in the two types of viewing situations and as a result the psychic results are not identical.[5]

Should the associationist (and also spiritualist) adopt the physiological approach, the hypothetical psychic and unconscious operations would not be necessary. In this vein James writes:

> Our rapid judgments of size, shape, distance, and the like, are best explained as processes of simple cerebral association. Certain sense-impressions directly stimulate brain-tracts, of whose activity ready-made conscious percepts are the immediate psychic counterparts. They do this by a mechanism either connate or acquired by habit.[6]

Thus a brain mechanism, whether innate or acquired, directly determines a concomitant mental event, and no other mental state need be interposed between the mechanism and the psychic fact.

JAMES'S EMPIRISTIC THEORY
OF PERCEPTION

Two theories of perception, which are developed concurrently, can be discerned in James's writings. An important difference between them is that one is partly empiristic and the other completely empiristic. For the purpose of exposition the two theories will be designated "first theory" and "second theory."

"FIRST THEORY"

One of James's basic goals was to give explanations of perception in terms of innate and acquired brain mechanisms so as to be consistent with the psychophysical postulate. Thus an acquired perception would represent a combination of "sensational and reproductive brain-processes" without any psychic factor intervening between the brain processes and the percept.

James defines sensations as the "FIRST *things in the way of consciousness.* They are the *immediate* results upon consciousness of nerve-currents as they enter the brain, and before they have awakened any suggestions or associations with past experience." He points out that it is almost impossible for adults to realize the nature of sensation because of acquired "memories and stores of associations," an "absolutely pure sensation" only being realizable very early in the life of the infant. One sense-impression leaves behind a "vestige" or "trace" in the brain so that the next impression, on interacting with it, would determine a somewhat different conscious state. Thus the same nerve currents entering the brain ("sensorial processes") produce different conscious reactions as a function of stored memories or associations.

The important original "spatial qualities" which James attributed to sensation are indicated thus: "Every thing or quality felt is felt in outer space. It is impossible to conceive a brightness or a color otherwise than as extended and outside of the body. Sounds also appear in space. Contacts are against the body's surface; and pains always occupy some organ." Although only exteriority, localization, and extension are here indicated as attributes of sensation, James also includes distance, form, size, motion, and binocular solidity.

The ambiguous relationship between the "retinal magnitude" or "retinal shape" and the magnitude or shape of the external object is the basis for James's empiristic approach. Thus the constancies of size and shape are included among the perceptions that would be acquired. He also regards the perception of the solidity in drawings, such as those inserted in a stereoscope, as acquired. Parenthetically, when James undertakes to explain the acquired perceptions he often speaks of "retinal sensation" or "overlooking the retinal magnitude" as though subscribing to the opinion that the retinal image or impression is itself perceived. However, he merely means to indicate, as was often the case in his period, that visual sensation is to be regarded as a function of the retinal impression to the exclusion of the effects of eye-movements.

According to James, when an object is present it elicits a sensation, its neural accompaniment leaving a record in the brain so that when later revived or activated, the same sensation is reproduced even though the object is now absent. Moreover, such an "imagined" sensation generally is fainter than the original sensation and may even be revived when an object is stimulating the retina. He supposes that an imagined sensation can "overpower" the present sensation, and that it can have a "quasi-hallucinatory strength." This supposition is essential, for in his theory an acquired perception represents the revival of previous sensation. If the revived sensation were only a faint copy of the original, an acquired percept would not have the vividness of an immediate sensation. Although accepting the traditional opinion that an "idea is a faint revival of some direct sensation," he justifies the concept of "quasi-hallucinatory strength" by supposing an object is immediately stimulating the sense. What he means is that the sensory currents, on being diverted into some vestige, enable the reproduction of a sensation with the same power and vividness of a present sensation. When those sensory currents are absent, on the other hand, the revival of the reproduction in imagination is weaker.[7]

"*The consciousness of particular material things present to sense*" is the way James defines perception. It differs from sensation in that "associative processes" are involved; sensorial currents arouse "processes in the hemispheres which are due to the organization of that organ by past experience." Thus James seems to imply that there is no reference to "things" in infancy, though this is the fact that characterizes the consciousness of adults, and apparently contradicts the earlier statement that "everything is felt in outer space" as an attribute of sensation. The inconsistency is conspicuous when he states, "Infants must go through a long education of the eye and ear before they can perceive the realities which adults perceive. *Every perception is an acquired perception.*" Perhaps the inconsistency can be resolved by considering the changes in the size and form of the retinal sensation as an object is moved in different ways. The infant in not yet having acquired any associations would experience such changes in retinal sensation whereas the adult would perceive an object which tends to be stable in size and form. Thus, a long education for the infant might be necessary even though the given sensational attributes are supposed.[8]

James enunciates several general principles and conclusions concerning the development and nature of the perceptual process which we shall exemplify in his discussion of shape constancy and the Necker Cube.

Shape constancy. A "table-top" yields an "infinite number of retinal sensations" when viewed from different positions but only one sensation is square-like, all other sensations having "two acute and two obtuse angles." Correspondingly, a circle also produces an infinity of sensations of which only one is a true circle. An important explanatory principle of James's, paraphrased, states: In our dealing with an object we always choose that one of the infinity of sensations which constitutes its real form. In conformity with this principle James says that the "mind chooses" the square or circle and ignores the perspective views. Suppose that a circle, when viewed from a particular position, gives rise to the sensation of an ellipse. While still looking from the same position, this sensation is ignored and another chosen. The substitute—that of a circle—is reproduced from memory, and James calls it the "imagined sensation." He explains the substitution of one for the other in the following way. He defines "the normal position" in viewing an object with both eyes. The head is upright, the optic axes are symmetrically converged in a horizontal plane, and the plane of the circle (or object) is perpendicular to the plane of the axes with their intersection coincident with the center of the circle. The sensation thus obtained is that of a circle and it is the one later imagined or recalled even when viewing the circle from a non-normal position.

James now supposes that the sensation derived from the normal position has an "extraordinary pre-eminence" over all other sensations. This sensation, when revived or imagined, supersedes or becomes the substitute for a present sensation. Although the sensation derived from the normal viewing position is a rare occurrence, as the definition of this position indicates, its pre-eminence would confer a power not possessed by the other sensations of the infinite class. If the present sensation had prevailed in consciousness the true form of the object would not be perceived. The present sensation has the role of a "sign" which suggests the imagined one, its suggestive effect being the result of "experience or custom."

While learning shape constancy, the perspective views and the real form are perceived as a series of "continuous gradations." A circle "may slide" into an ellipse of any degree of eccentricity, a square into a trapezoid or trapezium. The normal position of viewing determines the choice of the one sensation indicative of real form. The "real form of the circle is deemed to be the sensation it gives," writes James, "when the line of vision is perpendicular to its centre." He continues, "all its other sensations are signs of this sensation." Thus when the plane of the circle is oblique to the line of vision, the sensation is that of an ellipse. In having learned that this sensation is a member of a wide class of sensations from the same object, it functions as a sign of the previously experienced sensation of a circle. The imagined sensation is so vivid, as already noted, that James calls it "quasi-hallucinatory." James proposes a similar analysis of size constancy, the normal position being defined in reference to a standard viewing distance.[9]

Necker Cube. James observes that the Necker Cube is an "ambiguous perspective" projection of two "natural objects." Thus face ABCD (Figure 1.1) may represent the closer face of one actual cube or the more distant face of another cube. He supposes that the natural objects themselves have been originally perceived as solid objects. Now the "lines drawn on our retina by solids" are similar to those which the outline diagram itself produces. Since we perceive solids many more times than the line diagram of the cube, "we perceive the diagram solid." The shift in appearance results from the ambiguity of the retinal sensation, for two natural objects are "suggested." Although "accidental circumstances" in brain activity are the basic cause for this shift, James also says that imagining one or the other face to be forward causes it to be seen that way. A similar explanation is given for the perception of solidity when looking at the inside of a theatrical mask. In this instance, however, we perceive relief only since the human face, always a convex object, produces a retinal impression similar to that of the mask.[10]

"Two languages." James's explanation of perceptual facts would suggest an adherence to the traditional point of view he has previously criticized. Thus he says that an imagined sensation can overpower a present sensation or that the mind can "choose" one sensation rather than another. Moreover, there is the implication that an acquired perception is a compound event: a present sensation and an imagined sensation. However, two kinds of language prevail in James's discussion of perception and sensation: that of psychology or "common sense" and that of physiology. In the first language, descriptions are rendered

in the ordinary terminology of his period or stated much as the lay-man might in dealing with perception. When acquainted with the fact of reversibility of solid form in the Necker Cube, he probably would say that the mind in some way is responsible for it because there is no change in the objective stimulus. But perceptions in the language of physiology are to be explained in terms of processes in the brain and sensory organs. These processes are wholly deterministic physical events; there is no "choice" in such events. If the state of the brain at a given moment is completely known, as well as the laws governing brain action, the immediate next state ought to be predictable when some nerve current enters the brain. By virtue of the "law of nature" as expressed in the psychophysical postulate, these brain states cause those mental events which we know, as well as causing the way in which one mental event follows another. In line with this kind of thinking, James has extensive discussion of those neural processes which might explain acquired perceptions. A nerve current beginning with stimulation of a sensory organ enters some part of the brain which determines sensation. The sensorial process leaves behind its vestige or copy in some other part of the brain, which remains when the stimulus is removed. Later and under given conditions the ves-tigial process is revived or reproduced, causing an "imagined sensa-tion." When James asserts that the present sensation is replaced by the imagined one, thus apparently implying a double or compound event in consciousness, he means this to be understood in reference to brain events. The vestige of an often repeated sensorial process forms a "deeply entrenched system of organized paths in the brain" so that the same sensorial process is sidetracked into the paths leading to the ves-tige instead of terminating in the part of the brain which would cause a present sensation. The reproduction of the vestige then determines the so-called absent or imagined sensation, the single event in con-sciousness.

James says that the two natural objects, which the diagram of the Necker Cube ambiguously represents, determine two alternative orga-nized brain processes of about equal strength. The incoming nerve currents produced by stimulation from the diagram may be side-tracked into one organized process or the other. The particular brain process which is revived depends on accidental physiological circum-stances. But the spontaneous changes in the physiological conditions in the brain are such that the alternative brain-process is reproduced.

According to James, when two organized brain-processes are possible each one typically acts as a unit. In regard to phenomena of this type he says, "What we more commonly get is first one object in its completeness, and then the other in its completeness. In other words, *all brain-processes are such as to give what we may call* FIGURED *consciousness.*" Thus a particular brain-process gives rise to the figured consciousness of one face of the diagram appearing forward, and the alternative brain-process gives rise to the figured consciousness of the other face appearing forward. Now when James says that an act of the imagination alters the reversibility of the perceived solidity of the diagram he means that that act increases the prepotency of one brain process over the other, this process then determining a particular figured consciousness. Moreover, the reason why "it is easier to perceive the diagram solid than flat" is also explainable physiologically. "Those lines," he writes, "have countless times in our past experience been drawn on our retina by solids for once that we have seen them flat on paper." The vestige of the brain process that results from frequent viewing of a natural object is more deeply embedded in the brain than the vestige which results from viewing the diagram. The incoming nerve current, therefore, flows to the former rather than the latter vestige. In respect to the perception of solidity of the hollow mask, the nerve currents can only flow to the single vestige representing the many times the human face has been perceived in relief.[11]

The physiology of shape constancy presents a special problem which we shall raise and attempt to resolve from the standpoint of James's theory. Let us suppose that shape constancy has already been learned and that we are viewing a square obliquely. The retinal image has two obtuse and two acute angles, and it is to be supposed that its concomitant sensorial process in some way corresponds. How is it that the sensorial process leads to the reproduction of that brain process which would produce the imagined sensation and consciousness of a square rather than that of some other geometric shape such as a trapezoid? One might suppose that the present sensorial process ought to elicit the vestige corresponding to it more readily rather than the vestige of a square. Moreover, the fact that a square-like retinal image is a statistically rare event would seem to make it unlikely that its corresponding vestige would be excited by a trapezoidally shaped retinal image. But we have already observed that James invoked the "extraordinary pre-eminence" of the sensation obtained in viewing the object in the "normal position" to explain such facts. Its physiological translation would mean that the vestige of the corresponding sensorial process also has a pre-eminence over all those other vestiges derived from a non-normal viewing position. Supposing that the action of the brain is such that the pre-eminent vestige is more deeply rooted in the brain, the nerve currents which enter the brain will determine its reproduction irrespective of viewing position.

It would seem that when James himself resorts to psychological language this is done for the sake of exposition, having already supplied sufficient detail to show that the physiological language is the one expressing his intention. The specific steps in any physiological explanation he proposed are recognized by him to be hypothetical in character. His general aim is to demonstrate the feasibility of physiological explanation for the purpose of combating the mentalistic interpretations of perception that were quite common in his period. Such interpretations, in positing some event of the mind without a correlate in the brain, violated the psychophysical postulate. On the other hand, James explicitly evolved his theory so as to be consistent with this postulate. Moreover, in these examples of acquired perceptions it may be noted that James's account is sensationalistic. Thus to explain the perception of solidity of either the Necker Cube or the hollow mask, the sensation or original perception in three dimensions of an actually solid object is supposed.[12]

Unresolved Problems in James's Theory

When James maintains that a natural object such as the cube is originally perceived solid, he implies that shape constancy—seeing the right angles of a face slanting away—is also a matter of sensation. Moreover, he implies that size constancy is not learned since the rear edge of the cube appears to be of the same size as a forward edge. Nevertheless, he contends that both constancies are acquired. When he discusses the table top in relation to the acquisition of shape constancy, this top can be regarded as the face of a cube. He, therefore, should also have said that the perception of the top is not learned. Moreover, to say that the table top gives us the retinal sensation of "two obtuse and two acute angles" is equivalent to the assertion that the sensation of the top is bi-dimensional, an implication James overlooked. The hypothetical normal position in viewing an object is essential to James's

explanation of shape constancy. But this concept entails a self-contra-
diction and is also inconsistent with the actual facts in viewing objects.
When a square object produces a square retinal image, its plane is perpendicular to the line of sight. But this is only true in monocular
viewing, for in binocular viewing the image in the other eye is not
square-like. In typical binocular viewing of objects, moreover, neither
retinal image is a square. The "normal position" does not accurately
describe the actual viewing of a wide class of objects such as a table
top. For instance, no one ever looks at a table top in accordance with
his definition.

The problems in James's theory can be understood in relation to
the constancy hypothesis. When James rejected Helmholtz's explanation of color contrast and "rule" of modification, it is evident that he
also rejected the constancy hypothesis. Furthermore, when he gave a
physiological explanation for this phenomenon, the positing of a factor of judgment was unnecessary. His postulation of a sensation of solidity when the object itself is solid is another example of the repudiation of the constancy hypothesis. But James's discussion of the
constancies of size and shape and the Necker Cube involves the very
same assumption of the constancy hypothesis. If he had rejected this
assumption in these instances, he would have supposed that a retinal
image composed of two obtuse and two acute angles and the intersecting lines of the retinal image projected by the diagram would respectively give rise to the sensation of a square and the sensation of solidity. Therefore, on the condition of the acceptance of the constancy
hypothesis, such notions as the choice of one of an infinity of sensations, the pre-eminence of a particular sensation, and the normal position of viewing, were theoretical necessities. Although these notions
were expressed in a psychological language, the problems they imply
ought to be exhibited in a complete translation into the language of
physiological explanation—a defect in one language is not altered by
the fact of translation into another. We shall illustrate this point in
reference to shape constancy.

Adults see the table top as a rectangular surface slanting away in
space. The imagined sensation which is supposed to represent this perception could not convey the third dimension because it is a reproduction of the pre-eminent and bi-dimensional retinal sensation. When
expressed in James's physiological language the same difficulty remains
even when the pre-eminent vestige derived from the normal viewing

position is supposed. The sensorial process arising from the bi-dimensional retinal image can only determine a vestige in the brain having the very same characteristic. Therefore the imagined sensation which is the concomitant of this vestige could not account for the perceptual fact. Although James had raised a question concerning the change in form of projected after images in relation to "imagined sensations" and currents in the brain, he provided no decisive answer. Suppose that after having viewed a circle in the frontoparallel plane for a brief time we look at some slanting wall. The projected after-image is "actually *seen* as an ellipse" although the retinal image remains circular. What he did not explain is the choice of the vestige corresponding to the imagined sensation of an ellipse rather than the direct and pre-eminent vestige corresponding to the sensation of a circle. There is a further difficulty. When the after-image is projected upon planes whose degree of obliquity varies until the frontoparallel position is reached, we see a gradation of ellipses of different eccentricities and finally a circle. Apparently the very same retinal image has the power to evoke a large number of vestiges. What then determines the flow of the presumably same sensory currents along different paths so that one rather than some other vestige is reproduced? We might suppose, as James did, that the perception of the slant of the plane is an essential condition for the perception of a particular shape. This factor, however cogent, is psychological and not physiological. It would have to be shown how the retinal effects corresponding to the physical slant of the wall combine with those of the circular retinal image so as to elicit the appropriate vestige.[13]

The introspective criterion accepted by James in refuting Berkeley's theory could have resolved some of the problems in his own theory. Thus the perception of the table top as a rectangular slanting away surface could have been regarded as an original fact of consciousness, inasmuch as we do not perceive the distorted shape corresponding to the retinal image. His failure to apply the criterion in this instance may have been influenced by the evidence he cited pertaining to the recoverability of retinal sensation. He points out, as others had done before him, that the artist or draftsman can learn to see forms and magnitudes which correspond to the retinal images. Thus when the image is in the shape of an acute angle, the naive person perceives a right angle whereas the artist may perceive an acute angle. However, this evidence is not decisive. Its most direct interpretation suggests that training may modify a perception. The fact that the altered percept may correspond to some of the characteristics of the retinal image does not prove that the original perception was its counterpart. The effects of such training must be limited, for it seems improbable that the artist would perceive the table top as a trapezoidal surface in the frontoparallel plane or that he would perceive the sizes of objects in conformity to the relative sizes of their projected retinal magnitudes. Moreover, James has apparently fallen into the psychologist's fallacy in his interpretation of the trained individual. As a psychologist he notes that the retinal image (the objective fact) is the same before and after training, and infers that the mental effect before training would be the same as the mental effect after training.[14]

"SECOND THEORY"

The apparent denial of any sensation of extension or space is a significant feature of James's "second theory" of perception. Thus James describes the original consciousness of a baby as being totally chaotic or a "primordial chaos." In a famous statement he declares, "The baby, assailed by eyes, ears, nose, skin, and entrails at once, feels it all as one great blooming, buzzing confusion. . . ." Although this statement pertains to the baby's inability to discriminate among the different senses, it also refers to a single sense. Thus the baby cannot discriminate colors into the orderly and distinctive things which characterize his later consciousness. He merely has the "vague feeling of a total vastness" which has no subdivisions of parts. Apparently James supposes sensations to be originally homogeneous, for in this context he says, "The first time we see *light,* in Condillac's phrase we *are* it rather than see it." [15]

"Attention" is the agent, according to James, that determines the subdivision of the total vastness into parts. He says:

Millions of items of the outward order are present to my senses which never properly enter into my experience. Why? Because they have no *interest* for me. *My experience is what I agree to attend to.* Only those items which I *notice* shape my mind—without selective interest, experience is an utter chaos. Interest alone gives accent and emphasis, light and shade, background and foreground—intelligible perspective, in a word. It varies in every creature, but without it the consciousness of every creature would be a gray chaotic indiscriminateness, impossible for us even to conceive.[16]

In his view "attention carves out objects" such as "constellations" in the sky, and so on. This process is similar to the sculptor who chisels out a specific form: "The mind, in short, works on the data it receives very much as a sculptor works on his block of stone." Apparently the stone is to be regarded as the mass of sensations and the sculptor as attention which carves out the object. To explain the causal role of attention James asserts that attention must be directed to each part of the "vague total" so as to enable its emergence as a distinctly perceived entity. The singling out of a part or element may be influenced by "practical or instinctive interests." Thus, "the infant notices the candle-flame or the window, and ignores the rest of the room, because these objects give him a vivid pleasure." But as a more basic principle James says, *"Only such elements as we are acquainted with, and can imagine, separately, can be discriminated within a total sense-impression."* In relation to this principle, therefore, the infant must have had a prior acquaintanceship with the candle-flame as an element in order for interest to be attracted to it when it becomes part of an overall total. The meaning of this principle can be more readily understood in the case of the individual who, on listening to music for the first time, may hear the various sounds composing a string quartet as a uniform or undifferentiated sound. In order to hear the sounds produced by the four instruments in their individual character as sounds, it is necessary for him to hear each instrument in isolation from the others. Then upon again hearing the quartet and imagining how a violin sounds, he is able to detect its quality and so distinguish it from the sounds of the other instruments. Evidence of this type is advanced by James to support his contention that the differentiation of the visual field from its previous state of chaos is the result of attention. However, he does not relate the discussion of these issues to possibly pertinent evidence based on the life of infants or young animals.[17]

Difficulties in the Theory

If the vague total is initially an undiscriminated chaos, it would seem impossible for the infant to establish acquaintanceship with any element and, therefore, no element could emerge as a distinctive entity. For the same reason the principle James sets forth is not applicable. The infant cannot obtain any prior acquaintanceship with an element since the element itself is part of the vague mass. Nor can instinctive interest be a determining factor in the segregation of an element, for the object of interest must first be perceived before it can be discovered to be interesting, or before attention can be directed to it by virtue of that interest, or before it can be a source of pleasure. The simile of the sculptor and stone is inappropriate, for the sculptor must have some conception of what it is he wishes to shape. Should we bring a slab to him and instruct him to chisel the likeness of a friend whom he has never seen, he cannot perform the required task. And if we consider sensations to be raw and unshaped data, the mind cannot carve out objects since it has no prior conception of their shapes. These difficulties are readily apparent when Thorndike, in a text of 1905 with an introduction by James, refers to the "obscurity of a fog" in a discussion of James's theory. Having referred to the "big, blooming, buzzing confusion," Thorndike says:

> The progress of the mind is by the differentiation of vague feelings into more and more definite and detailed feelings. The clean-cut reds and blues, A flats and C sharps, sweets and sours, hards and softs which we call elementary sensations are the result of slow growth. The world of sense comes not as a building constructed of small pieces of bricks and mortar and glass, but as a landscape gradually clearing up from the obscurity of a fog. The child comes to feel hot, cold, red and green as we come to distinguish the constituents of a salad-dressing, the sounds of the different instruments in an orchestra, or the characteristic odors of a slum.[18]

It is not easy to understand how attention or interest can contribute to the clearing of the fog so as to enable the perception of objects.

The chaos of the infant's consciousness when considered from the standpoint of the psychophysical postulate would imply a similar chaos in the concomitant brain processes; if there is no subdivision of parts in consciousness, there ought to be none in the brain. Moreover, a sensorial process—the input of excitations in the brain determining states of consciousness—presumably is chaotic. And insofar as a reproductive process comes into existence, it also would be chaotic since it would copy the sensorial process. Although James said that the arousal of distinct neural processes by things is an "indispensable" condition for visual discrimination, he regarded distinctness in neural processes as "insufficient." [19]

According to James, attention makes us "perceive, conceive, distinguish, remember." He defines attention as a reproduced sensation, an "image" or "preperception" of the thing which we keep in mind. Thus the imaging of "red" may cause us to see that color in an object which does not clearly contain it. He also affirms that *an object once attended to will remain in the memory,* whilst one inattentively allowed to pass will leave no traces behind." Apparently, an unattended object can have no influence on the way some other object, or even the same one, is subsequently perceived. We have already observed that attention so conceived cannot be responsible for the breaking up of the vague mass into parts; the infant by definition or hypothesis does not yet have an image of any part.[20]

The following passage may indicate a way of reconciling the two theories of sensation: "Experience, from the very first, presents us with concreted objects, vaguely continuous with the rest of the world which envelops them in space and time, and potentially divisible into inward elements and parts." Since the "objects" are there all along in the original consciousness, though potentially, their characteristics do not have to be learned. Directing or focusing attention to one or another such object then serves to actualize its existence as a distinct thing of consciousness. However, how the conception of potential divisibility would nullify the problems stated above is not apparent. Thus the objects shrouded by "fog," as in Thorndike's metaphor, would be potentially present, but attention could never be directed to any of them.[21]

These ideas of James were popular in his period. Thus Sully and Höffding respectively refer to original consciousness as a "blurred or confused mass" and a "single chaotic sensation," attention being an important factor in the discrimination of the elements. Condillac had long before set forth a similar doctrine. Thus in denying any natural articulation and ordering of units in the original state of consciousness, James follows traditional formulations. On the other hand, he breaks away from tradition in his critique of the "associationists" and "spiritualists" and asserts that the perception of three dimensions is a primitive fact of consciousness. But the very principle at the basis of his critique, that space perception can never be explained on the assumption of an original nonspatial quality, may be directed to the second theory. *If the original consciousness does not contain ordered and distinctly articulated units, no process of attention, discrimination, or analysis can lead to their subsequent emergence.*[22]

FINAL ASSESSMENT

Although James's lifelong interest was philosophy rather than psychology or physiology, he wished to treat psychology as a "natural science" in the *Principles of Psychology*. States of consciousness are to be accepted as such without any special assumption concerning their origin in atomistic psychic states or psychic activity, and they are to be correlated in every instance to brain states. In this vein he says in the preface to the *Principles*, "This book consequently rejects both the associationist and the spiritualist theories; and in this strictly positivistic point of view consists the only feature of it for which I feel tempted to claim originality." Accordingly, all explanation is to be referred to physiological conditions rather than one state of mind causing another state. For this reason G. S. Hall, who reviewed the *Principles* in 1891, noted James's "Cartesian surrender to physiological mechanism." But the surrender was incomplete he says, for James found it necessary to posit the causal role of psychic processes. James's ambivalence toward the relation of mind to body, or equivalently toward the psychophysical postulate, is partly responsible for the apparent inconsistencies in the treatment of perception. Much as he tried to keep his belief that conscious processes steer neural events in abeyance, it asserts itself in his discussion of attention. He said that attention, although determined by brain states, could tip a neural process in one direction or another when neural processes would be in a state of balance. Attention, therefore, is to some degree a cause of a subsequent psychic fact though mediated by a neural process. Since the way in which attention modifies neural processes is not explainable by or correlatable with brain events, the psychophysical postulate is partly given up. James conceded this to be the case in the discussion of these issues and he classified himself as a believer in a "spiritual force" in contrast to mechanistic or materialistic explanation.

For James the deviation from the postulate was necessary for explaining the subdivision of the initial chaos into parts in terms of attention and also for establishing the thesis that the mind was "active" rather than "passive" in perceiving. If the mind is presumed to be passive then physiological mechanism is the only cause of perception. On the other hand, the assumption of an active mind represents a departure from the exclusive importance of physiological mechanism. Thus an active mind not only "attends," but also "chooses," "selects," and "discriminates." [23]

That the study of consciousness is a field of study in its own right is the central unifying theme in James's writings. And from the standpoint of psychology in his period it represented an important contribution, for it was this basic theme which led to the rejection of any theory that proposed introspectively nonverifiable assertions concerning the content of the "mind" or states or consciousness, and formed the basis of his appraisal of the relation of consciousness to physiology.

Some physiologists, says James, in the course of their investigations and expositions ignored consciousness as a source of important data for physiology, attacked the "subjective method" of psychology, and supposed that a science of psychology must be "founded on physiology." On the contrary, says James, "the truth really [is] that the subjective method has not only given us almost all of our fundamentally secure psychological knowledge, but has also suggested all our interpretations of the facts of brain-physiology." For instance, the subjective method reveals that conscious states follow one another in certain sequences, physiology takes its "cue" and finds the basis for them in given tracts and interconnections of fibers in the brain. Without prior knowledge of consciousness and its various states, it would be impossible for the physiologist even to know which part of the brain should be studied. "Without introspective analysis of the mental elements of speech, the doctrine of Aphasia, for instance, which is the most brilliant jewel in Physiology would have been utterly impossible." Clearly the discovery of aphasia and its special conditions hinged on a conscious although aphasic individual, and also upon knowledge of speech patterns obtained by the psychologist on the basis of his own conscious states. With this information the physiologist seeks the conditions in the brain responsible for the defect. Should he suppose that each brain cell represents an idea or that a particular connection between two cells represents a mental association—having observed the brain to consist of a mosaical network—he is led to the erroneous conception of consciousness as consisting of a bundle of ideas tied together by associations. In further evaluation of the relation of consciousness to physiology, James considers two possibilites. On the one hand, what the physiologist regards to be knowledge of the nervous system and its functioning may be questioned. On the other hand, introspection may afford the possibility of a different hypothesis concerning brain action. For instance, in having insisted that perception is an integral thing in an article which appeared in *Mind* in 1884, he says:

> If we are ever to be entitled to make psychological inferences from brain-processes, we should make them here in favour of the view I defend. The whole drift of recent brain-inquiry sets towards the notion that the brain always acts as a whole, and that no part of it can be discharging without altering the tensions of all the other parts. The best symbol for it seems to be an electric conductor, the amount of whose charge at any one point is a function of the total charge elsewhere.

Thus it is not necessary to suppose that brain processes be construed as independent events giving rise, in the traditional conception, to independent conscious effects. These brain processes in their mutual interactions may produce a unified brain process, the conscious effect being that of an integral thing.[24]

In the extensive discussions of the psychophysical postulate, James elaborates its meaning and implications which otherwise might have remained vague. A departure from the postulate, as in the traditional associationistic theory of perception, is the basis for the postulation of those psychic acts for which there is no evidence. An adherence to the psychophysical postulate, on the other hand, shows that the explanations are to be in terms of innate or acquired physiological mechanisms. When he partly abandons the postulate he stipulates the conditions of divergence and the reasons which justify it. Thus he clarifies the particular problems that await solution irrespective of the opinion entertained in respect to the postulate.

Finally, James's critical spirit itself constituted a contribution of importance. The willingness to seek out hidden assumptions whether in philosophy or in science, to consider the evidence for and against, to select assumptions which to him made more sense although in defiance of tradition, gave cause to others to re-evaluate their point of view. His abrasive and direct expression, sometimes and erroneously described as "vituperative," jarred many a philosopher and scientist accustomed to more dispassionate discussion. Moreover, he often appealed to his own experiences for evaluating some point whereas the experimentalist usually resorted to the consciousness of some other person. Some of these features were noted by Hall in his review of the *Principles,* "Its personal frankness, which also accounts for such denunciatory epithets for divergent psychologists as we have quoted, is unequalled in the history of the subject." Hall's observation would have been irrelevant to James since he accorded the same privilege to those who examined his own assumptions. Any assumption was to be held provisionally, ready to be given up when a better one came along. The spirit of James is exemplified in the series of articles on space perception published in *Mind* in 1887, the critical reaction by the editor Croom Robertson, and James's reply. James had set forth his position later to be published in the *Principles.* He argued against the theory of a muscular consciousness of space as advocated by Bain and Mill, and affirmed the necessity for supposing an original perception of space. In reply Croom Robertson noted, "The service, indeed, should first be acknowledged which Prof. James has rendered to English psychology in forcing attention to questions which it has been too much the insular habit, since the days of Berkeley, to slur over with a merely general profession of Berkeleyan theory." He concluded that an original space perception is impossible, that perception must have a "tactile base," and that the Berkeleyan theory "remains inexpugnable." After voicing several objections to Croom Robertson, James asked, "May not the supposed impossibility be rather an assumption and a prejudice, due to uncriticised tradition?" [25]

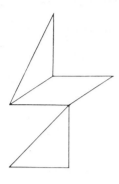

13 EVALUATION

I do not believe that, after this description of certain physical and physiological facts, I need defend the strict distinction between percepts and physical objects any further. But why is it so difficult to convince people that this distinction is necessary? . . . Part of the trouble, I suspect, arises from the fact that even distinguished authors sometimes confuse one particularly important perceptual entity with the corresponding physical object.   Köhler, 1966

If the [Berkeleyan] doctrine be false," said Mill in reply to Bailey, "there must be something radically wrong in the received modes of studying mental phenomena." Although Mill did not think that there was anything wrong in the traditional methods of study; the criticisms of Condillac (1746), Bailey, Abbott, Spalding, and James indeed did indicate that something was radically wrong. The following exposition assumes this body of criticism to be correct. Inasmuch as the traditional methods to which Mill referred in 1842 generally prevailed through the end of the nineteenth century, the critical reaction beginning with Condillac was relevant until that time. We shall only consider the

247

"formation of associations," "evidence," and the distinction of "mental and physical facts."

FORMATION ON ASSOCIATIONS

For the purpose of evaluating the hypothesis that the infant at first sees the world as a plane, a man born blind whose sight has been perfectly restored to both eyes will be supposed. Further, the traditionally hypothesized variety of color he would see in the first instance of vision will be considered as disposed on a flat surface at some distance in apparent space. According to Berkeleyan theory, sensations of eye-movements, whether of convergence or accommodation, do not originally denote different degrees of depthness. The explanation of the perception of solidity, which is presumed to be acquired through the sense of touch or the actual palpation of the object, presupposes that every part of the object be touched. The surgeon's face, which may be selected as the object whose perception must be learned, is perceived by the normally sighted adult as a molded surface composed of many subsurfaces in various orientations in depth. The tip of the nose appears closer than other parts of the face from a given viewing angle, the eyeball is perceived as a convex surface, and the pupil is perceived as a dark circular and flat form at some distance behind the surface of the cornea. When the resighted man looks at the surgeon's face for the first time, he sees it as a flat surface and, in shifting his gaze to the ear lobe, he perceives the surface of the rear wall as a plane continuous with the perceived lobe. When he raises his hand, touches the surgeon's face, and moves his hand across it, he sees one contoured color in motion in the same plane as the various shaped colors composing the face. Inasmuch as the parts of the face are at different physical distances from the resighted man, the motion of his hand could be graded in proportion to these distances. This motion, it is said, gives rise to a graded series of muscular sensations. These sensations, moreover, presumably become associated with the color sensations which arise from the different parts of the face that are touched. Since every part of the face must be touched, the orbs of the eyes, the nostrils, the lips, and so on, must be explored. In some way the muscular sensations become linked to color sensations, so that ultimately these parts are perceived as graded surfaces. This explanation, however, is inherently implausible. For instance, the hand covers a relatively large portion of the face, a fact which would prevent the formation of the necessary associations. In probable recognition of this problem, the tip of the forefinger was regarded as the organ of exploration. This assumption, however, merely serves to postpone consideration of the difficulties in the explanation. The eyelash bends back when touched, the surgeon would never permit his cornea to be touched, and his pupil is untouchable. The surgeon's head could not crystallize as a distinct visual entity until the rear wall, which at first is perceived as contiguous with the head, is perceived at some distance away from the head.[1]

Locke pointed out an important fact in the discussion of the acquired perception of the globe when he noted that the alteration by the judgment led to the changed appearance of the original variety of color into a "uniform color" as well as to the changed appearance from a bi-dimensional to a convex figure. What "variety of color" refers to is not readily described because we perceive the globe as convex. Nevertheless, in accordance with Locke's hypothesis of an original perception of the globe as a flat and variously colored circle, it may be supposed that the variety of color of the "gold" globe refers to the bright and dark appearances which correspond to the portion of the globe directly reflecting light and to the portion in shadow. These appearances would be perceived as two distinct juxtaposed patches bordered by a circle in the plane. But when "altered by judgment" the appearances are not perceived, for they have been transformed into the convex appearance of a uniform gold color. Similar changes in appearance may be observed in the "conversion of relief" which occurs when a theatrical mask or a plaster impression of a medal is viewed. The phenomenal change in the colored appearance of the globe obviously could not be the result of touch; color perception is uniquely visual. Inasmuch as the same consideration applies to the perception of the human face, this alone suffices to invalidate the traditional explanation of this perception.[2]

Faintness, rounding of contour, confused appearance, retinal magnitude, and sensations of convergence and accommodation have been some of the standard traditional "signs" of visual distance. Each sign is presumed to acquire its signification through association with "locomotor" sensations in walking to and touching an object. The previous analysis of the first two signs discussed in Abbott's critique of Berkeleyan theory, in Chapter 11, applies to the other signs as well. For instance, a particular sensation of convergence or a particular retinal magnitude would serve as the sign for amount of locomotor sensation. However, the association of the sign and its significate could not be acquired. By the time the walk has been accomplished and the object touched, the size of the angle of the optic axes has increased and the correlated sensation of convergence is different from the sensation of convergence before the walk was undertaken. Similarly, the size of the retinal magnitude, as a consequence of the walk, has increased. The wrong measure of the signs, as it were, would be associated with the locomotive sensation of distance.

Obviously empiristic theory, when considered in relation to its own premises, could not account for the acquisition of percepts in terms of associations. Moreover, psychological chemistry or even innate principles attributed to the mind could not successfully remedy this defect in the theory. Since the sensory data would be haphazard series of mental events and since these data would not contain those characteristics necessary for the formation of a percept, the mind would be unable to synthesize them into the final form known to us as the perception of an externalized, three-dimensionally shaped and colored object. In James's metaphor of the Kantian machine shop, the mind could not tool percepts since it would not have the necessary raw materials upon which it could exercise its operations. Thus the argument initiated by Condillac in 1746 and executed in greater detail by Bailey and Abbott, and to a lesser extent by James, decisively undermined the empiristic contention that visual percepts developed from, and were decomposable into, associations of color-sensations with muscular and tactile sensations. Furthermore, it should be observed that this argument is independent of the appeal to consciousness, or James's introspective criterion.[3]

THE EVIDENCE

The point of interest in discussing questions of evidence concerns the selective interpretation of some experiment or datum, the neglect to state the conditions relevant to the interpretation of some datum irrespective of theoretical interest, and the omission of evidence possibly contradictory to the theory.

The Resighted

The possibility of impairment to the optical apparatus and its relevance in evaluating the theoretical significance of the new sensations of the resighted had been pointed out by Condillac, restated and further developed by Bailey, and finally emphasized by Abbott. Abbott called attention to the fact that the Cheselden patient was viewing with but one eye and that its lens was missing, and he asked, "It is not imagined that we perceive distance by magic without any physical antecedent, and why may not the lens be one of the conditions of existence of such an antecedent?" Yet we find that those who cited the evidence of the resighted as favorable to the empiristic theory generally failed to state the special condition of the eye and its possible relevance to the theory. Furthermore, in some of these discussions the reader unfamiliar with the material will have the impression that the patient's vision had been restored to both eyes rather than to one eye, which was in fact the characteristic feature of the majority of the cases at the time observations were made. It was generally known that distance perception was better in binocular rather than monocular viewing. Thus the fact of monocular vision might have been partly responsible for the deficiency in distance perception exhibited by the resighted. The typical assumption at the basis of the interpretation of these cases was that the new sensations were identical either to those of normal infants or adults, hence the mere possibility of defective vision on being resighted would invalidate the assumption.[4]

Cheselden case. The standard attribution of the boy's seeing all objects as though in a plane or as flat pictures is false, the actual statement in the report pertaining to paintings and not to solid objects. But even in allowing this attribution, an interpreter of the case should have noted that the surgeon's face, the boy's cat and dog, and his own face when looking into a mirror, would have looked squashed out and quite different from their later appearances. In any case the acquired perception of the solidity of the human face would be a necessary condition for perceiving the solidity of a painting; if the picture of the face alone were to be touched, the picture should always look flat. However, there is no evidence in the report that the perception of the face, or any perception, had developed by means of the sense of touch.

Abbott, in referring to the generally accepted relationship between apparent distance and apparent size, observed that "if objects were seen as in contact with the organ they would appear small." What he means is this. The apparent area of the surgeon's face, after the distance perception corresponding to two feet has been acquired, would increase over 500 times. He remarked that there was no evidence for change in apparent magnitude, and further, that should the boy have learned to perceive magnitude, he would have expressed surprise much as he had in discovering the discordancy between the senses of sight and touch. These and other comments of relevance which Abbott pointed out, were ignored in subsequent discussion of the data.[5]

Wardrop case. When taken at face value the data are in contradiction to Berkeley's theory and the Cheselden case, especially in respect to the behavior of the woman in reference to the coach on her return home after the operation. "She exclaimed, 'What is that large thing that has passed by us?'" It would appear, from the mere asking of the question, that the thing she saw had, as it were, an objective reference. She did not feel the thing as touching her eye, in the eye, or in her mind. Furthermore, her judgment of the thing as external, and also as large, was arrived at independently of touch. Wardrop's statement that her blindness had been more complete than any previously reported case of restored vision was generally accepted by those who might have discussed the case. Therefore, it ought to have superseded any previous case in the theoretical discussions of vision, especially after Bailey and Abbott had stressed its importance. But this did not happen.

We shall cite several interpretations of this case in reference to Berkeley's theory and the standard Cheselden case. (1) We may observe that Wardrop regards his case as confirmatory of Berkeley's prediction of what a man born blind will see on gaining sight in reference to the prediction stated in Section 79 of the *Essay*. He does not refer his case to the prediction of Section 41, 'objects seeming to be in his eye or rather in his mind'. If Wardrop had wished to, he could have presented his case as a contradiction to Berkeley's theory by having cited Section 41. But even Section 79 is not necessarily verified in his data. According to this section, she ought not have been able to assert the judgment of magnitude represented by her saying "large thing" when the coach went by.

(2) Bailey had cited several passages of the Wardrop data which in his opinion contradicted Berkeley's theory. In his review of 1842 Mill

singled out the woman's perception of motion (when the glass was moved away from her), which he said would have been decisive if the experiment had been a "fair" one. "But," he continued, "the patient was of mature years, and the trial not made till the eighteenth day after the operation; by which time a middle-aged woman might well have acquired the experience necessary for distinguishing so simple a phenomenon." Mill, however, failed to consider the implications of his assumption that all objects are originally perceived in a plane. Let us suppose that the experiment had been tried on some preceding day when she did not yet perceive the longitudinal motion. She would have seen the table as an up-ended distorted quadrilateral shape and she would have seen the glass as a flat object shrinking in size and moving in the apparent plane of the table. How muscular experience could transform this initial perception to the perception of the eighteenth day is not readily understandable.

(3) Taine quoted the cases by Cheselden and Nunneley, and another case which has not been discussed in this text, as evidence for his theory that the new sensations of those with restored vision would be localized at the surface of the eyeball.

The next case discussed is Wardrop's, which Taine, in his extensive quotation of events through the end of the first day, regards as the "most instructive" because the woman's blindness had been more complete than that of other cases. However, he failed to note a possible contradiction between the three previous cases of the resighted and the woman's comment about the coach. Perhaps this failure can be explained by the qualification "usually" when he introduced the three cases as evidence for "touching the eye." His theory of localization of sensation, however, did not seem to allow for any exception— obviously the woman did not touch the coach. Further, Taine regards the case as providing evidence for his theory that visual sensations are the same before and after the operation. Thus he quotes and interprets a portion of the data: " 'In the course of the evening she requested her brother to show her his watch . . . and looked at it for a considerable time, holding it close to her eye. She was asked what she saw; and she said there was a dark and a bright side.' In fact, these two sensations of brightness and darkness alone corresponded to her former sensations, since till then she had never been able to do more than distinguish light and darkness." However, Taine did not continue with the quotation so as to include the woman's pointing to the hours of twelve and six of the watch, reactions which contradict his contention pertaining to the similarity of new and former visual sensations. This is a simple illustration of the selective citation and interpretation of evidence to fit a preconceived theory rather than changing the theory to fit the evidence.[6]

Franz case. From the time Abbott called attention to the existence of the Franz case to English philosophers in 1864, it became the basis for sharp criticism of Berkeley's theory by followers of Hamilton's philosophy. This criticism was directed principally at the theory of Bain and at the theory advocated by Mill in the early editions of his *Examination of Sir William Hamilton's Philosophy*. Mill, who had previously neglected to cite the Franz data, replied in a later edition in which he quoted an incomplete account of the case second hand from McCosh and conceded that his theory would have to be substantially changed providing that the case had been "correctly reported." He said that what he had "called a rudimentary conception of figure by the eye, must be more than rudimentary; it must be, in its way, considerably developed; and it must be such that 'after attentive examination' it could be recognised as corresponding with the circles and quadrangles already known by touch." His acceptance of the data in one phase of the discussion of this case was obviously provisional. For instance, he pointed out that this case was in contradiction to the case of Nunneley, and that McCosh failed to state whether the boy had been "completely blind" before the operation. After further discussion it was evident that Mill in his summation of the case, in which he stipulated the correct reporting of the case, was willing to grant the possibility of the original perception of bi-dimensional forms. He could not have conceded the possibility of the original perception of relative distance or three dimensions, for which there was some evidence in Franz's report as we have pointed out in Chapter 10, because such features of the case had not been excerpted by McCosh.[7]

The principles governing the selection of one case rather than some other case and the selection of one aspect rather than some other aspect of the very same case were never stated in any clear and consistent fashion. In a review of some of the criticisms of Berkeley's theory in 1872, Bain, who evidently regarded the Cheselden report as decisive, did not evaluate other cases. In another review of criticisms of the same theory in 1901, Fraser considered the case-study material in more detail. He quoted the Cheselden case but, for reasons that were not explained, he did not regard it as philosophically satisfactory. He listed several subsequent cases as the "most important" of the cases that had been published in the *Philosophical Transactions,* this list including the Wardrop case but excluding the Franz case. He then quoted the Nunneley case because it "is one of the last and most philosophically described of any I have met with." However, he did not explain why this case was better than any other case. Hamilton accepted the portion of the Cheselden case dealing with "touching the eyes," rejected the portion concerning the boy's behavior toward the cat and the dog and other features of the case, and ignored the cases of Wardrop and Franz.[8]

The extensive body of criticism and cross-criticism that had developed over these and other cases was partly justified. The degree of pre-operative blindness was usually unknown; the surgeon might have asked leading questions without realizing that this could have influenced the patient's descriptions; the meaning of the patient's phraseology insofar as it was the patient's own rather than a paraphrase by the surgeon, was often ambiguous; essential features of experiments which would aid in interpreting the results usually were omitted; the surgeon's interest in examining a patient was guided not only by the desire to secure information as to the character of the new sensations but also, and perhaps more important, by the desire to determine the degree of correlation between these sensations and tactual data in accordance with the Molyneux problem. In ordinary circumstances such evidence would be bracketed and judgment suspended since no clear and uncontested decision is possible. But the followers of Berkeleyan theory in the period under consideration did not and probably could not adopt an attitude of objective neutrality. For the cornerstone of their theory was that external reference and perceived relative distance were acquired. To have set aside the case studies of the resighted would have deprived the theory of the only evidence that could have been cited in support of it, as well as the means for effective reply to the objections raised by critics.[9]

Ignored Evidence

In 1795 Adam Smith referred to observations of the visually guided behaviors of young birds which, in his opinion, demonstrated that they "evidently enjoy all the powers of Vision in the most complete perfection." Although he did not particularize the details and interpretation of their behaviors, he provided sufficient information about the point he wished to make.

The nests of many birds are built in inaccessible places, and are physically removed at a considerable distance from surrounding objects such as trees. Their construction, moreover, restricts the amount of light-stimulation which the nestlings receive. A swallow, for instance, may achieve its physical maturity in a nest that has been placed in a small opening in the side of a cliff or under an eave. During the period of its development, it of course receives light-stimulation; however, its range is severely restricted relative to the stimulation which it will receive when it is completely mobile in respect to surrounding objects. Light reflected from a distant tree will not stimulate it at all, and it does not have the opportunity of learning the shapes or distances of blocked-off objects while in the nest. But when the bird leaves the nest for the first time, it immediately flies to the tree and perches on a limb.

Several aspects of this visually guided behavior are of interest. On approaching the limb, the bird decelerates its flight speed and extends its claws, a reflexive action which prevents injury. The action of deceleration, beginning at a particular distance before the limb is reached, shows that distance is perceived. Its flight and deceleration are controlled by the perception of the actual location of the limb toward which it flies, rather than by a point twelve or twenty-four inches above or below the limb. A perceived mislocation would mean not only that the limb is missed but also that the deceleration is an inappropriate action. The fine appreciation of distance is indicated by the relation of the path of the motion of the extended claws to the limb. This path includes the limb only, and certainly not a portion of space one inch below.

Other perceptual facts characterize its vision. The limb as a perceived entity is separate from other perceived things. As a thing it appears detached from and ahead of the empty space immediately above and below. The bird avoids other objects such as the trunk of the tree; it doesn't collide with them. Finally the reversal of the retinal image seems to offer no obstacle to the complex sequence of actions and the correct response to the limb. The fact that the bird has had visual experience before leaving the nest is of no importance. Even if it is supposed that its discrimination of the twigs composing the nest or per-

ception of objects in its immediate vicinity are learned, generalization to explain the behavior subsequent to its departure from the nest is impossible. Since the bird does not fly while in the nest, the later coordination of action and vision is a unique achievement independent of learning. Smith cited further and similar observations pertaining to birds which nest on the ground, such as goslings and ducklings, and to young "quadrupeds," such as calves and foals.

The fact that the observations before Spalding were derived from the behavior of animals in their natural environment does not impair their theoretical importance. The visually guided behavior of birds nesting off the ground cannot be explained in terms of past experience nor can they be referred to any sensory modality other than the visual. Naturalistic observation may even be more advantageous than experimental observation since the conditions of an experiment may so impair the animals that a scientific interpretation of their behavior would be dubious. Spalding himself, in having obtained evidence for experimentally induced disturbance in behavior, pointed out the value of naturalistic observation. He also stipulated an important methodological point when he said,

Further, it would seem that any early interference with the established course of their lives may completely derange their mental constitution, and give rise to an order of manifestations, perhaps totally and unaccountably different from what would have appeared under normal conditions. Hence I am inclined to think that students of animal psychology should endeavour to observe the unfolding of the powers of their subjects in as nearly as possible the ordinary circumstances of their lives.[10]

These observations, whether naturalistic or experimental, in themselves suffice to refute Berkeley's theory for the reasons already discussed by Bailey. The failure to observe any contradiction between the animal evidence and Berkeleyan theory is a remarkable feature of the empiristic school. Thus Smith in his exposition of Berkeley's theory, in the course of which the *Molyneux Premise* was stated as justification for the nonperceivability of distance, nevertheless cited the observations of young animals without noting any contradiction to the premise. Hamilton is of special interest since he noted the contradiction between Berkeley's theory and evidence. He argued: "If in man the perception of distance be not original but acquired, the perception of distance must also be acquired by them [animals]. But as this is not the case in regard to animals, this confirms the reasoning of those who would explain the perception of distance in man, as an original, not as an acquired, knowledge." He proceeded to quote Smith's observations *in extenso,* which he did not contest, but nevertheless refrained from drawing the conclusion dictated by his own syllogism, namely, that perception of distance in man is an original perception.[11]

It would appear that the selection and interpretation of evidence was guided by the conviction that Berkeleyan theory was "unshakable," as Mill said in his 1842 review of Bailey, and "unexpugnable," as Croom Robertson was to say in reply to James in 1888. Even Charles Darwin apparently was in the grip of this tradition although his approach to scientific theory in general, and the theory of evolution in particular, was guided by evidence as the foremost consideration. In 1877 he provided a "biographical sketch" of the development of one of his children in *Mind.* In respect to vision he said:

His eyes were fixed on a candle as early as the 9th day, and up to the 45th day nothing else seemed thus to fix them; but on the 49th day his attention was attracted by a bright-coloured tassel, as was shown by his eyes becoming fixed and the movements of his arms ceasing. . . . At the age of 32 days he perceived his mother's bosom when three or four inches from it, as was shown by the protrusion of his lips and his eyes becoming fixed; but I much doubt whether this had any connection with vision; he certainly had not touched the bosom. Whether he was guided through smell or the sensation of warmth or through association with the position in which he was held, I do not at all know.

We may observe that Darwin stipulated "touch" as a condition for the visual perception of the bosom in the interpretation of the protrusion of the lips and fixity of the eyes of his son. He might have been correct that these reactions were the result of some concomitant circumstances, but this possibility already represents an interpretation based on a theory of vision rather than on evidence. Simple experiments could have excluded the possible causal role of smell, warmth, or position, and the theoretical significance of touch could have been decided on the grounds of evidence. Although the description of the infant's reaction to the candle is somewhat different, protrusion of the lips not being mentioned, we may observe that this reaction is independent of touching of the candle.[12]

Mental and Physical Facts

The distinction between mental and physical facts was traditional in the history of philosophy and was generally accepted by the scientist as well as the philosopher. However, the failure to observe this distinction strictly in discussion of visual perception is an important reason for ambiguity in empiristic explanations. A mental fact may simply refer to that consciousness or awareness we describe as seeing a book on the desk. We always attribute various characteristics to the object we see, its color, and the spatial attributes of form, size, and so on. And when specifically questioned we may also say that the book at which we look is an objective external thing, for there is no subjectivity whatever in our perception. This is still true even when we identify the book as belonging to us, in contrast to its being a library book, for our claim to ownership pertains to a thing although also referring to the self. This point is more decisive when language is not yet available for the purpose of describing perceptions. Thus a young child who understands questions but who cannot yet speak may point when asked, "Where is your toy?" Indeed from the perceiver's standpoint the book at a distance is not even mental. The phrase "mental fact" merely defines the topic for the purpose of scientific discussion. Such a perception, considered as a mental fact, may be termed a phenomenal object and the distance at which we see the book, phenomenal distance. Actually the mental fact should be described as a phenomenal book at a distance, inasmuch as when we see the book we also see it at some distance. For the purpose of convenience, however, it is customary to separate object and distance in phenomenal descriptions. The domain of physical facts refers to stimulation, excitation, retinal image, and other similar terms, as well as to the external object.

The confusion between the two types of facts is apparent in such recurring phrases in the history of perception as the "mind interprets the retinal image," the "mind compares one retinal image with another image," the "mind overlooks the retinal image," "we perceive retinal images," and the "retina sees things." The retinal image of course is a physical fact, but the realization that "image" refers to an aggregate of excitations or electrochemical events makes the confusion more conspicuous. Although no theorist said that the mind could interpret and compare sets of excitations, the former assertions convey that very implication. Since everyone seemed to know that "retinal image" had the meaning of a collection of excitations (or motions), "image" must have had a meaning other than that of exclusively referring to a physical fact. And when the various contexts of its use are examined another meaning is evident, namely, one which pertains to a mental state. For instance, the perception of the retinal image, or the image which is interpreted by the mind, is equivalent to Reid's "visible figure" or James's "retinal sensation." But not all uses of "retinal image" can be readily reconciled to its dual meaning even in the writings of the same author. Nor, in fact, would the assertion pertaining to the perceivability of the visible figure escape the confusion.[13]

The constancy hypothesis represents an important reason for the confusion of mental and physical facts. Thus the bi-dimensionality and perspective changes of the retinal image were at the basis of the opinions that the original perception of any object is bi-dimensional and that an original perception varies perspectively in size and shape. This assumption may well have been responsible for phrases such as "the mind interprets the retinal image." The law of isolated conduction, which on the basis of independent conduction of excitations to the brain asserts that sensations are independent, represents a similar confusion. The following are other traditional examples of the confounding of mental and physical facts: that the small size of the images on the physical retina implies that the size of the original percepts are small; that a child, because his eyes are smaller than those of the adult, sees things as smaller; that the double images, one on each retina, and their inversion require learning to see an object single and upright; that excitations conducted to the brain cause "sensations in the brain," the sensations being mind-localized. The confusion of phenomenal and external objects is exemplified in theories which suppose the "extradition" of sensation and the "spreading of color over objects." Since neither sensation nor color can leave the mind to enter physical space, the so-called object necessarily must be the phenomenal object. A similar consideration applies to the projection of an after-image on a wall. The wall necessarily is a phenomenal, rather than physical, wall.

Such confusions are related to the inferring of mental states from physical facts. Inferences of this kind are unjustified since knowledge of a mental state can only be obtained through someone who is conscious, and who makes this known to the scientist either through his verbal report or actions.

Other basic recurring terms in the literature of perception which also have dual meanings include *sensation, distance, sign, visible object, visual field, field of vision,* and *light.* Thus *visible object* may be descriptive of the external object or of the original perception, and *sensation* may refer to nervous excitations or to the psychic concomitant of excitations. Since the meanings of a particular term are often freely interchanged by a theorist without an explicit reference to the shift, ignorance of this fact may account for the apparent self-inconsistency in his theory and the failure to understand the explanation that he might give for the acquisition of some perception. However, knowledge of this fact does not always successfully resolve such problems. A few of these points will be illustrated in the specific contexts in which they arise.[14]

The discussion of the problem of the inverted retinal image by the physiologist Starling was typical of the approach to this problem toward the end of the nineteenth century. In reference to "localisation and projection" he said:

> Much discussion has been wasted on the question why we see things upright while the images on our retina are inverted. The answer is a simple one. We do not look at nor are we conscious of the image on our retina.

When we say that we see anything we are not expressing merely a sensation, but we are giving an interpretation of certain sensations in the light of long experience which has involved a large number of sensations besides that of vision. Thus a new-born child sees, *i.e.* receives images on its retina which excite impulses in the brain, but it is unable to interpret anything that it sees. In the first few months there is indeed no connection between the visual sensations and eye movements; it is only about the third month after birth that the child will follow a lighted candle or bright object with its eyes, and this association of ocular movements with retinal impressions gradually extends also to many other movements. The continual and at first apparently aimless movements of the infant bring in a flood of muscular and tactile impressions which only after many trials are recognised as corresponding with sensations arriving from the eyes. It at first finds that with the right hand it can touch objects lying on the right side of the field of vision. It becomes conscious therefore, not of the left side of its retina, but of a series of objects which have distinct relations to its right hand, and of a certain *thing seen* outside itself. The projection and localisation of visual impressions are therefore not intuitive or innate qualities attached to stimulation of each point of the retina, but are the result of experience, the testing and comparing of visual sensations with tactile and muscular sensations from all parts of the body. From these experiences we learn to associate stimulation, say, of the right side of the retina with the presence of objects lying in front of and to the left side of the body, and to project our visual sensations in this direction. If, for instance, we press the finger, with closed eyelids, on the outer side of the right eyeball, a luminous ring, or phosphene, will be seen apparently towards the left, *i.e.* the region whence the pressed-upon part of the retina will be normally stimulated by rays of light.

Apparently, Starling maintains that the infant's consciousness of seeing an object on the "right side" is caused by tactile sensation, for he indicates that this sensation precludes consciousness of the left side of the retina. If we suppose for the sake of argument that the tactile sensation is absent or not yet associated with visual sensation, considering only what the infant might see initially, the infant is either conscious or nonconscious of visual sensation. If the infant is conscious of visual sensation, presumably he would be conscious of different parts of the retina. This implication would contradict the opinion expressed in the first few sentences of the quotation. If the infant is nonconscious of visual sensation, then the meaning to be accorded to the infant's "seeing" before any interpretive act is obscure.

Starling seems to define the initial seeing by the infant physiologically, namely, in terms of the reception of retinal images and the excitation of impulses in the brain without reference to a mental state. Obviously, this definition is inadequate, since the infant would be put in the position of having to interpret impulses in its brain. Further, if these impulses initially would cause nonconscious visual sensations, it should have been explained as to how the impulses arising from tactile stimulation could give rise not only to conscious tactile sensation but also to the consciousness of visual sensation.

Toward the end of the quotation the "presence of objects," which Starling does not define, is asserted to be one term of an association. If "visual presence of the object" (phenomenal object) is intended, the proposed explanation would beg the question because upright vision is presupposed, as in the infant's seeing the mother's face as erect. If "tactile presence" is intended, the explanation would be incomprehensible because seeing is not the same as touching. And if "physical presence" is intended, the explanation would be meaningless because no association can be formed between an event in the retina or the brain and another event in physical space external to the body—the nervous system does not extend from the body to the physical object.

The pressure phosphene has always been a thorny problem for scientific interpretation. The localization of the luminous ring in phenomenal space, in the traditional language, exemplifies a "subjective appearance," inasmuch as no object in physical space corresponds to it. If this appearance can be scientifically interpreted as expressive of an innate or intuitive fact, the innateness of the phenomenal localization of an object when physically present and stimulating some portion of the retina would be implied. If the action of radiant energy and pressure on the eyeball produce similar effects on the retina, they ought to give rise to the same or similar visual sensation. Starling implicitly conceded the necessity of the implication because the antecedent learning of phenomenal localization when the physical object is present was regarded as the factor at the basis of the localization of the phosphene. Thus the infant would learn to see, or to become conscious of, an object to the right when light rays stimulate the left side of its retina so that when pressure is exerted on the same side, he will see the luminous ring to the right. Without this antecedent experience, therefore, the applied pressure would not cause the phosphene. However, there is no way of ascertaining in Starling's account what the conscious reaction, if any, might be. In any case, however successful Starling's explanation may be, it fails to account for the shape of the phosphene as a "ring" in contradistinction to a square or triangle.

These and other problems in Starling's explanation partly arise from the failure to maintain a consistent distinction between mental and physical facts. In his text "sensation" generally refers to a mental fact, while other terms refer not only to physical facts but also imply the mind's appreciation of them. He suggests, as others said explicitly, that sensation is projected along the physical path of physical light rays. Such facts, however, are not appreciated by an infant or any other perceiver, nor can sensation detach itself from the body to be projected. To say we learn to associate stimulation of the right side of the retina with the presence of objects may have as much meaning as to say we learn to associate impulses in the right cerebral hemisphere with the presence of objects, or to say we learn to associate impulses in the auditory nerve or auditory cortex with a Beethoven sonata. Of course, much depends on the meaning of the undefined concept "we learn." If this concept refers to the formation of associations considered as physiological events in the brain, then all terms when defined physiologically are homogeneous. Thus one could say that the impulses in the brain arising from stimulation of the retina become associated with the impulses arising from, or correlated with, movements of the muscles of the eyes or limbs. Homogeneity in terminology can also be attained by referring associations to the linkages between sensations, the translation of these linkages into neural terms being deferred. Starling seems to adopt the latter approach but he is inconsistent since the projection of sensation involves heterogeneous terms in the association, including on the one hand a psychic fact and on the other, stimulation and light rays.

As long as the reversal of the retinal image is regarded as a problem in the explanation of seeing things upright, the distinction between mental and physical facts becomes difficult to maintain. For the denial of external reference, as is evident in the Starling quotation "*thing seen* outside itself," is an important reason for the existence of this problem. Since phenomenal distance is rejected as an original datum of sight and since the dimensional characteristics of visual sensation and retinal image are presumed to be similar, there is the tendency to suppose that sensation and image possess the same orientation. And for this reason it was sometimes said that the infant at first sees upside down. However, this opinion was usually rejected on a number of different grounds. But the persistence of the problem and difficulties in its solution indicate its unsuccessful resolution. Indeed it may even be the case that this assumption of the original seeing of objects upside down underlies Starling's own thinking, but he avoids its explicit statement on the supposition that the infant at first is nonconscious of visual sensation.[15]

When Starling turned to the discussion of after-images in the pages following the quotation, he was concerned with the change in their size as a function of distance. He explained this fact in terms of a comparison of the "judgment of retinal-image size" with the "muscular effort of the convergence and accommodation which are present at the same time." However, he did not relate this explanation to his discussion of localization and projection of sensations. Actually, upright vision and the so-called "projection of after-image" are interdependent facts. If one is the product of association, so for the other. When we look at a triangle and turn away to look straight ahead at some surface, the after-image has not only the shape of a triangle but also the same orientation as the previous percept. If the experiment could be tried with an infant prior to the formation of any association, this fact ought not to characterize his visual experience, inasmuch as phenomenal distance was presumed not to be an original visual datum.

The distinction between personal and scientific standpoints, although often neglected, is useful when properly observed for resolving some of the problems of perceptual theory. From the personal standpoint such physical facts as rays of light, retinal image, stimulation and excitations, the nervous system and brain are wholly irrelevant. Not only do none of these facts betray themselves in the phenomenal object but also knowledge of them is a relatively late acquisition in the history of science, and for many not known at all. Such facts, therefore, could not be terms of any association. This distinction has been generally acknowledged in reference to the reversal of the retinal image, but it is equally applicable to rays of light and excitations. Thus the projection of sensation or retinal image and the perception of retinal image or blood vessels are meaningless, inasmuch as some physical entity is presupposed.

The physical facts of which we spoke are known only to the scientist. However, he has knowledge of the other domain of facts as well, namely, mental facts, either as reported by the viewer or through his own self-observation as a viewer. He then correlates the two kinds of facts, and he ascertains the physical condition of the body or external physical facts which are the concomitant of a mental fact. Now just as from the personal standpoint no statement can be advanced concerning the concomitant physical processes of some percept, so too in respect to any inference drawn from the scientific to the personal standpoint. Both types of data, each drawn from its own source, are essential. The participant in an experiment on after-images reports various changes in the size and distance of what for him is a luminous patch on some surface. The scientist knows that the magnitude of the after-effect of retinal stimulation remains constant. He can measure the physical distance of the wall from the viewer and, under the guidance of the viewer, he can also measure the dimensions of the luminous patch. Thus he is enabled to ascertain the relations among these various measures. The concept of projection is unnecessary in these determinations. Moreover, he can hypothesize that convergence and accommodation of the eyes are correlated with the size of the luminous patch and he may secure evidence for it. Thus excitations in the brain arising from muscular action of the eyes in conjunction with visual excitations would become an important physical concomitant of the changes in phenomenal size. But should he conjecture that the excitations derived from muscular action of the eyes have sensation as their concomitant, its verification only can be ascertained phenomenally from the personal standpoint.

In another experiment he focuses rays of light on the white part of the eye from the side and he anticipates that the shadows cast on the retina by blood vessels will give rise to visual sensation. The subject who is looking at some surface straight ahead verifies this anticipation, for he says that he sees some dark and narrow squiggly lines. To say that the "blood vessels are perceived" is an incongruous expression, unless the scientist wants this to be a descriptive statement from his own standpoint in the sense that the perceived lines represent the effects of cast shadows. Interesting in this regard is the subject's report that the lines he sees quickly disappear, a fact which the scientist could not have predicted. However, the scientist discovers that by moving the light source to and fro, the percept does not fade away; in this instance, the subject sees the lines moving.

From the scientific standpoint it is known that "luminous points" in particular spatial positions will stimulate opposite parts of the retina by means of light rays. The subject reports the positions of the luminous sources, which for him are phenomenal objects, and the scientist in coordinating these reports with the objective facts ascertains a correspondence. The subject says "I see a light to my left" and the scientist knows that this is in agreement with the placement of the source to the left. He can summarize the results of his investigation in relation to some law such as the "law of visible direction." There is no implication that the law, although correlating two types of distinct data, is ever descriptive from the personal standpoint. If the scientist should assert this implication, he would return to the incongruity that we project our sensation along the paths of lights rays or that we perceive the direction of light rays. Moreover, as long as he is concerned with establishing the correlation, the reversal of the retinal image presents no special problem.[16]

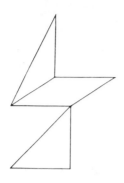

14 THE GESTALT THEORY OF PERCEPTION

Time forbids more than a few very slight personal memories of Profes-
sor Köhler. While I was working at Wesleyan University with Profes-
sor Dodge (1920–1924) there appeared a paper in the Psychological
Bulletin by one Koffka, whose name we just knew as a foremost young
German psychologist. It is hard to imagine the shock it gave to our
laboratory. Most of the fundamentals of psychology seemed to be abol-
ished. Particularly Sensation, which had already been slightly rocked
on its pedestal, had now been toppled off entirely. It is hardly possible
to realize what effect this had upon us in those days. I doubt whether
there is anything that could so astonish the psychological world of
today. Titchener, who visited our laboratory in 1923, the year after
Koffka's paper, asked the writer: "What are they proposing to start
from?" From this source we learned of the group in Germany who
were engineering this revolution and of the arch-revolutionary
Köhler. Humphrey, 1962

Gestalt psychology began as a movement in a series of experiments
performed by Wertheimer in 1912 which dealt with "apparent" or
"stroboscopic" motion such as we see at the cinema. Previous investiga-

tors had already studied apparent motion, but the special importance in Wertheimer's approach was his novel psychological and physiological interpretation of his own further experimental results. Köhler and Koffka, two subjects in these experiments, became convinced of the correctness and importance of the new approach in discussions with Wertheimer, the three forming the nucleus of the gestalt movement. The principles they formulated became the basis for numerous experiments undertaken by them and their followers in the investigation of the perceptual phenomena of the visual and other sensory modalities, and also for speculation concerning processes in the brain that might be the cause and correlate of perception. They argued that gestalt principles required a revision of basic categories in the study of perception, thus the movement was occasionally called the "gestalt revolution." As with any revolution an extensive critical reaction by psychologists and physiologists has arisen in the past half-century. Since the presentation and evaluation of gestalt principles requires knowledge of many experiments on vision performed by psychologists and physiologists and also knowledge of other fields such as neurophysiology, the present discussion should be regarded only as an introduction to gestalt theory.

For the purpose of exposition, we will regard Wertheimer, Köhler, and Koffka, and their principal followers as a team, drawing upon one or another as our need may arise. The progressive changes in the gestalt movement will be ignored in order to stress those principles and observations which they regarded as important in understanding the basic issues in a theory of perception.

Generally gestalt theory represents a reaction to empiristic and nativistic theories and is intended as their replacement. According to gestalt psychologists, both theories have the constancy hypothesis as a common assumption and many detailed examples of this assumption are provided. Furthermore, they maintain that the important defects in empiristic and nativistic explanations are ultimately traceable to this assumption, and they say that an adequate theory of perception requires its repudiation. The critique of the "traditional" theories from the standpoint of the constancy hypothesis is a conspicuous feature in their statement of gestalt principles and in the experiments undertaken by them. This is so much the case that disengaging principles and experiments from critique is not feasible from a practical standpoint, and thus they ought to be discussed together. In making some initial assumptions of our own, however, it is possible to defer the explicit discussion of the gestalt critique of traditional concepts. In any case, a proper estimate of the critique presupposes knowledge of some of the principles and results which they have emphasized.[1]

A preliminary statement of some of the basic tenets and assumptions of gestalt theory will simplify its exposition. (1) Phenomenological investigation is adopted as the essential means for ascertaining the facts of "direct experience"—facts of consciousness in the older vocabulary—which are to be explained in reference to theory. The principal facts of such investigation are collectively subsumed in the concept of *organization*. It is supposed that organization is the direct result of sensorial processes and for this reason organization is regarded as a "sensory fact." Sensory organization, says Köhler, is "not the product of learning."

(2) The psychophysical postulate is to be strictly observed; every fact of direct experience is "blindly coupled" to a concomitant process in the brain. The gestalt version of this postulate is the principle of isomorphism. In accordance with this principle, the spatial attributes of a perception are identical with or resemble the dimensions of the cerebral pattern corresponding to it. The cerebral pattern, moreover, is presumed to be similar in some degree to the external object. Therefore an isomorphic relationship to some extent prevails between pattern and object. The qualification "in some degree" is necessary because of exceptions that will be apparent later. Finally, it is held that the isomorphic relationship between perception and object is preserved to some degree. The relationship between perception and object is important in determining the other two isomorphic relationships. For instance, Köhler notes that a phenomenal circle has perfect symmetry about the common center, a phenomenal fact which is similar to the objective stimulus. Since a cerebral process is the immediate cause of the phenomenal circle, this process also ought to be characterized by similar symmetry. In subsequent discussion the "isomorphic principle" will refer to the relationship of percept to brain pattern.

(3) All nervous processes are physicochemical events, hence the laws of physics characterize their formation. Those processes in the brain which have concomitant conscious effects are described as "psychophysical" or "psychophysiological." An external object at a "molecular level" consists of swirling molecules; however, physical laws pertaining to the attraction of molecules suffice to explain their cohesion

and the formation of the object as a distinct and segregated entity. Inasmuch as psychophysical processes are events in nature, the laws governing their organization into specific coherently shaped patterns are those of physics. In specifying the cerebral "laws of organization" the gestalt psychologist partly adopts a "conservative approach," that is, he accepts the usual explanation of the transmission of retinal excitations to the visual cortex. The transmission is such that the spatial distribution of excitations in the cortex "resemble," or are similar to, the spatial distribution of the excitations in the retina. Because of this similarity, the visual cortex is regarded as the "cortical retina." The degree of resemblance, which is far from being exact, is usually expressed as a one-to-one correspondence between the excitations of the cortical retina and the retina of the eye. However, and this is where gestalt theory departs from the conservative approach, the cortical distribution is regarded as a mosaic of molecular processes which cannot account for visual percepts. Therefore, their physiological organization into a macroscopic unified cerebral process is essential for explaining phenomenal organization. It is in the full recognition of the problem of physiological organization, the stipulation of its possible laws, and the explanation of how physiological organization might occur, that gestalt theory makes its most important and unique contribution to the history pf perceptual theory.[2]

THE PHENOMENOLOGICAL APPROACH

Asks Koffka in formulating the basic question of any perceptual theory, "*Why do things look as they do?*" Before the "why" can be discussed, he says, one must first know how they look. An accurate description of the "looks" or appearances of things is essential and a prescription is offered for this determination. Any commitment to a theory dictating how things ought to look or how they are to be explained is to be set aside in this phase of an investigation because ascertaining the "facts of direct experience" is the important first task. After having gathered the facts one may then proceed to propose a theory which explains them, but this step should not be undertaken prematurely for otherwise important facts may be overlooked. Moreover, direct experience must be accepted as a primary fact and any descriptive statement must be verifiable in reference to direct experience.

This procedure defines the "phenomenological method." Says Koffka, "For us phenomenology means as naive and full a description of direct experience as possible." Phenomenology is to be stressed because a "good description of a phenomenon may by itself rule out a number of theories and indicate definite features which a true theory must possess." Thus a theory which supposes "muscular and tactile experience" as a component of perception or a theory which supposes a percept is the "sum of a mosaic of visual sensations" is falsified on phenomenological grounds. In contrast, a true theory must regard a percept as a unitary and genuine fact of visual experience. Gestalt phenomenology has still another feature, namely, the prescription that direct experience must be the starting point of a theory. Some of the reasons given in justification of this prescription are similar to those cited in our previous discussion of the distinction between mental and physical facts, and we shall omit them. The phenomenological approach is not only a criterion for excluding a given theory and indicating the direction of another, it is also an important tool for the discovery of basic principles and the means for understanding the nature of the cerebral counterparts of percepts.[3]

In having noted the common confusion of mental and physical facts, gestalt psychologists introduce a terminology as a precaution for avoiding it. *Proximal stimulus* refers to the distribution of retinal excitations or retinal image, and *distal stimulus,* to the external object producing it; a thing or object when prefixed by "visual" always refers to the phenomenal object. Thus visual things have color, size, and shape and they are distributed in visual space. Their distribution in visual space defines what is meant by "phenomenal" or "visual" field.

The first task of a theory is the setting forth of the important characteristics of the phenomenal field. This aspect of gestalt theory is only descriptive, no explanation of the characteristics being intended. Nevertheless, analysis of direct experience leads to the formulation of certain "laws" or "principles" which are phenomenologically verifiable. Their formulation arises from a background of theory which will be discussed later.

Organization

Köhler defines the concept of organization thus, "In most visual fields the contents of particular areas 'belong together' as circum-

scribed units from which their surroundings are excluded." He is looking at his desk and he sees among other things "a pencil, an eraser,
[and] a cigarette." These "visual things" are the shaped and segregated entities to which the definition of organization pertains. The
pencil is a particular circumscribed unit set apart from other units and
also set apart from the surface of the desk, that is, it is detached from
the surface and is somewhat closer to him. Köhler's direct experience
also informs him of other facts, for instance, that the "eraser" is between the two other visual things. Moreover, these visual things have a
third dimension and they are externally referenced. Since in general
we all see what Köhler sees, organization is a general property of the
visual field. Let us again consider the pencil. The fact of its phenomenal segregation from the background exemplifies what is usually
termed the figure-ground relationship, figure referring to the pencil
and ground to the surrounding surface of the desk. We observe that
the pencil is bounded by a contour, two parallel lines closed at one
end by a short line and closed at the other end by two lines coming to
a point. This contour belongs to the pencil as a visual thing and de-
limits the shape of the yellowness of the area inside this thing.

An important characteristic which is implicit in this description of
the seeing of objects is the "one-sidedness" of the contour of a visual
thing. The contour defines or shapes the thing, rather than shaping
the adjacent surface of the desk. If the contour of one thing were to be
perceived as belonging to the contour of another thing, we would no
longer see objects as we do. Thus, if one edge of the pencil were perceived as "belonging to" the eraser, both pencil and eraser would not
be perceived as distinct things. Köhler points out that in looking
down the street we see buildings as visual things and the expanse of
the sky as ground. The edges shape the buildings rather than the sky.
On the other hand, if the edges shaped the sky, the buildings would
not be perceivable objects. In this instance the shaped sky would appear somewhat closer than the adjacent darker areas which previously
were perceived as belonging to the buildings. The one-sided function
of a contour in defining the visual things which correspond to the objects of the natural environment is a typical feature of the figure-
ground relationship. And if this were not so, it would be difficult to
understand how we could respond to objects adaptively. When the
pencil is the visual thing we can directly respond and pick up the corresponding object. But should the same area be perceived as the

ground, the picking up of the pencil would be a difficult achievement because no visual thing would correspond to it.

These and other characteristics of percepts can be verified in looking at diagrams. The fact that the diagrams are "artificial" rather than "natural" objects is of no theoretical significance to gestalt psychologists.

Figure 14.1: Two *F*'s, one the mirror image of the other, may be perceived which, on continued looking, disappear and we perceive instead a cross with a base. (On further inspection, the two percepts reverse.) This fact exemplifies the one-sidedness of contour and also the reversibility of a figure-ground relationship. The edges separating the central black area from the adjacent white areas to the left and right may be considered as the counterparts of the physical contours of some natural object. The corresponding phenomenal contours shape the central black area when the cross and base is the visual thing but the same edges determine phenomenal contours shaping the white areas, the *F*'s then being perceived. Moreover, when the *F*'s are perceived they appear as somewhat closer than the surrounding black and white areas; the white areas corresponding to them recede when the *F*'s are no longer perceived. When an *F* is perceived, complete contours may be observed as though faint lines had been drawn. Since the contours have no counterparts in the distal stimulus they are called "subjective."

Figure 14.2: On inspecting this figure for some time an *E* and its mirror image may be seen. Furthermore, the reversibility of the two percepts may be observed. Thus, if an *E* to the left and its mirror image to the right were the first percepts, the mirror image on the left and the *E* in its usual orientation on the right might then be perceived. Other percepts are possible, three "birds flying in formation vertically" or lines disposed as though a road sign at an intersection. What is important, however, is that these percepts are mutually exclusive. An *E* and its mirror image on the same side of the vertical cannot be simultaneously perceived; evidently, the phenomenal contour corresponding to a particular zig-zag line can have only one direction. We may also observe that when the three "birds" are seen, the zig-zag lines merely divide adjacent white areas; the phenomenal contours do not have any apparent sidedness. In respect to the subjective contours, there is a shift in their location from above to below the zig-zag lines corresponding to a change from *E* to the mirror image, both being on

FIGURE 14.1

FIGURE 14.2

FIGURE 14.3

FIGURE 14.4

FIGURES 14.1-14.4. One eye viewing, and also increased distance, may help in getting the perceptual effects. (Figure 14.3 is reproduced from G. Kanizsa, "Margini quasi-percettivi in campi con stimolazione omogenea." *Rivista di psicologia,* 1955, 49, 7–30, with permission of the author and the editor of the journal, C. L. Musatti.)

the same side of the vertical. There are no subjective contours when the "birds" are perceived.

There are further facts of interest. Particular areas of a perceived figure appear brighter than other areas in correlation with sidedness of contour, and their location changes in the reversal of figure and ground. The portions of the white areas immediately above the three zig-zag lines appear brighter than the areas immediately below when an *E* is perceived on the left, but when the mirror image is perceived on the same side, the brightness shifts to the white areas below the lines. Furthermore, there is a perceived fluctuation of relative depth which is correlated with changes in the sidedness of contour and location of the brighter areas. Finally, when the *E* and mirror image are perceived simultaneously the three pairs of lines are perceived as a unified or organized entity.

Figure 14.3: This figure, recently published by Kanizsa, is the one that is usually regarded as the most interesting figure of this sort. An erect triangle is perceived as somewhat in front of an inverted triangle. We may observe that main stretches of the phenomenally contoured surfaces have no counterpart in the diagram. Some of the facts discussed in relation to the preceding two figures are also descriptive of the percept to which this figure gives rise.

Figure 14.4: The reader is invited to observe the different diagrams and to describe the perceptual effects without being informed as to what to expect. Some of the perceptual effects will only become evident on prolonged observation.

Percepts and the Geometry
of Physical Units

Lines are drawn on paper with a ruler or compass and certain areas may be shaded. Physical units can be varied in size as well as in the distances between them. Such units which are the remote causes of percepts, are not significantly responsible for the characteristics of percepts. Köhler pointed out that although this is readily conceded in the perceived third dimension of the Necker Cube because the distal stimulus is flat, it is equally true for other features of a percept such as shape. Subjective contours and reversibility of figure and ground certainly illustrate this point. However, it would also be the case when the lines of a distal stimulus were continuous. A contour is phenome-

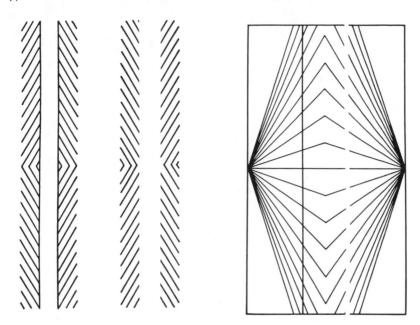

FIGURES 14.5. The illusion of the apparently "bent" parallel lines is also obtained when these lines are not physically present. (Reproduced from S. Tolansky, *Optical illusions,* 1964, with permission of the publishers, Pergamon Press. Some of the lines in Tolansky's diagram have been erased in order to show that the illusion occurs with subjective contours.)

nally related to the points "inside" rather than to those "outside" it. The one-sided function of contour is an exclusive perceptual fact because sidedness does not characterize the physical unit itself. The perceptual effects produced by certain drawings, however, may seem to be a contradiction. With a straight edge, four lines of the same length are drawn so as to form a closed figure, and with a compass another closed figure is drawn. The first figure gives rise to the perception of a square and the second to a circle, percepts which correspond to the geometry of the figures. However, the mere geometry of diagrams could not account for the percepts because when they are drawn on white paper with white chalk, a uniform or homogeneous white surface is perceived. Clearly inhomogeneity in the physical unit is essential, thus a gray pencil is used in drawing on a white surface. But even in allowing such inhomogeneity, the drawing itself could not account for the one-sidedness of contour. When the context of a unit is appropriately

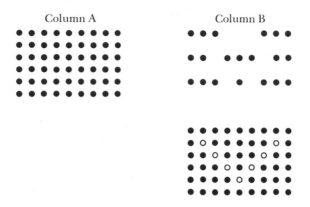

Figure 14.6

altered by the inclusion of other lines or shaded areas, the same unit elicits a different percept. Thus a physical straight line may appear curved rather than straight; square-like and circular physical shapes may appear distorted; a series of appropriately drawn concentric circles will be perceived as a spiral. But given inhomogeneity, the necessary degree of contextual isolation, and the sidedness of contour, the characteristics of a percept do correspond significantly to those of the geometrical arrangements. Two drawn circles, for instance, produce corresponding percepts and when the distance between their centers is increased, we perceive them as further apart.

Wertheimer introduced many physical units for the purpose of illustrating the thesis that mere geometry is insufficient for explaining a percept. Some of these arrangements are set forth in Figures 14.6–14.9. In Column A of these diagrams, we see a rectangular array of dots or also such geometric forms as two squares and a straight line touched by a diamond. These same arrangements contain many other possible arrangements which generally do not have any counterpart in a percept. Some of these other arrangements are set forth in Column B, where for the purpose of emphasis those in Column A have been altered by deletion of some dots, substitution of circles for other dots, and by physical separation of some sub-units.

We do not perceive the groupings of dots in Figure 14.6A as we do in Figure 14.6B. Yet from a geometric standpoint these and many other possible groupings are contained in 14.6A. The rectangular array of dots contains all the letters of the alphabet in a physical sense,

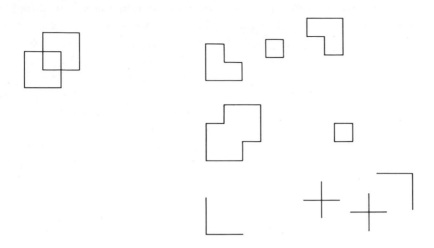

FIGURE 14.7

FIGURE 14.8

FIGURE 14.9

but we only perceive an entity which is describable as a rectangular array of dots. The units or groupings that we do perceive are termed "natural" or "spontaneous." These are the units we perceive when looking at figures naively, without analyzing them for the purpose of discovering some other unit. Thus the seeing of a diamond touching a straight line in Figure 14.8A tends to be the spontaneous percept. After the sub-units in Figure 14.8B are indicated, it may be possible to see them in the previous arrangement. This percept, the consequence of an "analytical attitude," is not spontaneous or natural. Even if we are successful in seeing two sub-units, the "spontaneous" percept tends to be dominant. In Figure 14.9A we do not spontaneously see the words WOW and MOM. The diamond shape bordered by two parallel lines in the same figure gives rise to the perception of the letter K only when this possibility is suggested, although the corresponding sub-unit is geometrically present. There is, of course, a limit to what can be achieved with the intention to look for something. For instance, the V is not a perceived entity in the rectangular array of dots. We can imagine its existence by tracing out the path of the relevant dots, but we do not see it.[4]

Factors or Rules of Organization

Since specific percepts are spontaneous or natural, notwithstanding the number of "theoretical" or "logical" organizations to which physical arrangements could give rise, their formation or selection must be accounted for. Thus Wertheimer, having asked whether "such arrangements and divisions follow definite principles," stated a number of principles, also termed "factors" or "laws." He verified these principles in relation to appropriately chosen drawings of shapes and dots and the characteristics of percepts.

Proximity. Says Köhler: "Other things being equal, items which are near one another unite most readily in one group, and this group tends to have its boundary where distances become greater." When the dots in the first row in Figure 14.6A are considered as the items, the others being covered, no particular grouping other than equidistant dots is perceived. However, with appropriate increase in distances between the third and fourth dots, and between the sixth and seventh dots, we would perceive three groupings of three dots each. Thus in the first row of 14.6B we perceive two groupings, the third group not being represented. Changes in distance will determine other perceived groupings. For instance, should the vertical distances between the successive rows of Figure 14.6A be increased, we would perceive horizontal groupings of dots. A corner dot tends to be united to the next member in the same row because it is closer to it, rather than to the dot immediately below. Suitable alteration in the distances of the dots in the rectangular array will determine the percept of a *V* as a distinct entity. Proximity is also a factor in the percepts of other diagrams, such as the one pertaining to the two *F*'s. When the distance of the vertical bars from the center is increased the *F*'s are not perceived, and correspondingly the subjective contours disappear.

Similarity. Says Köhler: "In the formation of a perceptual group *like* items tend to unite, and where a new kind of item begins there the unitary group tends to end." For instance, the annuli in Figure 14.6B are perceived in the form of a *V*. In substituting green dots for these annuli and red dots for the black dots, the same form is perceived providing the color vision of the perceiver is not defective.

When similarity and proximity "compete" the former factor is said to have the advantage in the formation of some grouping. Thus when the alternate rows of the rectangular array of Figure 14.6A are replaced by the same size green dots, one tends to perceive horizontal rather than vertical groupings.

However, the factors of proximity and similarity are not sufficient to account for all spontaneous percepts. If the vertical sides of the two "squares" in Figure 14.7 are considered as the "items," the two factors should favor the grouping of the two left verticals or the two right verticals. Instead, one left side is perceptually united to a more distant right side. Thus additional factors such as "direction" and "closure" are invoked. For instance, in Figure 14.8 we perceive a straight line since this percept preserves the sameness of direction. This same factor is also operative in the perception that arises from Figure 14.7 so that a horizontal line, which intersects a vertical line, is seen as the side of a square. Similarly in Figure 14.7B we tend to perceive the two lines of the plus sign as intersecting perpendicularly rather than as two right angles with a common vertex. "Closure" favors the perception of "self-enclosed units." Thus, in Figure 14.9 we perceive two contiguous circles rather than the *S*-like figure and its mirror image. However, this factor in itself is indecisive in respect to Figure 14.7, for some of the part organizations in Figure 14.7B also form self-enclosed units. In this case, however, the factor of "direction" is determinative.

The discussion of factors of organization is intended to be illustrative, for these and still other factors are said to be effective in the perceptions which arise from a wide variety of arrangements. The most general point of gestalt psychology is that we tend to perceive those forms or "wholes" which are most simple and most regular as conditions will permit. For instance, in reference to Figure 14.7, the percept of criss-crossing lines in a plane is not simple nor is the percept of a central square inside an octagonal shape regular. The favored organization in this case is the percept of two square forms in the depth relationship similar to that of the Necker Cube.

Wholes and Parts

The concept of "wholes and parts," which is often regarded as the central concept of gestalt psychology, may be somewhat obscure when considered apart from its origin in nineteenth-century controversies. Hence for the purpose of concreteness, this concept will be related to the discussion of percepts and units or arrangements. The nine units of Figure 14.7B are geometrically present in the arrangement to the left. For the purpose of definition the percept arising from each of the units in isolation in the column to the right will be called a part, and the phenomenal squares arising from the arrangement to the left will be called wholes. It may be observed that the parts are not phenomenally present in the wholes. Furthermore, the identification of the wholes as "squares" is contingent on the seeing of squares. Naive persons who view the arrangement to the left never give the description or identification of "octagon" and "small square." The phenomenal absence of the parts would account for their failure to produce such identification. However, much depends on the definition of part or whole. If a *V* percept, such as might arise from a particular arrangement of black dots, is called a part, this part is no longer phenomenally present or identifiable in the perceived rectangular array in Figure 14.6A. But if the percept that arises from a single dot is the "part" and the *V* percept is the "whole," this particular part is still phenomenally present and identifiable in the whole.[5]

FIGURE 14.10. David Brewster reported the observations of W. H. Wollaston who altered portions of a portrait in order to show that the "direction of the nose" is the principal feature of a portrait that produces the apparent direction of the eyes, and also that a "total difference of character may be given to the same eyes by a due representation of the other features." The portion of the head which is above the nose is identical in both pictures. (Reproduced from Brewster, 1851.)

Generally the perception of natural objects would involve the same factors of organization. Thus the segregation of a particular object in the phenomenal field depends on the similarity and proximity of the contours, its dissimilarity from adjacent surfaces, and distance from another object which may have similar contours and color. Köhler points out that perceived natural unities are destroyed by camouflage. Here too, however, factors of organization would be the basis of their destruction.[6]

Motion

Thus far only stationary percepts have been considered, however, the perception of an object in motion is another characteristic of the phenomenal field. When an object is in actual motion we often perceive a motion corresponding to it, hence it might be supposed that the moving stimulus is the cause of the perceived motion. But gestalt psychologists have argued that this is an incorrect supposition, and to make their point they repeat the discussion of the relationship of percept to the geometry of arrangements. "Apparent" or "stroboscopic" motion, however, may suffice to establish the gestalt thesis because the stimuli at the basis of this motion are statically presented. Accordingly, this discussion will be restricted to stroboscopic motion for the purpose of illustrating some facts of perceived motion as well as factors of organization.

In an experiment on stroboscopic motion the stimuli are presented intermittently and sequentially. For instance in Figure 14.11A the left vertical line is flashed on and then off before the right vertical line is flashed on and a short time later, off. When this cycle is repeated with optimal durations, a to and fro motion of a single object is perceived. If the durations are not optimal we may perceive two lines either simultaneously or successively. In Figures 14.11B, C, and D the perceived movements for the paired stimuli are respectively transverse, a rotation of 90° in the plane, and a 180° rotation in the third dimension. Although the units are identical, the perceived movements are diverse. Apparently the orientation of one stimulus relative to the other is a significant determinant of perceived movement. Other experiments have shown that the factors of organization are relevant. Thus when the distance between paired stimuli is increased the perceived motion disappears (factor of proximity). In Figure 14.11E the movement occurs between the two vertical lines rather than between the left vertical and the right squiggly line (factor of similarity). However, when the right vertical is blocked off, the movement takes place between the remaining pair of lines.

Finally, the perceived duality of parts in nonoptimal conditions generally is not observed in the perceived unitary motion in optimal conditions. The blocking off of the right vertical line in Figure 14.11E is an exception, the parts being identifiable even when the apparent motion is perceived.[7]

FIELD THEORY

The phenomenal facts of organization, the factors of organization, and so on, represent a description rather than an explanation of the phenomenal field. These must be related to their immediate cause in

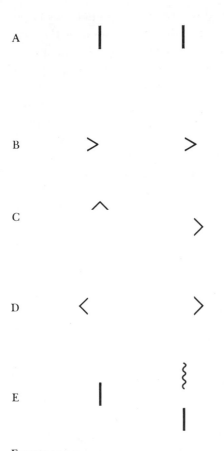

FIGURE 14.11

brain processes in order to explain perception. Lawful relationships govern the occurrence of these processes, and gestaltists, principally Köhler, proposed a number of hypotheses concerning their nature. According to him, direct experience is an essential prerequisite in physiological investigation, but he acknowledges that direct experience in itself cannot provide any information concerning brain states. Therefore, he pointed out that a "leading principle" is necessary for making "inferences from given properties of direct experience to the properties of concomitant physiological processes." This principle is the concept of "psychophysical isomorphism" and it refers to the spatial resemblance of percept and its brain correlate. In accordance with this principle direct experience would allow for the formulation of specific physiological hypotheses. Generally, the organization of the phenomenal field into things distributed in space is regarded as having its isomorphic counterpart in the cortical organization of brain processes. In looking at his desk Köhler has the percepts of a pencil and cigarette, and in his brain there would be two "cortical things" in different locations. When the percepts are farther apart, as may happen when the transverse physical distance of the two objects is increased, there would be a corresponding increase in the separation of the two cortical things. The perception of the shapes as three-dimensional entities on the top of the desk, which is the ground, would have its correlate in shaped three-dimensional cortical things detached from the cortical representation of the surface of the desk. The percept of a square, it is said, would have a "square-like pattern of excitation" as its partner in the brain. In effect, the principle of isomorphism allows for the translation of statements concerning phenomenal facts into statements concerning brain events. Thus the perceived depth of the Necker Cube and its perceived reversibility, stroboscopic motion whether laterally or in depth, the one-sided function of contours, subjective contours, and so on, are presumed to have correspondingly similar counterparts. The principle of translation would also apply to the phenomenal similarity of shapes and the nonidentifiability of a part in the whole. Finally, on the hypothesis that sensory organization is not learned, the organized processes in the brain likewise are not the product of learning.[8]

Koffka's question pertaining to "looks" is transformed into a new question. Why do cerebral processes have the specific properties as dictated by the isomorphic principle? Koffka considered three possible answers and rejected them. First, it may be supposed that their cause lies in the organized properties of external objects. This is incorrect because whatever organization they might possess would be lost in the transmission of reflected light rays to the retina. The order of rays reflected from different points is, of course, preserved in the retinal distribution, but this fact is not especially significant. Bundles of rays do not have contours and even if it were possible to imagine their existence, they do not have a onesided function.

Second, since the rays stimulate the retina it may be supposed that the distribution of retinal excitations and its local organization is the answer. But this is also wrong. For then the tri-dimensionality of a percept, figure-ground reversals, stroboscopic motion, subjective contours, and other perceptual facts could not be explained. There is a more basic reason for rejecting the possibility of local organization. The discussion of "percepts and the geometry of arrangements" is again applicable, the geometry of arrangements now referring to the geometry of retinal excitations. These excitations would have a theoretically large number of possible organizations but the perceived organization is considerably delimited. Moreover a given retinal "contour" would not confer a one-sided function. The excitations "inside" possess no more intrinsic relation to the "contour" than do the excitations "outside." In short, perceived shape as a segregated entity has no counterpart in the retinal distribution. This distribution is to be regarded as a mere "mosaic" or aggregate or excitations. Each excitation, or some circumscribed number of excitations, is independent of any other, and the change of one excitation has no influence on any other. Thus the principle unifying the excitations into one group or another is absent. Koffka resorted to the analogy of a photographic negative to make his point. No physical image or picture is in the negative; there is merely a variation in the density of particles, a density measurable by an instrument. Should a corner of the negative be torn off, there is no change in the density of the particles in either portion; thus the distribution of densities is a mosaic.

Finally, the transmission of retinal impulses to the cortex is considered by Koffka. Since the conduction is along isolated paths and since the distribution of excitations in the "cortical retina" is a mosaic, the same argument repeats itself. Hence this possibility also must be rejected. The gestalt explanation of the organization or "spontaneous articulation" of the molecular processes into the macroscopic processes or cortical things which are the correlates of percepts lies in "field theory." [9]

The general problem and its resolution in terms of field theory may be stated in a preliminary way in reference to stroboscopic motion. Supposing that the intermittent distal stimuli give rise to two cortical processes at different locations, these processes, in accordance with the isomorphic principle, ought to influence each other so that the phenomenal fact of a single moving object would have a brain correlate. The transmission of the influence of one process to the other process is presumed to take place through a field which pervades cortical tissue and includes the two processes. Their interaction would be such that a single psychophysical process would move from one location to the other. If there were no field effect, the facts of phenomenal motion would be inexplicable, since two intermittent but stationary objects ought to be perceived.

Köhler points out that impulses in brain cells are known to be accompanied by direct currents which pervade the neighboring tissue. The field theory proposed by him is based on this fact. He supposes that these currents interact and he further supposes that the interactions are the basis for the formation of an electrochemical field. The nature of this field or "medium" would explain not only the transmission of influence but also other facts of cerebral organization. In modifying one of his examples for the purpose of exposition, we may suppose a small white disk superimposed on a large and uniform gray ground in the frontoparallel plane is the distal stimulus. The areas of retinal distribution of excitations may be divided in two, one corresponding to the disk and the other to the ground. The retinal distribution is inhomogeneous at the common boundary because the level of activity is higher in the inside area than in the outside area. The projection of retinal excitations to the brain gives rise to a similar difference in cerebral activity. As a concomitant of the different levels of cerebral activity, which is thought to be electrochemical in nature, there is a difference in electric potential which has an abrupt drop at the boundary. The presumed potential difference, it is also said, causes electric currents to flow which loop from one area to the other at all points of the common boundary. The density of electric current is greater inside the boundary than outside and is maximum at the boundary. This would account for the formation of a macroscopic figure segregated from the ground, the correlate in direct experience being the perception of a white circle on a gray surround. The explanation of other perceived contours is similar. Thus when a thin black line on a white ground is the distal stimulus, the contour process in the brain corresponding to the line is the region of greatest current density. Furthermore, the interaction of nervous impulses, though adjacent, is as essential to the explanation of perceived contour as it is to the explanation of stroboscopic motion.

If it be supposed that cortical activity is in a steady state when the eyes are closed, this state is momentarily disrupted when the eyes are opened and stimulated by an object. However, a new equilibrium is achieved; the contour which is formed represents the best or simplest resolution of the unbalanced forces that conditions allow. The projection of retinal excitations in the brain is regarded as an important "constraining condition" in the achievement of equilibrium. When the common boundary dividing the two retinal areas is circular, the projected boundary is approximately circular. The electrochemical interactions at the basis of cerebral organization will give rise to the contour process tending to have the most regular form, in this instance a circle. Processes in nature also may lead to a circular shaped figure, as in the case of oil that has been dropped on water and floats on its surface. Initially and momentarily the oil may have a very irregular shape because the cohesive forces between the molecules are then in a state of disequilibrium. Equilibrium is attained when the area of the oil is the smallest possible, a requirement implying that its form be that of a circle. And if we imagine the possibility of placing a square shaped film of oil on water, its shape will become circular for the same reason.

A similar principle, though the events in the brain are electrochemical, is said to be a factor in the formation of cortical contours. However, this principle is apparently contradicted by the fact that we see a square and not a circle when the distal stimulus is a square. Thus the central projection of a retinal boundary constitutes an important fact in the understanding of form perception. However the principle is not abandoned since it is supposed that the cortical square-like contour represents the resolution of the cohesive forces within a circumscribed area which would tend to produce the circular contour, and of the constraining forces of retinal origin which would tend to produce a square contour. The cohesive forces, it is supposed, are not of sufficient strength to overcome the other. This way of approaching the problem is thought to be necessitated and justified by certain perceptual facts. For instance, the after-image produced by a distal square stimulus tends to become circular. The boundary of the retinal after-effect does not change in having glanced away from the stimulus, but its strength as a constraining condition when projected to the brain is weakened. Thus the balance of forces is altered, the forces of cohesion assert themselves in the achievement of the final steady state, and the after-image tends to assume the shape of a circle. However, even when the restraining forces are supposedly of undiminished strength, other perceptual facts suggest that mere projected retinal boundary does not suffice to account for perceived contour. Thus a straight line is perceived as straight, but when in the context of intersecting lines it may look curved. The intersecting lines would determine new cortical forces which in their interaction with the constraining forces produce a contour process corresponding to the actual percept.[10]

Subjective contours. The phenomenal fact of subjective contours suggests that the formation of psychophysical contours does not require an objectively complete figure. Several cerebral organizing factors have been invoked to explain their formation, for instance, the tendency of cerebral processes to complete the best shape most appropriate to given conditions.

Phenomenally, the three angles of the Kanizsa diagram tend toward completion in the form of an equilateral triangle as the simplest and most stable figure. Further, it may be observed that the subjective contours which join the sides of the angles are straight rather than curved or irregular in shape. Other incomplete diagrams provided by Kanizsa give rise to completed curved subjective contours such as an ellipse or circle. Similar effects can be observed in viewing phosphorescent painted slender rods in a dark room. Two parallel rods of equal length, one directly above the other, will give rise to a faintly specked luminous surface between the perceived rods, and faint contours will join their ends so that a complete rectangle is perceived. When one rod is displaced laterally, a parallelogram is perceived with a filled-in surface between the rods. Likewise two rods which are bent in the arcs of a circle, but which do not physically connect, will give rise to the perception of a complete circular surface.

The explanation of such phenomenal facts in terms of cerebral processes would be stated so as to be consistent with the isomorphic principle and field theory.[11]

Satiation. The one-sided function of phenomenal contour is said to be related to the greater density of currents in the brain area shaped by a contour process, relative to the density of currents in an adjacent area outside the contour process. The phenomenal contour which arises in viewing natural objects is usually stable, just as in looking down the street the sky is ordinarily perceived as ground and the buildings as figures. Hence the cortical organization which corresponds to this contour also would be stable. On the other hand, drawings such as Figure 14.1 show that a percept can be unstable (figure-ground reversal), thus there would be a corresponding instability in its brain correlate. Let us suppose, in respect to an unstable percept, that the organization of cerebral processes initially favors a particular contour or figure process. One problem to be explained is the origin of forces or stresses which would upset this equilibrium so that when a new one is achieved, a contour process belongs to the adjacent area. The stresses are said to be the product of cerebral factors rather than of changes in retinal excitations. Köhler introduced the concept of *satiation* for the purpose of explaining their origin.

He points out that physiological investigation of the nineteenth century had shown that when direct currents are made to pass through cells, these cells become increasingly resistant to the flow of current and that the current is deflected to adjacent cells. This discovery, he says, also applies to those direct currents whose inferred existence is presumed to be the basis of vision and which are generated by the activity of brain cells. Thus in applying the concept of satiation to the phenomena of figure-ground reversal he says: "These facts point to the possibility that prolonged occurrence of a figure process in a given area leads to gradual changes in this area which oppose the further existence of the process in the same place; in other words, a figure process seems to have some effect by which it tends more and more to block its own way." The field of a "percept process" is pervaded with "electric currents." The density of current is greatest within the contour process itself, of decreasing magnitude toward the center of the circumscribed area, and also of decreasing magnitude into the adjacent area. Since the strength of satiation is a function of density, those cells whose activity gives rise to the percept process will obstruct the current flow differentially. Considering only a comparison of the inside and adjacent areas, a continued inspection of a diagram will lead to a greater degree of satiation of the active cells inside, relative to the active cells outside. As the correlate of the differential satiation there is a gradual shift in the relative density of current. When a critical point is reached there is a "sudden change" in the percept process, its phenomenal counterpart being a reversed figure-ground relationship. The re-reversal is to be explained in similar terms.

The causal role of satiation is also applicable to stable percepts, but its possible influence is not readily observable in the ordinary circumstances of viewing objects and many diagrams. The conclusions of Köhler and Wallach in their re-interpretation of a discovery by Gibson exemplify this effect. Gibson found that a curved line seems less curved when inspected for a few minutes and that upon its removal and substitution of a straight line in the same place, the new line looks curved in the opposite direction. According to Köhler and Wallach, satiational effects produced by inspection of the curved line are asymmetric in the areas adjacent to the length of the contour process, being greater on the concave side; moreover, the satiational effects are of such a nature that the ends of the contour process undergo a greater displacement away from the satiated areas than does its center. Thus the line appears less curved on continued inspection of it. The contour process corresponding to the straight line is displaced in a similar fashion, hence a line of opposite curvature is perceived. Furthermore, the inspection of a straight line, when considered as the first "object," also produces satiational effects, but these are symmetrically disposed about the contour process and so, in this instance, there is no perceived distortion. Generally the changes in perception of figures as a function of previous perceptions are referred to as "figural aftereffects." [12]

Necker cube and stroboscopic motion. Koffka developed a field theory of "space perception" by contrasting it to Berkeley's theory, and he quoted the *Molyneux Premise* as its basic postulate. At the time of writing (1930) it was generally conceded, he says, that the binocular perception of the third dimension was "innate" and that the spatial perceptions arising from monocular stimulation were acquired. Furthermore, he noted the belief that the binocular spatial perception arising from the observation of three-dimensional objects was regarded as the basis for the acquired monocularly derived depth perceptions of either natural objects or diagrams. For instance, the binocular perception of a cube viewed from different positions would influence the perception of its planar representation so that this representation gives rise to the perception of solidity and also the perceived reversibility in depth. He disagreed with these interpretations, his thesis being that the "laws of organization" sufficed as explanatory principles. His physiological explanation of the binocular perception of relative distance and solidity is too complex, hence only his explanation of monocular depth perceptions of bi-dimensional distal stimuli will be considered. In this regard Koffka exemplified his thesis by an extensive discussion of the Necker Cube, and also of stroboscopic motion. He submitted for consideration a regular hexagon with its diagonals and another version of the Necker Cube, regarding them as retinal projections of the "same wire-edge cube." He noted that although both represented the retinal images of the wire cube, the hexagon tended to be perceived as flat and the other as a three-dimensional figure (Figure 14.12).

In the explanation of these different perceptual effects the "laws of good shape and continuation" are deemed sufficient. In reference to the cortical distribution of excitations or forces which arise from the hexagonally shaped retinal image, the laws favor a bi-dimensional organization which is "perfectly simple and symmetrical." Phenomenally, the "law of continuation" refers to the fact that we perceive three diagonals and not lines broken at the common vertex. To perceive it as a cube, on the other hand, the diagonals indeed would have to be "broken up" and the corresponding cortical representation then would be tri-dimensional. With continued observation of the hexagon we may in fact perceive a cube, and also the "broken lines" at the common vertex. Koffka, however, is concerned with the "first perception" and, in any case, the cube-like percept is unstable. Thus the "law of continuation" tends to favor the more stable perception of a bi-dimensional figure. In reference to the traditional version of the cube, Koffka says "the plane figure is very irregular, without any simple plan, and therefore very hard to see." But if the plane figure were to be seen, several juxtaposed, irregularly shaped closed figures would be perceived, the corresponding cortical counterpart being similar. Such a cerebral plan, however, is not favored by the "forces" of organization. Instead, as the result mainly of the "law of good shape," that tri-dimensional organization is achieved which is the correlate of our actual percept. The cube-like percept has a good shape in the sense that it is bounded by six regular surfaces in a unified and symmetrical pattern. Furthermore, it may be observed that the "law of continuation" could not favor a bi-dimensional organization because the central lines of the figure are

FIGURE 14.12. (Reproduced from Koffka, *Principles of gestalt psychology*, 1935, with permission of the publishers, Harcourt, Brace & World.)

broken. The perceived reversibility of the Necker Cube may be explained in reference to satiational effects.

In dealing with stroboscopic phenomena Koffka first takes up the case of motion perceived in a plane. The physiological explanation of apparent motion involves the translation into cerebral terms of those organizing factors previously discussed phenomenologically, and additional concepts such as "attraction." For instance two cortical processes are more likely to attract each other when they are similar or closer than when dissimilar or more distant. Koffka then proposes to explain the perceived rotation in the third dimension of the angles pointing away from each other (Figure 14.11D) and invokes two other principles of organization: a psychophysical contour tends to retain its shape in moving from one location to another, and a moving process tends to select the shortest path. First the possibility of a horizontal motion in the plane may be considered. For this to happen a continuously deforming contour process would be required. Thus for the left-pointing angle to apparently move and become a right-pointing angle, its vertex would have to gradually turn inside out. Koffka considers this to be an unlikely possibility because too much "energy" would be consumed in the distorting process. Therefore the first principle tends to prevail physiologically. Although the preservation of shape cannot occur in a side motion through the plane, nevertheless there are two possible paths in which the same shape can be retained. The two paths correspond to the perceived rotation of an angle in the plane and to the perceived motion of an angle in the third dimension. The cortical path representing the first motion is said to be longer than that representing the second. In accordance with the second principle, therefore, the cortical path for the perceived motion in depth prevails. Thus we see a single angle moving to and fro in the third dimension in front of the plane. The motion is also subject to satiational influences, for with continued observation the angle is perceived as moving behind the plane. Thus the satiation of a given cortical path makes it a functionally longer one, and the moving cortical process takes the path of an unsatiated region.[13]

Two Criteria for Field Effects

Toward the end of the last century simultaneous color contrast was often explained nonempiristically in terms of local retinal processes and their direct effects in the brain. Those who opposed this explanation at the time, but still accepting a nonempiristic explanation, cited the results of experiments in binocular color contrast. For instance, when a white rectangle superimposed on a large black ground is viewed with crossed eyes, one sees two rectangles; on placing a red filter before the right eye and a gray filter before the left eye, the "white" rectangles appear respectively reddish and greenish. Since the perceived green could not have originated in the local retinal processes of the left eye, it was concluded that interacting physiological processes in the brain were responsible for the color. Thus gestalt psychologists, beginning with Wertheimer, have emphasized interocular perceptual phenomena as constituting an important theoretical reason in favor of field theory. In his early work Wertheimer had considered the possibility of explaining stroboscopic motion nonempiristically in terms of the rise and decay of adjacent retinal processes resulting from the on-off presentation of stimuli; the explanation was rejected because the motion was still perceived when the items of the paired stimuli individually stimulated different eyes. He also gave a simple example of the point he wished to make. When a forefinger is raised and some distant point is fixated, upon alternately opening and closing the eyes the finger is perceived as moving from side to side. Köhler and Emery (1947) cited the results of an experiment in the stereoscopic viewing of two shapes in which they found that a contour was perceived, although no contour was perceived in the monocular viewing of one shape. An illustration of their point is given in Figure 14.13.[14]

The interocular criterion was supplemented by another criterion which is more general since it is independent of the way in which the retinas might be stimulated. According to this other criterion, the transmission of processes along lateral connections in the brain and the effects of the interaction of these processes at a particular locus are selective. For instance, phenomenally the factors of proximity and similarity are determinants of stroboscopic motion and, in accordance with the isomorphic principle, such factors ought to characterize their brain correlates. Let a represent the continuing cortical process produced by the momentary retinal stimulation of the first stimulus, and let b and c represent the cortical processes produced by the two items composing the next stimulus. Only a and b are to be regarded as similar. When a is equidistant from b and c, the transmission of its influence goes to b and interacts with b. However, when the distance from

L

L, R

R

FIGURE 14.13. The parts of the diagram placed in the left and right sides of a stereoscope are denoted by *L* and *R*. Subjects see a "subjective triangle" although in monocular viewing through one side of the stereoscope they do not.

a to *b* is sufficiently increased, the influence of *a* is transmitted to, and interacts with, *c*. By virtue of such selectivity, proximity and similarity are regarded as important factors in the organization of cerebral processes. Some of these arguments are explicit in a passage from Köhler which we quote not only because it is a succinct statement of the issues but also because other relevant arguments are introduced. In 1941 he said:

> Organization in this sense is not yet a generally accepted concept. To many it will appear mysterious until it has been interpreted in terms with which they are more familiar. Actually, no mystery is involved in this concept. To be sure, many details of organization need further elucidation, and the theory of organization is only now beginning to assume a more definite shape. The fundamental idea, however, which we have to use in this connection is simple enough: it is the concept of *interaction*. If under the influence of peripheral stimulation various processes develop in a given sector of the nervous system such events are not likely to remain separate and independent. They are likely to *interact*. Interaction among neural processes will tend to be specific and selective in the same sense as in interaction, say, in chemistry. Not every process will interact indifferently with every other process. As in all physical or chemical interaction, the specific properties of the interacting processes in their relations to one another will play a part in the determination of the result. It appears that in the case of perceptual organization *resemblance* is a condition which greatly favors interaction. Moreover, just as all interaction in physics is favored by shortness of distance so perceptual organization

follows the principal of *proximity*. Obviously, the forces involved in an inter-action are stronger when acting over short distances. This seems to hold in the nervous system as it does in inanimate nature.[15]

The Meaning of "Gestalt"

"The noun 'gestalt'," says Köhler, "has the meaning of a concrete individual and characteristic entity, existing as something detached and *having* a shape or form as one of its attributes." Phenomenolo-gically, a thing is segregated from other things and necessarily pos-sesses the attribute of form, such as its being circular or square-like. Others following the gestalt school of thought have defined "gestalt" as a "structured whole process" or as a "configuration." The attribute of form, which Köhler regarded as "real" and "concrete," also was sup-posed to characterize other sensory fields. At the inception of the *ge-stalt movement* in this country in the 1920s, the critical concept "ge-stalt" was interpreted by many American psychologists as a mystical term reeking with the obscurities of German metaphysics. Thus Lund, in an article of 1929 entitled "The Phantom of the Gestalt," said, "we again feel ourselves in the atmosphere of the Hegelian Universals and the Platonic Forms." This reaction was not without justification since *gestalt* was not (and still is not) clearly defined. Moreover, Koffka in concluding a lecture on "gestalt-theorie" in 1925 said, "It is unitarian, not in reducing every process to the mechanism of neural bonds or as-sociations, but in its attempt to give ultimately an explanation of de-velopment by means of the universal law of Gestalt." However, some aspects of the history of gestalt psychology furnish the meaning of "form," and indicate the sense in which "form" is to be regarded as "real" rather than as a "phantom."

Toward the end of the last century and the beginning of the pres-ent century philosophers and psychologists often drew a distinction between "sensible qualities" and "form-qualities." A melody was re-garded as a "form-quality" and the tones at the basis of the melody were regarded as "sensible qualities" or as "sensory elements." A fea-ture of melody that was particularly emphasized concerned its trans-posability. The key can be changed and we still hear the same melody. This fact was explained in terms of a form-quality which would re-main constant with changes in the sensory elements. Generally it was supposed that the form-quality represented the activity of the "mind." The stimulation of sense furnished the elements and the mind, perhaps by means of "unconscious psychical processes," supplied the non-sensory form-quality. The form-quality could not be a sensory element because we still perceived and recognized a melody as being the same although the constituent elements varied. Thus a melody might consist of six sensory elements or qualities *plus* the seventh element which would be contributed by the mind. Presumably the new element was the constant feature so that despite the variation in the data which the senses presented to the mind, the form-quality was unchanged.

In this same period it was pointed out that perceived spatial forms were also transposable. Suppose that a series of square distal stimuli, varying in size and reflected wave lengths, is placed one at a time in the frontoparallel plane at the same distance from the observer. A series of square-like forms, different in size and color, are perceived. As before, the sensible qualities which were produced by stimulation varied but nevertheless the "squareness," the form-quality contributed by the mind, remained constant. It was generally supposed that the sensible qualities, sensory elements, or sensations were "real." Therefore, by implication the form-quality was not real or genuine, inasmuch as it did not directly arise from sensory stimulation. Gestalt psychology rejected this concept of form, eliminating the special powers attributed to the mind, the unconscious psychic processes, and the sensory elements. Perceived form was regarded as "real" since it was supposed to be the immediate correlate of events in the brain. In the view of gestalt psychology the intercession of any psychic process between brain events and perceived form was superfluous. The problem of transposition was resolved in terms of field theory. For instance, the mosaic of retinal excitations would give rise to an identical psychophysical form process in the brain although the excitations might vary as in the above example of square-like distal stimuli.

Temporal and visual forms as "structured whole processes" or as "unitary configurations," emphasize the exclusion of sensations and superadded elements from their determination. When considered from the standpoint of the isomorphic principle, the psychophysical form process is also a "structured whole." This psychophysical event does not contain those molecular processes which, in previous theories, would have been the basis for sensation or sensible quality.

The "universal law." The "law" which, according to Koffka, asserts that "any configuration will become as perfect as the prevailing conditions permit" is related to the principle that the "whole" may determine the characteristics of the "parts."

The visual forms produced by the Kanizsa diagram may be regarded as two wholes and the perceptual effects of differential brightness produced by adjacent areas of the diagram as parts. From a phenomenological standpoint, the visual forms and the one-sidedness of contour are correlated with the perceptual effects. In accordance with the isomorphic principle such facts have representations in cortical processes. The local and identical processes arising from stimulation of the adjacent areas are so modified by the psychophysical contour process that they give rise to different perceptual effects. When the visual form fades away, there is no concomitant psychophysical form and the two local processes may now give rise to equal brightness effects. The retinal areas which correspond to the spaces between and about the rods in the experiment on phenomenally contoured surfaces in the dark room do not receive any stimulation. The processes aroused in the brain by the actual stimulation of the rods tend toward completion of a psychophysical form so that its concomitant visual form is a rectangle. Inasmuch as the "parts" inside and outside the visual rectangle are different, there would be a corresponding difference in brain processes inside and outside the psychophysical form. Presumably this difference in the brain would be the natural result of the formation of the whole contour process.[16]

Mach's famous "bent card" demonstration is a further illustration. A small white rectangular card is folded down the middle so that the crease, which is vertical, is more distant than the two edges. With continued monocular fixation of some point in the crease, a phenomenal inversion in depth takes place. That is, at first the crease appears to be more distant than the two edges, but after phenomenal inversion it appears closer. Mach also pointed out that when one side of the card receives more light than the other side, no noticeable difference in the illumination is perceived in "unprejudiced observation" before inversion. After the phenomenal inversion takes place, "the light and shade stand out as if painted thereon." Although the difference in the intensity of the retinal excitations corresponding to the two sides remains constant, nevertheless, as the concomitant of two tri-dimensional psychophysical form processes, this intensity difference gives rise to distinct differences in perceived illumination.[17]

The Memory Trace

Today we instantly recognize someone whom we have met some time ago. Evidently the previous encounter has left a record or "trace" in the brain which today is called forth automatically and without effort. According to gestalt psychology, a percept process in the brain taps the trace. There are, however, innumerable traces in the brain; how is it that the percept process selects the right trace? Köhler, who asked this question, said that this happens because the percept process "resembles" the trace. At the time of the first encounter the percept process left behind a trace which resembled it. Since today the present percept process is similar to the past percept process, it arouses the trace corresponding to it. The trace, moreover, generally has the same features of organization as the percept process which produced it. Evidently, the percept process is regarded as an event prior to the tapping of the trace. Such considerations already show why gestalt psychologists exclude the role of empiristic factors as determinants of primitive organization. If the percept process were "unorganized" in the way indicated by James, its trace, supposing a trace to be possible, would also be similarly unorganized. The repetition of the same percept process would arouse the same trace. No matter how frequently this sequence occurs, the organization of the percept process could not take place. If the visual field were not organized in a figure-ground relation, no traces could lead to its organization. Since organization of the visual field must be accepted as a sensory fact, according to gestalt psychology, the role of empiristic factors can only modify one organization into another and "better" organization. In general, the influence of such factors is circumscribed; the modification of one organization into another depends on specific conditions which themselves refer to other basic principles of sensory organization. Under certain conditions, according to Köhler, satiation might lead to a permanent modification of a perception. The influence of satiation would not be mediated through memory traces since the cortical region in which the percept process itself presumably occurs is permanently modified as the result of direct currents passing through it. The effects of satiation are not arbitrary, they depend on specific features of the organization of the percept process in relation to the characteristics of the cortical medium. The modification of the perception, moreover, is independent of the "associations" presupposed by the empirist to explain changes in visual appearance.[18]

The concept of "constancy hypothesis," introduced by Köhler in 1913, is in his opinion the leading and often "hidden assumption" in empiristic theory. The same "local stimulation" of the retina, in accordance with this assumption, would give rise to the same sensation or sensory experience irrespective of other retinal stimulations. In an extended discussion in 1947 Köhler expressed the opinion that "no grounds have ever been given for this radical assumption" and the further opinion, "it seems to be the expression of an *a priori* belief about what ought to be the nature of things, experience to the contrary notwithstanding." Practically all psychologists, he says, reject Helmholtz's explanation of color contrast, believing that contrast is the outcome of the interaction of nervous processes. Yet in having made this concession they fail to realize that a "fundamental principle in the whole field of sensory experience can no longer be held." Köhler continues: "When in the future an experience is found to be at variance with local stimulation, we shall have to consider the possibility that, just as contrast, such an experience depends upon a set of stimuli rather than upon local stimulation alone." He provides several examples pertaining to the spatial characteristics of visual experience, such as shape and size, to illustrate its meaning. Thus *interaction,* as the fundamental gestalt principle characterizing nervous functioning, represents the replacement of the constancy hypothesis not only in the explanation of qualitative experience such as color contrast but also of spatial experience.

Köhler maintained that a special assumption concerning nervous processes was the basis for the continued acceptance of the constancy hypothesis, despite phenomenological evidence to the contrary. According to this assumption, which he calls the "machine theory," processes are conducted along insulated and independent pathways to the brain where, still retaining their independence, they give rise to sensory experience. Since it is generally believed that physiologists have verified this conception of nervous functioning, according to Köhler, the proponent of the constancy hypothesis can justify his position by saying it is consistent with established facts. On the contrary, says he, physiologists have not actually established what the facts are. Moreover, the machine theory not only makes it impossible to account for direct experience but also necessitates an empiristic approach to perception. The machine theory in his view must be rejected and replaced by field theory. Köhler regards Descartes's "mechanical interpretation of organic functions" as the prototype of subsequent neurological theories. Many neurophysiologists have made this point, hence Descartes's theory can be selected for the purpose of exemplifying Köhler's thesis concerning the inadequacies of the "machine theory." [19]

The cerebral image will be considered as a direct function of the retinal image, the pineal gland always being stationary. The filament from a specific retinal element to a point in the inner cavity of the brain and its corresponding pore at the pineal gland will be called a conduction unit. The stimulation of such a unit causes a motion which upon being propagated to the pore, causes the emission of nervous fluid. As the concomitant of this flow, the mind has a sensation. A conduction unit is capable of transmitting a variety of motions which depend on the intensity and quality of the light so that each type of motion produces a nervous flow corresponding to it. All conduction units are anatomically distinct, hence the motions they transmit to the pineal gland are also distinct. Since the pineal gland consists of a mosaic of pores and since the emission of fluid is correlated to sensation, the fluids composing the mosaic are each independent of the other. In the chapter on Descartes it was noted that the cerebral image contains the same defects as exist in the retinal image. For instance, the retinal image has no representation of relative distance; hence there can be no such representation in the cerebral image. The cerebral image, moreover, has other defects such as those that arise from intermittent stimulation of adjacent areas of the retina, as in stroboscopic motion, and the absence of any retinal stimulation corresponding to "subjective contours." An additional feature of Descartes's theory, which was emphasized by Malebranche, states that the memory image resembles the cerebral image. Therefore whatever defects exist in the cerebral image must also exist in the memory image.

This model necessarily implies an empiristic approach in the attempt to understand the phenomena of sensory experience. When neurons, impulses or excitations, and the visual cortex are substituted in this model, we have the main features of the machine theory which

Köhler asserts to be the case in the much later theories of nervous functioning. Furthermore, it may be observed that nineteenth-century theories substituted the analogy of the telegraph and telephone exchange for Descartes's hydraulic analogy. Thus Descartes's conception of the nervous system and its functioning anticipated "connectionism," as exemplified in the theory of Bain, and the law of isolated conduction.

In order to explain the formation of a retinal image, Descartes supposed that an external object by means of pressures exerted by light rays impresses or imprints an image which, although imperfect, resembles the object to some degree. Apparently he presupposed that the retinal image was a coherent entity segregated from those motions of the retina which are to one side or another of the image. Thus just as the external object is segregated from its ground or from other objects in its vicinity, so too is the retinal image. Actually, however, the motions of the retinal image, the motions of an adjacent image, and the motions between the images, constitute a mere mosaic. If it is supposed that a group of motions have a contour, this contour would be as indifferently related to the motions inside the area corresponding to the retinal image as it would be to those motions outside. That is, the retinal contour, if one exists, does not have any one-sided function. Therefore, for this reason alone, there cannot be any resemblance between the retinal image and the object. Thus Descartes, in regarding the image as a segregated entity, took for granted an important fact that called for explanation. However, his notion that the motions in the retina have a contour is false. For those motions, which are presumed to form the contour of an image, are also indifferently related. One motion of the "contour" would have the same geometric relationship to an adjacent motion of the "contour" itself as it would to another motion to one side of the "contour." Since the same consideration applies to the formation of the cerebral image, Descartes's theory cannot account for sensory organization. In effect, the posited retinal and cerebral images do not exist. In substituting impulse or excitation for motion, a similar point can be made for later "connectionistic" theories.

But allowing the possibility of a retinal image for the purpose of examining its implications, another problem arises. When objects approach, recede, or rotate, their retinal images undergo sudden and incessant perspective transformations in form and size. The motion of the head back and forth or from side to side, the motion of the eyes, and the motion of the body toward or away from objects, will produce similar changes in the images. When considered in relation to "sensation" or original perception, the infant's perceptual world would be one of "chaos." But from the standpoint of the perceptions of the adult, his phenomenal spatial world of tri-dimensional things is orderly and stable. The unresolvable problem then arises of how we can account for phenomenal order when the original phenomenal world is chaotic.[20]

Experience Error

The assumption that the "retinal image" is a segregated entity represents the error of attributing characteristics of phenomenal facts to the distribution of retinal excitations. The phenomenal object is a square-like object distinct from its ground, it is then supposed that the distribution has corresponding properties. In having made this error, the theorist supposes that he has explained the characteristics of the percept. In effect, the very fact that should be explained, namely, sensory organization, is presupposed. Köhler who called attention to this error, labeled it the "experience error." He defined it as follows:

> This error occurs when certain characteristics of sensory experience are inadvertently attributed to the mosaic of stimuli. Naturally, the mistake is most frequent in the case of very common sensory facts, in terms of which we tend to think about almost everything. And it is most persistent so long as any problems involved in these facts remain utterly unrecognized. Physiologists and psychologists are inclined to talk about *the* retinal process which corresponds to an object, as though stimulation within the retinal area of the object constituted a segregated unit. And yet these scientists cannot fail to realize that the stimuli form a mosaic of entirely independent local events.

Gestalt psychologists themselves often talk of a "retinal image" or "retinal pattern" but they intend this to be an "abbreviation" only. The same is sometimes true for those having a different theoretical outlook; however, this happened only after gestalt psychologists had emphasized the importance of the "experience error."

Other examples of the experience error. (1) Phenomenally we know that we look at objects involuntarily rather than at the "holes" be-

tween them. This fact has been explained in terms of reflex movements of the eye. Thus it is said that the eye moves so that the retinal
areas which correspond to the distal stimuli are each brought into the
foveal position. However, the retina is also stimulated by the "holes"
between the distal stimuli. Since the proposed explanation ignores the
theoretical problem implied by this fact, it presupposes that the retinal
areas are segregated entities. To facilitate discussion of the next two
examples, the language of "retinal shapes" will be used.

(2) Consider the empiristic explanation of form perception, such as
the V percept of Figure 14.6, in terms of eye-movements. When one retinal shape is in the foveal position, it is supposed that the eye can
move in the right way so as to bring the retinal shapes necessary for
the V percept to the foveal position. However, there is no principle
that would guide the motion of the eye so as to lead to the selection of
the retinal shapes corresponding to the "white" circles rather than the
retinal shapes corresponding to the "black" dots. Unwittingly the
theorist, himself seeing a V, supposes the existence of a corresponding
over-all retinal shape. Also, he supposes that the excursion of the eye is
guided by the similarity of those individual shapes corresponding to
the "white" circles. Thus on the basis of his direct experience the
theorist inadvertently supposes the principle of organization by "similarity," but he attributes this organizing principle to the peripheral
events of the retina and the eye.

(3) When we see two squares as in Figure 14.7, it is natural to suppose that two square-shaped retinal images correspond to them and to
ignore the "theoretical" possibilities of other retinal shapes in the
proximal distribution.[21]

Empiristic Theory and Evidence

Gestalt psychologists have employed many arguments to contest the
evidence and its interpretation, which have been held to favor empiristic theory. One argument accepts a stated explanation of some perception as an acquired perception. As the next step of the argument, it is
pointed out that when the distal stimulus is varied the explanation requires an increasing number of supplementary hypotheses to account
for the original evidence. Finally, it is concluded that the explanation
is either incorrect or implausible. We may consider the supposition
that tri-dimensional perceptions of actual cubes may account for the

tri-dimensional perception of the Necker Cube. This hypothesis, however, required another and additional hypothesis for the purpose of explaining perceived reversibility. For instance, it was said that we see actual cubes either from below or from above, and that this experience transfers to the viewing of the diagram so that the perceived reversibility is accounted for. However, when we look at Figure 14.7, depth and reversibility are perceived although the diagonals of the standard Necker Cube are missing. It may now be supposed that the two squares are sufficiently similar to the traditional diagram of the cube so as to arouse those same processes which are responsible for the perceived depth effects of the latter. But when a circle is substituted for a square the same depth effects are perceived, and this is still true for a broad range of substitutions. In such instances, therefore, there is no similarity to the traditional diagram. The original explanation is to be abandoned or modified in the sense that other actual objects in the environment must be found, the perceptions of which would then explain those obtained from the substitute diagrams.

Familiarity with the letter E is said to be the basis for the E percept of Figure 14.2. Thus the three zig-zag lines to the left of the vertical in this diagram would be sufficiently similar to parts of the letter so that they would elicit the memory trace of the letter. However, supplementary hypotheses were invoked in order to explain the subjective contours and the apparent enhancement of brightness. First, a raised or block form of the letter was substituted for the letter characterizing our ordinary reading experience. Second, illumination was regarded as coming from a light source placed to the left of an object or above it. According to this hypothesis, shadows are cast either to the right or below the corresponding and adjacent illuminated portions of perceived raised objects. Through experience we have learned to associate the light-shadow gradient to the placement of the light source. This association exerts its influence on a present perception either through an "assumption," which may be unconscious, or by mediation of traces in the brain. The zig-zag lines, which represent the "shadows," elicit the memory trace of the block form. Thus we have the E percept, a perception which is consistent with the hypothesis pertaining to the placement of the light source. However, since the same zig-zag lines give rise to the mirror image of E, further supplementary hypotheses become necessary. For instance, a common object in the environment must be sought which would leave another trace to be elicited by the same lines. But should this be the case, the light source would be to the right since the lines would represent shadows. Hence some correction in the hypothesis concerning the typical light-shadow gradient becomes necessary. Whatever the nature of its correction, it must be compatible with the fact that, in respect to all the lines of the diagram, an E and its mirror image may be simultaneously perceived. Therefore, the perceiver would have to make two contrary assumptions as to the placement of the light at the same time. The trace hypothesis also would require some modification because the same three zig-zag lines give rise to alternating percepts. Although mutual incompatibility of two traces might be invoked as a factor, the simultaneity of different percepts would seem to require some other hypothesis. Furthermore, we may alter the lines by changing the angles, making them curved, and also changing their orientation. Since the perceptions vary in these circumstances, it is necessary to find objects in the environment which may account for them.

Since similar considerations as in the above apply to the F and ꓤ percepts, and the percept of the Kanizsa diagram, it may possibly be the case that phenomenally contoured surfaces are not explainable by the light-shadow gradient hypothesis. Of course, the empiristic explanations may still be correct despite the addition of further hypotheses. But when we observe that subjective contours are instances of general phenomena which are not restricted to the specific characteristics of distal stimuli, it is plausible to suppose that their explanations involve general principles. The same point can be made for the depth effects of diagrams such as the Necker Cube and its variations. Moreover, the possibility of general principles is strengthened when it is realized that the constancy hypothesis is responsible for the empiristic explanation and its complications. Inasmuch as this assumption was inadequate in the explanation of other perceptual phenomena and is the "hidden assumption" that may deter the search for principles, it can be set aside.[22]

Evidence from anthropology. What often is regarded as "evidence" actually is not evidence in its usual meaning. Thus no data were ever cited to show that the Necker Cube is at first seen flat and later three-dimensionally or to show the causal influence of "knowledge" of the light-shadow gradient in perception. By the very nature of the case it may be difficult to obtain the necessary data since it can be said, perhaps with some justification, that the perceptual learning takes place so early in the life of the child that experiments to demonstrate the role of empiristic factors cannot be undertaken. However correct this position may be, actual evidence does not exist. Therefore, what may be regarded as "evidence" ought to be bracketed until confirmed by investigation. Furthermore, the "evidence" is contingent on the acceptance of a particular theoretical orientation. If this orientation is rejected, the "evidence" need no longer be accepted. In any case, "evidence" of this sort drawn from the field of anthropology has been interpreted as demonstrating the pervasive influence of culture as a determinant of sensory organization. This evidence will be discussed for the purpose of illustrating additional arguments of gestalt psychologists in the evaluation of the empiristic approach. A general principle relevant in the interpretation of this evidence should first be considered.

In previous discussion of "memory trace" it was noted that a percept process is the antecedent condition for trace selection and for recognition. There is another factor of importance, namely, that we can often name or label that which we recognize. Sometimes, however, we may have difficulty in producing the name although we recognize the person we see or the melody we hear. Such facts suggest that trace arousal is an essential but not sufficient condition for the process at the basis of naming. When a person with a particular color defect looks at a chart with an arrangement of various hues he fails to say that he sees the number two. The percept process corresponding to the seeing of the form does not occur in his brain by virtue of his color defect. Since there cannot be any selection of a trace, he does not report "two." For a person with normal vision, on the other hand, the prior existence of the percept process determines the course of events ultimately leading to the "two" label. A similar interpretation can be made of the perception of the triangle and the report of it as in the Kanizsa diagram and other facts that have been discussed. One conclusion that can be drawn is that the naming process cannot influence the percept process. Names or labels do, in fact, have to be learned, but this learning is contingent on the percept process. In ordinary language, without referring to processes and traces in the brain, the issue may be stated as follows. In order to report the seeing of a "triangle" the triangle first must be seen.

Some of the anthropological evidence has been interpreted in the context of the importance of cultural variation in language on seeing.

Sapir succinctly expressed this point of view when he said, "we see and hear and otherwise experience very largely as we do because the language habits of our community predispose certain choices of interpretation." The names and labels of things vary from culture to culture and consequently the members of different cultures see the world differently. What is contended is not that the name for the very same percept varies, but rather that the *looks* of things are changed.

To illustrate the linguistic hypothesis, an example concerning a cluster of seven stars in *Ursa Major* is sometimes advanced: we see a "dipper," whereas members of other cultures see such shapes as a "bear," "plough," "seven plowing oxen," and so on. The difference in label presumably alters the percept so as to conform with the label or the shape suggested by it. However, this supposed change in percept was a mere assertion since no evidence or justifying explanation was advanced. According to the *Oxford English Dictionary*, this cluster is called the "Big Dipper" in this country and in England the "Big Bear," "Plough," and "Charles's Wain" (wain means wagon). Surely the perceptions of the English do not vary according to the label nor are they different from the perceptions of Americans. It is difficult even to understand from a theoretical standpoint how the phenomenal arrangement of seven stars might be influenced by the "bear" label. This label is derived from Greek mythology wherein Callisto was transformed into a bear and transferred to the heavens. Obviously the Greeks perceived the seven stars in a specific arrangement segregated from neighboring stars in order to attach a particular name to the grouping in the construction of the legend. Their percept was the same as that of today. They called it the "big bear" while other cultures named it "plough," "seven plowing oxen," and so on. Some cultures must exist in which the cluster of seven stars is not named, yet their members undoubtedly perceive the same arrangement of stars as do persons in cultures which have labeled it.

Another and more widely discussed example of the linguistic hypothesis concerns the influence of the verbal classification of colors on the perception of color. Some primitive cultures have a single color name for designating colors for which we use different names. On the basis of color designations the conclusion was drawn that primitives do not discriminate or see differences in colors as we do. For instance, in reference to the natives of New Guinea it was said, "Their color classifications are so different that they saw yellow, olive-green, blue-green, gray and lavender as variations of one color." The members of another culture, it was said, do not see blue and green as distinct colors because they have the same color name for both. Apparently the members of such groups are to be regarded as functionally color-blind; if they had been given the opportunity to look at a color chart they would not see the form "two" as we would. The explanation that might account for this "evidence" is vague; the possibility that sensory mechanisms are involved in color vision, although acknowledged in other contexts, is not included as a factor in the color perception of natives who are adults. An explanation must presuppose that the children at first see colors distinctly because they have not yet acquired color names. A child's seeing of two colors which we would describe as yellow and green can be denoted by Y and G and their common name by L. The learning of names and their connections to "things" and "colors" requires repetitions. During such trials the child learns to attach L to Y end also to G. An explanation must further presuppose that L so affects Y and G that some other and possibly intermediate color is perceived. This implies that Y and G are unnoticed sensations. For if this were not the case, the adult native would be conscious of the original colors, which would be immediately followed by the intermediate color. Furthermore, since the color different from Y or G was not a term in the formation of the connections, it is not apparent how this color could have been linked to Y or G.

Actually this "evidence" represents the anthropologist's interpretation based on his knowledge of color names in a particular culture and his point of view that cultural influences are so pervasive that they affect concepts, values, and also sensory perceptions. The simpler way of viewing the problem is that primitives attach different labels to colors although they see the same colors as we do. The fact that they may have one color name for different colors should not cause any theoretical difficulty. In our culture individuals may be referred to by a class name such as "actor" although we see them as being different from one another in complexion, stature, and weight. When the evidence is considered from the standpoint of processes in the brain, its explanation is impossible. The sensory processes corresponding to Y and G are prior to the processes of recognizing and labeling. Thus there is no way in which the labeling process could affect the sensory process.

Other evidence relates to the influence of "customs" on perception. For instance, the resemblance between father and son is acknowledged by natives of the Trobriand Islands but the resemblance between two brothers is denied, it being considered a grave breach of custom to hint at any fraternal similarity. The anthropologist who described this custom had observed a "striking resemblance" between two brothers and when he called the attention of the natives to this fact "they refused to admit it." This example has been interpreted to mean that the natives as a result of their custom did not *see* any resemblance between the two brothers. This interpretation, however, has the same difficulties as in the above two examples. Further, it is difficult to believe that they would fail to see any resemblance in cases of identical twins. Thus it is more plausible to suppose that they did see a resemblance but refused to admit it publicly. Similar facts are true in other and presumably more advanced cultures. For instance, the twice-married husband usually does not tell his new wife that she bears a striking resemblance to his former wife although this resemblance is evident to him and others, since she would regard the comparison as offensive.[23]

EVIDENCE FOR GESTALT THEORY

One kind of evidence for "field theory" was generated by framing predictions based on the principles of organization in contrast to predictions based on the assumption of the constancy hypothesis of "machine theory." It is in this vein that the extensive experimental investigations of those principles in respect to stroboscopic motion and figural after-effects with human subjects are to be understood. Their successful results, not having been predicted by adherents of the "machine theory," led to a considerable broadening of perceptual investigation. Since the two theories were regarded as mutually exclusive, the verification of predictions were interpreted as important evidence for field theory.

Early in the history of the gestalt movement (1915) Köhler investigated animal perceptions for the purpose of testing the two theories; the constancies of brightness and size, and transposition were the main problems. He interpreted the results of his experiments both as proof of field theory and as a demonstration of its generality. Subsequently, others confirmed the results by extending the range of animal species and problems. As further evidence of field theory, Köhler and his colleagues (1949 and later) obtained results which seemed to indicate that "direct currents" are correlates of the cortical patterns at the basis of perception. We shall only discuss the evidence obtained from animal experiments.[24]

Animal Experiments

Köhler chose animals as subjects for his experiments because of the prevailing assumption that "judgment" and "reasoning" were the basis for the acquisitions of the constancies of brightness and size. On the premise that such intellectual processes were minimal in chickens and young apes, he tested them and concluded that such percepts were not learned. However, the results were challenged on the grounds that his subjects were too old at the time of test. In subsequent investigation young apes were no longer regarded as suitable subjects because by the time an experiment became feasible, it could always be argued that they had gained the necessary experience so that what might be regarded as an "innate" perception was in fact acquired. Thus there was a shift to animals lower down in the evolutionary scale. In 1935 Koffka reported a later experiment (Götz) which he regarded as decisive. Götz, having trained three-month-old chicks to select the larger of two grains equidistant from them, showed that they continued to do so even when the larger grain was placed at such a distance that the area of its retinal image was 1/30 that of the smaller but closer grain. Said Koffka, "Chicks must be geniuses if they can discover in the first three months of their lives that something that looks small is really bigger. Since we do not believe that they are endowed with such miraculous gifts we must conclude that they select the bigger because it looks bigger, even when, within wide but definite limits, its retinal image is smaller." This conclusion was later criticized on the grounds that he minimized the intellectual abilities of chicks. It was considered possible that the chicks of three months had acquired sufficient ability to succeed in the task assigned to them.

Lashley and Russell (1934) in their investigation of distance perception contributed evidence which supported gestalt theory. They kept rats in darkness from birth until the time of test at the age of about 100 days, and they found that the rats, after a short period of training in light, successfully jumped from one platform to another for food even though the distance was varied randomly from trial to trial. Their performance did not much differ from rats raised under normal conditions. They conclude, "the visual perception of distance and gradation of force in jumping to compensate for distance are not acquired by learning, but are the product of some innately organized neural mechanism." Lashley (1938) undertook a more extensive investigation of the rat's ability to respond to a variety of stimuli, and he said that many of the gestalt principles of organization were confirmed. However, in this experiment the rats had not been dark-reared. The methodology and interpretations of both experiments were later challenged.

For the purpose of resolving some of the questions that had been raised in reference to Lashley's work and to the gestalt interpretation of animal evidence, I undertook a series of experiments with ducklings. My assumption was that the "closer to a birth a perceptual datum is manifested the more likely that autochthonous factors are the principal causal agents."

The eggs of ducklings were kept in a dark incubator and when they hatched, the ducklings remained in darkness until the time of tests at about the age of fifteen hours; an age when they would be ready to respond to food as an incentive. When not in an experimental situation they were again returned to darkness. The objects of the experiments were simultaneously presented and their positions were varied from trial to trial. A duckling first had to learn to displace an object for food, such trials being included in the evaluation of its performance. The mean number of trials will be indicated in order to give some idea of the rapidity of learning to select an object for food.

Brightness constancy. The relevant stimuli were medium and light-gray blocks of the same size. In a preliminary task the animal learned to consistently select the medium gray ($M+$) and avoid the light gray (L) when both are evenly illuminated. In the next and critical phase another and fixed light source was introduced to one side which provided extra illumination to the object placed on that side. The intensity of the light was such that $M+$ reflected back more light than did the L, which was in relative shadow. This fact was determined photometrically or by the use of a reduction screen. The screen has two apertures so spaced that when positioned before the two objects, the experimenter can see parts of them. When the light intensity is optimal he sees the portion of $M+$ as considerably brighter than that of L. Without the screen, however, $M+$ is seen as darker than the other, inasmuch as the additional light source provides extra illumination both to the object and its background. The four ducklings in this experiment learned to select $M+$ within three days of hatching (mean, 65 trials). Moreover, after mastery of the selection of $M+$ in the first phase of the experiment they generally required no further learning in the selection of the correct object in the critical trials entailing one-sided lighting (mean for critical phase, 5 trials). One duckling completed both phases of the experiment before the age of sixteen hours. Since the animals did not have the opportunity to acquire any experience of the factor of uneven illumination, the immediate transposition of successful response from the preliminary phase to the critical trials could not have been the product of learning. Therefore, brightness constancy evidently is a primitive "sensory fact" for these animals.

Form. Geometric figures of equal area pasted on identical size blocks were the objects for an experiment with another group of four ducklings. The triangle was the positive object when contrasted to the square, diamond, and parallelograms, the trapezoid being omitted for these trials (Figure 14.14). All learned to select the triangle within three days of hatching (mean, 55 trials), one duckling achieving success after 20 trials in the one hour it had been in the experimental situation. Since the number of trials for success was relatively small, the animals obviously perceived a difference between the triangle and the other forms. This conclusion is strengthened by the fact that the trials preceding success comprised learning the displacement of the triangle, becoming adapted to the situation, and associating the triangle with food. Moreover, the results suggest that the animal responded to the triangle as a unitary figure. The altitudes of the four negative forms clearly could not have been the basis for successful response. Moreover, the possible part perception of an angle of the triangle could not have been critical because the acute angles of the triangle and the parallelograms were equal. It is possible that the animal may have perceived the two base angles and the included side as a unit, thus distinguishing it from the others. But when the trapezoid was substituted for the

FIGURE 14.14

square and food placed under it instead of the triangle, the ducklings persisted in their selection of the triangle. Since in this instance the sub-units were the same, it seems probable that the triangle was perceived as a whole. There is a further result of interest. When the duckling left the cage and proceeded to the tray on which the five blocks had been placed with spatial separations among them, it always directed its strike to an object and never to the space between the blocks. Apparently, the blocks themselves were "things" to the duckling irrespective of its correct choice of the triangle or incorrect choice of another form.

Size constancy. In an earlier experiment size constancy was demonstrated in one duckling at the age of six days and in another at the age of twelve days. Not knowing the perceptual capabilities of ducklings at that time, I obtained them at the age of two or three days; thus they had been exposed to the visual stimulation of objects before participation in an experiment. Moreover, the training in size constancy had been preceded by an experiment on brightness constancy for the first duckling and for the other, extensive training in the selection of a wide variety of triangular forms. Although probably not decisive for these reasons, nevertheless the experiments indicate the range of complex achievements of which these animals are capable at a time when the supposed intellectual processes have not yet expressed themselves.[25]

Interpretation of Animal Experiments

The significance of the results of my experiments and the results of other animal experiments will be interpreted mainly from the standpoint of the arguments Köhler advanced in his own investigation of animals. According to him, empiristic theory presupposes that the same local stimulation gives rise to the same "sensation." In a training procedure the fact of the uniformity of sensation makes it possible for this hypothesis, under prescribed conditions, to explain the formation of an association between sensation and the response of approach or avoidance. Thus in the preliminary phase of the brightness constancy problem the animal learns to select $M+$ and to avoid L. In the critical trials this hypothesis can explain the animal's choice of $M+$ when away from the light because it would arouse the same sensation. The problem arises when $M+$ is placed on the side with the extra illumination because the local stimulation has changed, thus giving rise to a distinctly different sensation. The change in sensation was conceded in the empiristic explanation because a compensation for the level of illumination through some acquired judgment was postulated in order to account for the continued correct selection of the object. Supposing this to be the case, $M+$ always would arouse two different sensations which correspond to its placement toward or away from the light. In having learned to compare these sensations with those arising from the different intensity levels of the backgrounds of the distal stimuli, the correct choice of $M+$ irrespective of position might be explained. These comparisons would be unconscious because in human consciousness there is no trace of their existence.

The terms "sensation" and "consciousness" are not essential to the explanation. Thus the sensory process in the brain corresponding to $M+$ in the preliminary phase would instigate, by means of acquired connections, the conduction of impulses along those neurons which control selective responding. However, this connection would not be available in the critical phase because $M+$ gives rise to another and distinct sensory process. Therefore, the acquisition of other connections must be supposed in order to account for the correct responses in these trials. Since, in fact, the animal directly transposed its response from the preliminary to the critical phase, both the psychological and physiological explanations are incorrect.

In Köhler's view *interaction* is the necessary concept for understanding the animal's performance. The local stimulation from $M+$ in the preliminary phase is accompanied by local stimulation from its background. The sensory effects in the brain to which the local stimulations give rise interact and the product of the interaction, which is an organized process, is the antecedent of the animal's ability to respond to the stimulus. The local stimulation produced by $M+$, to be sure, is different when this stimulus receives extra illumination, but so also is the local stimulation produced by its background. Their sensory effects are different from those in the previous instance, nevertheless the interaction is such that the resulting organized process is similar to the previous organized process. And this would explain why the animal is able to transpose its response. Says Köhler in 1947 in the modification of a well known formula, "The right psychological formula is therefore: *pattern of stimulation—organization—response to the products of organization.*"

There is still another side to the problem, namely, that of "looks" on the human level. We perceive an object to be "gray" despite a wide variation in the over-all level of illumination. The fact that $M+$ looks much brighter than L when both are viewed with a reduction screen is of no importance, since the local stimulation from the ground is common to the different local stimulations from the apertures. The fact of "looks" is not explained in the physiological approach here described, since this approach is concerned with relationship of stimulus to response. On the other hand, the "organized process" in the brain is the basis not only of the animal's response but also of "looks" on the human level.[26]

Finally, we may again consider the relevance of animal data in the understanding of human vision. Human infants are born relatively immature and by the time they are old enough to be the subjects for experiments dealing with complex perceptual phenomena, maturational processes and the possible effects of learning are so confounded that no decisive answer in respect to causation of percepts may be possible. Hence experiments with the young of those animals born in a relatively mature state afford the means for eliminating the variable of postnatal maturation and the confounding effects of experience. The fact that the optics of image formation are the same across species and the fact of similarity in the structure and functioning of the nervous system suggest the reasonableness of generalizing from lower to higher forms.

Furthermore, in their experiments physiologists generally suppose that the validity of hypotheses concerning nervous functioning is not restricted with respect to species. For instance, interaction effects obtained in the eye of the horse-shoe crab are presumed to provide information on interaction effects in the more complex human visual system. Arguments of this sort, however, often do not seem to be binding since chicks and human infants obviously are different. Moreover, an argument derived from evolution may be regarded as decisive against generalization. The nervous system of man might be more "plastic" than the nervous system of a lower form such as that of a bird, which might be characterized as "rigid." Man is the product of a long evolutionary history, thus a nervous system might have evolved with different basic properties. The human brain has a cortex, part of which is important for vision, whereas the bird's brain does not. Avian vision may be correlated with sub-cortical structures which are fixed and not amenable to the influence of learning. Human vision, on the other hand, may involve other parts of the cortex which register the effects of experience, thus influencing the final outcome of processes originating in the visual cortex. Köhler, although familiar with the evolutionary argument, nevertheless refers to animal data in stating that "sensory organization appears as a primary fact which arises from the elementary dynamics of the nervous system." [27]

Köhler and other animal experimenters such as Lashley have noted that their own percepts share many important similarities with those of their subjects. The experimenter draws the figures or prepares the objects which are to be the visual "stimuli" for testing animal vision. These stimuli represent the properties of his own phenomenal organization. When preparing figures such as triangles and squares, and so on, for a visual discrimination experiment, he draws them with India ink on white paper without hesitation. If the thought of using white chalk occurred to him, he would dismiss it because the figures then would not be easily discriminable from the ground. That is, he prepares them in such a way that their effects in his nervous system would give rise to phenomenally segregated wholes. Similarly when drawing two straight lines for an experiment in length discrimination, he makes sure that they look discriminably different to him. In testing a properly chosen animal he discovers that these same stimuli give rise to a phenomenal organization similar to his own insofar as he can judge on the basis of the response he observes. Should he rank stimuli in order of difficulty from his phenomenal standpoint, he would find that the order is similar in the animal. If animal percepts were fundamentally different from human percepts, he would not even know what stimuli to prepare. For instance, to find out whether animals are subject to "illusions," such as the horizontal-vertical illusion, he himself must be subject to them, for otherwise he would not conceive of the possibility of such a test. Finally, the constancies of brightness and size are similar in animals and humans. Thus the human eye is used as an instrument, as it were, to calibrate the relative intensities of illumination in an experiment on brightness constancy.

The gist of the argument pertaining to the similarity of animal and human percepts seems to be the following. The organization of the physiological processes in the brain and the "laws" which characterize them are similar. Furthermore, the demonstration of the innateness of those animal percepts which are similar to human percepts implies that these human percepts are innate, inasmuch as the causes in the brain are similar. In short, the verification of field theory at a lower level implies that the same theory is valid at a higher level, notwithstanding the fact that different brain centers are the basis for vision.

On the other hand, it may be said that however similar the organization of cerebral processes may be, organization in humans could represent the product of learning factors, although this is not the case in lower forms. Field theory may indeed characterize the nervous functioning of lower forms, and machine theory that of higher forms. However, should this be the case, birds would have to be placed above man in the evolutionary scale, inasmuch as physiological interaction is usually regarded as an indication of higher nervous functioning. Furthermore, a discontinuity in the evolution of nervous systems and the principles governing their functioning would be implied.[28]

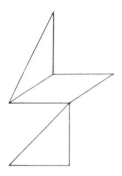

15 CONNECTIONISM: HULL AND HEBB

Now, gentlemen, we shall pass from peaceful affairs, if we may say so, to matters of war, to Mr. Köhler. We are at war with him.
Pavlov, 1935

The idea that one has to learn to see a triangle must sound extremely improbable. Hebb, 1949

An important feature of the behavioristic approach to perception which was developed by the founders of behaviorism, Watson and Pavlov, and its principal exponent in this country, Hull, is the connectionistic view of the nervous system. Further, they adopted the "telephone metaphor," or some variant, to describe the nervous system and its functioning. In their theories "stimulus" and "response" and the connections formed between them in the nervous system are the basis for explaining perception (and also behavior). Still another important feature is that perception is defined in relation to "response" or the "motor activity" in reaching for and manipulating objects rather than in relation to "direct experience."

Although Watson was most influential in the development of behaviorism in this country we shall omit discussion of him. Subsequent behaviorists regarded his expositions as too "crude," thus causing behaviorism to be vulnerable to criticism and even "ridicule." In any case he didn't say much about perception and when he did, traditional empiristic formulation was followed. Pavlov also treated the topic of perception cursorily but what he said is more interesting. By way of illustrating the possibility of the objective investigation of sensory functioning so as to exclude any reference to the causal role of psychic factors, Pavlov, in 1927, said:

> Are not Helmholtz's famous "unconscious conclusions"—in his *Physiological Optics*—in reality conditioned reflexes? We may take as an example the case of a drawing imitating the visual character of a relief. In actual experience, of course, the tactile and muscular stimuli proceeding from a relief represent the initial and fundamental stimuli: the visual stimuli provided by its areas of light and shade form the signalling conditioned stimuli, which only subsequently obtain a vital significance by being constantly reinforced by the tactile and muscular stimuli.[1]

Although this quotation was not explained, it apparently supposed an original bi-dimensional visual field. Presumably the connections established between the visual stimuli proceeding from actual three-dimensional objects and the "fundamental stimuli" not only determine the tri-dimensional perception of such objects but also the perceived relief of a drawing. The visual stimuli of the drawing, being similar to those of the actual object represented, would elicit the same tactile and muscular stimuli. Since the connections referred to paths between cortical cells, Helmholtz's concept of "unconscious conclusions," suggesting the possible causal role of psychic activity, was not necessary. Pavlov earlier had made a similar point in a discussion of size perception in 1908, and again in 1934 in opposition to gestalt theory.

The "war" with Köhler pertained to his criticism of the basic conceptions of the theory of conditioned reflexes such as stimulus and response and the specificity of neural connection. Pavlov argued that the physiological mechanisms he proposed were sufficient to explain those facts presumably requiring gestalt formulations, "We clearly see that due to association a system, an organization, or in Köhler's terminology, a gestalt, arises. Consequently, it is the associations which form the gestalt and not the gestalt which forms the associations." The "phenomena of the subjective world" could be decomposed or analyzed into smaller units and thus were not necessarily the unanalyzable wholes as Köhler had contended. In asking "What is perception?" Pavlov said:

> Some fifty or sixty years ago when I was studying in the seminary, and when there was not even a sign of the gestaltists, I learned from the same old professors and psychologists all about perception and what distinguished it from sensation, which is a more elementary process. The course of psychology at the seminary taught us that sensation is a kind of purer, so to speak, physiological stimulation, produced by a certain external agent on the sense organs; perception, however, is that which arises in the brain, when this stimulation is not single, but connected with other stimulations and old traces. It is this that enables us to get an idea of an external object. Such is perception. The final result of internal elaboration constitutes its very essence.[2]

He goes on to say that a half-century before the inception of gestalt psychology Helmholtz had accurately explained the facts physiologically and concludes, "Perception, if considered profoundly, is simply a conditioned reflex; however, since Helmholtz knew nothing of conditioned reflexes he called them unconscious conclusions."

It would appear that Pavlov did not appreciate the significance of gestalt doctrine. First, sensation and perception are used in the double meaning of referring to phenomenal facts and also to physical events in the brain. Second, a percept is not phenomenally analyzable into elementary sensations. In his example of the perceived relief of a drawing, there is no awareness of a sensation either of flatness or of muscular movement. He suggested, of course, that the visual and fundamental stimuli, being integrated or elaborated in the brain, may have the perceived relief as the immediate psychic correlate. This being the case he might then have accepted the gestalt argument pertaining to its phenomenal unanalyzability. However, this possibility of re-interpretation would have been inconsistent with the theory of conditioned reflexes. When a dog is taught the habit of salivating to a buzzer, its response is directly visible to the experimenter or indirectly apparent by means of some recording device. The connection between auditory stimuli and the salivary response is presumed to function with machine-like regularity so that whenever the buzzer is sounded, the dog salivates, other conditions being equal. And in the case of perceived relief, the muscular response ought to be visible to the experimenter or, more importantly, there ought to be some subjective awareness of it. Perhaps the connectionistic view of the nervous system was unduly restrictive. For instance, in reference to the telephone metaphor: electrical impulses arrive at some point in the switchboard or exchange; a connection is closed between this point and another point; the impulses are shunted along and pass through a wire to the destination where they cause vibrations in the diaphragm of the receiving phone. Apparently a muscular response of some sort should be elicited because it is part of the closed input-output neural circuit.[3]

Hull recognized the difficulties in the Watsonian and Pavlovian approaches, especially those pointed out by gestalt psychologists, and he proposed to correct them.

HULL

In the *Principles of Behavior* (1943) Hull adopted an approach similar to Euclidean geometry for the purpose of deducing the laws of habit formation. He set forth a series of "postulates" often in the form of equations and derived a number of "laws," which he then used as the basis for quantitative empirical investigation. Some of the motives which account for the unique features of the *Principles,* almost twenty years in the writing, are described in Hull's posthumously published "idea books." In an "idea book" of 1926 he said, "It has struck me many times of late that the human organism is one of the most extraordinary machines—and yet a machine. And it has struck me more than once that so far as the thinking processes go, a machine could be built which would do every essential thing that the body does (except growth) so far as concerns thinking, etc." And he also conceived of the possibility of constructing a machine that would exhibit the characteristics of conditioned reflexes. He expressed the hope that he might make a "major contribution to the theory of knowledge," undertook the study of such philosophers as Locke, Berkeley, Hume, and Kant, and he observed that "all have started from introspective experience as the more primary and more basic, and attempted to derive a system with which to explain action and human nature as well." Including gestalt psychologists in this same category of philosophers he continued,

The moral of the whole thing is that innumerable attempts to derive a satisfactory (i.e. scientific) theory of knowledge and of thought and reason from conscious experience as such have failed. In the place of this I propose to develop a system which starts from exactly the opposite end. I shall invert the whole historical system. I shall start with action—habit —and proceed to deduce all the rest, including conscious experience, from action, i.e., habit.[4]

His "strategy," is to set aside conscious experience until after a thorough investigation of the "numerous action mechanisms" and discovery of basic principles; this having been done, the nature of perception and other "phenomena of conscious experience" can be deduced.

When he was at the University of Wisconsin in 1926 Hull arranged a visiting professorship for Koffka, having been previously unsuccessful in securing a fellowship to study with him in Germany. Koffka, says Hull, spent a good deal of lecture time in Wisconsin attacking Watsonian behaviorism, then at its peak in this country. While generally agreeing with him, Hull, rather than being convinced of the correctness of gestalt doctrine, was converted to "neo-behaviorism." Hull's meeting with Koffka was personally significant. Having been worried that his age was a handicap to achieving a major contribution, and having noted the relatively late age of some philosophers at the time of their first important contribution with some encouragement, Hull in 1930 said, "In some ways I really have an advantage over these men in that I started on these meditations at least six years ago, i.e., when I was 40. More especially I was roused to violent activity by contact with Koffka, at Madison during the year 1926–1927, when I was 42." Apparently Koffka had so crystallized the difficulties of behaviorism that Hull believed they could be resolved. He thought the postulational approach might afford the possibility of deducing conscious experience, and the laws of behavior and the hypothesis of "afferent neural interaction" would remedy the defect inherent in Watson's connectionism. Thus the important aspects of the *Principles* and the posthumous *Behavior System* (1952) evolved as the "neo-behavioristic" answer to gestalt theory.[5]

AFFERENT NEURAL INTERACTION (1943)

The neural interaction hypothesis is the second postulate in the *Principles*. When an objective source of "stimulus energy" (S) stimulates a sensory surface, an "afferent neural impulse (s) is generated and transmitted to the brain. When S is removed the impulse s continues its activity in the brain for "some seconds" though gradually decaying until it ceases. We may consider two sources of energy, S_1 and S_2, to be simultaneously stimulating a sensory surface. According to the hypothesis their neural impulses "interact with each other in such a way as to change each into something partially different." The modified impulses are indicated as $\breve{s}_1$ and $\breve{s}_2$. If the two sources act independently of one another, at an interval exceeding five seconds, their respective impulses cannot interact. The important point to note in the following discussion of interaction is that $\breve{s}_1$ although somewhat different from s_1 nevertheless "partly resembles" it. The degree of resemblance is defined by Hull in reference to the variation in magnitude of a conditioned response as an inverse function of quantitative differences in stimuli, these stimuli being on the same continuum as the original stimulus which was used to establish the conditioned response. Thus the smaller the difference between the original stimulus and a substitute stimulus, the greater the magnitude of the conditioned response elicited by the substitute stimulus, and the greater the degree of resemblance between the neural impulses which are evoked by the original and substitute stimuli.

Simultaneous color contrast and the results of an experiment by Humphrey, the so-called "Humphrey's Arpeggio Paradox," are the two important examples of afferent neural interaction which directly or indirectly pertain to conscious experience in the *Principles of Behavior*. The first example was cited in order to illustrate the meaning of the interaction hypothesis; the second example was discussed in detail in order to show how this hypothesis might resolve Humphrey's paradox in accordance with behavioristic principles.

Hull points out that a gray patch superimposed on large blue or red backgrounds will appear respectively yellowish or greenish. The neural impulses arising from the gray patch, he says, will interact with those arising from the backgrounds so that there is a difference in conscious experience. Apparently Hull introduced the afferent neural interaction hypothesis for the purpose of circumventing the problems imposed by the acceptance of the constancy hypothesis. Our immediate question is whether this interaction hypothesis successfully accounts for the facts of color contrast and whether the difficulties of the constancy hypothesis are obviated.

We may denote the neural impulses of the gray in isolation as s, and the neural impulses of the gray when placed on the background as $\breve{s}$. Hull, in various discussions of neural interaction, made it clear that a component of s would be contained in $\breve{s}$. Therefore as a composite event $\breve{s}$ may be written as $d{\cdot}s'$, where d and s' respectively represent the part different from and the part resembling s. Moreover, the composite event represents the brain correlate of the induced color. When this color is a yellowish gray, the yellow would correspond to d and the gray to s'. The gray patch when viewed either in isolation or on the blue background apparently gives rise to a similar conscious experience. However, the results of other color experiments have shown that the induced color does not have to have a trace of the conscious effect of a stimulus viewed in isolation. In such instances, therefore, the neural counterpart of the color should be single rather than composite. That is to say, the result of interaction would have no resemblance to s.

The presumed presence of s' in s would indicate that Hull did not reject the constancy hypothesis and did not avoid the implications of its acceptance. That the assumption of the composite nature of the modified impulse was essential is conspicuous in the discussion of the "paradox." [6]

In his *Nature of Learning* (1933) Humphrey provided an extensive account of the results of experiments on conditioned reflexes in order to show that the underlying connectionistic hypothesis of "fixed paths" led to difficulties which, in his opinion, could be resolved from the standpoint of gestalt field theory. In this context he reported the results of his own experiment, one acknowledged to have had its parallel in Russian laboratories. He trained subjects to raise their hand when an "active" note was sounded, this being accomplished by pairing a slight shock to the hand with the sound. They were also taught not to raise their hand when inactive notes, these not being paired with shock, were sounded. Through extensive practice the "conditioned reflex became very stabilized"; the active note was always followed by raising of the hand and the inactive notes never. He advanced two predictions as to what the results might be when the active note was included in a "melody or arpeggio." According to the doctrine of "fixed paths" the neural effect of this note would remain the same and therefore the conditioned response should be elicited. On the other hand, the phenomenal experience of the active note sounded in isolation is different from the phenomenal experience of the same note when included in the context of a melody; the presence of the active note in the melody, moreover, may not even be recognized. Thus, there is no reason to suppose that the subject would raise his hand when the active note is included with others in the context of a melody. Moreover, according to Humphrey, the neural processes evoked by the active note are different. This being the case, the neural process corresponding to the active note, when included in the context of other notes, would not activate the path of the conditioned response. Behaviorally the results of the experiment confirmed the second prediction. When included in the melody of "Home Sweet Home" fourteen times, no subject responded to the active note whereas all subjects responded when it had been sounded in isolation. After having considered and rejected possible interpretations from the standpoint of the connectionistic theories of Pavlov and Watson, Humphrey concluded: "We are again making the same point as the Gestalt psychologists, who claim that the melody is a unitary configuration." In accordance with the "isomorphic principle," he said, "there must be unity in the correlative physiological processes." [7]

Hull simplified his theoretical re-interpretation of the results by considering the case of three notes, the active note being temporally between the others. He pointed out that when the first and inactive note is struck, it is still vibrating when the active one is struck. And this note in turn is vibrating when the next inactive note is sounded. Although the vibration of the first inactive note might have ceased by the time the second inactive note was struck, the neural impulses aroused by both notes would temporally overlap since "some seconds" must elapse for the first neural impulse to decay to a zero value. Since the three neural impulses are to some degree contemporaneous, they are modified as a result of their mutual interaction effects. In order to explain the absence of the conditioned reflex to the active note when included in the context of the two inactive notes, Hull first explains the formation of "habits" when the three notes are individually presented. According to him, three separate habits, one positive and two negative, are learned at this stage. For the purpose of convenience the habits may be represented as follows:

$$\text{Habit 1 (positive): } s_A\text{-----}R$$
$$\text{Habit 2 (negative): } s_1\text{-----}R$$
$$\text{Habit 3 (negative): } s_2\text{-----}R$$

Reading down the column, the s's refer to the neural impulses of the active and inactive notes; R refers to the conditioned response. When the habits are in the process of formation s_1 and s_2 excite R because they vary quantitatively from s_A. With further practice, however, their tendency to excite the conditioned reflex is inhibited because the hand is never shocked when the inactive notes are struck. The three habits are characterized by certain magnitudes of strength, and a positive number and two negative numbers are assigned to them as their measure. Since either negative habit does not interfere with the positive habit, the overlap of impulses being absent by virtue of the presentation of the three notes in isolation, the conditioned reflex is elicited in its appropriate degree of strength when the active note is struck. But when the notes are presented in close succession, as in the arpeggio, the overlap in the neural processes causes the simultaneous activation of the three habits.

Hull points out that the overlap alone, interaction effects being temporarily set aside, will diminish the magnitude of the positive habit because this habit is in competition with the two negative habits. But when the effects of the neural interaction of the three impulses are duly considered, he says, the absence of the conditioned reflex is explained. The absolute magnitudes of the three habits are decreased because the modified neural impulses are somewhat different from the corresponding processes elicited by the notes in isolation. For instance, *Habit 1* in the arpeggio is activated by $\breve{s}_A$ rather than by s_A. Since $\breve{s}_A$ is partly different from s_A, the magnitude of the habit is diminished. Hull then works out the arithmetic so that the net effect of the sum of the strengths of the negative and positive habits is a relatively small number. Its size is such that the tendency of $\breve{s}_A$ to excite *Habit 1* fails to exceed a threshold value. In other words the subject does not raise his hand, although he had done so when the active note was presented in isolation. Hull concludes, "Thus Humphrey's configurational problem finds a natural and consistent explanation in terms of habit dynamics."

The "configurational problem" first may be considered from a physiological standpoint. Humphrey, in following Köhler, argued that the identity of the neural process of a stimulus presented in isolation may no longer be evident in the organization of neural processes when this stimulus and other stimuli are presented in the context of a melody. This organization, moreover, is presumed to be a structured whole process rather than being composed of three discrete processes. It was for such reasons they argued that the conditioned reflex would be absent when its corresponding stimulus is in the context of other stimuli. For Hull, on the other hand, the configuration consists of a combination of the three modified neural processes $\breve{s}_A$, $\breve{s}_1$, and $\breve{s}_2$. Moreover, he presupposes that each original neural process is to some degree the same in its modified correlate (for example, s_A partly resembles $\breve{s}_A$). Evidently Hull has shifted the meaning of the term "configuration."

The shift in the meaning of "configuration" from that intended by Humphrey might have taken place because Hull's meaning of the concept is essential to the explanation of the summation effects of the three habits. According to Hull, every habit whether positive or negative involves a response. Hence the summation effects would take place on the response side rather than on the afferent side of a connection, and the individual presence of each of the three $\breve{s}$'s becomes a prerequisite for the evocation of habit. Moreover, the part resemblance of $\breve{s}_A$ to its corresponding s_A is likewise essential. It is this factor of resemblance which enabled Hull to say that the conditioned reflex tends to be aroused although the active note is part of an arpeggio. The $\breve{s}_A$ can be denoted by $d \cdot s_A{}'$, where $s_A{}'$ represents the component of s_A. Adapting Hull's description of the formation of habits to this notation, the component impulse would travel along the same path as s_A had done when the connection was originally established and thus would excite the conditioned reflex. A similar point can be made for the other $\breve{s}$'s and s's. We may observe that Hull's explanation of the summation of habits and concept of "configuration" presuppose the constancy hypothesis.

The configurational problem also has a phenomenal aspect which Humphrey always discussed in relation to physiological processes in the brain. Phenomenally the individual presentation of notes give rise to a succession of discrete tones but in the context of a melody they are perceived as a coherent unit. He supposed their neural correlates to be correspondingly different, and he discussed other perceptual facts in a similar fashion. When Hull discussed the arpeggio paradox his interest was in explaining the behavioral facts—the presence and absence of the conditioned reflex—and he did not refer to conscious experience. Nevertheless we may consider the phenomenal facts from the standpoint of Hull's discussion of the neural events at the basis of the paradox. When the notes are in isolation their neural processes do not overlap, and consciously the subject experiences discrete tones. In the second presentation the discreteness of the modified impulses can be regarded as the physiological condition for a phenomenally experienced unitary configuration. The special problem arises in the fact that the subject may not recognize the previously active tone in the configuation. This nonrecognition suggests that $\bar{s}_A$ is qualitatively rather than quantitatively different from s_A. If the difference were quantitative the component of the original neural impulse present in the modified impulse should give rise to some recognition.

The difference between Humphrey and Hull may be clarified in relation to the hypothetical results of the following possible experiment. Subjects have been trained to raise their hand when a gray stimulus is presented in isolation; when the stimulus is superimposed on a blue background they do not raise the hand. Humphrey might say that the subjects see a saturated yellow whereas previously they saw gray. The neural correlate of the induced yellow is similar to the neural correlate of the perceived yellow produced by an objective "yellow" stimulus, and qualitatively different from the neural correlate of a perceived gray. The neural correlate or process of the induced yellow will not have any tendency to activate the conditioned reflex. Hull, on the other hand, might say that the neural correlate of the yellow would tend to activate the conditioned reflex since it contains a component of the original process produced by the gray in isolation. For Humphrey the product of interaction in the brain leads to a new result whereas for Hull, the product is always partly new and partly old.[8]

"BEHAVIOR SYSTEM" (1952)

Whatever the theoretical strength the concept of afferent neural interaction may have, Hull did not express adherence to the empiristic approach to perception in the *Principles* of 1943. Actually there are indications of the acceptance of nonempiristic theory. For instance, he apparently accepted the results of Lashley's experiments with rats which Lashley had interpreted as evidence for the innate organization of the rat's "visual field." In referring to these results, Hull cited the importance of the neural interaction hypothesis and in this context said the "interaction occurs between different parts of the retina." Since retinal interactions could hardly originate in factors of learning, it would seem that Hull shared Lashley's interpretation. However, in the *Behavior System* Hull seemed to accept the empiristic approach.

In outlining the future development of behavioristic theory, he maintained that the topic of perception "should be reworked from a behavioral point of view." The "laws peculiar to perception" should be deducible from the same principles governing the formation of habits. The fact that this approach was contrasted to gestalt theory would suggest that the "laws" pertain to the laws of sensory organization. Although Hull only treated the topic of "space perception" in the *System*, his followers have attempted to work out explanations of the usual gestalt laws of organization in accordance with behavioral principles.[9]

The empiristic explanation of the ability of "organisms" such as rats and higher animals to correctly respond to objects is the principal aim of the chapter "Behavior in Relation to Objects in Space." An animal on receiving stimulation from an object must learn to run in the direction of the object, to bring its body in contact with the object, and to manipulate the object. When the object is food the locomotive actions of the animal are reinforced, and the animal will tend to repeat them when again receiving stimulation from it. On the other hand, the animal learns to avoid an object when it leads to pain. "Receptor adjustment," the muscular activity of the eyes, is regarded as an important preliminary step in the acquisition of the locomotive behaviors. The animal must open its eyes "to see an object" and direct them so that corresponding retinal points will be stimulated. The receptor adjustment guarantees optimal stimulation of the retinas. Hull said that such receptor adjustment also must be learned. According to him, muscular activity of the eyes and size of the retinal image are connected with locomotive and manipulation movements. In the context of this discussion Hull apparently accepted the empiristic explanation of seeing or visual perception. He cited as evidential support an investigation reported by Riesen in 1947.

Riesen reared two chimpanzees in almost total darkness from birth until sixteen months of age. At the end of that time they were brought out into an environment of light and their reactions to objects tested. Although having some reflexes the animals did not blink when an object moved toward their eyes nor could they fixate their eyes on any object. According to Riesen, the animals were "blind" or failed to "see." His most important conclusion for our immediate purpose is the statement that the "organization of perceptual processes" in normally reared chimpanzees and human infants is learned. Although there are several ambiguities in the report, Riesen, in effect, implies that higher organisms must learn to see. Hull's interpretation of this investigation, in the context of the importance of receptor adjustment, is:

> Intimately connected with receptor adjustment is the matter not only of stimulus reception, but of *perception*. The specific question of *space* perception, for example, especially concerns us here. As we shall see, this very frequently depends on stimulus intensity. Other things equal, the more intense the vibrissae stimulation becomes, the shorter will be the distance to the redolent object; the more intense a radiant heat becomes, the shorter will be the distance to the hot object; the louder a sound becomes, the closer will be the sounding object. In the case of an object seen by the eye, the larger the image on the retina becomes, the closer will be the object and the more the two fixating eyes will converge; i.e., the greater the tension on the internal recti becomes, the closer will be the object.
>
> How does the animal acquire a knowledge of these space relationships? A great deal of light has been thrown on this subject, at least so far as higher organisms are concerned, by Riesen's classical study of chimpanzees which lived in darkness from birth until the age of sixteen months. With these animals, apparently, space perception is learned, and the learning is acquired rather slowly through an indefinitely large amount of trial and error in which the complex stimuli of visual space are closely associated with manualmotor and locomotor space movements. For example, as an object in the hand is brought toward the eye its retinal image grows larger and the convergence of the optical fixation becomes greater; and the same thing occurs as the organism walks toward an object, though in this case the optical image of the whole surrounding landscape grows larger. Here we have a motor sense of space being associated directly with the corresponding visual cues. Riesen's study strongly suggests that in higher organisms these space cues normally receive an immense amount of reinforced practice during the first weeks of life. Lower organisms, however, require far less practice.[10]

This extract which is not free of ambiguity can be interpreted in two ways.

Interpretation 1: Organisms must learn to respond correctly to the spatial characteristics of objects. We have already said that this is the basic theme of the chapter from which the extract was taken. Since the first paragraph of the extract expressed this theme, *"space* perception" would relate to the muscular responses made by an animal in reference to objects. Thus "learning to perceive" would have the meaning of learning those muscular movements which are correctly related to the distance and size of an object. Thus Riesen's chimpanzees would learn to blink their eyes, fixate an object, and to reach out to grasp an object.

This interpretation incurs the following difficulty which is derived from Abbott's criticism of empiristic theory: a given convergence of the eyes or a particular size of the retinal image could not become associated with the locomotive movements in running or walking to an object because when the object has been reached, the degree of convergence and image size have changed. Nevertheless in a certain sense Interpretation 1 is correct. Let us suppose for the sake of argument that perception as "direct experience" is not the product of learning. The human infant on seeing a nursing bottle at a distance may have to learn to extend its arm the right distance and to engage in those muscular actions so that the hand can conform to the shape of the bottle. Moreover, the infant may have to learn to bring the bottle toward itself in such a way that the nipple touches the lips. Through such actions the infant learns to pucker its lips although the bottle it sees is held at a distance, and to recognize it. A portion of the Riesen data deals with visual recognition and can be interpreted in a similar way.

Hull's discussion of "discrimination learning" in lower animals presupposes the central effects of sensory stimulation to be a prior event in the explanation of the consistent choice of one stimulus and the consistent avoidance of another stimulus. On the human level the phenomenal discrimination of black from white or square from circle would then be an antecedent condition for discovering that one leads to an incentive and the other to shock. Since the "discrimination" is presumed to be the direct outcome of afferent processes, Hull evidently regarded it as not learned. Therefore, the Riesen experiment cited by him, but not interpreted in detail, could have been introduced for the purpose of illustrating the importance of response learning.

Interpretation 2: Organisms must learn to see. The movements in reaching and manipulating objects, and the movements of the eyes in fixating an object, would be an essential factor in the development of visual percepts. This interpretation would be consistent with another portion of the Riesen data and the theoretically stated possibility of deducing the laws of organization from behavioral principles. If this was Hull's aim, he would be expounding the traditional empiristic theory of perception. In which case, the difficulties of this theory which have been described in previous chapters would apply to Hull's theory.

Moreover, the meaning of the afferent neural interaction hypothesis in the *System* would become theoretically ambiguous. Having been originally introduced for the purpose of overcoming objections by Koffka and Köhler and of providing the possibility of reconciling behaviorism and gestalt psychology, the laws of perceptual organization presumably are to be explained in terms of empiristic factors. When induced color was cited as an example of afferent interaction in 1943, figure-ground organization was implicitly presupposed as the outcome of interacting afferent processes; the perception of the form of the patch is a correlate of the perceived color. If the Riesen data are interpreted as referring to phenomenal change, from an initial failure to see to a later ability to see, then induced color and the seeing of form are learned. Thus the theoretical role of the interaction hypothesis in 1952 is not clear.[11]

HEBB

Hebb strives to reconcile connectionism and the field theory advocated by Köhler and Lashley in developing his theory of perception in *Organization of Behavior* (1949). According to him, connectionism—with its assumption of acquired and rigid connections between the cells of the sensory and motor systems in which the brain has the function of a telephone switchboard—could not explain the facts of perception, and Hull's proposed revision in terms of the neural interaction hypothesis was inadequate. His own theory, says Hebb, is connectionistic of the "switchboard variety" but the connections are not between "afferent and efferent pathways" in a direct way. A principle of flexibility, missing in traditional connectionism, is introduced which, in his view, removes the theory from the objections of gestalt psychologists and other field theorists. Field theorists, especially Köhler, regarded excitation patterns as independent of a fixed locus in the brain and they denied the very conception of the formation of connections. Thus they constructed a theory which was inconsistent with the known facts of nervous functioning. On the other hand, his neurophysiological theory, although conceded to be somewhat speculative, would be consistent with such facts. However, field theorists, Hebb continues, have made it abundantly clear that sensory organization cannot be wholly acquired and some aspect of it must be regarded an "innate." Since this degree of limited acceptance did not necessarily imply acceptance of Köhler's theory of brain action, Hebb concludes that a reconciliation with his connectionism is possible. The reason why the gestalt contention that perceptual organization is "wholly innate" cannot be accepted in his view lies partly in physiological facts and partly in evidence.

The fact of a one-to-one correspondence between retinal excitations and the resulting excitations in the visual cortex, he says, implies an "isomorphism" between retinal and cortical patterns. Field theorists have relied upon this fact in "accounting for the perception of square as a distinctive whole," and if they are right, the perception of the square would be innate. However, physiological evidence weakens this argument. For instance, when each "corner" of a square is viewed in succession the shape of the cortical pattern undergoes considerable variation; nevertheless we tend to see a square shape. Köhler had invoked satiational processes for the purpose of correcting the anatomical distortions in the cortical patterns, but this resolution of the problem was inadequate. Further facts and reasons are adduced by Hebb to show that field theory and its assumption of an isomorphic relationship between perception and events in the visual cortex could not provide an adequate basis for a theory of perception. Thus Hebb, on the basis of physiological facts and their theoretical interpretation, arrives at the general conclusion that perception probably is to some degree the product of learning. The evidence, in his view, removes the probability and makes the conclusion certain. The results of Riesen's experiments show that the animals had no "visual perceptions" and were "avisual" even after many hours of visual stimulation, and that the improvement in their ability to perceive was the outcome of experience. It is said that Senden's monograph (1932) which dealt with human material corroborated these results, a conclusion which Riesen had emphasized in his original report. Senden had compiled all known cases of those born blind whose sight had been surgically restored. Hebb reports that these data indicate that some patients only saw an "amorphous mass of light" in their first exposure to objects and that subsequently they saw definitely shaped objects. Both reports are said to provide important evidence for the necessity of perceptual learning in normal human infants.[12]

A patient described by Senden is the basis for Hebb's concession to an innate factor in perception and explanation of acquired perceptions. Hebb maintains that the figure-ground relationship is "primitive," innate, or an amorphous mass of color. He cites the case of a patient who could not distinguish a square from a circle but who could do so when he looked at the corners successively. In having fixated a particular vertex he was able to perceive the angle clearly, and likewise for the other vertices, thus making the distinction between the two figures possible. But should his eye have fixated some other point of the square, perhaps its center, he would have perceived an amorphous mass.

We may consider an infant who has not yet learned to perceive a whole form and suppose, as does Hebb, that he is looking at a drawing of a triangle. At first the infant may perceive amorphous light but when his eyes fixate a vertex, he sees an angle. In further fixations he sees a line, another angle, and so on. Such part perceptions define what Hebb calls "perceptual elements." The infant repeats these actions many times so that the perception of the triangle as a whole emerges as the outcome of a prolonged process of learning. However, the triangle percept would not be immediate and unitary even after it has been acquired. Says Hebb in stating his fundamental thesis, "the perception is additive, a serial reconstruction (though very rapid and 'unconscious' for the normal adult)." Eye-movements are always essential in the synthesis of the perceptual elements into perception. When the neurophysiological basis of the percept is theoretically elaborated, Hebb supposes that the order of the events in the brain corresponds to the order in the percept. The neural representations of the perceptual elements are assembled additively by means of anatomical connections or "growths" which develop among them as the result of eye-movement. Actually a perceived triangle, it is said, comprises six part perceptions: three sides and three angles. Thus six neural representations are involved in the development of the perception. However, in order to simplify theoretical discussion, Hebb excludes the perceptual elements corresponding to the three sides.[13]

Experience is also regarded as essential for the perception of an angle or line. To obtain some insight into the reason for this assumption, we may consider the patterns of excitation in the visual cortex. What has been said in respect to the distortions suffered by those patterns when the gaze is directed to different parts of an objective square also applies to a line. When we look at the left end, right end, or some other point above and below a straight horizontal line we perceive a straight horizontal line. If this perception were innately determined, some uniformity in the projective patterns in the visual cortex would be necessary. But since the required uniformity does not exist, the perception of the straight line is not wholly innate. For similar reasons, the perception of an angle is partly experiential. However, Hebb presupposes the perceptual element of an angle to be a given in the exposition of theory; to simplify our own discussion we shall suppose this element to be innate. His neurophysiological explanation of the development of a triangle percept is intricate and its presuppositions are not always clearly related to phenomenal and other facts. A synoptic presentation of the physiological detail suffices for our purpose.[14]

THE ACQUIRED PERCEPTION OF
A TRIANGLE

Let us return to the excitation pattern in the visual cortex which, according to Hebb, is not the immediate correlate of perception. When the impulses of this brain pattern are transmitted to another part of the brain such as the "association cortex," a similar problem arises in an even more important way. The connections between the visual and association cortices, it is said, are "diffuse" and "random" so that there is no point to point correspondence between the impulses in those two areas. The cells in the association cortex are so anatomically intertangled and "disorganized" that the nervous activity in them could not be the immediate correlate of perception. Whatever isomorphism had existed between cortical and retinal patterns is lost in the transmission of impulses to the association cortex. Thus the problem arises of how to explain the physiological organization of those scattered impulses so that they can correspond to the known facts characterizing the perceptions of normal adults. Although the plan of the nervous system might seem to offer insuperable obstacles to the physiological organization of excitations, Hebb points out it may have several advantages. The excitations at specific cells in the visual cortex can be transmitted along many alternative paths to the association cortex, and likewise the nervous activity at specific cells within the association cortex may be transmitted to other specific cells within this cortex in many different ways. Thus there would be a flexibility of action which makes it possible to say that excitations have specific locations in cells but without being confined to the same cells in repetition of stimulation of the retina. Inasmuch as the evidence shows that the excitations arising from eye-movements are important in perceptual development, according to Hebb, the connections between those excitations and visual excitations could only take place in the association cortex.

It seems evident that in the way in which Hebb has conceptualized the action of the nervous system, the perception of a line or angle, apart from the other reason arising from the variation in the pattern in the visual cortex, must be learned. Processes in the visual cortex are called "sensory" and those processes in the association cortex which contribute to the formation of physiological organization are called "nonsensory." Thus the brain correlate of an acquired perception would comprise sensory and nonsensory processes. The neural representation of a perceptual element, which we have presumed to be innate, consists of a pattern of cells whose excitations give rise to the part perception. In our account we shall suppose that it is already independent of a particular and same cellular pattern. Representation thus defined is approximately equivalent to Hebb's "cell assembly." In order to diversify our language we will also refer to it as a cortical unit. The physiological processes of learning to perceive begin when two such units are activated at the same time or nearly the same time. The concurrence of action makes it possible for linkages to be formed between them. These become firmly established so that the activation of one unit immediately activates its partner, the excitations passing through the linkages to the other unit.[15]

The only acquired perception of which Hebb treats in detail is that of a triangular form. This form and the perceptual elements which lead to its formation are depicted in Figure 15.1. The same letters will be used to denote the physical stimuli, and also the cortical units corresponding to the elements although the units are not angles. We may consider the eyes to have already reflexly fixated vertex a. This fixation is momentary since the eyes tend automatically to follow the sides so that they again fixate momentarily at either one of the other two vertices. Chance factors determine the actual path taken, so that all vertices are fixated in turn although the order need not be identical from trial to trial. We have said that the eye-movements follow the side but this is somewhat inaccurate; actually, the eyes move erratically in lateral directions while changing fixation points of the vertices. During

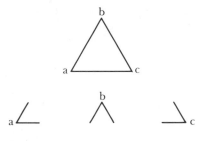

FIGURE 15.1

the course of these movements retinal stimulation will give rise to a succession of cortical units. To get some idea of how linkages might be formed, we consider the vertex *a* as momentarily fixated to be followed by fixation of the vertex *b*. When the eyes have moved to the latter vertex the excitations of cortical unit *a* have a continuing existence so that they overlap temporally with the present excitations of cortical unit *b*. The simultaneity of excitations enables linkages to be developed between the units. The rapidity of eye-movements is essential to the formation of the acquired connections, for if this were not the case the simultaneity of excitations would be impossible; thus if the eyes moved relatively slowly two discrete and detached perceptual elements would be perceived. The unification of the three cortical units does not yet explain the perception of the triangle, for their order is chronological. Adults in looking at a triangle perceive it as a simultaneous whole rather than as a rapid succession of part perceptions.[16]

Thus Hebb has the traditional problem of nineteenth-century empiristic theory: to explain the contemporaneity and indivisibility of a perception although its constituent sensations are successive. Its resolution is implicit in the postulation of a "*t* structure" which represents the "synthesis" of the cortical units so that its conscious correspondent is the "perception of the triangle as a distinctive whole." The *t* structure is of such a nature that its activation is simultaneous, hence the perception of the triangle at a specific instant is not divisible into parts. It appears to Hebb, however, that certain kinds of data require a succession of part perceptions. For instance, in having referred to such data, he says, "the perception of the whole as such is momentary, and alternates with perception of the various parts." [17]

The concepts of *schema* and *phase sequence* are important in

Hebb's general neurophysiological theory. A "schema" involved in the perception of a triangle consists of a temporal sequence of cortical units and t's such as represented in the following:

$$a\text{-}b\text{-}t\text{-}a\text{-}c\text{-}t\text{-}b\text{-}$$

When motor linkages are included between successive pairs, the progression defines a "phase sequence." This sequence is said to account for the evidence which suggests the alternation of part perceptions and the perception of the whole. Moreover, the sequence is intended as the representation of the cortical events at the basis of the perception of a triangle. The effects of eye-movements in the brain (motor linkages) enable the transition from one term of the sequence to the next. Still another problem of those nineteenth-century theories of perception which emphasized the importance of eye-movements, as does in fact Hebb's own theory, concerned the simultaneity of perception and the momentary perception of objects when illuminated for only a very brief time interval. For Hebb eye-movements are responsible for the progression of terms, but they are not involved in the t structure itself. Although part perceptions necessitate eye-movement, the perception of a whole does not. Nevertheless, what he says is interesting since it is reminiscent of Lotze's theory. Writes Hebb:

> In terms of the schema, the alternate perception of whole and parts is an alternation of activity among a, b, c, and t, with corresponding directions of fixation (except for the entity t, which is accompanied by no determinate eyemovements; since the *average* values of the six eyemovement vectors associated with the three part perceptions of the triangle add up to zero, but also fluctuate from moment to moment, their resultant would fluctuate in direction and amount, and would produce neither a fixation of gaze nor any predictable change of fixation).[18]

Let us suppose that when we look at the three separate angles in Figure 15.1 our perception of them is simultaneous. Obviously the three part perceptions do not constitute the perception of a triangle. And should we describe what we see, we might say that we see three angles in one instance and a triangle in the other. Although both types of perception are simultaneous, they are not the same. Therefore the t structure in addition to having the property that would account for simultaneity must have some other property. In fact Hebb ascribes this additional property to t and that is why he calls it a "new structure." The introduction of t into his system was in response to gestalt theory. In having discussed the formation of connections among the cortical units, he says that the structure resulting from them must be "new" and not a "sum or hooking together of a, b, and c." The notation abc in his view does not adequately represent the new structure since it would suggest the idea of summation; to avoid the implication of summation t is introduced as the designation of the new structure. He then observes, "As *Gestalt* writers would say, this is something other than the sum of its parts; but unlike *Gestalt* theory, the schema derives the distinctiveness of the whole from the perception of the parts." However, Hebb does not discuss how the concatenation of a, b, and c can give rise to t and the important properties ascribed to it.[19]

Hebb provides many examples of the importance of t for the purpose of explaining those facts which usually were interpreted as supporting field theory. For instance, he points out that, according to gestalt theory, an incomplete triangle, with a small portion of an angle missing, may be perceived as a whole triangle. Field processes in the brain supposedly tend naturally toward completion; familiarity with the figure is not essential in this explanation. On the other hand, Hebb contends that thorough familiarity with the figure is a necessary condition for the perceived "closure." He explains this fact by supposing the two present vertices a and b are fixated in succession. Cortical units a and b are activated, which in turn excite the third unit c although no retinal stimulation corresponds to it. The excitations in the three units momentarily excite t, thus causing the perception of a complete triangle.[20]

Hebb's explanation of visual perception in the *Organization of Behavior* is developed only in reference to the acquisition of the perceived whole form of a planar triangle. Other perceptual facts are discussed, but they presuppose the validity of the explanation of the triangle percept. However, there is no discussion of the constancies of size and brightness, external reference, of the perceptions of size, relative distance, solidity, and other facts of classical interest. Obviously the explanation of the perception of the triangle is intended as a basic model but there is no indication of the way this model might be applied to the acquisition of other percepts. The human face is an object of principal interest to the infant. Apparently the perception of the face would evolve from successive acts of fixation, and the phase sequences to which they might give rise. Yet the acquisition of this perception seems impossible. Since Hebb did not discuss the perception of the human face, the success of the theory may be evaluated in explaining the perception of a triangle. If the theory cannot account for this perception, it cannot explain any other perception.

The after-image of the form of a triangle does not depend on eye-movements, providing the gaze remains relatively stationary. There are always rapid and slight erratic eye-movements but they do not affect the constancy of the retinal pattern of after-stimulation nor do they influence the perceived form. Depending on the conditions of original stimulation an after-image can last for as long as three minutes. During a substantial portion of the period of observation, say the first minute, we perceive the same form. At no time do we ever perceive the alternation of part perceptions and a whole perception. Of course, it may be said that the constancy of the retinal pattern is the basis for the persistence of the perceived whole form, but this is not the contention under examination—eye-movements were regarded as critical in the perception of form because their central effects would activate the sequence of cortical units and t. The more important possibility concerns the nature of the t structure. Since the retinal pattern is constant, the summation of eye-movement vectors might have a zero value during the period of observation. Thus the t structure would be directly activated and would remain activated for this period. Hence, there would be no reason to suppose alternating part and whole perceptions. But since the excitation of t is contingent upon the activation of the cortical units, as the definition of phase sequence and the explanation of closure make clear, the same problem arises. Toward the end of the period of observation the countours become fuzzy and perhaps only parts of a triangle are perceived, but such facts are not relevant to the particular point under discussion.

When we look at the diagram of Figure 15.2 we see one whole triangle slightly ahead of another whole triangle. Presumably each percept has a t corresponding to it, but it is not easy to understand how the existence of the two t structures can be explained in terms of zero summation of eye-movement vectors. A similar problem arises in explaining the six small triangles that are perceived when the retina is stimulated by the same diagram. Let us consider the formation of these percepts in early life, supposing that the complex diagram rather than the simple diagram of a triangle is the first figure. Since there are

FIGURE 15.2

thirty angles in the diagram we may suppose that they give rise to a similar number of perceptual elements. Thus each perceived triangle would represent the integration of three perceptual elements; the principle governing the ordering of the elements would lie in the reflex motions of the eye. After the eye has fixated the lowest vertex it rapidly moves to the next fixation point which, in the diagram, is represented by either of the two intersections of the first horizontal line and the two sides. Since this and other intermediate fixation points eliminate the possibility of explaining the percepts of two whole triangles, only the possible formation of the percepts of the small triangles need be considered. Consider the perceived triangle of which the vertices are the lowest vertex in the diagram and the two intersections just described. The perceptual elements which must be ordered through eye-movements correspond to the three "inside" acute angles. When the eye fixates the lowest vertex it gives rise to one perceptual element, but in moving on to the next fixation point it may give rise to one of four perceptual elements; of the four elements only one can belong to the particular perceived triangle in the process of formation. The principle governing the selection of the correct element is not apparent, and a similar problem arises when the eye fixates any of the remaining ten fixation points. We have chosen the complex diagram to make our point but the same problem of choice of the correct element in the perception of adults would exist even on the supposition that the simple diagram was the first figure and the perception corresponding to it was developed. When the adult eye rests on one of the six intermediate intersections, one of the four possible elements still must be selected. Further, the assumption that the motion of the eye from one fixation point to another is random compounds the complexity of the problem. These difficulties can be translated into corresponding difficulties in the formation and activation of cortical units or cell assemblies.[21]

We may consider the performance of ducklings in selecting the triangle in the experiment on form. The theory under consideration supposes that the principles of neurophysiological functioning are generally valid throughout the phylogenetic series; the differences in brain structure only alter the speed of learning. Since Hebb maintains that what is ordinarily regarded as instinctive behavior also may involve some learning, perhaps a few seconds, it may be possible to say that ducklings originally perceive parts which are assembled into a whole through very rapid learning. This possibility, however, does not seem to be a likely one. Each of the quadrilaterals in the form experiment ought to give rise to eight perceptual elements and the triangle to six (the sides are also included in this count). Thus the duckling must learn to assemble the elements unique to each form. Those forms, however, were selected so that would have common elements, a factor contributing to the difficulty of finding the right combinations. At the same time, moreover, the duckling is learning to discover the form associated with food and to adapt to the experimental situation. Furthermore, one duckling achieved criterion after an over-all total of 20 trials, a number smaller than the total number of 38 perceptual elements. Thus whatever might correspond to the t structure in this duckling's brain, could not have been the result of cell assemblies and their acquired connections.

The problem of succession and contemporaneity does not seem to be completely resolved by the t structure. The a, b, and c are the neural correlates of part perceptions, and t the correlate of a unitary perception. However, we are not aware of such part perceptions in looking at a triangle, nor does Hebb say we should for he indicates that these may be "unconscious." Apparently the theory presupposes the equivalent of the concept of unnoticed sensation. Moreover, the phase sequence is a recurrent series of the units and t, but since the psychic concomitants of the units are not noticed we ought to experience gaps in consciousness. Yet in direct experience there are no interruptions interspersed with the momentary perception of a whole. To suppose that the rapidity of the serial and additive reconstruction of parts may go unnoticed does not quite help since t is also a term in the rapid sequence. To avoid such problems we may suppose that t, whatever its origin in learning, is at present the only cortical structure. Thus the central effect of retinal stimulation would directly tap t without the mediation of a, b, or c; consciously we experience a unitary whole, and there is no need to account for "unconscious" part perceptions. This alternative, however, was evidently not acceptable to Hebb since he said that the "gestalt argument" could not be answered if the perception of a whole figure is as immediate and indivisible as it appears to the adult, and to sustain his theory against this argument he also said that "prior recognition" of parts is a factor in the perception of the whole.[22]

Empirists have often cited the discrepancy between perception and retinal pattern as the theoretical justification of the proposition that we learn to see. The important assumption at the basis of this line of thought is the constancy hypothesis. Hebb's empiristic approach can be understood in terms of the implied acceptance of this assumption stated in a somewhat different form, namely, as the discrepancy between the distorted patterns in the visual cortex and perception. Two factors are responsible for the distortion: the anatomical organization of the pathways of the fibers between the visual cortex and retina, the perspective changes in the retinal pattern and the place of the retina receiving stimulation. Since, according to Hebb, sensory processes which are identified with activity in the visual cortex cannot account for perception, nonsensory processes which are identified with activity in the association cortex must be invoked in order to explain perception.

THE EVIDENCE AND CHANGE
IN POINT OF VIEW

Since the critical points of the data of the resighted discussed in previous chapters are relevant to Hebb's citation and interpretation of the Senden material, we shall consider the chimpanzee data only. Subsequent to the publication of his report in 1947, Riesen discovered that the two animals had incurred optical damage as the result of being reared in the light-deprived environment for sixteen months, and he reported that the deterioration in the visual functioning of one of them approached blindness, although the animal had been placed in a normal environment for over three years after the termination of the experiment. He reported such facts and the results of additional experiments in 1950. During this period Riesen evidently changed his interpretation of the data. In 1947 the data were related to the hypothesis of learning to see, whereas in 1950 they were related to the hypothesis on the effect of "disuse" or absence of visual stimulation on visual functioning.

At about the same time Walls interpreted the findings of the animals' vision as symptomatic of optic atrophy and raised a question concerning the possibility of damage to the brain structures important in vision. In his view, "When they seem to have to 'learn to see,' they may indeed have been learning how to salvage some usefulness from wrecked visual equipment." Apparently for him such data were not directly relevant in understanding the visual development of normally reared human or chimpanzee infants. In another observation of interest Walls pointed out that many prisoners who had been confined in cells deprived of all light in "Devil's Island" for periods as long as five years (one had been so detained for over ten years), emerged from their confinement "totally blind." The blindness, it was later discovered, could be prevented by alternating twenty days in the lightless environment with ten days of semi-darkness. If these reports are correct, visual stimulation is as essential for the maintenance of normal vision in those who have been previously reared in normal environments (the prisoners) as it is for the development of normal vision in early life (the chimpanzees).

Obviously Hebb could not have known of the possibility and facts of damage in 1949 when the Riesen (and Senden) data were interpreted as evidence for visual learning in both abnormally and normally reared animals. However, after 1950 Hebb continued to regard these data as support for his theory, although accepting the new results of "cell loss and chemical deficiencies" in light-deprived chimpanzees and acknowledging that the same might be true for those with congenital cataracts. Quite possibly Hebb considered the Riesen and Senden data as relevant because the 1949 thesis of "learning to see" was given an additional meaning. In 1949 it referred only to the acquired connections between perceptual elements, and later also to the "importance of sensory stimulation in development."

It is plausible to suppose, as Hebb did, that continued sensory stimulation in the developmental period after birth is important to the emergence of the final perceptions characterizing the normal adult. The infant chimpanzee may see quite differently than he does in later life as a function of exposure to a normal environment, and visual stimulation is necessary for the development and maintenance of neural structures. All this may be called perceptual learning and accepted as such. But this type of learning does not imply "learning to see" in the meaning of the acquisition of connections among perceptual elements. Therefore, the evidence adduced in support of the importance of sensory stimulation might be irrelevant to the second type of perceptual learning.[23]

Although sensory stimulation is undeniably important, its significance requires some evaluation. For instance, prior visual stimulation did not seem to be essential to the reactions of Spalding's chicks when placed in a lighted environment. Some restriction on the scope of "sensory stimulation" is therefore necessary. An obvious basis for the restriction lies in the high degree of maturity of these animals at the time of hatching or shortly afterwards when they become subjects for a visual experiment. Human and chimpanzee infants, on the other hand, are born relatively immature. Since an important part of their maturation takes place after birth, sensory stimulation is important for their visual achievements. But the role of such stimulation may still fall in the nonassociational rather than in the associational type of perceptual learning. For the purpose of illustration we may imagine a human freak born at the same level of maturity in respect to his optical and visual system as that of a one-year-old child. Should the freak see as well as the child, we may surmise that the perceptions of the child do not exemplify the second type of perceptual learning. The infant's percepts may be regarded as the direct outcome of postnatal maturational processes although in this instance visual stimulation is a factor.

A chimpanzee is a visual and social animal and when deprived of sensory stimulation it is reared in an abnormal environment. Maturational processes, therefore, do not pursue their normal course. When compared with normally reared animals his responsiveness to objects is different and his vision may be abnormal. If the condition is severe enough he may never recover the visual functioning characteristic for his species and he may even become blind. Thus for the development and maintenance of normal perceptions it is essential that an abnormal environment be avoided. Although this conclusion may appear to be a near equivalent to the statement that learning or sensory stimulation is part of perceptual development, there are some differences. Consider, for instance, the change in perception after the deprived animal has been restored to a normal environment. The perceptual change or development may be quite different from that of the animal that has always remained in the normal environment. The blink reflex, which was absent in one sixteen-month light-deprived animal when brought into the light, manifested itself for the first time in the fifth day when the face was threatened with a blow; the reflex became consistent only after many hours of visual stimulation. This result has been interpreted to mean that the blink reflex is learned in both abnormal and normal animals. But the course of its development is not the same. The abnormally reared animal flutters its eyes rapidly in a way quite different and for a longer period than does the normal chimpanzee after birth. Although the final blink response may be the same, the preceding responses in its development are different.

In another often cited experiment a chimpanzee was raised with its forearms and forelegs inserted in cardboard tubes so as to prevent any manipulation of objects or touching of various parts of its body for the first thirty months of its life. On removal of the tubes the performance of this animal was compared with that of a normally reared animal in various tasks. With vision blocked off, the normal animal immediately responded to pain when pricked with a pin whereas the other animal gave no sign of disturbance. A normal chimpanzee will feel pain and react to it a few months after birth but the experimental animal failed to do so at the age of thirty months. The control animal needed 200 trials to establish a coordination between a left turn of the head and the touching of its left hand whereas the experimental animal was not completely successful even after 2000 trials. Obviously the wide difference in the reactions of the two animals is a function of the restrictive condition, and is not quite relevant in understanding the development of normal animals. Generally, therefore, any direct inference from the behavior of an animal raised in an abnormal environment to the development of an animal raised in a normal environment is unwarranted.[24]

It often happens that when a lower animal is transferred from its habitual to a new environment, its behavior undergoes a change. He may "freeze," not eat, and so on. A certain period of adaptation is required before his previous behaviors return. When chimpanzees are kept in darkness for a considerable time, this, their first environment, becomes the habitual one. An important fact characterizing this environment is the not seeing of objects. His experience with objects is based only on touch or whatever feelings he may have from limb movements. Then a lighted environment becomes the new or strange environment in contrast to the preceding one. A period of re-adjust-ment is therefore necessary for becoming acquainted and familiar so that the environment loses its quality of strangeness. Thus he may spend some time in merely looking, and when he moves, the move-ments might be tentative and halting. And this could still be true even if light deprivation had not produced physical damage. But in its in-troduction to the new environment the animal as a necessary condi-tion for the experiment becomes the subject of visual tests almost at the outset of entry into it. Thus the opportunity for re-habituation is precluded. Moreover, accounts of some of these animals indicate that their whole personality has been deranged. A proposed test of vision can hardly be considered in isolation from these other factors. In any case a further complication is introduced in the interpretation of the data.

For instance, we may consider the results of the following experi-ment with a chimpanzee that had been light deprived for seven months and a normal chimpanzee of the same age. A large plaque con-sisting of black stripes on a yellow background was moved in the direc-tion of the chimpanzee's line of sight, and when it touched the lips the chimpanzee received a slight electric shock. The normal chimpanzee learned to avert his head at the approach of the plaque after two trials whereas the light deprived chimpanzee required thirty trials. Although this difference does not seem remarkable in view of the previous his-tory of the animals, it may be and has been interpreted as evidence for perceptual learning. However, another interpretation is possible, the difference between the abnormal and normal chimpanzees pertains to learning to respond rather than learning to see. Both animals see the forward motion of the plaque. One animal takes two trials to acquire an association between an avoiding response and the visual item while the other takes thirty trials to establish a similar association.[25]

Animals are reared in a restricted environment for the apparent purpose of disentangling the effects of maturation from those of expe-rience or learning in normal perceptual development. Thus if the de-velopment is adversely affected in these animals, it is presumed that learning has been responsible for, or has contributed to, the normal development of animals not subject to the restriction. This procedure presupposes that maturational processes and experience are indepen-dent variables. However, this separation is unrealistic and the results of isolation experiments are indecisive for the same reasons as dis-cussed above.[26]

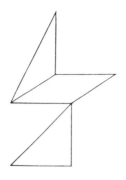

16 FUNCTIONALISM: AMES AND MURPHY

The fact that what we are conscious of in perception has had its origin entirely *in past experience and does not exist in its own right in the objects we are looking at is a difficult one to believe.* Ames, 1946

So wherever our needs differ we literally see differently.
Murphy, 1947

The "functionalist" approach or also the "New Look" to perception became a popular movement in this country after World War II. According to this approach, functional factors such as needs, values, purposes, motives, expectations, significances, and personality dynamics were important causal determinants of perceptual organization. Gestalt psychology, it was said, had emphasized the "structural," "autochthonous," or intrinsic factors of organization and ignored the "functional" factors. Moreover, it was thought that the rapidly accumulating evidence showed that the gestalt theory of perception was wrong on factual grounds. For instance, one experiment seemed to show that poor children saw certain coins as larger in size than did rich children.

Gestalt theory could not explain this result because it would predict that poor and rich children should see the coins as of the same size since the structural factors of organization for both groups are presumed to be identical. On the other hand, it seemed reasonable to suppose that poor children, in having a greater need for coins, saw them as larger. "Past experience," it was said, was another functional determinant which had been disregarded by gestalt psychologists. The proponents of functionalism, however, did not reject the role of structural or organizing factors in the brain. They proposed an "eclectic" theory, unifying the principles and findings of gestalt psychology with those of the new trend.

It was necessarily the case that functionalism should ally itself with empiristic theory. Thus the explanation of the difference in the perception of coins by poor and rich children had to entail previous experience with coins. Moreover, needs and strivings, it was said, always characterize the "organism" from the beginning of its life. At no time can the organism ever be regarded as "empty." Hence, the functional determinants would be effective in the organization of perception at the moment the child first receives visual stimulation. This is why functionalists inclined to the acceptance of the hypothesis that "we learn to see" and embraced the evidence which seemed to support it. Ames and Murphy had an important role in the reinstatement of this hypothesis within a functional framework.[1]

AMES

After a career in physiological optics, a field in which he made important contributions, Ames turned to the resolution of the philosophical and psychological problems which in his opinion were implicit in the traditional theories of perception. In about 1945 and 1946 he devised a number of "demonstrations" for the purpose of illustrating such problems. In the philosophical or epistemological phase he was concerned with the problems arising from the errors or deceptions of sense, and in the psychological phase the problems arising from the fact that retinal images are defective representations of the characteristics of objects. After conferences and discussions with psychologists, philosophers, and educators who had observed the demonstrations, he and his collaborators evolved a theory which came to be called *transactionalism*.

John Dewey who participated in the development of the theory provided the key term "transactional." The epistemological importance he ascribed to the demonstrations is evident in a letter to Ames in which he said, "I think your work is by far the most important work done in the psychological-philosophical field during this century—I am tempted to say the *only* really important work." Ames's apparent goal in formulating a transactional theory of perception was to synthesize various branches of science and philosophy. In a preliminary exposition of this theory in 1947 Cantril said, "Ames' approach and demonstrations are a natural development and enlargement of Helmholtz's methodology that followed in his mind from integrating with Helmholtz's contribution certain scientific contributions since Helmholtz, especially those of James, Freud, Whitehead, Dewey, Gestalt psychology, and the findings of modern physics." The task of integration involved the functional determinants which have been described above.[2]

The contribution from Helmholtz is acknowledged by Ames when, in referring to Helmholtz, he says, ". . . in the simplest percept there is involved a complex, integrative, judgment-like process based on experience." And he quotes Helmholtz: "These inductive conclusions leading to the formation of our sense-perceptions certainly do lack the purifying and scrutinizing work of conscious thinking. Nevertheless, in my opinion, by their peculiar nature they may be classed as *conclusions*, inductive conclusions unconsciously formed." Helmholtz's influence in the formulation of transactional theory is apparent in the importance which Ames has ascribed to the concept of "unconscious assumptions." However, Ames failed to recognize the constancy hypothesis as another traditional influence in the development of his theory. This assumption is particularly evident in the theoretical discussions of the demonstrations by Ames and other transactionalists. Inasmuch as expositions of transactional theory have been vague, we can gain a clearer idea of what the theory is about by discussion of the demonstrations. Many of those who witnessed them became convinced of the importance of "unconscious assumptions" in the formation of percepts. A few of the demonstrations will be described and interpreted from the standpoint of Ames's theory; the degree of emphasis is the same as exists in his writings. Monocular viewing is supposed throughout.[3]

THE DEMONSTRATIONS

1. The three chairs. Three apparently identical chairs are seen when external objects are viewed through the same number of peepholes. An "artificial eye," consisting of a ground glass and lens, is inserted in each of the three peepholes labled *A, B,* and *C.* The image of a chair depicted on one ground glass is the same as the two other images. Since the ground glass is conceived as corresponding to the retina, we are in a position to observe the counterparts of the retinal images. They are very small, inverted, two-dimensional, and the angles formed between the legs are not 90°. But when we again look through the holes—the lens and ground glass having been removed—we perceive the "chairs" to be much larger, erect and in three dimensions. We also perceive the angles between legs and seat to be 90°. This phase of the demonstration proves that the percept cannot be derived from the retinal image.

Let us now turn to look at the external objects behind the peepholes. Behind *A* we see a three-dimensional chair constructed with strings ("legs") and a white rectangular cardboard ("seat"). These parts are connected much as a real chair would be. Behind *B* we see a "bit of jumbled three-dimensional nonsense." "Chairness" is not perceived because the strings "are all of different lengths at different angles." They are neither connected one to the other nor to the seat, the seat merely being a painted white diamond on a rear wall. The object behind *C* consists of connected strings and a cardboard arranged in the same plane. In this instance a flat chair is perceived. The lengths of all parts and their distances from the peepholes are so chosen that the images of the objects projected on the ground glass "retinas" are all identical. The conclusion drawn from this phase of the demonstration is that "visual perceptions are not determined by objects." The ground glass and the lens are re-inserted in each hole. From the ground glass images alone it is clearly impossible to ascertain the nature of the external objects. The object could be any of the three behind the holes. In fact, the class of possible objects projecting the same image is of infinite size. A similar point is made for perception. Potentially there are an infinite number of possible percepts for a given retinal image. Actually, though, only one perception prevails; when we look through the peepholes we see the same "chair," and not the "jumbled nonsense" or the two-dimensional chair. It is claimed that the origin of the single perception lies in past experience since this perception cannot be derived from the external object or from the retinal "physiological stimulus-pattern."

2. *The distorted room.* When we look at a normal room a particular retinal image is projected from a given viewing position. The construction of an infinite number of artificial rooms, whose images imitate that of the normal room, is theoretically possible. The edges formed by the intersection of walls, the edges of window frames, and other details must be properly selected in respect to their dimensions, angles, and distances in reference to some fixed point. When thus constructed its retinal image is identical to that of the normal room. If the artificial eye is placed at the two positions, there is no perceivable difference in the images on the ground glass. The left vertical edge of the rear wall can be more distant and longer than the right edge, the floor can be sloping rather than horizontal, and the window frames can have trapezoidal rather than rectangular shapes. All such differences do not reveal themselves to the artificial eye, since the distorted and normal rooms project identical images. The geometry, though more complex, is the same in principle as in the preceding demonstration. However, the distorted room looks like a normal room when it is viewed from the reference point; the rear wall and window frames are perceived as rectangles, and the floor looks horizontal. Since the same conclusions apply here as those in the demonstration of the three chairs, we turn to other considerations.

While always looking from the same reference point we are asked to undertake a variety of actions. We project an arm into the room and spill liquid from a container on the floor. We perceive the liquid flowing to the left on a horizontal plane. We reach down to place a ball on the left, giving it an impulse to the right. We perceive the motion of the ball to the right and then to the left, but always on an apparently horizontal floor. When given a stick and asked to touch the left edge of the rear wall, we are surprised to discover that we must push the stick out further than we anticipated on the basis of its perceived distance. And when asked to touch the rear right edge, we find that the stick collides with that edge rather than merely touching it. If such actions were to be performed in a normal room, completely opposite results would be achieved. For instance, the ball would continue to move to the right until it stopped.

The discordancy between perception and action makes us realize that the room's true shape is other than what it appears to be. We undertake actions on the basis of perception and we find no agreement. However, from the results of those actions we can deduce the plan of the room. The liquid flowing to the left and the movement of the ball to the right and then to the left enables us to figure out that the floor slopes to the left. This conclusion which is the result of reasoning does not alter our perception, for the floor still continues to look horizontal. This fact is explained in saying that so much experience in perceiving and acting in relation to normal rooms has been gained in the past that mere knowledge and brief discordant actions are not sufficient to outweigh it. What happens if action is allowed to continue? In continued exploration of the room with a stick, the actions become "successful." This means that the subject succeeds in touching its various parts without collision or other error. More importantly, continued successful action alters the appearance of the room so that it looks distorted whereas before any action it looked normal. For instance, it is claimed "there is a growing body of evidence which indicates that as he continues to act and experience the consequence of his action, he sees the room more and more in its true shape even though the stimulus pattern on his retina has remained unchanged."

One of Ames's basic contentions is that the normal appearance of a room in the usual environment is the product of past experience based on numerous successful actions. We have formed an "unconscious assumption" of what a room ought to look like so that when we are actually looking at a distorted room, this too looks normal until further action leads to an alteration in appearance.

3. *The two balloons.* Two illuminated balloons are viewed in a semi-dark room. Their relative brightness and relative size can be varied independently. In this variation the centers remain equidistant from the viewer. When the balloons are of the same size but one is brighter than the other the former appears closer than the dimmer one. The explanation is advanced that an "unconscious assumption" of identical brightness is made by the viewer. In line with this assumption the apparently brighter balloon must be closer than the other and for that reason it is perceived as closer. When their brightnesses are made the same and the relative size varied, the larger balloon appears closer than the smaller one. This time the "unconscious assumption" of identical size is made and operates so as to cause the apparently

larger balloon to appear closer. When the balloons are of the same brightness and size they are perceived at the same distance. The equality in perceived distance is caused by the assumption that apparently identical objects are the same distance away. There is a final result of interest. The relative size of the balloons can be continuously varied —as one becomes larger the other becomes smaller. The brightness remains the same throughout. A motion toward and away is perceived, the balloon of increasing size moving forward and the one of decreasing size moving away. The viewer supposes that the objects are identical in size and that the changes in the relative size of the retinal patterns are indicative of their positions in space. Thus when a balloon increases in size there is a corresponding increase in the retinal image. Instead of perceiving an object of increasing size, the change in image size is interpreted to mean that the same-size object is coming closer. The effect of these assumptions causes the phenomenal motion of an object moving toward the perceiver.

The unconscious assumptions of the perceiver originate in his past experience. Consider for instance two similar objects of the same size placed at the same distance away. The retinal patterns are of course identical. Through action he learns that these images indicate two similar and equidistant objects. When the distance of one is doubled he learns through additional action to interpret the difference in the relative size of the images as indicative of the actual locations in space. When translated into perceptual terms this means he perceives two objects of the same size and at the same distance away in the first instance and two objects of the same size but at different distances in the second instance.

4. Rotating rectangular and trapezoidal windows. The windows slowly rotate about a common vertical axis in a continuous clockwise direction (the direction is defined looking at the apparatus from above). The vertical dimensions of the trapezoid are chosen so that in respect to a fixed viewing distance the retinal projection of its short edge is always smaller than that of its long edge. The trapezoid is perceived as having an oscillatory motion; the apparent motion recurrently shifts from a clockwise to a counterclockwise direction and vice versa. Thus when the gaze is directed to the right side of the axis of rotation the right edge seems to be moving forward and then going away. On the other hand the rotating rectangle is always perceived in a clockwise direction. Of all the demonstrations devised by Ames, no other equals it in scientific and popular interest. With relatively simple apparatus anyone can observe the discrepancy between the apparent and real motions of the trapezoidal window, and the agreement of apparent and real motions of the rectangle rotating below it on the same axis. Thus, according to Ames, the contention that both types of motion are the result of unconscious assumptions can be readily verified. If it had not been for the discovery of oscillatory motion of the trapezoid, it was thought, the role of unconscious assumptions might have gone undetected because of the correspondence of the phenomenal and real motions of the rectangle.

The principal features of phenomenal motion reversal can be observed by cutting out a small trapezoid from a piece of paper and gluing one end of a toothpick to it. Hold it up before the eye so that the sides are equidistant, the short side being to your right. Now wait, while continuing to fixate the same point, until the short edge appears more distant than the long edge. When this happens slowly rotate clockwise through a small arc. You will observe that the phenomenal motion is counterclockwise; although the right edge is physically moving toward you it appears to be moving away. In another phenomenal fact of importance in understanding Ames's theory the trapezoid looks like a rectangle oblique to the line of sight when its short edge appears to be more distant than the long edge, whereas before the reversal in the apparent relative distances of the edges it looked like a trapezoid.

According to Ames the phenomenal motion of the rectangle is learned in childhood and he envisages its acquisition along the following lines. He points out that the typical forms in the environment are rectangular rather than trapezoidal. In walking through doors, locating windows, and perhaps handling objects, the rectangular forms almost always project "trapezoidal" retinal patterns. It is only in the rare instances when the line of sight is perpendicular to the plane of a rectangular form that the retinal image is also rectangular. By engaging in actions or executing his purposes in relation to objects the "observer" has learned of their actual forms. Says Ames,

> He [the observer] learned to interpret the particularly characterized retinal images that exist when he looks at doors, windows, etc., as rectangular forms. Moreover, he learned to interpret the particular degree of trapezoidal distortion of his retinal images in terms of the positioning of the rectangular form to his particular viewing point. These interpreta-

tions do not occur at the conscious level; rather, they are unconscious and may be characterized as *assumptions* as to the probable significance of indications received from the environment.

This past experience is responsible not only for the perceived rotation of the rectangle but also for the apparent oscillation of the trapezoid. In Figure 16.1 and its accompanying description we have set forth some of the details of this learning as described by Ames. The following synopsis may give the reader some insight into the nature of this complicated explanation.

Hold up a rectangular card and view it with one eye so that it is perpendicular to the line of sight. The projected retinal image is rectangular. We interpret the equality in its vertical edges as indicative of equal physical distance of the sides of the card. By virtue of this interpretation in conjunction with previous actions we have undertaken in respect to rectangular objects, and also in relation to unconscious assumptions, we perceive the card as a rectangular surface with equidistant sides. When the card is turned slightly in a clockwise direction the corresponding retinal pattern is trapezoidal, the difference in the vertical lengths being relatively small. Still unconsciously assuming that the pattern is rectangular, we interpret the long edge of the image as indicating that the right side of the card is somewhat closer than the left side, and we perceive a rectangular surface slightly inclined to the line of sight with its right side phenomenally closer to us. We do the same for each slight clockwise turn of the card. When the card is continuously turned from its broadside position there is a succession of retinal images, each causing us to see a rectangle with a particular degree of slant, or, in other words, we see the card moving clockwise. Go back to the trapezoidal cut-out and hold it so that the right side is slightly closer. Its projected trapezoidal retinal pattern gives rise, because of past experience, to the unconscious assumption of a rectangular configuration. Since we have learned that the nearer side of a rectangle cannot project a retinal edge smaller than the other retinal edge, we suppose the short edge to represent the far side of the trapezoid. Thus we see it inclined opposite its true direction. Since the same is true for a further clockwise turn of the trapezoid we perceive the short side as being somewhat more distant than we did in the previous instance. Hence in continuous turning the trapezoid seems to be moving counterclockwise when in fact it is moving clockwise.[4]

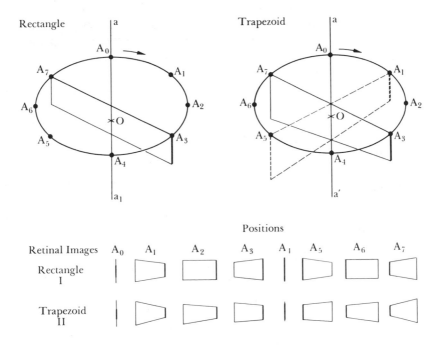

FIGURE 16.1. The diagram depicts the retinal images projected by the rectangle and trapezoid, which are in constant clockwise motion about the vertical axis aa_1. The viewing is monocular with the line of sight perpendicular to the frontoparallel plane at the point O. The motion of the rectangle begins when the leading edge (thickened for emphasis) is at position A_0, successively assuming positions A_1, A_2, and so on. The corresponding retinal patterns are represented in Line I (image reversal is ignored). The leading edge of the patterns is shortest when the corresponding edge of the rectangle is at position A_0 and longest when at position A_4. The relative difference of the lengths of the vertical edges diminishes until they are equal as in A_2, the rectangle being viewed broadside, and increases again (inversely) until the difference is maximum as in A_4. The retinal image is rectangular only twice in a complete revolution of the rectangle, all other images being shapes of varying degrees of trapezoidalness except for the two positions when the rectangle is viewed endwise. The horizontal dimensions of the images are minimum in endwise viewing and maximum in broadwise viewing. This variation makes the horizontal dimension an "ambiguous cue" as to the direction of the objective motion of the rectangle since it is identical for the 90°

excursion from A_0 and the minus 90° excursion from A_4. The explanation of the retinal images projected by the trapezoid in Line II is similar except for the fact that they are never rectangular in shape. (Figure 16.1 is an adaptation from Ames.)

We may consider Ames's explanation of the continuous phenomenal clockwise motion of the rectangle. By virtue of actions undertaken in relation to rectangular objects in early life, the "observer" has learned that the varying retinal patterns represent the projections of an objective rectangular form of unchanging shape. In this period of life he has learned the following: (i) The shorter vertical edge of the retinal image always indicates the more distant side of the rectangle. (ii) The variation in the relative difference in the lengths of the vertical edges of the image indicates different slants of the objective surface. Thus when the leading edge of the rectangle has turned slightly from position A_0, the relative size difference in lengths produced by a slightly inclined surface is maximum, and he sees a rectangular surface sharply inclined to his line of sight. Since the relative size difference is zero when the leading edge is at A_2, the equality in retinal edges enables him to see a rectangular surface perpendicular to the line of sight. In between these two positions he perceives the rectangular surface as having different degrees of inclination. Since there is a continuous change in the relative size difference, he perceives motion through an arc of 90°. The explanation of the continuation of perceived clockwise motion is similar through the remainder of the excursion of the rotating physical rectangle. (iii) The relative difference in the vertical lengths of the image is more reliable as a cue than is the variation in the horizontal dimension of the retinal patterns. Let us suppose that the "observer" paid no attention to the relative difference when the retinal images vary A_4 to A_5, and further suppose that he attends to the increase in horizontal dimension. Although still assuming that the retinal pattern is a rectangular configuration, he cannot judge whether the objective motion is clockwise or counterclockwise. If he supposes a counterclockwise motion, he discovers that this motion does not correspond to the actual motion. Thus he learns that the relative size difference is more reliable even though he has noticed the expansion and contraction of the horizontal length of the retinal patterns. (The expansion is the same on either side of A_4.)

What he has learned in early life transfers to the present situation as an adult when now receiving stimulation from the rotating rectangular window, and, in correctly interpreting the changes in retinal patterns in conformity with the assumption of rectangularity, he perceives a steady clockwise motion. This learning also influences his perception of the motion of the rotating trapezoid, inasmuch as the retinal images of Line II generally are similar to those immediately above them in Line I. For this reason the "observer" interprets them as "rectangular configurations."

We shall explain the reversal of apparent motion through a small arc, supposing it to take place when the leading short edge of the trapezoid has just left the physical position A_2 on its way to the next position. When rotating in the arc A_1A_2 the relative size difference in the vertical dimensions of the retinal image have the same role as they did in the rotation of the rectangular window, thus he perceives a clockwise motion. But should the "observer" retain this assumption in the excursion A_2A_3, he would have to give up the assumption of rectangularity of the image since the projected edge of the physically closer side of an actual rectangle is never smaller than the projected edge of the more distant side (compare images in the A_3 column). On the other hand, he wishes to continue with the assumption of rectangularity. The problem of "choice" is resolved by suppressing or ignoring the cue of relative size difference and adopting the change in horizontal dimension as the cue. We may note that the contraction in the horizontal dimension of images A_2 and A_3 (Line II) corresponds to the contraction in the images in the line above. But the "observer," having retained the assumption of rectangularity, interprets the trapezoidal pattern A_3 of the second line so that its right edge would be projected by the more distant side of a rectangle. As a consequence, instead of perceiving the leading edge of the trapezoid in its correct position at A_3 he perceives the motion of the leading edge as moving away from A_2 to A_1, rather than coming forward from A_2 to A_3, as would have been the case had he been viewing an actual rectangle. We may observe that the reversal of apparent motion is compatible with the contraction of the horizontal dimension of retinal trapezoidal patterns or images.[5]

Further Points in Ames's Theory

Ames in a letter to John Dewey says, "We would not perceive distance but for the assumptions that similar things are identical and that things are wholes, etc. We would not perceive motion but for our assumption of size constancy." Thus he supposed that before the acquisition of any assumption neither distance, things, nor motion would be perceived. This is already quite clear in the discussion of the demonstrations pertaining to the chairs, distorted room, and rotating windows. The observer's interpretation of the retinal pattern before experience would be determined by the characteristics of the pattern. The hidden assumption of his theory that the world is originally perceived flat, helps us understand the major features of the theory and its development. Whether Ames would have denied external reference cannot be readily determined from any specific statement, but its denial seems to be implicit in the recurrent phrase the "observer interprets the retinal patterns." The balloon demonstration indicates that brightness constancy is acquired. Ames observes that the oscillatory motion of the trapezoid is perceived at a distance of about twenty-four feet in viewing it with both eyes. At this distance stereoscopic vision, if effective, should cause us to see a continuous clockwise motion, as in the monocular viewing of a rotating rectangle. His explanation of the ineffectiveness of stereoscopic vision suggests the unconscious appreciation of each of the retinal images, thus implying that single vision is the consequence of psychic activity. There is no clear statement in Ames's writings which would indicate the acceptance of the belief that visual direction is learned. But from the fact that the retinal pattern, which the observer interprets, is reversed together with the presupposition that unconscious assumptions cause us to see things as they are, we may infer that the world would appear upside down to the observer should he be but conscious of his first interpretive act of the retinal pattern and later on remember it. We may consider some of the assumptions which are fairly explicit.[6]

Assumption 1 (the retinal image): The physiological stimulus pattern represents an infinity of external configurations. This assumption underlies the demonstrations pertaining to spatial characteristics and also the balloon demonstration. For instance, consider a light source to produce a given intensity of excitation on the retina. This same level of intensity can be related to an infinity of radiant sources. A very distant source can be a strong radiator whereas one that is very close can be an appropriately weak radiator.

Assumption 2 (number of perceptions): An infinite number of possible perceptions may be related to the same stimulus pattern. This is the first assumption turned inwards, as it were. A given trapezoidal retinal pattern could make us see a variety of trapezoids or a rectangle in any one of infinite possibilities of perceived size and slant. Another assumption is essential for "we never see an infinity of configurations; we see just one."

Assumption 3 (choice): The organism chooses just one perception from the infinite number that may be related to the retinal pattern. The choice, psychological rather than physiological, originates in past experience—purposes, assumptions, and effectiveness of actions. We shall refer to the entirety of such experiences as the *assumptive complex.* We may consider the possibility that there is no choice in perception. Whatever the origin of the assumptive complex everyone sees the three chairs when looking through the peepholes, and the same observer, who may look repeatedly, continues to see what he had seen in the first trial. Thus this perception seems to be necessary and not selected by the observer or organism. The assumptive complex, however, has other features which do indeed make choice possible. The observer, it is said, "unconsciously relates to the stimulus pattern some sort of weighted average of the past consequences of acting with respect to that pattern." Thus, there is choice because the weighted average is probabilistic. We have already noted this feature in the explanation of the phenomenal motion reversal of the trapezoidal window, the observer who at first utilized the cue of relative size difference in the vertical dimensions of the retinal image rejects it and chooses another and more probable cue. Every perception, according to transactionalist theory, is accompanied by some process involving the weighting of cues. This process, the interpretation accorded to the retinal pattern and the choice of assumption, occurs "unconsciously" or in the "subconscious mind." [7]

Perception and Action

The relation of perception to action has two distinct meanings in Ames's theory. It is maintained that we "act on the basis of our perceptions" and it is then shown that the actions are "fallible." In trying to touch various parts of the distorted room with a stick for the first time all sorts of errors are made. When we suddenly thrust out the stick to touch part of the distant wall, we discover that we have banged against it rather than merely touching it; or we may find that we have not thrust it far enough for touching the part. Apparently, our actions are undertaken in relation to the apparent uniformity of the distance of the wall. More generally, if we try to judge what is "out there" in external space on the basis of a percept our judgments are liable to be erroneous. The judgment that "three chairs" are behind the peepholes is false because there is but one "chair" actually present. The second and more important meaning, however, relates to the thesis that action determines the percept and also modifies the assumptive complex. The change in the appearance of the distorted room which they report, exemplifies the thesis. But action is a necessary determinant of all perceptions. It is through action that the individual learns that there is but one object with given characteristics in space rather than an infinity of possible objects, and learns to select a particular perception from the potential class of infinite perceptions. It is through action that he learns to interpret the retinal patterns so that perception may develop. Without action, it is said, perceptions could never develop. "Action" in transactionalist theory has the meaning of bringing the body in contact with objects so as to discover their properties either by mediation of its organs, such as the hands, or by a stick.

EVALUATION

Since Ames's theory resembles nineteenth-century empiristic theory in many important ways, it is subject to the same criticisms. Therefore, we shall not restate the objections to the leading assumptions of the theory which imply that the world originally is perceived flat and that touch (or action) is the basis for the acquisition of perceptions.

Evidence

It was not until 1954 that experimental evidence was submitted in verification of the claim that action changed the appearance of things. In that year Kilpatrick, an associate of Ames whose writings were helpful in the interpretation of transactional theory, reported the results of an experiment involving distorted rooms. The results, he says, represent a limited confirmation of the theory. Some subjects who comprised an "action group" had the opportunity to touch the walls of the distorted room with a wand or to throw a ball at some designated spot whereas other subjects comprising a "no-action group" merely observed the actions performed by someone else. Both groups at first saw the distorted room as a normal room but reported a gradual alteration in its appearance in the direction of distortion. No subject ever saw the "true shape of the distorted room" since the degree of practice was limited, but this is not important for our present purpose. Kilpatrick reports that there was no difference in the degree of altered appearance between the two groups, and that the results of the no-action group are "clearly contrary to hypothesis." He further points out that the "notion that gross overt action is necessary for such perceptual modification to occur is clearly wrong." Since a few years previously it had been contended that active touching was responsible for alteration in appearance, obviously a basic revision in the theory was necessary, a task which Kilpatrick undertakes, but his proposed revision is inadequate and we shall ignore it.

The important theoretical question is how the passive watcher can benefit from observing the actions performed by someone else. Their viewing positions are necessarily different and so are their respective retinal patterns. Presumably the passive watcher learned to associate the consequences of someone else's action to the interpretation of his own retinal pattern. How this association might be acquired and how, on the premise that it has been acquired, it would contribute to "learning to see" the distorted room in the direction of its true shape, are not explained. Moreover, it is said that the subjects of both groups generalized the alteration in appearance to a "normal room"—that is, this room tended to look distorted. Apparently a life-long experience and accumulated habit in dealing with normal rooms can be upset by an experiment involving only four brief learning sessions. Yet those who designed and constructed the distorted rooms and who were completely familiar with their characteristics for a period of years never reported any change in their perceptions. To be sure it is reported that there was some change in perceptual appearance of the action group. But the theory cannot draw much comfort from this result until it is demonstrated that active touch changes the perceptions during the time in childhood when "learning to see" presumably takes place; or even to indicate in a hypothetical fashion the steps which would describe the learning process that leads to the perception of a "normal room" on the premise that what is originally perceived corresponds to the characteristics of the retinal pattern. For these reasons, a repetition of the experiment would be necessary before any theoretical significance could be ascribed to the results.

We will consider some of the evidence inconsistent with the theory.

The retinal patterns in the eye of a chimpanzee and bird are the same as those for man. Yet insofar as can be judged from their responses to objects, they see as well as humans do. The results of experiments with lower animals show that such concepts as assumptive complex, choice, and interpretation of retinal patterns are redundant in the understanding of human vision unless one wants to attribute to animals a subconscious mind and the ability to weigh cues unconsciously. Even this attribution, which in fact no one has proposed, is precluded because the very young of many animals respond to objects as proficiently as they will in later life. Although in transactionalist writings the term "organism" is often used in referring to the description of retinal patterns, thus suggesting the generality of the theory, lower animals are excluded from the theory. But this exclusion is fortuitous because the retinal patterns at the basis of the theory in the acquisition of human perceptions are similar in lower animals, nor has any justification been advanced for restriction of the theory. We may observe that the above stated Assumptions 1 and 2 are unrestricted or unqualified in respect to species. Moreover, other results have been reported which contradict the importance of the assumption of rectangularity in the explanation of the perceived motion of the rotating rectangular and trapezoidal windows.[8]

Conceptual Structure

Says Ames, " [The observer] *keeps assuming different rectangular configurations as the trapezoidal window rotates.*" [9] This statement implies that each degree of trapezoidalness of the retinal pattern necessitates the assumption of a rectangular configuration unique to it. In this way a particular rectangle slanting in space at a given degree of inclination to the line of sight is perceived. Since there is a continuous series of retinal patterns interposed between the two patterns corresponding to endwise and broadside viewing, the observer apparently is called upon to make a near infinite number of assumptions. A similar comment applies to the rotating rectangular window, since each relative size difference in the vertical dimensions of the pattern requires a unique interpretation by the observer. Thus when it is sometimes said that the observer makes the assumption of a rectangular configuration, this expression should be regarded as a generic category subsuming the near infinity of assumptions. A similar number of assumptions are necessary for the interpretation of the absolute lengths of the edges of the retinal patterns for achieving the perception of "real size." Moreover, in the re-reading of Assumptions 1, 2, and 3 we observe that the necessity for an infinite number of assumptions is basic to the theory. Therefore, the observer must unconsciously weigh an infinite number of cues and possibilities before making the choice of that particular assumption which represents the probabilistic best fit for the retinal pattern. If it were not for God, said Malebranche, the individual perceiver would have to engage in an infinite number of reasonings and assumptions. Ames's theory is similar except that the reasonings and assumptions are attributed to the subconscious mind rather than to God.

The violation of the psychophysical postulate is implicit in the theory. Various properties are attributed to the mind as a causal agent in the formation of perceptions in apparent independence of physiological processes in the brain. There is no suggestion in Ames's writings that the assumptive complex is regarded as a shorthand expression for brain processes nor is there any suggestion as to the importance of such neural events approximately describable as memory traces, whether visual or tactual in origin, which might obviate or mitigate the violation. If the theory could be translated into physiological terms its most distinctive features would have to be given up. The language of "choice," subconscious mind, values, observer interpreting retinal patterns, and so on, would no longer be meaningful. Actually Ames did not express any interest in the psychophysical postulate, nor is such an interest apparent in his associates. We may return again to the assumption of the mind and the abilities attributed to it. Nowhere is there any discussion of the ways in which the mind might have acquired the abilities to construct perceptions from the chaos of raw material provided by retinal patterns and movements of the body.

Interposed between the perception and the retinal patterns is the "observer" who interprets the patterns. Ames's account of the way in which one learns about rectangular forms presupposes monocular viewing, but objects are viewed with two eyes and, consequently, there is a corresponding number of retinal patterns. Thus the observer ought to be called upon to interpret two patterns. The perception or interpretation of the retinal image is an important feature of the transactionalist's explanation of perceptual development. Evidently mental and physical facts are confounded. But whatever the meaning the "interpretation of the retinal pattern" was intended to convey, it may be re-interpreted as representing adherence to the constancy hypothesis. The observer, as it were, interprets the characteristics of the perception corresponding to the retinal image rather than the image itself. This reformulation, however, does not resolve the problem of two retinal images, since the "interpretation" of these images would be replaced by two perceptions.

Moreover, returning to the assumption of monocular viewing, Abbott's argument is effective in refuting the notion that the specific characteristics of a retinal pattern, such as the relative size difference of its edges, can be related to the characteristics of the distal stimulus through action. When the "observer" has walked to the object in order to touch it, the characteristics of his present retinal pattern are different from those of the retinal pattern before he started his walk.

That the organism "chooses" a perception as in *Assumption 3* was regarded as the most probable or reasonable conclusion which follows from *Assumptions 1* and *2* that are considered as premises. This syllogism represents the confusion of personal and scientific standpoints. The first premise entails a comparison between proximal and distal stimuli, but this comparison can only be ascertained by the scientist. The second premise, however, involves a comparison of the proximal stimulus or retinal pattern as known by the scientist and a perception which is only ascertainable by the perceiver who, in turn, reports it to the scientist. Having both types of information available, the scientist concludes that the characteristics of the perception do not correspond to the characteristics of the retinal pattern. The discrepancy is, of course, the classical problem in perceptual theory, and does not in itself constitute a confusion of the two standpoints. But when the transactionalist argued that an infinite number of perceptions are potentially available to the perceiver, and inferred that the perceiver chooses a particular perception from this class, he attributed to the perceiver a knowledge of facts known only by him as a scientist.

This line of thinking is related to another syllogism: *Premises:* (a) Perception cannot be derived from the properties of external objects. (b) Perception cannot be derived from the retinal pattern. *Conclusion:* Perception is derived from past experience. However, another conclusion is assertable, namely, that perception is derived from cerebral processes. Thus the gap between perception and retinal pattern may be

explainable in physiological rather than psychological terms. Therefore, the syllogism is insufficiently motivated so as to oblige its acceptance.

An important clue in understanding the emphasis on the psychological factors of past experience and the omission of brain physiology
is provided by the following observation of the science writer R. K.
Plumb, who had witnessed the demonstrations in Princeton in 1954
and paraphrased their significance on the basis of information supplied by his guide. He says:

> Viewed from the historic point of view of psychology, the new devices
> contradict the traditional Gestaltic concept of vision. This held that the
> viewer reconstructed in the complex of nerve cells within his brain a
> three-dimensional, diminutive facsimile of what his eyes beheld. By
> "thinking about" the three-dimensional model, the beholder figured out
> what he was seeing. The new idea has it that the viewer needs no three-
> dimensional picture, that objects are flat in the brain as they are flat in
> the visual experience. The new idea is that it is experience in judging
> sizes, shapes, brightnesses and motions that tells the viewers what he is
> looking at.

We may observe that the rejection of the two isomorphic relationships of perception and brain correlate, of brain correlate and external
object, implies the acceptance of the bi-dimensionality of brain pattern
and of visual experience. Apparently brain physiology is irrelevant because its study would at most show that the brain pattern is bi-dimensional, thus not affording the grounds for understanding perception
anyway.[10]

The "Trapezoidal Motion
Illusion" Reconsidered

A general explanation of phenomenal motion reversal, and of
other facts related to this phenomenon, are controversial at the present
time. Nevertheless it is possible to state common principles from a descriptive point of view irrespective of theoretical orientation. We may
observe that a description of the conditions correlated with the phenomenal facts of motion is an essential preliminary step for their explanation. The unquestioned acceptance of the phenomenological approach is a prerequisite condition in undertaking the task of descrip-

tion; the physical fact of retinal excitation patterns is a second condition. The physical fact known only to the scientist cannot in itself be the basis for any prediction concerning a phenomenal fact. Thus he can but judge of the perceptual effects to which the patterns give rise only insofar as such effects are reported by the perceiver. When the scientist says, as he often does, that a given excitation pattern is an "ambiguous cue" to motion he must be referring to his knowledge of the relationship of that pattern to the distal stimulus, since there is nothing whatsoever ambiguous in the perception which is correlated with this pattern. "Judgment" as a condition for perceived motion is impermissible from a descriptive standpoint because it is introduced as an explanatory concept. Moreover, "judgment," which actually represents the scientist's own judgment as to what ought to be perceived based on mere knowledge of excitation patterns, cannot be verified phenomenologically. The approach here suggested is noncommittal in respect to the empiristic or nonempiristic origin of the perception.

First, we may consider the phenomenal continuous rotation of a rectangle. To simplify discussion, some of the relevant features are depicted schematically in Figure 16.2. In ascertaining the perceptual effect produced by the stationary distal stimulus the scientist finds out that the perceiver sees a slanting surface with the right edge closer. Since the perceived surface corresponds to the inclination of the distal stimulus, the latter may be considered as its representation. Some of the perceptual depth effects corresponding to the retinal excitations are indicated in the representation. The distal stimulus is turned to a new position. The perceiver reports that he sees the right edge of the slanted surface as being somewhat closer, and its representation may also be depicted by the distal stimulus. The scientist records the fact that the same excitations can give rise to different perceptual depth effects. Insofar as the perceiver continues to see a slanted surface with the right edge closer than the left edge when the distal stimulus is in continuous rotation for the given arc, the rotation of the perceived surface corresponds to the objective fact.

A problem seems to arise in the case of the trapezoid because its perceived slant does not correspond to the slant of the distal stimulus. From the descriptive standpoint, however, there is no problem because phenomenally there is no discrepancy. The perceiver, the viewing conditions being optimal, sees the right edge of the slanting surface as

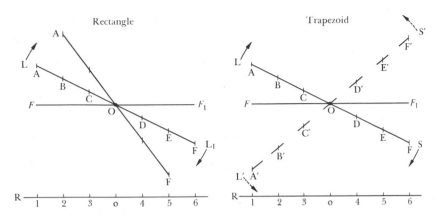

FIGURE 16.2. Both diagrams are schematic cross sections of Figure 16.1. *Rectangle:* LL_1 represents the distal stimulus at a particular inclination before being turned; $A, B, C, \ldots$, represent points on LL_1; and $1, 2, 3, o,$ $\ldots$, represent points on the retina R. The retina on being stimulated gives rise to the perception of an inclined surface. Since this perception corresponds to the inclination of the distal stimulus, LL_1 will also denote its representation. When the distal stimulus is rotated through the indicated arc, the retinal points $2–5$ receive stimulation. This stimulation gives rise to a perceived surface at a slightly greater degree of inclination, and its representation is denoted by the distal stimulus in its new position. On continuous rotation through the small arc, the succession of retinal excitations on either side of o converge toward o; the perception of a rotating surface corresponds to this convergence. Since the diagram is cross-sectional, these excitations actually represent trapezoidal patterns of varying shape. We may observe that the excitations of two successive retinal points such as $2, 3$ give rise to different relative perceptual depth effects.

Trapezoid: Although the distal stimulus is inclined as depicted by LS, generally the slant of the phenomenal surface is quite different $(L'S')$. In this instance the distal stimulus does not denote any perceived surface. We may observe that the excitations of $1, 2, 3, \ldots$, give rise to the perceptual effects A', B', C', and so on, rather than A, B, C, and so on, as would have been the case if the distal stimulus had been a rectangle. Moreover, when the distal stimulus is turned clockwise through an arc the perceived surface rotates counterclockwise, or equivalently, the distance of S' recedes while also having a lateral motion to the left. No additional principle is necessary in the understanding of the apparent motion reversal from a descriptive point of view because it represents a special case of the motion of the perceived rectangle. In both instances, the excitation paths converge toward o and the changes in the trapezoidal retinal patterns are similar. The description of the so-called "real" motion of the perceived rectangle involved the phenomenal fact of slant as a necessary condition, and the same is true in the description of the so-called apparent motion reversal of the trapezoid. From the standpoint of the perceiver the "real" and "apparent" motions both represent his perceptions, and phenomenologically there is no distinction between them. The terms "real" and "apparent" are introduced by the scientist who has knowledge of the inclination of the distal stimulus and of the perception as reported by the perceiver.

FF_1 represents a section of the frontoparallel plane. The angles F_1OF' and F_1OF (trapezoid), respectively negative and positive, are defined in relation to the motion of a horizontal line about O in a counterclockwise direction for the first angle and in a clockwise direction for the second angle. In the diagram pertaining to the rectangle, the rotation of the horizontal line forms two angles with OF_1 and both are positive. For the sake of exposition let us suppose that LL' represents the distal stimulus and AF the perceived slant. When the distal stimulus turns clockwise, the motion of the perceived right end moves toward the viewer and laterally to the left. In this instance there is no apparent motion reversal, notwithstanding the discrepancy between the perceived slant and the slant of the distal stimulus, and the descriptive analysis of this motion would be similar to the previous analysis of the rectangle. We may observe that the two angles formed by the two sides with OF_1 remain positive. We may infer that the oppositeness of signs is an essential condition to the apparent motion reversal of the trapezoid.

---

more distant than the left edge and so reports it. Insofar as he continues to see the right edge as more distant than the left edge in the steady clockwise rotation of the distal stimulus, he sees the surface rotating counterclockwise (or the apparent right edge recedes and the apparent left edge moves forward).

The following condition may be inferred as essential to apparent motion reversal. The angles formed by the representations of the distal stimulus and of the apparent surface in reference to the representation of the frontoparallel plane are of opposite signs, or equivalently, corresponding points on the representations are on opposite sides of the represented frontoparallel plane. Should the angles be of the same sign, as would happen with the "rectangle" because its perceived slant generally is in agreement with the actual slant, no apparent motion reversal occurs.

Inasmuch as the description of apparent motion reversal of the trapezoid is contingent on the description of the perceived motion of the rectangle, the problem of "explanation" is whether the perceived slant (and motion) of the rectangle is learned or not learned.[11]

MURPHY

The dominant theme of Murphy's *Personality* (1947) is based on a formula of the nineteenth-century philosopher Herbert Spencer, who maintained that evolution could be explained in terms of a transition from an original homogeneity to heterogeneity. This conception applied not only to the evolution of the human race but also to the physical and mental development of every human being from the time of the formation of the zygote to the achievement of complete development at some unspecified time after birth. Moreover, the postnatal history of each psychological function exhibits the transition from homogeneity to heterogeneity. Murphy's delineation of three stages of perceptual development is based on this formula.[12]

The first stage pertains to the just-born infant. Says Murphy, "The mind as a whole is a blur; there are no sharp outlines within it." The impressions from different senses merge into a "global mass." The incomplete development of the central nervous system is partly responsible for this state of affairs. The emergence and differentiation of "elements" mark the second stage of development. The infant can sort out his impressions according to their sensory modalities and he can distinguish the elements for the same sense. Thus he responds differentially to sounds and also colors and shapes. Murphy points out that neural maturation contributes to the emergence of the second stage but generally its importance is minimized and "learning" or "experience" emphasized. The movements of the hands and eyes are presumed to be significant in the breaking up of the original visual mass into its constituent elements. Although the visual elements are not explicitly defined, it is apparent that they correspond to the sensations of traditional empiristic theory based on the presupposition of the constancy hypothesis. Thus he maintains that the constancies of size, shape, and brightness, and the perception of the third dimension are the products of learning. Whatever the infant sees at this stage corresponds to the characteristics of retinal stimulations and patterns. The third stage is one of "integration"—the elements are articulated into "organized totals." The three stages are not necessarily sequential or chronological. For instance, while the infant is "disentangling" the mass into specific elements he is at the same time engaged in the process of ordering them into an organized unit. Although manipulation of objects and other motor responses constitute one important factor in perceptual development, needs and autisms are said to be another and more basic factor.[13]

According to Murphy needs have an existence prior to perception. He says, "Needs determine how the incoming energies are to be put into structured form." Presumably the energies refer to the effects of retinal stimulation, and depending on the nature of the need, they are structured one way or another so that we see that which we wish to see. When perception conforms to the need, gratification is secured, and that is why need is so important in perceptual development. Without needs the transition from the first to the second stage would be impossible. The concept of *autism,* which is closely related to the concept of *needs,* was adopted from the psychiatrist Bleuler who said, "This detachment from reality, together with the relative and absolute predominance of the inner life, we term 'autism.' " Psychotics grossly misinterpret various features of the world including simple instructions of the physician, and they may confuse an idea with a perception. The guiding consideration is an inner or psychotic wish which they themselves accept as real. In thus justifying the introduction of a new concept, Bleuler was concerned with thought processes. Murphy extended the meaning of the concept to perception. According to him, perception evolves from the wish to procure gratification and the wish to avoid frustration. Autistic factors become important in the transition from the second to the third stage. Sensory elements have already emerged, and these are not altered by the pressure of needs or wants. They are, however, available for ordering in one arrangement rather than another arrangement of elements and for the accenting of one element so that it can emerge as the figure against the background of other elements. But this does not imply that the final perceptions are completely contingent on personal factors, as Murphy pointed out, because objects in the environment are stable and the infant must learn to adjust to them since otherwise he could not survive. Thus his perceptions tend to be realistic, although he learns to see under the pressure of inner factors.[14]

Several examples from adult experience are provided in justification of the thesis that factors of learning, rather than neural maturation, are primarily responsible for the transition from the first stage to the second stage. In tasting tea we ordinarily have the experience of a single uniform taste even though it may be composed of a variety of blends. However, the tea taster trains himself to recognize the individual components in the blend and thus for him the tea does not have the uniform taste it does for us. On hearing the Japanese language for the first time, we have the impression of a "melodious blur." But in having learned a few words we can detect their presence, and the blur, as a result, is differentiated into elements. Since maturation is complete, the uniformity of tastes and sounds represents a general characteristic of consciousness and the functioning of the nervous system; hence the emergence of the elements would be the result of learning. These instances of perceptual learning in the adult typify the perceptual development taking place in the infant. The apparent uniformity of the adult state of consciousness occurs when we are confronted with novel situations or "unfamiliar things." For the infant, however, every situation is at first novel, hence his sensations form a "massive blur." [15]

Clearly Murphy's theory recapitulates James's second theory of perception. For instance, the first stage of perceptual development corresponds to the "one great blooming, buzzing confusion" James attributed to the baby's mind, and "needs"—the factor Murphy emphasizes to explain the crystallization of elements in the second stage—corresponds to James's "attention." Since the same objections to James's theory apply to Murphy's theory, the second stage of perceptual development could not have evolved from the first stage. Murphy's description of the spatial characteristics of the visual elements or sensations of the second stage is contingent on the assumption that the child sees all objects as flat. Therefore, in our view, neither autistic factors nor motor responses could ever explain the emergence of perceptions in the third stage.

An early discussion of perceptual development in 1935 provides further insight into the reasons at the basis of the three stages which were elaborated in 1947. According to Murphy, the simultaneous stimulation of different spots of the retina leads to jumbled-up nonspatial qualities. To explain the emergence of spatially ordered three-dimensional visual patterns, the local sign theory of Lotze and the muscular movements in reaching for or feeling objects are cited. Local signs, in his view, also account for localization of sensation according to the part of the body that is touched or irritated. It would seem that Murphy presupposed a "projection theory" of visual sensation. Although the theory of local signs is not mentioned in 1947 and in later expositions, nevertheless it probably represents a continuing influence.[16]

The main underpinning of his theory, especially as stated in 1947, rests on the results of three experiments performed by himself and his collaborators. An important methodological requirement to be observed in designing an experiment for the purpose of demonstrating the influence of need in the formation of some percept is that the objective stimulus typically must be marginally presented. The experimental room may be quite dark, the stimulus may be exposed for a brief interval tachistoscopically, or its contour may be somewhat obscured by placing it behind a translucent screen. Thus the subject is prevented from getting a "good look." If the mode of presentation of the stimulus allows for a firm and distinct percept the factor of need may not exert an influence; a "perceptual habit" may be so strong that it overrides the possible effect of a competing need. Thus marginality of the situation is essential to the experiment.

In one experiment subjects looked at "long" and "short" lines in a semi-dark room. In the training period the seeing of the long lines was accompanied by reward and short lines by punishment. After a certain number of trials the reward and punishment were discontinued, and the subjects were now asked to report on the perceived lengths of the lines. The result of the experiment indicates that all lines looked longer than they did before the administration of reward and punishment. In a second experiment subjects looked at a variety of forms placed behind a translucent screen after varying periods of hunger; it was reported that the greater the degree of hunger, the more likely a given stimulus would be perceived as a food object. The third experiment which indicates that a figure-ground relationship can be altered by reward and punishment will be discussed in more detail.

Contour lines were drawn within each of two circles, the lines forming two complementary human profiles. Division of each circle at the contour leads to a total of four profiles. In Figure 16.3 one pair is shown and we shall gear our discussion to this pair alone.

Some subjects received a monetary reward when Profile *A* was shown and had the reward withdrawn (punishment) when Profile *B* was shown. For other subjects the reverse was true: Profiles *A* and *B* were respectively punishing and rewarding. The purpose of the experiment was to determine whether the subject would perceive the profile previously associated with reward when the two profiles were brought together so as to form an inclusive figure. In all trials the stimuli were exposed tachistoscopically for ⅓ second. The subject was informed that the learning of the associations of names and perceived profiles was the purpose of the experiment. The subject successfully learned the names of the two perceived profiles, although the seeing of one profile led to consistent reward and the other to consistent punishment. After these training trials the two profiles were recombined into a single circle, and the subject was instructed to give the name associated with the profile which he saw. It was reasonably supposed that the naming was contingent upon the percept. If, for example, the subject saw Profile *A* in the combined figure he produced the name appropriate to it rather than the name of the unseen Profile *B*. The two combined figures were randomly presented in over 32 post-training trials without any reward or punishment. It was reported that up to trial 16 the subjects perceived that profile which previously had been rewarded.

The result was interpreted as confirming the hypothesis that autism had been active in establishing a figure-ground relationship. Its general implication for the stages of perceptual development lies in the hypothesis that autistic factors can only alter structural relations, they

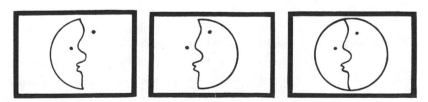

FIGURE 16.3. (The figures are from R. Schafer and G. Murphy, "The role of autism in a visual figure-ground relationship. *J. Exp. Psychol.*, 1943, 32, 335–43. Reproduced by permission.)

cannot create a percept from unformed raw visual data. In the post-training trials there are two possibilities of structural relations or organizations: one given profile is figure and the other ground, and conversely. Autistic mechanisms determine the organization that is to prevail. The perceived form, either of the half or full circle, is itself not the product of autism. Similar facts are thought to characterize perceptual development in early life.[17]

The three experiments were held to be consistent not only with the theory of autism but also with the related thesis *"we learn to perceive* in much the same way that we *learn to act."* In general we learn those responses which lead to reward and inhibit those which lead to punishment. And this same consideration was supposed to be true in the learning of percepts. Actually an examination of the methodology of the experiments shows that the results were not decisively established. Generally the hypothesis under test was vaguely stated, and it was not related to the conditions of the experiment. It was perhaps for this reason that the authors of the experiments inspected the data in order to ascertain the degree to which a hypothesis had been verified and why they found it necessary to introduce additional hypotheses in order to account for those results that they had not anticipated. For instance, in the experiment on figure-ground reversal, it was found that the hypothesis of autism was not verified subsequent to trial 16, and ancillary hypotheses were called in for the purpose of explaining the results. The choice of the critical number was adventitious in the sense that it was not stipulated in advance of the experiment, its selection being guided by the data themselves. The risk inherent in this procedure is that the results declared to be "significant" actually may represent artifacts of the procedure itself. This problem and some other problems that have arisen in the interpretation of the results will be ignored in further discussion, inasmuch as our interest concerns their theoretical significance.[18]

If the subject had viewed the combined figure before the training trials the theory at the basis of the experiment implies that he would have perceived Profile *A* in some trials and Profile *B* in other trials, the exposure time being too short for figure-ground reversal during a single trial. Moreover, he would have learned to recognize and correctly name them. What has to be explained is the way in which the reward administered during the training trials gave an advantage to one perceived profile rather than perceived alternating figures in the post-training trials. In previous discussion we have observed that a percept process is an antecedent condition to the processes of recognizing and naming. A similar point can be made in respect to the process at the basis of reward. In other words, the seeing of an object is a prerequisite to the anticipation of reward. From the standpoint of the theory of autism we tend to see that which is gratifying and we tend not to see that which is punishing. If the seeing were conscious it would lead to the paradox of reward or punishment as an antecedent condition to seeing. However, in the theory under consideration, the influence of autistic pressures is said to be expressed unconsciously. In reference to his "unconscious" the subject at first sees one or the other profile and selects the rewarding rather than the punishing profile. Since the unconscious perceptions require an evaluation before the right one is perceived and recognized consciously, an evaluator is essential. Thus Murphy suggested the possibility of a "pre-perceptual observer" to explain the results. This type of explanation leads to additional problems while possibly resolving others. Consider, for instance, the training trials when the profiles are individually presented. The association of one profile with punishment does not prevent its conscious perception in these trials although this perception presumably is suppressed when the profile is combined in an inclusive figure in the post-training trials. The role of an autistic mechanism necessarily must be restricted, but the reason for this restriction is not evident.[19]

A predator may be regarded as the administrator of actual or potential punishment. If the intended prey were guided by considerations similar to the human wish to avoid seeing the unpleasant or punishing things, it would not long survive on catching a glimpse of the predator. And if it did manage to survive the attack, it is reasonable to suppose that the animal would more readily engage in actions leading to escape in another encounter. Similar facts, of course, characterize human actions. In instances of this kind it appears that not only does the percept guide the appropriate action but also that it creates the need.

Autistic mechanisms, according to Murphy, are more effective in children, because they are less realistically oriented than are adults and the possibility of alteration of perceptual organization is therefore greater. Although no clear example of the acquisition of perceptual organization or its modification is provided, we may surmise the following in respect to the infant who is somewhere in the second stage of development. If he sees his mother's face in profile as a segregated and stable unit from the background, figure-ground organization is not the product of learning. On the other hand, should he see the ground as "things" and the face as a "hole," each alternating with the other as in figure-ground reversal, the acquisition of figure-ground organization in terms of actions, rewards and punishments, and needs would be impossible.

When a theoretical structure becomes increasingly complex relative to the data it was intended to explain, one considers the possibility of a simpler hypothesis. The foundation of Murphy's general theory of perceptual learning lies in the results and explanation of the three experiments. We will take another look at the data.

In one experiment subjects gave estimates of the magnitudes of lines in terms of inches. It is conceivable that reward and punishment influenced the judgment of length rather than phenomenal length. Thus a shift in the estimate of a given line from five to twelve inches may merely have represented an alteration in how long the subject thought the line to be and not that the line *looked* quite short in one instance and very long in the other. In the experiment pertaining to the need for food the subjects were instructed to "verbalize an association with every picture you see." The experimental subjects—those who had gone without food—were also promised a meal after the experiment. It is not unreasonable to suppose that these subjects, college students, were concerned with food and that they might have thought that the topic of the experiment itself concerned their interest in food in some way. On being exposed to a series of stimuli, therefore, they tended to respond with food associations rather than merely to describe their percepts.

Consider, for example, the letter X. If one sees this letter on a sign while driving, it signifies the possibility of danger ahead. On the other hand, this same letter signifies a multiplication sign in an arithmetic book. The need to drive safely or the need to understand the book changes our interpretation. In both instances, however, the letter still looks the same in the sense of two intersecting straight lines. The fact that the stimuli in the experiment were "ambiguous" increases the scope of different associations or significances. In being hungry, the stimulus reminds us of food and we so report it, whereas in being well fed we report some other association. The picture we see in both instances remains the same perceptually but we think and say different things about it. No positive evidence was adduced in either experiment that would suggest the fact of any phenomenal change. Since such a change represents an interpretation by the experimenters, another interpretation of the same data is feasible. The results of the experiment on figure-ground alteration may be explained in similar terms. During the training trials the subjects could have learned to associate the direction of a given profile with the name or rewarding character of the profile itself. This acquired association was then carried over into the post-training trials. For instance, the "nose" of Profile A points to the right. This distinctive part cue could have been associated with the name without the subject perceiving the profile as a figure. The mirror image of the profile could have been presented along with the original direction of the profile in the post-training series as one way of "controlling set," as the authors of the experiment themselves acknowledge. Since the stimuli were exposed for only $\frac{1}{3}$ second, the subjects would not have had the time to search for the distinctive cue, whether pointing to the left or to the right. Correct naming in these circumstances might be indicative of a perceptual effect. These three experiments evidently do not oblige the acceptance of the interpretation conferred upon them by their authors. Since there is no proof of a phenomenal change, the simplifying alternative gains in plausibility.

The fact that marginal situations form the core of the experimental procedures suggests the ever-present possibility that perception is not the only factor involved. Such marginal perceptual situations allow for the maximum play of interpretive or judgmental factors. The subject does not get a clear visual impression since the exposure time may be too short or the stimulus too ambiguous. Therefore, he is constrained to interpret the "stimulus situation." Such reconstruction, moreover, may be related to his needs. Thus a complicating factor is introduced into the experimental design. Is perception itself influenced by needs or is only the interpretive process accompanying a percept so influenced? A decisive answer may be impossible to obtain as long as the experimental situation is of a marginal character. This impasse, of course, cannot be resolved by enabling the subject to secure a firm view of the situation. For when the stimulus is well-defined, inherent processes of organization are presumed to prevail and the possible influence of need abolished. In this instance, therefore, a theory of autism is not being fairly tested. But since the main direction of research by adherents of an autistic theory has involved marginal situations, its conclusions cannot be regarded as decisive.[20]

It is sometimes said that the distinction between interpretation or judgment and perception is a matter of definition and that the exclusion of the role of interpretive factors on perception is equivalent to a definition of perception independent of such factors. Actually the distinction is conceptual in the same sense that it does not rest on the way words are to be used. Moreover, the possibility of an interpretive act altering a perception can be given a definite meaning, and its influence can be ascertained through experiment. Let us return to Descartes's distinction between seeing and judging and the example of the two ships. The ships are perceived to be at the same distance and of the same size. On the basis of these phenomenal facts and knowledge of the ships, one ship is judged to be more distant than the other. We observe the following: (a) the judgment of distance is contingent on the phenomenal facts; (b) the judgment of distance is contingent upon previous experience or knowledge; (c) phenomenal distance and size are not altered by the act of judgment. We may also observe that if the viewer has no knowledge of the ships he cannot judge their distance, and that upon obtaining the necessary information he can do so.

This example justifies the conceptual distinction between perception and judgment. Of course, it is possible to include judgment in the definition of perception. And this makes it possible to say that the perception of the viewer, as in Descartes's example, has been altered by judgment and past experience, although the phenomenal content of distance and size has not changed. However, empirists traditionally, including Murphy, believe that judgment may and does change the phenomenal content. Hence the distinction re-emerges, but the theorist does not often distinguish the two meanings of perception. And for this reason it is difficult to tell whether the evidence which is cited to show a change in perception refers to the meaning in which judgment is included as a matter of definition, or to the meaning of change in phenomenal content. To avoid this confusion it is desirable to have a term which refers exclusively to phenomenal content. *Perception* would qualify as the appropriate term.[21]

NOTES

1. See Lucretius for an early discussion of errors of sight. The Necker Cube is named after Necker, who first reported the phenomenon in 1832. The horizontal-vertical illusion was discussed by Malebranche (*Recherche,* Vol. 1, p. 93). In addition to the drawing of lines for the purpose of illustrating this illusion, he also suggested an experiment with two pieces of straw of the same length.

2. Crombie; Graham, pp. 28f.; Kline, Ch. 10; MacCurdy, Ch. 9; Richter, pp. 107–21; Ronchi, 1952. The quotation from Leonardo da Vinci at the head of the chapter is from Richter, p. 110.

3. R. W. Darwin, pp. 346f. Said Darwin in anticipation of Emmert's Law: "Thus when you view a spectrum on a sheet of white paper, if you approach the paper to the eye, you may diminish it to a point; and if the paper is made to recede from the eye, the spectrum will appear magnified in proportion to the distance."

The problem in the explanation of the moon illusion—another classical problem concerning perceived magnitude—arises from the equality (or near equality) of the retinal images of the zenith and horizontal moons. On the assumption of the constancy hypothesis, the moon in its two positions originally would be seen as of the same size. In actuality, however, the image of the zenith moon is slightly larger because the moon in this position is closer to the observer by approximately the radius of the earth. The sizes of the retinal images usually were regarded as equal in order to simplify theoretical discussion of the illusion (cf. Molyneux, 1687).

The constancy hypothesis was the basis for the empiristic approach to perceptual phenomena that do not involve spatial characteristics—for instance, brightness. The retinal effect produced by light reflected from an object gives rise to a perceived brightness irrespective of the retinal effects produced by light reflected from the background or from other objects; when the retinal effect varies, according to changes in illumination of the object, the perceived brightness also varies. Three sheets of paper designated as "black," "gray," and "white" respectively appear black, gray, and white when observed in uniform illumination. These sheets selectively absorb incident light so that the intensity of reflected light is least for the black paper and greatest for the white paper. The variation in intensity produces corresponding graded retinal effects, and these effects, in accordance with the constancy hypothesis, give rise to the seeing of black, gray, and white. Furthermore, when the white paper is placed in shadow so that the intensity of reflected light is less than that reflected by the gray paper, the white paper, in respect to original perception, should appear grayer than the gray paper. However, for the adult it looks white. Similarly, the black paper when reflecting the direct rays of the sun looks black, and white paper in the shadow looks white. This perceptual phenomenon, which exemplifies *brightness constancy,* likewise arises in the viewing of actual objects under conditions of variable illumination. Coal looks black in sunlight and in dim light. (See Arnheim, pp. 247f., and Köhler, 1947, pp. 75f., for further discussion.)

4. Brewster, 1856, Chs. 1, 4, 5; Giraud-Teulon, 1861, Sec. 100–15, and 1868; Helmholtz, *Optics,* Vol. 3, Sec. 33; Panum; Wheatstone, 1838, 1852. Whewell suggested the concept of "nearly corresponding points" in 1840 (Bk. 4, Ch. 2).

Wheatstone reported an experiment which, in his view, invalidated the eye-movement theory (1838). After having obtained two after-images by looking through a stereoscope, he observed either a single after-image or two after-images. He noted that the single after-image was three-dimensional, as though he were again viewing the original figures that gave rise to the after-image through the stereoscope. Inasmuch as the single after-image required the optic axes to be converged in the right way, he concluded that the perceived third dimension could not have been the result of eye-movement. Thus, his experiment and interpretation anticipated the theoretical conclusion of the later experiment with an electric spark (Dove's experiment, 1841; see Helmholtz, *Optics*). Giraud-Teulon subsequently noted that the Dove experiment was unnecessary, because in the momentary flash of lightning during a storm we perceive objects extended in three dimensions (1868).

Chapter 2 (DESCARTES)

1. *Discourse on method,* Pt. 5; *Meditations* (VI).

2. *Passions,* Arts. 31–35; *Meditations* (VI); *Principles philosophy,* Pt. 4, Art. 196; a letter of 1637, Alquié, pp. 791 f.

3. *Principles philosophy*, Pt. 4, Art. 189.

4. The "psychophysical postulate," which is not Descartes's term, is implied in the quotation at the head of the chapter, *Passions*, Pt. 1, Art. 13. See also *Passions*, Pt. 1, Art. 34, and *Dioptrique*, Discourse 6.

5. *Passions*, Pt. 1, Arts. 21, 26; *Rules* (XII); *Dioptrique*, Discourses 5, 6; *L'Homme*, p. 443.

6. There is no justification for the usual opinion that Descartes found it necessary to re-invert the cerebral image in order to explain upright vision. This opinion is based on diagrams which were included in the text of *L'Homme* by others, Descartes's own having been lost. See Pastore and Klibbe.

7. Cf. *L'Homme*, p. 434 and pp. 448–67, and Alquié's footnotes to these pages.

8. See preceding note for references, and also *L'Homme*, pp. 423–27. In *L'Homme* the limits of the effectiveness of movements of convergence and accommodation are respectively "15 or 20 feet" and "3 or 4 feet" whereas in *Dioptrique*, Discourse 6, they are "100 or 200 feet" and "4 or 5 feet."

9. *Meditations* (VI); *Principles philosophy*, Pt. 4, Art. 196.

10. *Passions*, Pt. 1, Art. 50.

11. *Meditations* (VI).

12. See note 2 for references.

13. *Passions*, Pt. 1, Arts. 23–25, 33.

14. *Ibid.*, Pt. 1, Arts. 13, 50.

15. *Dioptrique*, Discourse 6; *Rules* (XII); *Meditations* (III, VI); *Principles philosophy*, Pt. 1, Arts. 66–71, and Pt. 2, Art. 196.

16. For discussion in the text of Descartes's natural geometry, see *Dioptrique*, Discourse 6. Also see *L'Homme*, pp. 428f. "Natural geometry" in *L'Homme* pertained only to the binocular perception of distance; reasoning and the mind's ability to pay attention to locations along a straight line were not mentioned. As Descartes proceeded to develop a physiological explanation of perception in this text, movements of the pineal gland were proposed as the mechanism at the basis of distance perception, and there was no further reference to geometry. In *Passions of the soul*, in which Descartes set forth the physiological explanation of single vision which was implicit in *L'Homme*, natural geometry was not discussed.

Descartes's "geometric" explanation of perception was derived from Kepler (Graham, pp. 39f.; Ronchi, 1952, 1957, 1963; R. Smith, "Remarks," p. 4; Turbayne, 1962). For instance, said Smith: "The vulgar account of objects appearing erect notwithstanding the inversion of the pictures upon the retina, is also Kepler's; who tells us that the mind perceiving an impulse of the ray Pp on the lower part of the retina, considers this ray as directed from an higher point of the object; and likewise perceives the impulse of the ray Rr upon the higher part of the retina, to be directed from the lower part of the object." According to Smith, Descartes adopted a similar solution of the problem of inverted retinal images.

17. For Gassendi's criticism and Descartes's reply, see Haldane and Ross, Vol. 2, pp. 198–202, 231.

18. Rohault, Pt. 1, Chs. 28–32, in Clarke, same chapters. Figure 2.1 was reconstructed before Rohault's work was examined. Insofar as Rohault followed Descartes, the frontispiece would represent an independent verification of our interpretation of Descartes.

Chapter 3 (MALEBRANCHE)

1. *Recherche*, Vol. 1, pp. 19, 79, and Vol. 2, p. 240; *Search after truth*, Bk. 1, Chs. 6, 10.

2. *Dialogues*, p. 154.

3. *Search after truth*, Bk. 3, Pt. 2, Ch. 7, also p. 144 of the *Illustration* to Ch. 7.

4. *Search after truth*, Bk. 1, Chs. 7, 10–12; *Réponse*, Ch. 1, Secs. 4, 9.

5. *Réponse*, Ch. 1, Sec. 4.

6. *Search after truth*, Bk. 1, Ch. 9, Sec. 3.

7. *Recherche*, Vol. 1, pp. 97, 113 f., Vol. 3, p. 328; *Éclaircissement*, Sec. 27; *Réponse*, Ch. 1, Sec. 2. See also N. Smith.

8. *Search after truth*, Bk. 1, Chs. 7, 14; *Réponse*, Ch. 1. See N. Smith. Malebranche also regarded interposition of "images," as in the case of the moon illusion, as a factor in the perceived sizes of the "child" and "giant."

9. *Search after truth*, Bk. 1, Ch. 7, Sec. 4.

10. *Dialogues*, p. 129. "Visual direction" and "situation" are synonymous.

11. *Éclaircissement*, Sec. 43.

12. *Search after truth*, Bk. 2, Pt. 1, Ch. 7, and Pt. 2, Ch. 2.

13. *Ibid.*, Bk. 3, Pt. 2, Chs. 3, 6, 11.

14. *Ibid.*, Bk. 1, Chs. 10, 12, 14.

The substitution of innate properties attributed to the "mind" for the properties Malebranche attributed to God directly led to one form of nonempiristic doctrine (cf. Porterfield, Vol. 2, Bk. 5, Chs. 3–5).

Chapter 4 (LOCKE AND MOLYNEUX)

1. Locke, *Examination of Malebranche's opinion*, Secs. 9, 10, 18, 38–41.

2. *Ibid.*, Secs. 11, 12.

3. Locke, *Essay*, Vol. 1, p. 185.

4. *Ibid.*, Ch. 9; Leibniz, p. 136.

5. Locke, *Essay*, Vol. 1, pp. 211 f.

6. *Ibid.*, Ch. 8; also Vol. 2, pp. 38 f.

7. *Ibid.*, Vol. 1, p. 187.

8. For the Synge solution and comments of Molyneux and Locke, see Locke, *Familiar letters*, pp. 370–78.

9. Leibniz, pp. 137–41.

10. Molyneaux, 1692, Proposition 31.

11. *Ibid.*, Proposition 28.

12. *Ibid.*, Pt. 2, Ch. 7.

Chapter 5 (BERKELEY)

1. *Essay*, Secs. 9–12.

2. *Ibid.*, Secs. 88, 90.

3. *Ibid.*, Secs. 17–20; *Alciphron* (Dialogue VII), Secs. 16, 17; *Three dialogues* (Dialogue I) in Calkins, pp. 243f.

4. *Essay*, Secs. 2, 50, 60, 88; Graham, pp. 109f.; Koffka, 1930; N. Smith, p. 199; Russell, 1948, p. 51.

5. *Essay*, Secs. 44, 79–83; R. Smith, Vol. 1, Secs. 97, 98. According to Molyneux (1687), to whom Berkeley refers in Sec. 75 of the *Essay* in a discussion of the moon illusion, the moon's apparent magnitude is 30′.

6. For other contemporary interpretations of Sec. 41 by philosophers, see Hicks, Johnston, Luce (1934, 1963), and Warnock. Graham, pp. 94f., traces the history of the meaning of "in the mind."

7. *Essay*, Sec. 120. Said Le Cat: "We learn to see while in the arms of our wet-nurse, she is our first object. . . ." (Vol. 2, p. 620).

8. *Essay*, Secs. 45, 54.

9. *Ibid.*, Secs. 16–27, 45; 1733, Sec. 66.

10. *Essay*, Secs. 54–60, 77; 1733, Sec. 59.

11. *Essay*, Sec. 153.

12. *Ibid.*, Secs. 143–45; *Alciphron* (Dialogue IV), Secs. 10–12.

13. *Essay*, Sec. 102.

14. *Ibid.*, Secs. 59, 147, 148.

15. *Ibid.*, Secs. 126, 145, 146, 159; *Alciphron* (Dialogue IV), Sec. 12.

16. *Essay*, Secs. 86–120; Turbayne, 1955; Walls, pp. 6–13.

17. *Essay*, Secs. 49, 108, 111, 117, 127, 132, 133; 1733, Secs. 42, 44. Also see Cassirer, p. 109; and Luce, 1934, p. 33. Says Cassirer: "The *Essay towards a New Theory of Vision*, which forms the prelude to Berkeley's philosophy and contains all of his ideas implicitly, is nothing but an attempt at a complete systematic development and elucidation of Molyneux's problem."

18. *Essay*, Sec. 135; Bourdon, p. 380.

19. *Essay*, Secs. 129, 130, 156; Bailey, 1842, Ch. 4.

20. *Essay*, Secs. 83, 136; Armstrong, pp. 42f.; Condillac, 1746; Fraser, 1871, p. 471.

21. *Essay*, Secs. 157, 158. In respect to Berkeley's repudiation of Locke, Fraser asks: "Does Berkeley mean to hint . . . that the only proper object of sight is *unextended* colour—that even *superficial* extension is invisible—and that, apart from an experience of certain sensations and exertions in the motor organs, all *visibilia* are perceived as unextended points?" (1891, p. 242 n.).

22. *Essay*, Sec. 145.

The confounding of visible ideas and feeling of motion, which Berkeley supposed, implies that consciousness is a delusion (see Chapter 8). Berkeley's "appeal to consciousness" in the rejection of natural geometry was turned against Berkeley's own theory. N. Smith: "If we apply Berkeley's own favourite mode of argument, and inquire whether, on looking into the mind, we can discover any such signs as data existing prior to our perceptions, the answer must be negative. We do not first apprehend the signs of distance and from them gather their meaning. The perceptions arise in consciousness, as Malebranche insists, with all the apparent immediacy and sensible force of a simple feeling of pain. On Berkeley's theory, however, strictly interpreted, we can perceive nothing but the signs" (pp. 199f.). Also see Armstrong, p. 20.

23. 1733, Sec. 71. In an appendix which only appeared in the second edition of the *Essay* in 1710, Berkeley alluded to the account of a resighted person who had been operated upon by Roger Grant and which had been reported in *Tatler*, No. 55 (Fraser, 1901, Vol. 1, p. 210).

24. The Cheselden report was quoted in full or nearly so, or in extensive paraphrase, by Cheselden himself in various editions of his *Anatomy* subsequent to 1728 and also by Buffon, Condillac (1754), Fraser (1901), Hamilton, Helmholtz, Le Cat, Magendie, Mayo, McCosh (1892), Preyer, Priestley, and A. Smith. The Voltaire account of the case was republished in many different sources (cf. Diderot; Diderot's *Encyclopédie*, article, "Sens"; Condillac, 1746).

Voltaire (pp. 80f.) summarized and paraphrased the case in such a way that it suggested to Condillac (1746) that the boy at first saw things inverted. Buffon was of the opinion that infants see upside down, but he did not relate this opinion to the Cheselden report. R. Smith believed that things are originally seen double because of the formation of two images in the retinas, this opinion being stated independently of the report. Buffon followed Smith's opinion, but added that the report did not provide corroborating evidence. Priestley, who also adopted Smith's opinion, said: "The most extraordinary circumstance in this account is that objects did not appear double upon their first looking at them with both eyes, since a variety of other observations seem to prove that it is only by a ready association of ideas, in consequence of much experience, that we conclude an object is single, when there is a distinct picture of it in each eye" (p. 724). In speaking of "their," Priestley alluded to several other cases of those born blind whose sight had been restored by Cheselden. These cases were said to lead to the same conclusion, as did the account of the thirteen-year-old boy, of "their *learning to see*." Buffon expressed the same opinion, but he also said that Cheselden had reported his observations in *Tatler*, No. 55. This opinion, which apparently originated in Smith, has been carried down into the present century.

However, Cheselden published the account of only one case of the restoration of sight to a person who had been born blind—the case which is reproduced in Appendix A. Aitken's footnote to *Tatler*, No. 55 is of some interest in view of the occasional citation of the Grant case in contemporary literature. He pointed out that a controversy had arisen in 1709 over an allegation that Grant was an "impostor." The *Dictionary of National Biography* has the following entry:

"GRANT, ROGER (*d.* 1724), quack oculist, having lost an eye as a soldier in the German emperor's service, set up as an oculist in Queen Anne's reign in Mouse Alley, Wapping, and contrived to get appointed oculist to Anne and to George I, and to acquire considerable wealth. He is satirically referred to as 'putting out eyes with great success' in No. 444 of the 'Spectator' (30 July 1712). A sheet describing his professed cures is in the British Museum Library, and also an 'Account of a Miraculous Cure of a Young Man in Newington,' London, 1709, evidently written to discredit his pretensions. The latter pamphlet states that Grant was a baptist preacher, had been a cobbler, and was illiterate."

Chapter 6 (CONDILLAC)

Our account of Condillac's theory is based on the first edition of the *Traité des sensations* (in Le Roy; and, in Italian translation, in Carlini). Thus discussion of inconsistencies which developed in changes in the theory in subsequent editions could be avoided. The English translation by Carr, which is of the third edition, was useful in translating those portions of the first edition which were included in the third. Condillac provided a succinct and useful summary of his theory (1755). See Le Roy, and Carlini. All citations are to Condillac's 1754 treatise.

1. Introductory section, "Purpose of this work," Pt. 3, Chs. 3 and 4, Pt. 4, Ch. 8.
2. Pt. 1, Ch. 11, Pt. 3, Ch. 3.
3. Pt. 1, Ch. 11. Condillac's supposition of the mind as a "spiritual and indivisible" substance is apparent in the 1755 summary. A significant inconsistency in the third edition is that Condillac, although adhering to the concept of "mathematical point," insists that sensation of color is extended.
4. See note 2 for references, also Pt. 2, Ch. 2.
5. Pt. 1, Ch. 11, Sec. 8.
6. Pt. 3, Ch. 3, Sec. 11.
7. Pt. 3, Ch. 3, Secs. 15 and 16.
8. Pt. 3, Ch. 5.
9. Pt. 4, Ch. 8, Sec. 3.

Chapter 7 (REID, HAMILTON, MÜLLER)

Mansel and Veitch published the lecture notes that Hamilton had written in 1836–37, serving as the basis for his lectures on perceptual and metaphysical theory for the following twenty years, as *Lectures on metaphysics* in 1858 after Hamilton's death in 1856. Hamilton also developed a theory of perception in the many "notes" and "dissertations" to his edition of Reid's philosophical works (1846). Most of these have been collected in a single and convenient source by Wight. The work by Bowen presents Hamilton's principal ideas in an abridged form, including some of the "notes" and "dissertations." A portion of the notes and dissertations are included by Walker in his edition of Reid's *Essay on the intellectual powers of man*.

1. Reid, 1764, Ch. 6, Secs. 11, 12, 19, 20, 23. In Secs. 3 and 20, Reid includes the constancies of brightness and color among the acquired perceptions.
2. *Ibid.*, Ch. 5, Sec. 1, Ch. 6, Secs. 8 and 12, Ch. 7; Reid, 1785, Ch. 8.
Although Reid regarded sensation as a state of consciousness, generally direct knowledge of it would be impossible. Inasmuch as he said sensation "instanta-

neously passes through the mind," its conscious existence would not be noticed. Thus Reid must surmise the characteristics of sensation. In his theory, moreover, sensation is a "passive state" of the mind. All else involved "active powers" of the mind, which he supposed to be original or constitutional. Some of these active powers include: (a) the immediate forgetting of sensation, (b) the sensation suggesting the visible figure, (c) the non-noticing of the visible figure, (d) the visible figure and the color joined to it suggesting the perception. The active powers of the mind would not be noticed. In this chain of events, therefore, only the final event, namely, perception, would be noticed. Reid says: "The process of nature in perception by the senses, may therefore be conceived as a kind of drama, wherein some things are performed behind the scenes, others are represented to the mind in different scenes, one succeeding another. The impression made by the object upon the organ, either by immediate contact, or by some intervening medium, as well as the impression made upon the nerves and brain, is performed behind the scenes, and the mind sees nothing of it. But every such impression, by the laws of the drama, is followed by a sensation, which is the first scene exhibited to the mind; and this scene is quickly succeeded by another, which is the perception of the object" (1764, Ch. 6, Sec. 21).

3. Reid, 1764, Ch. 6, Secs. 8 and 12. In regard to the seeing of retinal images, Reid said, "Nor is there any probability, that the mind perceives the pictures upon the retina. These pictures are no more objects of our perception, than the brain is, or the optic nerve" (p. 237).

4. Hamilton, Lect. 13. See also Stewart, Vol. 2, pp. 141 f.; and Brown, Lects. 10 and 11.

5. Hamilton, Lects. 13, 26, 27, 28, 29, 36.

6. *Ibid.*, Lects. 15 and 25; Bowen, Ch. 11; Wight, p. 276.

7. Hamilton, Lects. 25, 27, 28, Appendix 3.

8. *Ibid.*, Lect. 29; Bowen, p. 386 n.

9. Wight, pp. 385–411, 430; McCosh, 1875, pp. 432 f.

Hamilton cites and interprets the case of the paralytic after Maine de Biran, who regarded it as evidence for Condillac's description of the "statue" as originally experiencing sensations to be mind-localized (pp. 96 ff., 386).

In 1823 Charles Bell quoted the opinions of the author (who was not identified) of a just published text on optics which are relevant to our interpretation of Hamilton's theory as presupposing the presence of the mind in the retina. The author said: "We know nothing more than that the mind residing, as it were, in every point of the retina, refers the impression made upon it, at each point, to a direction coinciding with the last portion of the ray which conveys the impression." Furthermore, an "operation of the mind" would enable the mind to trace the rays "back to the pupil." Since the rays crossed inside the eye, "erect vision" was made possible. Although the quotation contains the qualification "as it were," it would seem that the author found it necessary to suppose that the mind is distributed throughout the retina in order to explain the law of visible direction. The unnamed author might have anticipated Hamilton's later and less clearly stated opinions. Bell regarded such opinions as "obscure" and he proposed the motion of the eye as a substitute in his explanation of erect vision.

10. Müller, pp. 1380–86.

11. *Ibid.*, pp. 1082, 1163, 1211, and 1307.

12. *Ibid.*, pp. 1080–84, 1176.

13. *Ibid.*, p. 1080.

14. *Ibid.*, pp. 947, 1073 f., 1081, 1176.

15. *Ibid.*, pp. 1171 f.

16. Bowen, p. 383 n. The supposition of resemblance is implicit in Hamilton's and Müller's positive answer to the Molyneux problem (Hamilton, p. 391; Müller, pp. 1175 f.).

Reid developed two different solutions to the Molyneux problem. In both he supposed a person born blind who would be given his sight perfectly and who would see everything as flat. The first solution, which concerns the recognition of three-dimensional objects, is negative. Reid: "To a man newly made to see, the visible appearance of objects would be the same as to us; but he would see nothing at all of their real dimensions, as we do. He could form no conjecture, by means of his sight only, how many inches or feet they were in length, breadth, or thickness. He could perceive little or nothing of their real figure; nor could he discern that this was a cube, that a sphere; that this was a cone, and that a cylinder. . . . In a word, his eyes, though ever so perfect, would at first give him almost no information of things without him" (Reid, 1764, p. 203; Davis, p. 403).

The second solution, which is positive and concerns the recognition of drawings, is developed in reference to the distinguished blind mathematician, Dr. Saunderson. In the context of this solution, Reid wishes to prove the thesis of resemblance between visible figure and external object and to illustrate the erroneousness of Berkeley's concept pertaining to the heterogeneity of the ideas of sight and touch. Reid: "If Dr. Saunderson had been made to see, and attentively had viewed the figures of the first book of Euclid, he might, by thought and consideration, without touching them, have found out that they were the very figures he was before so well acquainted with by touch" (Reid, 1764, pp. 234 f.).

17. The philosopher Mansel, who combined the views of both Hamilton and Müller, apparently recognized the existence of a problem in the interpretation of the Cheselden data. After asserting that an infant "destitute of the power of motion" would at first "discern nothing but the images existing on the surface of the retina," Mansel indicated the placing of the hand over the eye as the "motion" which would lead to the projection of images. This sort of learning would bring the infant to the level of the Cheselden boy who, according to him, saw objects "as *on* not *in* the eye" (Mansel, p. 120). His explanation apparently presupposes the touching of the cornea as an essential condition for the projection of images.

18. Reid, 1764, Ch. 6, Sec. 17; Müller, p. 1197. What Reid and Müller stated explicitly is implicit in Berkeley's Sec. 41 concerning the first appearances that would be perceived by the hypothetical, resighted man.

Chapter 8 (MILL, BAIN, LOTZE)

1. Bain, 1868, pp. 1 f.; and 1872, p. 1, pp. 93 f. of Appendix.

2. Mill, 1889, pp. 291 f.

3. *Ibid.*, pp. 226 f.

4. *Ibid.*, p. 323.

5. *Ibid.*, pp. 301, 323f.

6. *Ibid.*, pp. 286, 301.

7. Mill, 1872, p. 558. Although Mill here writes of "psychological chemistry" or "mental chemistry," he does not refer to it as a law. For Mill's further discussion of what we have termed the "chemistry law" see 1859, and 1889, pp. 286 n., 357 n.

8. Mill, 1872, pp. 558f. The application of the "chemistry law" requires a good deal of interpretation since the clearest example of this law that Mill gave is that of the fusion of sensations of the spinning color wheel.

9. Mill, 1889, Ch. 9.

10. *Ibid.*, pp. 301f., 307, 311f.

Mill's reply to McCosh, who had criticized his interpretation of the paralytic, is instructive. McCosh's own opinion was that localization of sensation in parts of the body of normal people as well as the "feeling" of the phantom limb were not the result of association (1866, pp. 160f.). Said Mill, "In other words, we, naturally and intuitively, feel our sensations in a place which, in the case of an amputated limb, is not only outside our body, but may be at a distance of one or two feet from it: and this seat of sensation in the space outside our bodies follows us wherever we go. This is what Dr. McCosh would rather believe, than that the reference of the feeling to such a place is an illusion produced by association" (1889, p. 312). The feeling of sensation away from the body in the case of phantom limb experience has the same theoretical significance as does the "outness" or external reference of a phenomenal object—the visual perception of an object as though apart from and away from the body in space (see the chapter on Descartes). If Mill had recognized this theoretical similarity he would have been led to regard "outness" as the product of association because he apparently believed that the referral of sensation outside the body in cases of amputation *had* to be the product of association.

11. Bain, 1868, pp. 236, 372f.

12. *Ibid.*, pp. 384–94.

13. Bain, 1873, Chs. 3, 5, 6.

Bain said each association had to have its own track in the brain. It was in appreciation of the very large number of associations revealed by "mental science" that he wondered whether the brain, however large the number of cells and the possibilities for the formation of individual connections, could accommodate this learning. A circle alone might require "100 tracks," the human face many more, and so on. Then, too, there were other acquisitions to consider, such as those of other senses and language. Consistent with the law of concomitant variation, room in the brain had to be found for them all. He realized, however, that the number of acquisitions was too large. To eliminate this difficulty he proposed the principle of overlapping connections. These connections, however, were still sensory-motor (1873, pp. 104f.). Also see Spencer, Vol. 1, pp. 562f., for recognition of the problem of the very large number of neural connections that would be required to account for perceptions, and its resolution.

14. Bain, 1869. Bastian had criticized the theory of motor consciousness which Bain had developed in *The senses and the intellect.* This theory, according to Bastian, implied that the individual should have knowledge of the action of muscles in

thinking, speaking, and so on. He quoted the following statement from Bain as having this implication: "The tendency of the idea of an action to produce the fact, shows that the idea is already a fact in a weaker form. Thinking is restrained Speaking or acting."

15. Bain, 1872, p. 90.

16. Although Mill relied on Bain's explanations in the development of his theory and quoted them *in extenso* in his critique of Hamilton, he did not observe the absence of the statement of any "chemistry law" in Bain's theory. Similarly, Bain, who also quoted Mill's opinions in the exposition of his own theory, did not notice the important difference between his and Mill's theory.

17. Lotze, 1877; 1886, Secs. 28, 31; 1887, Sec. 277.

Lotze had also used another metaphor in which "consciousness" was compared to a "single vessel." He said excitations poured into this vessel where they would "mix indiscriminately together." In his view, if red and blue luminous sources stimulated distinct and separate retinal elements, the result in consciousness would be violet (Lotze, 1887, Sec. 280). This metaphor as well as the lens metaphor illustrate the similarity of Lotze's theory to Condillac's theory of 1754. Apparently Lotze was coping with the problems which Gassendi had raised in his criticism of Descartes. In the lens metaphor the seat of sensation would be represented by the focal point, that is, a mathematical point. This would then imply that the soul or consciousness is also a point. Although the chord example does not have a similar implication, it suggests that visual sensations are to be regarded as secondary qualities. Lotze's conception of the mind was interpreted in the nineteenth century as referring to a "punctual soul" (Lange, Vol. 3, p. 212). The diagram of the lens model is our own, as is the other diagram which follows.

18. Lotze, 1887, Sec. 277.

19. *Ibid.*, Sec. 278.

20. Lotze, 1886, Secs. 33, 34; 1887, Sec. 285.

21. Lotze, 1887, Sec. 286.

22. Lotze, 1886, Sec. 35; 1887, Secs. 283, 286, 287. In Sec. 286 Lotze seems to regard consciousness as delusory in reply to criticism of his theory: "My individual disposition cannot be communicated. I cannot therefore contradict those who tell me that they observe nothing of these feelings of movements, however much I may be convinced that they deceive themselves and, though they really have the feelings, do not recognise them for what they are."

See Ladd, 1888 and 1898, for a detailed discussion of Lotze's theory of local signs by a distinguished proponent and contemporary of Lotze; for contemporary discussion and evaluation, see Walls.

23. Bain's explanation of the perception of the small circle of one-tenth inch in diameter (which Mill accepted) is a further example of begging the question since it was never shown how the ocular sweep of a larger circle could transfer to the other circle. The patterning of eye-movements so as to conform to external shapes, such as a large circle or a horizontal line, may be considered in a similar way.

24. For critiques of the concept of "mental chemistry" other than that of James in Chapter 12 of this text see Bowne, pp. 139f.; Monck, pp. 68f.; and Titchener, pp. 30f.

Chapter 9 (HELMHOLTZ)

Citations to Helmholtz's popular lectures on "recent progress in the theory of vision" will be referred as *Vision* and will always refer to the Dover reprint of the English translation of the original German of 1871, or the French version of 1869. A citation to "section" will refer to the text on physiological optics, whether in French, German, or English. I wish to thank Mrs. Silvia Greenberg for important assistance in translating Helmholtz's German, and collating the German with French and English translations. Incidentally, Helmholtz expressed his authorization and approval of the French translation in the preface to *Optique physiologique*.

1. Secs. 26, 29, 33; *Vision*, pp. 171 f; Cesca, Pt. 2, Ch. 8.
Müller and Hering were Helmholtz's principal protagonists in discussion of his objections to nativistic theory. See Alison who speculated, for the purpose of explaining the correct perception of the orientation of objects, that the orientation of retinal impressions might be re-reversed both vertically and laterally in the "optic lobes," and Nunneley, pp. 325–29, who reviewed opinions pertaining to "erect vision from an inverted image."

2. Sully, 1878, p. 184; 1892, Vol. 1, p. 257. Wundt noted that Helmholtz, in respect to the importance attributed to the tactile sense, was in "absolute agreement" with the empiristic theories expressed by Berkeley and Condillac (Vol. 2, p. 196). The importance Helmholtz attributed to the sense of touch in the determination of spatial perceptions is particularly evident in *Vision*, pp. 174f., and in Sec. 30. See the historical part of Sec. 26 for Helmholtz's qualified approval of Berkeley and implicit acceptance of Reid's dichotomy of sensation and perception.

For a nontechnical exposition of Helmholtz's theory, see Sully, 1881. Sechenov, who discussed vision extensively in his various writings, apparently followed Helmholtz's empiristic theory (cf. "The Elements of Thought" and "Hermann von Helmholtz as a Physiologist" in Sechenov, *Selected physiological and psychological works*).

3. *Vision*, pp. 153f.; Cesca, Pt. 2, Ch. 8; Külpe, p. 370, Ribot, pp. 124f.
4. Secs. 26, 28, 32, 33; *Vision*, pp. 158, 172.
In Sec. 33 Helmholtz opposed the nativistic explanation of single vision and binocularly perceived solidity which is described in Chapter 1 of this text.

5. Sec. 26.
6. *Vision*, pp. 103, 120. Actually, Helmholtz's statement of the telegraph analogy preceded that of Bain's (Koenisberger, p. 72).

7. Secs. 26, 30.
8. Sec. 24; Sully, 1874, p. 68.
9. Lewes, who had set forth Helmholtz's explanation of color contrast, criticized a proposed physiological explanation thus: "But this hypothesis of retinal irradiation is in direct contradiction to the law of isolated conduction; nor have we any evidence whatever for supposing that excitation of one fibre can be propagated by cross action to neighbouring fibres. . . ." (p. 278 n.).

10. Sec. 30.

11. Sec. 30.

The motion of the windmill has two components, namely, the projections of the moving vanes to the sagittal and fronto-parallel planes. Phenomenally, the sagittal component involves motion of the vanes toward or away from the observer whereas the frontoparallel component involves the elliptical path described by the ends of the vanes. The illusion, in Helmholtz's discussion, pertains to the phenomenal motion in the frontoparallel plane; that is, when observation of the windmill is restricted to one side of the axis of rotation, the phenomenal motion is up or down. Boring (1942, p. 270) follows Helmholtz's explanation but he describes the phenomenal change in motion as being from counterclockwise to clockwise. In an analysis of this problem with Mr. S. Ferris, who also gathered the data of an experiment on this topic, it seemed to us that a phenomenal motion reversal could not be a function of perspective reversal.

The pattern of retinal stimulation formed in viewing the windmill is indeed ambiguous with respect to the plane of the physical vanes. But the succession of stimulations on the retina is not ambiguous with respect to the component of the physical motion of the vanes in the frontoparallel plane. Therefore, the phenomenal motion ought always be in an up direction irrespective of whether the right end of the vanes looks more distant or closer. A small black windmill, with vanes rotating in a counterclockwise direction at 11 rpm, placed at an angle in front of a backlighted translucent plastic sheet, was viewed monocularly at a distance of about 5.5 meters. The field of view was restricted; the photograph in the text depicts what the observer saw. Each of twenty-five college students who had no previous experience with this illusion, individually viewed the windmill. They were informed, just before observing the windmill, that they would see some object in motion and that they merely had to describe its nature. Two questions were asked of every subject during the period of observation. The questions were phrased so that the answers would provide information as to the occurrence of perceived perspective reversals and perceived motion reversals to the right side of the axis of rotation. All subjects reported that the right side always moved upwards although they all perceived perspective reversals.

The reader can verify this conclusion by viewing obliquely with one eye four small index cards (to simulate "vanes") placed on a phonograph turntable rotating at 33⅓ rpm. When perspective reversals are perceived the plane of rotation is seen as though from above or from below. Careful observation of the motion (tracing the motion with a finger will prevent confusion) will indicate that the phenomenal rotation is always the same.

For another interpretation of Helmholtz's explanation of the apparent motion of the windmill see Wallin, p. 21.

12. Smith's explanation was adopted by Porterfield, Vol. 2, p. 384; and Priestley, p. 699. Whewell says that by an "effort of thought" the obliquity of the sails "may assume one or the other of two positions; and as we do this, the sails, which in one instance appear to turn from right to left, in the other case turn from left to right" (pp. 112f.). Although the change in motion from left to right or from right to left was not explained, it would seem that Whewell supposed that the ap-

parent motion reversal takes place in the frontoparallel plane. Carr, 1935, p. 279, clearly supposes a phenomenal reversal of motion.

13. Sec. 30. The Necker Cube is discussed only in the *Optique*, p. 796.

14. *Vision*, pp. 174f.

15. Sec. 29; *Vision*, p. 157. Sully interpreted the results of the prism experiment as having demonstrated a phenomenal change (1874, pp. 68f.; and 1878, pp. 13f.). The context of Helmholtz's discussion of the experiment would suggest this interpretation.

16. Sec. 28. The quotation is a translation from *Optique*, p. 755.

17. Sec. 28. The "protrusion" cited by Helmholtz in his interpretation of the Wardrop report ("protrusion" is not mentioned in the report) would suggest that the resighted woman saw her brother's nose as three-dimensional rather than as flat. Hence Helmholtz might have believed that the monocular perception of solidity was an original perception, unless he supposed that the phenomenal protrusion had been acquired in the few days after the operation that preceded her recognition of the nose.

Helmholtz's interpretation of Wardrop's report as well as that of Cheselden's dealt with the Molyneux problem. The historical account of answers to the problem which Helmholtz gave, suggests his adherence to Locke's assumption pertaining to the original perception of a globe as a flat circle. He referred to the section of Locke's *Essay on human understanding* which not only has the Molyneux problem, and the answers to it by Molyneux and Locke, but also the discussion of the "idea of a globe received by sensation." He also referred to Jurin as concurring with Molyneux and Locke although Jurin arrived at a positive answer to the problem by changing some of the conditions of the problem (Jurin in R. Smith, *Remarks*, p. 27). Jurin, whose solution was similar to Leibniz's, presupposed that the hypothetical man of the problem at first would see the globe and cube as flat (see Chapter 5 of this text). However, he did not explicitly state the Locke assumption. Priestley, the next person cited by Helmholtz in his historical account, said: "I cannot help assenting to Dr. Jurin's solution. It is certain that pictures upon the retina give no idea of any thing more than flat surfaces; but then these have the same differences in the eye that they have in reality, by which they may, therefore, be distinguished from one another; so that a circle might be known from a square, though a square might not be distinguished from a cube, nor a flat circle from a globe, at least without attentively considering the change of their appearance in different situations" (pp. 720f.). Helmholtz did not dissent from the Locke assumption as expressed by Locke himself, as presupposed by Jurin, and as explicitly stated by Priestley. Hence it seems to us that Helmholtz also accepted the same assumption but without having made it explicit.

18. Sec. 28. The revision in local signs proposed by Helmholtz is that stimulation of adjacent points of the retina would directly give rise to separated colors in the visual field.

Chapter 10 (SUMMARY)

1. James, 1890, Vol. 2, p. 221 n.; Ribot, 1886, pp. 126f. Concerning the popularity of Berkeleyan theory, also see the survey by Janet. See Carpenter for a brief but nevertheless influential account of the principal points of empiristic theory.

2. Clifford, pp. 210f.; Pearson, pp. 53f.; Porter, p. 155; Wundt, *Outlines of psychology*, p. 325. Bernstein, pp. 19f., also discussed the "telegraph metaphor."

For further discussion by theorists who supposed that an original perception was composed of a mosaic of sensations see Brewster, 1856, Ch. 10; Sergi, pp. 200f.; Spencer, Vol. 2, p. 193; Wundt, *Animal psychology*, Lects. 10, 11, 12, and *Outlines of psychology*, Article 10, Secs. 13–35; Ziehen, p. 122.

3. Huxley, Chapter, "Bishop Berkeley on the Metaphysics of Sensation"; Burtt, pp. 311f.

4. Taine, pp. 293f., pp. 298f.; *Encyclopedia Britannica*, 11th edition, article, "Vision."

5. Dewey, pp. 164f.; Hall, 1877; Jackson, pp. 87f.; Taine, pp. 327, 340.

6. Höffding, 1891, pp. 201f.

7. Sully, 1881, pp. 75–81; 1886, pp. 114, 132; and 1892, Vol. 1, p. 190. Spencer, who supposed the decomposability of perception into component sensations, did not invoke the concept of "mental chemistry" (Vol. 1, Pt. 2, Ch. 1).

8. The assumption of an extended mind did not resolve the problems that had arisen in the explanation of perception. Thus Fichte and Walter, who made this assumption thought that the spatial dimensions of the extended visual sensation corresponded to those of the retinal image.

9. Sully, 1884, p. 152; James, 1890, Vol. 2, p. 79.

10. Sully, 1892, Vol. 2, pp. 333f.; Dewey, p. 165. Wundt: "We may observe the same phenomenon in the first months of childhood: the baby will reach for the moon or for the objects seen in the street through a third-story window" (*Animal psychology*, p. 173). Bourdon, p. 135, cited Helmholtz's recollection as evidence for the acquired perception of magnitude. Koffka who recalled a childhood experience similar to that of Helmholtz questioned Helmholtz's interpretation (1928, pp. 303f.).

11. Saisset, *Dictionnaire des sciences philosophiques*, article, "Sens." Höffding, 1891, p. 195, cited the cases of Cheselden and Franz as supporting Berkeley's theory, as did McCosh, 1892, p. 45. Neither Höffding nor McCosh referred to the Nunneley case. Mill, 1871, cited the Cheselden and Nunneley cases as a corroboration of Berkeley's theory but he did not refer to the Franz case.

Abbott, 1904, reported an interview of Franz's patient by Mahaffy in about 1874. The patient had practiced medicine and had studied the "psychological theory of vision, and entirely disagreed with the theory of John Stuart Mill." Abbott regretted the fact that the opportunity of questioning him on his recollections before and after the operation had not been fully exploited.

Chapter 11 (CONDILLAC, BAILEY, AND REACTIONS)

1. Condillac, 1746. See also note 24, Ch. 5.

2. Condillac, 1754, Pt. 3, Ch. 5, Sec. 8, regards the second paragraph of the Cheselden report as contradictory. The boy said that smooth and regular objects were most agreeable, although he could not discern shape and size. To "judge" that objects are agreeable, according to Condillac, their forms and sizes must be distinguished. He attributes this contradiction to Cheselden's not having expressed himself carefully.

3. Diderot evaluated Condillac's critique and concurred with the comments pertaining to the possibility of optical damage and the irrelevancy of touch. He supposed, however, that a globe and a cube would be originally perceived as a circle and a square.

4. Bailey, 1842, Ch. 2, Sec. 5, and Ch. 6; 1843, pp. 32 f.

5. Bailey, 1842, Ch. 2, Secs. 1, 5, 6; 1843, pp. 55 f.

Bailey also questioned Berkeley's concept of heterogeneity in relation to the supposed confusion of visible and tangible ideas. He said: "It is, in truth, most extraordinary in Berkeley to have imagined, that withdrawing the attention from the perceptions of sight to the conceptions derived from touch, should cause the mind to mistake the latter, on which its attention is concentrated, for the perceptions of the neglected sense. It will, perhaps, appear not less extraordinary, that he should have supposed any mistake of this nature to be at all practicable, when we reflect that, according to his repeated assertions, the perceptions and ideas of the two senses respectively are so totally unlike as not to have the least point of resemblance. How then could they be mistaken for each other?" (1842, p. 77).

Bailey apparently was the first philosopher to observe that Berkeley's theory implied that consciousness was a "delusion."

6. Bailey, 1842, p. 26.

7. *Ibid.*, pp. 39 f., 100 f.

8. *Ibid.*, Ch. 5, Sec. 2.

9. *Ibid.*, pp. 29 f., Ch. 5, Sec. 1; 1843, p. 52.

10. Bailey, 1842, Ch. 2, Sec. 2; 1843, p. 52.

11. Mill, 1842, p. 186.

12. Bailey, 1843, p. 50.

13. Brown, p. 286.

14. Bailey, 1842, Ch. 5, Secs. 3–7; 1843, pp. 58 f.

15. Bailey, 1843, p. 49; *Philosophy of the human mind*, Vol. 1, Letters 3, 7, 18, Vol. 2, Letters 16, 21.

16. Bailey, 1842, pp. 92 f., 105 f., 117; 1843, pp. 44, 48.

17. Bailey, *Philosophy of the human mind*, Vol. 1, pp. 148, 177.

18. Bailey, 1843, p. 44; *Philosophy of the human mind*, Vol. 1, pp. 157, 174–77.

19. *Philosophy of the human mind*, Vol. 2, Letter 1.

20. *Ibid.*, Vol. 1, Letters 5, 18, 20.

21. Bailey, 1852, p. 234; Whewell, pp. 287 f.

22. For further discussion of Bailey, see Pastore, 1965.

23. Mill, 1842, 1843. Mill had stated the "chemistry law" in the first edition of *System of logic* (1843). He seemed to return to his 1842 and 1843 statement of Berkeley's theory in 1871. See Ribot, 1877, pp. 314 f., for his evaluation of the Bailey-Mill controversy and defense of Mill.

Ferrier also responded to Bailey's critique of Berkeleyan theory; Bailey replied in his 1843 "letter." The "logic" of the *Molyneux Premise* constituted an important factor in Ferrier's defense of Berkeleyan theory. Some idea of the way he conceived of a basic problem in a theory of perception may be gained from his comment pertaining to perceived magnitude. He has pointed out that the image of a tower might be .01 inch when traced out in a picture plane and he says, "This is certainly not what you seem to see, but this is certainly what you *do* see" (1875, p. 343).

24. Abbott, 1864, Ch. 3; 1879; Fraser, 1864.

25. Abbott, 1864, Chs. 4, 11. In 1866 Simon wrote a spirited defense of Berkeley's theory. "It is necessary to speak of our two critics, Mr. Abbott and Mr. Bailey, who assert, against us all, that we can see distance, and to explain how they came to oppose (or shall I not say—to fancy that they opposed?) so very obvious a fact of consciousness and science, as that disputed in this assertion" (p. 431). The *Molyneux Premise*, in Simon's view, guaranteed the impossibility of the seeing of distance. It would appear that in 1866 Bailey and Abbott were the only critics of Berkeleyan theory who rejected this premise.

26. Spalding, 1873; Gray, 1962.

It was often believed, concerning the motive for Spalding's experiment in gumming the ears of chicks, that "projection of sensations of sounds" and the direction and distance of sounds were acquired perceptions; the explanation of such perceptions was similar to the explanation of acquired visual perceptions (cf. Bain, 1868, pp. 204, 352, 362; Adam Smith; Sully, 1892, Vol. 1, p. 206). Furthermore, the assumptions concerning the nature of original perceptions of both senses were similar. For instance, Adam Smith, who had pointed out that the boy of the Cheselden report should have said that he felt sensations "inside" his eyes, said: "A deaf man, who was made all at once to hear, might in the same manner naturally enough say, that the sounds which he heard touched his ears, meaning that he felt them as close upon his ears, or, to speak perhaps more properly, as in his ears."

Chapter 12 (WILLIAM JAMES:
THE "HAMLET" OF PERCEPTUAL THEORISTS)

James's *Principles of psychology* will be referred to by volume number only, and *Psychology: Briefer course* will be indicated by *BC*.

1. *BC*, Epilogue; II, pp. 216 f., 270 f.

2. I, p. 5, p. 129; *BC*, pp. 5 f.

3. I, p. 177; II, p. 582 n.; *BC*, Ch. 11; *Talks to teachers*, p. 119.

The influence of Hering in James's critique of traditional theories of perception and development of his own theory, especially in respect to the implications of the psychophysical postulate, merits further investigation (cf. Hering, 1913). The many quotations from Hering in James's *Principles* suggest such an influence.

4. II, p. 2, pp. 273 f.; *BC*, p. 151; Perry, Vol. II, Chs. 55, 56.

5. I, p. 521 n.; II, Ch. 17, pp. 218 f. 243 f., 278 f.; *BC*, Ch. 2.

6. I, p. 169.

7. II, p. 40, pp. 220, 258; *BC*, pp. 13 f.

8. II, pp. 76 f.; *BC*, p. 312.

9. I, pp. 285 f.; II, pp. 237 f., *BC*, pp. 334 f.

10. II, pp. 256 f.

11. I, p. 144; II, pp. 82 f., 258, 278.

12. II, p. 74, p. 582 n.; *BC*, pp. 317, 325.

13. I, pp. 645 f.; II, pp. 104, 238 f.; 265.

14. James might have presupposed that objects are originally perceived flat. In *BC*, pp. 343 f., he discussed the "overlooking of the retinal magnitude" and he said, "The hardest part of the training of a young draughtsman is his learning to feel directly the retinal (i.e. primitively sensible) magnitudes which the different objects in the field of view subtend. To do this he must recover what Ruskin calls the 'innocence of the eye'—that is, a sort of childish perception of stains of color merely as such, without consciousness of what they mean."

In *Elements of drawing* (p. 22 n.), Ruskin said: "The perception of solid Form is entirely a matter of experience. We *see* nothing but flat colours; and it is only by a series of experiments that we find out that a stain of black or grey indicates the dark side of a solid substance, or that a faint hue indicates that the object in which it appears is far away. The whole technical power of painting depends on our recovery of what may be called the *innocence of the eye;* that is to say, of a sort of childish perception of these flat stains of colour, merely as such, without consciousness of what they signify,—as a blind man would see them if suddenly gifted with sight." This quotation from Ruskin was cited by Porter to illustrate his point that by "vision only," a sphere or globe is perceived as a "flat surface" (p. 155 n.).

15. I, p. 448; *BC*, p. 14.

16. I, pp. 402 f.

17. I, pp. 288, 503; *BC*, p. 363; *Some problems in philosophy*, p. 50.

18. Thorndike, p. 22.

19. *BC*, p. 245.

20. I, pp. 424, 427, 442–47.

21. I, p. 487.

22. Sully, 1886, p. 99; Höffding, 1891, p. 199.

Many of our arguments pertaining to James's concept of an "original chaos" were developed by Gurwitsch, Ch. 2, Secs. 1, 2, 4. The italicized statement in the text represents a basic thesis of gestalt theory, namely, that an "organized" visual field cannot develop from an original "disorganized" visual field. Gurwitsch has made this point in his evaluation of James. Köhler contrasted the gestalt concept of "primitive sensorial organization" to James's concept (cf. Köhler, *La perception humaine;* 1931).

23. I, p. 448; Perry, Vol. II, Ch. 53; Gurwitsch, Ch. 2.

24. *BC,* p. 119; Perry, Vol. II, Ch. 53.

James anticipated features of the gestalt approach to the physiological explanation of perception when he said, in the analogy of an electric conductor, that the brain always acts as a whole. Although a similar theme is dominant from a general point of view in the *Principles of psychology,* James actually adopted the mosaic model of the functioning of the nervous system when he explained some fact in detail. In this regard see Wheeler, Perkins, and Bartley.

25. Robertson, 1888; James, 1889. Another tradition rejected by James was the "feeling of innervation" which had been widely adopted by physiologists and psychologists in the explanation of space perception. This feeling, he said, "is probably a wholly fictitious entity" (II, p. 236). His grounds for its rejection were phenomenological: *"There is no introspective evidence of the feeling of innervation"* (II, p. 499).

Chapter 13 (Evaluation)

1. In explaining the development of the spatial perceptions of a blind child, Sully, in order to illustrate the role of movement, said: "We will imagine that the child has only one finger-tip and not an extended hand, and so is able to have only one tactual sensation at a time. This sensitive point he can carry about just as the insect can carry its antennae from one object to another." Thus the child, according to him, would be able to learn the localization of the tip of the nose, and each of the eyebrows, of the human face. Sully made a similar assumption in explaining the spatial perceptions of a sighted child (1884, pp. 157–82).

The validity of our argument does not depend on the sense of touch, inasmuch as similar problems would arise in an empiristic explanation of perceptual solidity involving eye-movements.

2. Since the empiristic explanation of brightness constancy presupposes a similar transformation of appearance, brightness constancy cannot be acquired by means of the sense of touch.

3. Abbott's argument also applies to "retinal shape"—the original perception of form that corresponds to the shape of the retinal image—as a sign of real shape.

4. A. Smith although a proponent of Berkeleyan theory had pointed out that no certain inference could be made from the Cheselden case to normal infants because "disuse" and "gradual decay" could have "obliterated" any "instinctive power" at the basis of visual perception. For a later discussion of "damage" see Mach, p. 135, note 2. It was known that corrective lenses were essential for preventing "confused" visual appearances in operation for cataracts (cf. Rohault, 1671; Cheselden, 1795, p. 317. Many of the visual experiments with the resighted apparently were undertaken without such lenses.

5. Abbott, 1864, p. 145. He also raised the interesting question as to whether visual recognition could be possible in such circumstances (pp. 163f.). The Cheselden case was sometimes reported as though the surgeon had undertaken an experimental test of the Molyneux problem (cf. Voltaire, pp. 8of.; Ritchie, pp. 14f.).

6. Taine, p. 309. On p. 312, however, he did cite her behavior in relation to the watch. It is evident that Taine shifted the problem to one of recognition in his interpretation of this behavior.

7. Mill, 1889, p. 296 n.; McCosh, 1866, pp. 177f.; Ch. 10, note 11, of this text. See Mahaffy for further criticism of Mill's theory in respect to the implications of the Franz case.

8. Bain, 1872, p. 195; Fraser, 1901, Vol. 2, pp. 411f. Some philosophers argued that another case (Dufour's) was decisive (cf. Naville).

9. Bourdon, Ch. 13, summarized the ocular defects of the born blind immediately on regaining sight.

10. See Morgan, 1896, 1904, for descriptions of animals in naturalistic, as well as experimental, settings.

11. Hamilton, p. 395.

12. C. Darwin, p. 286.

13. Although the confounding of the two types of facts or events was a conspicuous feature of empiristic theory, "nativists" also fell into this confusion. James: "The *lower* half of the retina, which habitually sees the *farther* half of things spread out on the ground, ought to have acquired a habit of enlarging its pictures by imagination. . . ." (Vol. 2, p. 264).

14. When Bernstein says, "The entire field of vision is depicted on the retina as a plane surface" (p. 127), the "field of vision" obviously refers to objects in physical space. But when he writes of the "struggle between the fields of vision" (p. 149), "field of vision" refers to phenomenal events because he is describing the results of experiments in binocular rivalry.

15. Starling, p. 589. For explanations which are similar to Starling's, see Bernstein, pp. 78 f.; Dewey, pp. 167 f.

The well-known experiments of Stratton with himself as the subject, in which he wore lenses which produced an erect retinal image, were undertaken to determine whether erect vision requires the inversion of retinal images. Both his methodology and interpretation of results were effectively criticized by Hyslop in 1897. In the statement of the theory at the basis of the experiments which Stratton outlined in 1903, Ch. 8, it is evident that the problem of image-reversal, in his view, was contingent on whether the projection of visual sensation was innate or the result of experience and association. Inasmuch as he believed that "projection" was the product of association, upright vision also would be the result of experience. The results of his experiments, which were ambiguous, were misinterpreted, for it was commonly said that Stratton at first saw everything upside down and that this "appearance . . . gave place to a normal appearance after a few days" (cf. Ladd and Woodworth, p. 455). Stratton, however, did not report such results. In 1903, p. 147, he says there was no change in the orientation of the "visual scene." Higginson, 1937, has reviewed the literature of misinterpretation. The discussion of the problem of the inverted image continues into the present period. *Human physiology* (edited by Houssay), 1955: "The retinal image is inverted with respect to the object, but it is seen in the correct position. The 'righting' of the image is a psychological process, which is begun in childhood by the association of the visual image with other, especially with tactile, sensations" (p. 934). Best and Taylor, in their texts on medicine, have expressed a similar opinion (cf. Best and Taylor, p. 1667).

16. No decisive evidence was advanced in support of the contention that the so-called projection and localization of visual sensation was the outcome of association. The inability of the child to follow a lighted candle before the age of three months, supposing it to be a correct observation, is of ambiguous import. Thus the fact that he might do so in the third month may be the outcome of physiological maturation rather than association. Empirists often presupposed a "law" similar to the "law of visible direction." For instance, Giraud-Teulon, 1868, pointed out that Helmholtz had accepted the law of visible direction (see Helmholtz's *Treatise on physiological optics*, Vol. 3, p. 260).

Chapter 14 (THE GESTALT THEORY OF PERCEPTION)

1. The article by Koffka, to which Humphrey refers, introduced gestalt theory in this country in 1922. The source of the quotation is Humphrey's "personal memories" in a volume dedicated to Köhler, and edited by Asch and Pabst. Bentley, who had studied at Cornell University at the end of the last century with Titchener and who became his colleague, expressed an opinion similar to Humphrey's in 1928 (p. 166 n.). An examination of American textbooks in psychology published between 1900 and 1940, and also of articles and reports in the *American Journal of Psychology* and the *Psychological Review* for this same period, indicate that Berkeleyan-type theory had a quasi-official status. There are, of course, exceptions to this trend, Hyslop being an early notable exception. Important aspects of this trend, including developments in European psychology and philosophy, have been discussed and summarized by Bentley, 1902; Carmichael, 1925; Gurwitsch; Helson, 1925 and 1926; Higginson; and Koffka, 1922, 1928, and 1930. Parenthetically, Poincaré and Bertrand Russell offer an interesting contrast in the early period to the premises of gestalt theory, inasmuch as both presupposed the constancy hypothesis in developing their philosophical ideas (Poincaré, 1905, Ch. 4; 1913, Ch. 3, Sec. 6; Russell, 1912, Ch. 1).

2. Cf. Köhler, 1930, 1931, and 1938; Koffka, 1935, Ch. 2; Ellis; Humphrey, 1924.

3. For Koffka's now famous question see his 1935 text, p. 75, and for "direct experience" as a prescription see Koffka in this same text, Ch. 2. Also Koffka, 1928 Ch. 1; and Köhler, 1947, Ch. 1.

4. Wertheimer, Sel. 5 in Ellis; Köhler, 1925, 1941, 1947, Ch. 5; Köhler and Adams; Koffka, 1935, pp. 150–68; Arnheim, Ch. 2. A diagram in Abbott, 1864, p. 83, showed that the Zöllner illusion could be obtained without vertical lines. Figure 14.5 represents an adaptation of this idea to Hering's figure. The fact that the illusion is obtained with subjective contours weakens the general interpretation of illusions, when physical lines are present, in terms of overestimation of angles.

5. See preceding note for references.

6. Köhler, 1947, pp. 144 f., 157 f., 181 f.; Kanizsa in Kanizsa and Vicario.

7. Wertheimer, 1912; Koffka, 1930, 1935, pp. 286–301; the selections on motion in Ellis.

8. The discussion of the principle of psychophysical isomorphism in the text would imply that the percept and its brain correlate have similar structures. For instance, the third dimension of a percept would have a three-dimensional brain correlate. However, the principle, according to gestalt psychologists, does not imply this type of identity. Thus the phenomenal third dimension would have some representation in the brain, but without this representation being three-dimensional. Similarly, the brain correlate of a phenomenal square need not have the actual shape of a square. In actual application of the principle to specific problems, however, gestaltists proceed on the assumption that the percept and brain correlate have similar geometric characteristics. According to Köhler and Emery, this assumption, in respect to the third dimension, is adopted for "pragmatic reasons" in order to more readily visualize the nature of the brain correlate and those physiological events which might be responsible for its formation. This pragmatic approach is adopted in the subsequent exposition of gestalt theory in the text.

Köhler's justification of the principle of psychophysical isomorphism in part presupposes a "resemblance" between a phenomenal thing and the transphenomenal or external thing. This resemblance is mediated by events in the brain which, in his view, must resemble both phenomenal and transphenomenal things. If the psychophysical resemblance is not supposed, he says, the resemblance between phenomenal and transphenomenal things would be difficult to explain. He also maintains that there is no exception to the principle of psychophysical isomorphism. On the other hand, the isomorphism between the brain correlate and the distal stimulus need not be exact, inasmuch as there are many exceptions to the resemblance of phenomenal and transphenomenal things, such as subjective contours and the perceived solidity of the Necker Cube. Furthermore, he has said that strict observance of the psychophysical postulate implies the principle of psychophysical isomorphism.

For discussion of isomorphism: Köhler, 1938, Chs. 4, 5, 6; 1940, Ch. 2; and 1947, Ch. 2; Koffka, 1935, pp. 61 f., 275, 305; and 1938; Arnheim, p. 205.

The concept of psychophysical isomorphism has been the focus for theoretical and factual opposition to gestalt theory by physiologists and psychologists (cf. Bergmann; Jeffress; Lashley et al.; Piéron, 1933 and 1950; and Sperry, 1952). It is not yet known whether the various arguments are decisive.

9. Koffka, 1935, pp. 75–105.

10. Köhler, 1938, Ch. 6, Sels. 3 and 4 in Ellis; Koffka, 1935, Ch. 4.

11. Koffka, 1922, p. 557.

The Kanizsa diagram itself can be modified so that the subjective contours are curved. The alignment of the edges of two sectors constitute a condition for straightness of subjective contours (the three angles are not essential for the perception of an erect triangle). When the sectors are redrawn so that the edges are not aligned, a triangular shape with curved contours is seen.

The data for the results of the experiment with the phosphorescent rods were gathered by Mr. Robert Diamond and Mr. Saul Rosenberg of Queens College (un-published).

12. Köhler, 1940, Ch. 2; 1951; 1958; Köhler and Wallach.

13. Koffka, 1930; 1935, pp. 159f., 286–301.

14. Wertheimer, 1912; Köhler, Sel. 3, Ellis; Köhler and Emery, pp. 197f.; Higginson, 1926; Myers, pp. 268f.; Rivers, pp. 1098f.

Mr. Robert Diamond and Mr. Saul Rosenberg also gathered the data for the results of the experiment with the modified Kanizsa diagram of Figure 14.13.

15. Köhler, 1941, p. 492.

16. Köhler, Sels. 3, 4 in Ellis; 1929, Ch. 6; Wertheimer, Sel. 1 in Ellis; Bentley, 1902; Guillaume, 1937, Ch. 1; Gurwitsch, pp. 57f.; Helson, 1925, pp. 345f., 360.

17. Mach, pp. 208f.

18. Köhler, 1941; 1947, Ch. 8; Köhler and Fishback; Köhler and Wallach; Wallach, 1949.

19. Köhler, 1947, Ch. 4; S. Diamond, 1969.

20. Köhler, 1937; 1947, Ch. 4; Guillaume, 1964, Pt. 1, Ch. 1.

The implications of Descartes's theory are fairly evident in the Rohault frontispiece and its discussion in Chapter 2 of this text. Says Foster of Descartes in 1902: "If we read between the lines which he wrote, if we substitute in place of the subtle fluid of the animal spirits, the molecular changes which we call a nervous impulse, if we replace his system of tubes with their valvular arrangements by the present system of concatenated neurons, whose linked arrangement determines the passage and the effects of the nervous impulses, Descartes' exposition will not appear so wholly different from the one which we give to-day" (p. 268).

Pavlov in 1924: "In the main we base ourselves on Descartes' concept of the reflex. Of course, this is a genuinely scientific concept, since the phenomenon implied by it can be strictly determined. It means that a certain agent of the external world, or of the organism's internal medium produces a certain effect in one or other nervous receptor, which is transformed into a nervous process, into nervous excitation. The excitation is transmitted along certain nerve fibres, as if along an electric cable, to the central nervous system; thence, thanks to the established nervous connections, it passes along other nerve fibres to the working organ. Thus, the stimulating agent proves to be indispensably connected with the definite activity of the organism, as cause and effect" (*Selected works*, p. 178).

21. Köhler, 1947, pp. 162f.; Koffka, 1935, pp. 97f., 159, 181, 208; Guillaume, 1937, p. 52.

The nativistic approach to perception also is rejected by gestalt psychologists, for nativism, they insisted, supposed the "machine theory" as did the empiristic approach. Köhler points out that nativism referred its explanations to inherited anatomical arrangements, the arrangements which develop through maturation also being included in the meaning of "inherited." Nativism had achieved its most notable success in the explanation of single vision and many facts pertaining to stereoscopic depth effects. To illustrate the nativistic explanation of stereoscopic depth, a simple example adapted from Hering may be considered. When two horizontal lines of equal length are viewed in a stereoscope, each line stimulating one eye only, a single line is perceived in the apparent plane of the surface. To explain the absence of a depth effect, suppose that each line is subdivided into four equal seg- ments. The symmetrically disposed subdivisions about a common center are given equal numerical values but are opposite in sign, the center having the designation of zero. Thus for the right line the values beginning at the center and going to the right end are successively $+1$ and $+2$, whereas in going from the center to the left they are -1 and -2. For the left line the values are positive to the left of center and negative to the right. These numbers become the "depth values" of the retinal elements when the lines stimulate the retinas. The processes originating in the stimulation of corresponding retinal elements arrive at the same or nearly the same place in the brain; their depth values combine so as to produce a series of zeros (or absence of relative depth).

The concomitant of these hypothetical processes, as Hering himself regarded them, is the perception of a flat line. This theory would predict that the percep- tion arising from binocular viewing of the Necker Cube also ought to be bi-dimen- sional. But since this is contrary to fact, the empiristic hypothesis for this and other similar perceptual phenomena was adopted. Thus Hering also supposed as did the empirist that the same local retinal process ought to give rise to the same sensory experience. Furthermore, his explanation of stereoscopic depth presupposes that the summation of values in the brain is a constant function of the noncorre- sponding retinal numerical values. According to this hypothesis, the same relative disparity ought to give rise to the same depth effect. However, when Mach's bent card is viewed binocularly, phenomenal inversion in depth occurs although there has been no change in the "depth values" of the retinal elements. See Köhler, 1947, Chs. 4, 7; Köhler and Emery, pp. 195f.; Koffka, 1930; Linksz, pp. 386f.; Hering, 1942, Chs. 1, 6.

22. For examples of empiristic explanations of the Necker Cube, the "E" per- cept, and similar percepts, see Dashiell, pp. 297 and 403; Jastrow, Chapter, "The Mind's Eye"; Katz, p. 28; Linksz, pp. 612f.; Washburn. The role of "sensation" or "energy" derived from eye-movements, a frequently cited "cue" in traditional expla- nations of phenomena of this type (cf. Necker; Wundt, *Outlines of psychology*, pp. 260f.), is contradicted by the appearance of subjective contours in after-images. For instance, in getting a good after-image of Figure 14.1, one may observe the contours of the *F* and its mirror image, and also the reversibility of contours.

23. Crafts et al., Ch. 23; Hallowell, 1945, pp. 184f., and his chapter in Rohrer and Sherif; Herskovits, also in Rohrer and Sheriff; Klineberg, Ch. 8; Mead; Murphy, 1935, p. 171; Sapir. There is much ambiguity in statements of the "linguistic hy- pothesis." For instance, the concepts of "labeling," "conceiving," "recognizing," and "seeing" tend to be confused with each other. Segall et al. have reviewed the litera- ture and have pointed out some of the difficulties in the interpretation of cross-cul- tural data. It would seem that Malinowski, pp. 173f., whose work on the Trobrian- ders is often cited as showing the influence of culture on seeing, has been misinterpreted; he did not draw the conclusion that others have given to his work. The theoretical position of Boas, Ch. 11, also seems to have been misinterpreted.

Köhler selected the "big dipper percept" for theoretical discussion in order to point out that perceived form is a primitive sensory fact and that "acquired knowl- edge" and cultural factors have no role in its determination (cf. 1947, pp. 141f.,

151 f.). The analysis in the text follows from his comment: "The constellation of stars which we call the Dipper may remind one, say, of a 'wagon', but this can occur only *after* one has experienced some organized form which then and *as such* is seen to resemble a wagon" (Ellis, p. 391).

The "Helmholtz Rule" is important in the current interpretation of evidence in favor of an empiristic hypothesis. Gestalt psychologists, however, do not regard this rule as decisive (cf. Koffka, 1928, pp. 74 f.; Pastore, 1960).

24. In 1949 and 1952 Köhler and his associates reported the results of experiments which in their view provided evidence for patterned direct currents in the brain as correlates of spatial percepts. The results and their theoretical interpretation were brought into question by the experiments and discussions of Lashley et al., 1951; and Sperry et al., 1955. Köhler replied to their criticisms in 1958 and 1965.

25. Köhler, 1947, Chs. 4, 5, 6; Koffka, 1928, pp. 304 f.; and 1935, pp. 86 f.; Blanshard, pp. 106 f.; Pastore, 1958, 1959, 1962. The literature on the early perceptions of animals and infants is extensive (cf. Fantz; Walk and Gibson).

26. Köhler, Sels. 4, 18 in Ellis; Wallach, 1948.

27. Köhler, "Perception humaine"; Lashley, 1949; Hurwich and Jameson.

28. Köhler, 1947, p. 102; and 1950; Lashley, 1938 and 1947.

The extensive critical reaction to gestalt theory has not yet been systematically and objectively evaluated. Thus we do not know whether Koffka was wrong when, in a letter to Helson in 1926, but published by Helson in 1967, he said: "That our present explanations are wanting in ever so many respects is obvious. They may even be, in many cases, altogether wrong. But this does not in the least affect the general principle. I believe, you will agree to all this (not all, but the argument); but I find quite often that people believe they have refuted the Gestalt principle when they think they have refuted a special explanation given by the Gestaltists."

Chapter 15 (CONNECTIONISM: HULL AND HEBB)

1. Pavlov, 1927, p. 151; and 1955, pp. 563 f., 599.
2. Pavlov, 1955, pp. 215, 569–605.
3. *Ibid.*, pp. 440, 798. See also Ch. 14, note 20.
4. Hull, 1962, pp. 820, 837.
5. *Ibid.*, p. 836; and 1952. A substantial portion of Koffka's *Growth of the mind*, the first English edition of which appeared in 1924, is an extensive critique of the "behavioristic approach" as represented by Thorndike and Watson.
6. Hull, 1943, Chs. 3, 19. See also Hull, 1942, pp. 77 f.; 1945; and 1951, Ch. 22.
7. Humphrey, 1933, Ch. 9; and 1951, p. 153.
8. Hull, 1943, Ch. 19.

Hull said that he derived the concept of "afferent neural interaction" from Pavlov and that Pavlov was the first theorist to formulate this concept, subsequently being emphasized by Köhler (1951, p. 93). However, the gestalt concept of interaction was stated independently of Pavlov. Furthermore, Hull did not realize that his concept of interaction, which he regarded as similar to Köhler's concept, was actually different.

9. Hull, 1943, pp. 38, 189; and 1952, pp. 345 f.; Lashley, 1938.

10. Hull, 1952, pp. 215 f.

11. Riesen, 1947.

Generally, those behaviorists who followed Hull's system often unambiguously adopted the second interpretation. For instance, Taylor, who formulated a theory of perception within the Hullian framework with encouragement by Hull himself, speculates that the infant at first would see the world as an "undifferentiated fog" and that the infant's later perceptions would be the result of conditioning (Taylor, pp. 314 f.). Furthermore, such speculations imply that all the laws of perceptual organization would be the product of conditioning.

12. Hebb, 1949, Intro. and Chs. 1, 2.

13. *Ibid.*, pp. 17 f., 50, 80 f.

The exclusive interest of Senden in the analysis and interpretation of the data of the resighted was centered in the implications of the Molyneux problem. Thus he explored the conditions for the visual recognition, identification, and naming of those objects with which the patients were tactually familiar while blind. Although other cases are cited, besides those of Cheselden and Franz, in which the patients initially might have seen solid objects as flat, Senden was not interested in the problem of the visual development of perceived solidity. Nevertheless his report is confusing since the question of visual development was not clearly separated from the question pertaining to the way in which the visual recognition and naming of objects might develop in experience. When Hebb cites the Senden report, he does not himself maintain a consistent separation of the two questions. Therefore, it is often difficult to decide whether Hebb is interested in the question of "learning to see" or of "learning to recognize." I shall always interpret Hebb's theory as referring to the first question. The theory, moreover, is concerned with the bi-dimensional organization of perceived form. The fact that Senden reported that some patients saw things flat is not cited by Hebb. Wertheimer, 1951, in his review of the original Senden report, which he considered in relation to Hebb's theory, pointed out the confusion of visual development and visual recognition. Furthermore, it would seem that the Senden report could be interpreted so as to support a nonempiristic hypothesis (Lashley and Russell; Wertheimer, 1951).

14. Hebb, 1949, pp. 52 f.

15. *Ibid.*, Ch. 4. For discussion of another aspect of Hebb's theory see Wertheimer, 1961; the reply by Hebb, 1962; and Wertheimer's rejoinder, 1962.

16. The linkage refers to a "growth process or metabolic change" among cells which fire at about the same time (Hebb, 1949, p. 62).

17. Hebb, 1949, pp. 97 f.

18. *Ibid.*, p. 99.

19. *Ibid.*, p. 97.

20. *Ibid.*, p. 103.

21. Hebb's exposition of the development of the "triangle percept" presupposes the "experience error."

Taylor (p. 318) has argued that Hebb's theory should predict the development of a perception consisting of three lines that intersect at a common point rather than the perception of a triangle.

22. The presence of "parts" in the percept is implied in Hebb's analogy to "bricks and mortar" (1949, p. 83). The compositional aspect of the hypothesized neural structures at the basis of percepts is evident in the revision of Hebb's theory undertaken by Milner.

23. Riesen, 1950, and also 1958; Walls, pp. 67–71; Hebb, 1963, and 1966.

24. For the experiment of a chimpanzee with restricted limb movement, see Nissen et al. For Hebb's interpretation of this experiment, see his text of 1958, pp. 118f.; and text of 1966, pp. 153f.

Nissen et al. also undertook visual tests when the chimpanzee was about eighteen months of age, its limbs still encased in cardboard tubes, in order to ascertain whether its visual perceptions were defective (pp. 490–93). The results indicated that the chimpanzee's visual perceptions of form, size, solidity, and distance were not impared by the severe restriction imposed on the use of its limbs.

25. Nissen et al. indicate derangement in the personality of the chimpanzee whose limb movement had been restricted (p. 503). See Riesen, 1950, for the experiment pertaining to the chimpanzee's response to the plaque.

26. Hebb, 1966, pp. 148f., has expressed a more cautious attitude in the interpretation of the Senden data.

In 1963 Hebb interpreted the results of experiments with "stabilized images" that had been obtained after 1949 (cf. Pritchard) as providing important evidence for the cell-assembly theory. However, since such "stabilized images" have the same theoretical significance as do after-images, and since eye-movements are essential to the theory of 1963, the way in which the results can be reconciled with cell-assembly theory is not apparent.

Chapter 16 (FUNCTIONALISM: AMES AND MURPHY)

1. Blake and Ramsey; Canestrari and Marzi; Interrelationships between perception and personality: A symposium; Pastore, 1949; Prentice.

2. Cantril, 1947, p. 21; and 1960, p. 231.

3. Ames, 1951.

4. For discussion and interpretation of the "demonstrations" by transactionalists: Ames, 1946 and 1951; Cantril, 1950; Kilpatrick, Demonstrations in perception; Kilpatrick (ed.), Human behavior, pp. 1–17, 41–55; Lawrence.

5. The explanation which is developed in Figure 16.1 is based mainly on Ames, 1951; see also Kilpatrick, Demonstrations in perception. Says Kilpatrick: "When the short edge of the trapezoid is coming forward . . . we ignore or suppress the vertical dimension cues and utilize the width cues."

Transactionalists, in developing an explanation of phenomenal motion, seem to be influenced by the already known facts of phenomenal reversal and of the continuous rotation of the trapezoidal window. This knowledge is inadvertently attributed to the observer not only at a time in early life when he is presumably learning to see forms and motion but also as an adult when he sees an edge of the trapezoidal window moving toward and away from him. I have tried to avoid introducing this type of knowledge in my account. The observer can know of external facts only on the basis of his retinal patterns and his actions. Thus any psychological explanation should be constructed on the basis of data which are available to him alone.

6. Ames, 1951; Cantril, 1960, p. 197.

7. Kilpatrick (ed.), *Human behavior,* pp. 87–96. See also: Ames, 1951; Cantril, 1950; Ittelson and Cantril; Ittelson and Kilpatrick; Lawrence.

8. Kilpatrick, 1961, p. 185, cites two unpublished experiments which he says corroborate his original results. For results which are contradictory to the transactionalist interpretation of phenomenal motion reversal: Pastore, 1952; Canestrari; and Epstein, who has recently reviewed the literature.

Ever since the time of Wheatstone, it has been known that the phenomenal depth of a three-dimensional wire-edged cube, when held by means of a rod attached to it and when viewed monocularly, inverses so that the rear face appears closer than the front face. The shapes of the faces of the perceived inversed cube are nonrectangular rather than rectangular. It was also known that phenomenal motion reversal would occur in these conditions when the cube was rotated. Mach's "bent card" similarly gives rise to phenomenal nonrectangular shapes and phenomenal motion reversal. Furthermore, a rotating concave theatrical mask, when perceived as a convex surface, also produces the apparent motion reversal effect. Obviously such diverse facts contradict an explanation of phenomenal motion reversal in terms of trapezoidal retinal patterns or of a relative size difference in the vertical edges of these patterns, and of the unconscious assumption of rectangularity.

Transactionalists have performed many experiments, besides those dealing with motion and "normal rooms," some of which have been evaluated by Pratt; Pastore, 1954; and, most recently, Epstein.

Incidentally, a study of the visual perceptions of the "thalidomide" babies of a few years ago, and who are now sufficiently grown up to serve as subjects in experiments, would be of theoretical interest in evaluating the importance that has been attributed to "manipulative experience."

9. Ames, 1951.

10. Plumb, *New York Times,* Mar. 14, 1954, Section 1, p. 82.

11. The descriptive interpretation of phenomenal motion represents a development of the ideas I stated in 1952. The concept of oppositeness of signs can be related to the phenomenal motion reversal of the wire-edged cube, Mach's bent card, and the mask (note 8 above).

12. Murphy, 1947, Chs. 3, 14.

13. *Ibid.,* pp. 333, 338, 342, 619; Murphy, 1935, Ch. 10; and 1951, Chs. 10, 11.

14. Murphy, 1947, pp. 345, 365, 377 f.; Bleuler, p. 63.

15. Murphy, 1947, pp. 334, 338; and 1951, p. 150; Murphy and Hochberg.

16. Murphy, 1935, Ch. 10. The exposition and acceptance of Lotze's theory of local signs, including projection of sensation, can be found in many widely used American textbooks in the first few decades of this century (cf. Ladd and Woodworth). Murphy, evidently influenced by James, said in 1935, "Instead of the vast jumble of confusion which the world probably is to the newborn infant, most of it

is to us an orderly pattern of objects" (p. 165). This theme is still currently popular (cf. Burloud, Ch. 12; Elliot, pp. 174 f.; Kuhn, pp. 111 f.; Spitz, Chs. 3, 4; Taylor, see Chapter 15, note 11, of my text).

17. Levine, Chein, and Murphy; Proshansky and Murphy; Schafer and Murphy; Murphy, 1947, pp. 365–83, and 1951, Ch. 11.

18. Chein et al.; Luchins; Pastore, 1949, 1956; Rock and Fleck; Smith and Hochberg; Wallach, 1949.

19. Murphy, 1956; Murphy and Hochberg.

The concept of "need," "wish," or "attention" as an influential and decisive factor in the organization of percepts has been popular even since Condillac developed this concept in 1754. Rignano and McDougall criticized gestalt theory because, in their view, gestalt psychologists had neglected this concept. Koffka, in reply to McDougall, said: "In order that an object catch my attention it must first have entered my behavioural [phenomenal] world. To put conation first and perception afterwards is putting the cart before the horse, as Köhler has pointed out so clearly in his replies to Rignano and G. E. Müller" (1938, p. 228). Köhler's comment concerning the Big Dipper, Ch. 14, note 23, was in response to Rignano who had emphasized the importance of "emotion" in the organization of percepts. Thus the theory of autism as developed by Murphy represents another instance of "putting the cart before the horse."

20. Pastore, 1949; Chein et al.

21. A shift in Murphy's theoretical position is evident in his latest text on perception, which was written in collaboration with Solley. It is now maintained, "The infant does not experience what William James called a 'booming, buzzing confusion' nor is his perception completely vague and undifferentiated as Piaget, Werner, and Vernon among others would have us believe" (p. 131). Many of the basic notions of gestalt theory are accepted. However, a rapprochement between gestalt theory and the empiristic theories of Ames, Hebb, Helmholtz, Hull, James, Murphy's own theory of 1947, and the several variations in empiristic theory which developed in the 1950s, is attempted. Evidently the theory, as stated in 1960, is in a transitional state.

APPENDIX A

The Cheselden Case and
the Explanation of
the New Operation

VII. *An Account of some Observations made by a young Gentleman, who was born blind, or lost his Sight so early, that he had no Remembrance of ever having seen, and was couch'd between* 13 *and* 14 *Years of Age.   By Mr.* Will. Chesselden, *F. R. S. Surgeon to Her* Majesty, *and to St.* Thomas's *Hospital.*

THO' we say of the Gentleman that he was blind, as we do of all People who have Ripe Cataracts, yet they are never so blind from that Cause, but that they can discern Day from Night ; and for the most Part in a strong Light, distinguish Black, White, and Scarlet ; but they cannot perceive the Shape of any thing ; for the Light by which these Perceptions are made, being let in obliquely thro' the aqueous Humour, or the anterior Surface of the Chrystalline (by which the Rays cannot be brought into a *Focus* upon the *Retina*) they can discern in no other Manner, than a sound Eye can thro' a Glass of broken Jelly, where a great Variety of Surfaces so differently refract the Light, that the several distinct Pencils of Rays cannot be collected by the Eye into their proper *Foci* ; wherefore the Shape of an Object in such a Case, cannot be at all discern'd, tho' the Colour may :   And thus it was with this young Gentleman, who though he knew these Colours asunder in a good Light ; yet when he saw them

O o o   **after**

after he was couch'd, the faint Ideas he had of them before, were not fufficient for him to know them by afterwards; and therefore he did not think them the fame, which he had before known by thofe Names. Now Scarlet he thought the moft beautiful of all Colours, and of others the moft gay were the moft pleafing, whereas the firft Time he faw Black, it gave him great Uneafinefs, yet after a little Time he was reconcil'd to it; but fome Months after, feeing by Accident a Negroe Woman, he was ftruck with great Horror at the Sight.

When he firft faw, he was fo far from making any Judgment about Diftances, that he thought all Objects whatever touch'd his Eyes, (as he exprefs'd it) as what he felt, did his Skin; and thought no Objects fo agreeable as thofe which were fmooth and regular, tho' he could form no Judgment of their Shape, or guefs what it was in any Object that was pleafing to him : He knew not the Shape of any Thing, nor any one Thing from another, however different in Shape, or Magnitude; but upon being told what Things were, whofe Form he before knew from feeling, he would carefully obferve, that he might know them again; but having too many Objects to learn at once, he forgot many of them; and (as he faid) at firft he learn'd to know, and again forgot a thoufand Things in a Day. One Particular only (tho' it may appear trifling) I will relate; Having often forgot which was the Cat, and which the Dog, he was afham'd to afk; but catching the Cat (which he knew by feeling) he was obferv'd to look at her ftedfaftly, and then fetting her down, faid, So Pufs! I fhall know you another Time. He was very much furpriz'd, that thofe Things which he had lik'd

beft,

beſt, did not appear moſt agreeable to his Eyes, expecting thoſe Perſons would appear moſt beautiful that
he lov'd moſt, and ſuch Things to be moſt agreeable to his
Sight that were ſo to his Taſte.   We thought he ſoon
knew what Pictures repreſented, which were ſhew'd to
him, but we found afterwards we were miſtaken; for
about two Months after he was couch'd, he diſcovered
at once, they repreſented ſolid Bodies; when to that
Time he conſider'd them only as Party-colour'd Planes,
or Surfaces diverſified with Variety of Paint; but e-
ven then he was no leſs ſurpriz'd, expecting the Pictures
would feel like the Things they repreſented, and was
amaz'd when he found thoſe Parts, which by their
Light and Shadow appear'd now round and uneven, felt
only flat like the reſt; and aſk'd which was the lying
Senſe, Feeling, or Seeing?

Being ſhewn his Father's Picture in a Locket at his
Mother's Watch, and told what it was, he acknowledged a Likeneſs, but was vaſtly ſurpriz'd; aſking, how
it could be, that a large Face could be expreſs'd in ſo
little Room, ſaying, It ſhould have ſeem'd as impoſſible
to him, as to put a Buſhel of any thing into a Pint.

At firſt, he could bear but very little Sight, and the
Things he ſaw, he thought extreamly large; but upon
ſeeing Things larger, thoſe firſt ſeen he conceiv'd leſs, never being able to imagine any Lines beyond the Bounds he
ſaw; the Room he was in he ſaid, he knew to be but Part
of the Houſe, yet he could not conceive that the whole
Houſe could look bigger.   Before he was couch'd, he
expected little Advantage from Seeing, worth under-
going an Operation for, except reading and writing;
for he ſaid, He thought he could have no more Plea-

ſure

ſure in walking abroad than he had in the Garden, which he could do ſafely and readily.   And even Blind-neſs he obſerv'd, had this Advantage, that he could go any where in the Dark much better than thoſe who can ſee ; and after he had ſeen, he did not ſoon loſe this Qua-lity, nor deſire a Light to go about the Houſe in the Night.   He ſaid, every new Object was a new Delight, and the Pleaſure was ſo great,   that he wanted Ways to expreſs it ; but his Gratitude to his Operator he could not conceal, never ſeeing him for ſome Time without Tears of Joy in his Eyes, and other Marks of Affec-tion : And if he did not happen to come at any Time when he was expected, he would be ſo griev'd, that he could not forbear crying at his Diſappointment. A Year after firſt Seeing, being carried upon *Epſom Downs*, and obſerving a large Proſpect, he was exceedingly de-lighted with it, and call'd it a new Kind of Seeing. And now being lately couch'd of his other Eye, he ſays, that Objects at firſt appear'd large to this Eye, but not ſo large as they did at firſt to the other ; and looking upon the ſame Object with both Eyes, he thought it look'd about twice as large as with the firſt couch'd Eye only,   but not Double, that we can any Ways diſcover.

VIII. *An*

VIII. *An Explication of the Instruments used, in a new Operation on the Eyes, by the* Same.

A B R Eprefent the Figures of two Eyes, on which a new Operation was perform'd, by making an Incifion thro' the *Iris*, which had contracted itfelf in both Cafes fo clofe, as to leave no Pupil open for the Admiffion of Light. (*See Plate the* 2^d.)

The Perforation in the Eye A was made a little above the Pupil, the clofing of which enfued upon the putting down a Cataract, which not knowing how low it might be lodged, I made the Incifion a little higher than the Middle, left any Part of it fhould lie in the Way.

The Eye B was one I couch'd not long before, where the Patient had been blind but a few Years. At firft he thought every Object further from him than it was; but he foon learn'd to judge the true Diftance, the Caufe of which I fhall endeavour to explain by the lowermoft Figure, in which let the Circle H I K reprefent the Eye, H the Place where an Image through the natural Pupil I was reprefented from the Place M; now the artificial Pupil being at the Place K, the Object at L is now painted at the Place H, where the Object M was alfo to be perceiv'd; therefore it was, I fuppofe, that the Patient miftook the Place L for the Place M.

C is

C is a Sort of Needle with an Edge on one Side, which being pafs'd thro' the *Tunica Sclerotis*, is then brought forwards thro' the *Iris* a little farther than E. This done, I turn the Edge of the Needle, and cut thro' the *Iris* as I draw it out : The Handle of this Needle is half black, and half white, which though it is not of much Ufe in this Operation, is very much fo in couching Needles, we being thereby able to judge, of their Pofition, when we do not fee them.

F F is an Inftrument to keep open the Eye-lids. G is a Bit of Iron, which as it is moved backward, or forward, the Inftrument opens and clofes.

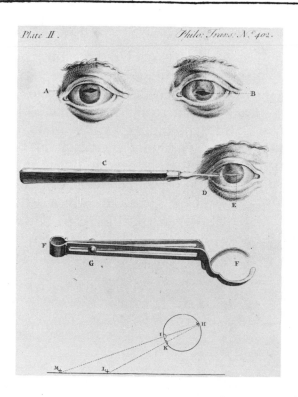

Plate II.   Philo: Trans: N.°402.

APPENDIX B

Case of a lady born blind, who received sight at an advanced age by the formation of an artificial pupil. By JAMES WARDROP, *Esq. F. R. S. Edin. Surgeon Extraordinary to the King &c. Communicated by the President.*

Read June 15, 1826.

As imperfections in the original structure of our organs of sense, which are remediable by art, are extremely rare, and as cases of successful operations on these organs essentially contribute to illustrate their functions, as well as to throw light on the operations and developement of the human mind, the following instance of vision being imparted to a lady born blind, by an operation at an advanced period of life, will, it is hoped, not be considered unworthy of being submitted to the consideration of the Royal Society.

The case, besides establishing the curious physiological fact, that the nerve of the eye can remain fit to receive the impressions of external objects, though totally excluded for a long series of years from the performance of that function, claims a much higher interest in a philosophical point of view; some of the facts here detailed confirming in a remarkable manner what Berkeley had predicated of "a man born blind being made to see," in the 79th Section of his "New Theory of Vision," published in the year 1709. He says, "a man born blind being made to see, would, at the first opening of his eyes, make very different judgements of the magnitude of objects intromitted by them from what others do. He would not consider the ideas of sight with reference to, or as having any connection with the *idea* of touch." It may also be observed, that in the present case the blindness was more complete, and the period at which vision was acquired was much later in life, than in any instance which has hitherto been recorded.

The lady, whose case forms the subject of this paper, was observed, during the first months of her infancy, to have something peculiar in the appearance of her eyes, and an unusual groping manner, which made her parents suspect that she had defective vision. When about six months old, she was placed under the care of a Parisian oculist, who performed an operation on both her eyes, with a view to afford her sight. The operation on the right eye was, however, followed by violent inflammation, and a collapse of the eye-ball, thus causing a complete destruction of the organ of vision. The operation on the left eye, though equally unsuccessful in attaining its object, was not followed by any alteration in the form or size of the globe. From the account stated by her friends, it was impossible to form any correct notion of the state of her eyes previous to the operations which were performed. It seems, however, extremely probable that the blindness, which was attempted to be remedied, had been produced by congenital cataracts, and that these operations had for their object the removal of the opaque lenses.

From the above early period she had continued totally blind, being able merely to distinguish a very light from a very dark room, but without having the power to perceive even the situation of the window through which the light entered; though in sunshine or in bright moonlight, she knew the direction from whence the light emanated. With regard therefore to the degree of sight, this lady was more completely blind then the boy in the celebrated case related by Mr. Cheselden, in the 35th volume of the Transactions of the Royal Society; for in that instance the boy knew black, white, and scarlet apart from one another; and when in a good light he had that degree of sight, which generally continues in an eye affected with cataract;

whereas in this lady, the pupil being completely shut up, no light could reach the retina, except such rays as could pass through the substance of the iris.

When she was placed under my care she had reached her 46th year. The right eye-ball was collapsed, but the left retained its natural globular form. The cornea of this eye was transparent, except at one point near its circumference, where there was a linear opacity, which had probably been the cicatrix of the wound made during the operation in her infancy. The anterior chamber of the eye was of its natural capacity, but I could not distinguish any vestige of a pupil, some streaks of yellow lymph being deposited in an irregular manner over the central part of the iris. There was every reason to believe that the retina was sound; for though she could not perceive objects, nor had any notion of colours, yet the circumstance already mentioned of her being able to distinguish between a very light and a very dark chamber, and between a gloomy day and sunshine, rendered it probable that the nerve was in a sound and natural state. Under this impression, I thought that the restoration of her sight by making an artificial pupil was practicable, and certainly well worthy of a trial. Accordingly, on the 26th of January, I introduced a very small needle through the cornea, passing it also through the centre of the iris; but I could not destroy any of the adhesions which had shut up the pupillar opening. After this operation she said she could distinguish more light, but she could perceive neither forms nor colours. The result of this first attempt justified the favourable views entertained of the state of the retina, and Mr. LAWRENCE, who at this time was consulted, coincided with me in this opinion.

On the 8th of February, a second operation was performed, which consisted in passing a sharp edged needle through the sclerotica, bringing its point through the iris into the anterior chamber, repassing it into the posterior chamber at a small distance, and then dividing the portion of iris thus included between the two perforations of the needle. Only a very slight inflammation followed,—the light became offensive to her,—she complained of its brightness, and was frequently observed trying to see her hands; but it was evident her vision was very imperfect; for although there was an incision made in the iris, some opaque matter lay behind this opening, which must have greatly obstructed the entrance of light.

On the 17th of February, a third operation was performed, which consisted in still further enlarging the opening in the iris, and in removing the opaque matter, by a needle introduced through the sclerotica. This was followed by a very slight degree of redness. The operation being performed at my house, she returned home in a carriage, with her eye covered only with a loose piece of silk, and the first thing she noticed was a hackney coach passing, when she exclaimed, "What is that large thing that has passed by us?" In the course of the evening she requested her brother to show her his watch, concerning which she expressed much curiosity, and she looked at it a considerable time, holding it close to her eye. She was asked what she saw, and she said there was a dark and a bright side; she pointed to the hour of 12, and smiled. Her brother asked her if she saw any thing more? she replied, "Yes," and pointed to the hour of 6, and to the hands of the watch. She then looked at the chain and seals, and observed that one of the seals was bright, which was the case, being a solid piece of rock crystal. The following day I asked her to look again at the watch, which she refused to do, saying, that the light was offensive to her eye, and that she felt very stupid; meaning that she was much confused by the visible world thus for the first time opened to her. On the third day she observed the doors on the opposite side of the street, and asked if they were red, but they were in fact of an oak colour. In the evening she looked at her brother's face, and said that she saw his nose; he asked her to touch it, when she did; he then slipped a handkerchief over his face, and asked her to look again, when she playfully pulled it off, and asked, "What is that?"

On the sixth day, she told us that she saw better than she had done on any preceding day; "but I cannot tell what I do see; I am quite stupid." She seemed indeed bewildered from not being able to combine the knowledge acquired by the senses of touch and sight, and felt disappointed in not having the power of distinguishing at once by her eye, objects which she could so readily distinguish from one another by feeling them.

On the seventh day she took notice of the mistress of the house in which she lodged, and observed that she was tall. She asked what the colour of her gown was? to which she was answered, that it was blue: "so is that thing on your head," she then observed; which was the case: "and your handkerchief, that is a different colour;" which was also correct. She added, "I see you pretty well, I think." The teacups and saucers underwent an examination: "what are they like?" her brother asked her. "I don't know," she replied; "they look very queer to me; but I can tell what they are in a minute when I touch them." She distinguished an orange on the chimney-piece, but could form no notion of what it was till she touched it. She seemed now to have become more cheerful, and entertained greater expectation of comfort from her admission into the visible world; and she was very sanguine that she would find her newly acquired faculty of more use to her when she returned home, where every thing was familiar to her.

On the eighth day, she asked her brother, when at dinner, "what he was helping himself to?" and when she was told it was a glass of port wine, she replied, "port wine is dark, and looks to me very ugly." She observed, when candles were brought into the room, her brother's face in the mirror, as well as that of a lady who was present; she also walked, for the first time without assistance, from her chair to a sopha which was on the opposite side of the room, and back again to the chair. When at tea, she took notice of the tray, observed the shining of the japan work, and asked "what the colour was round the edge?" she was told that it was yellow; upon which she remarked, "I will know that again."

On the ninth day she came down stairs to breakfast in great spirits; she said to her brother, "I see you very well to-day;" and came up to him, and shook hands. She also observed a ticket on a window of a house on the opposite side of the street ("a lodging to let"); and her brother, to convince himself of her seeing it, took her to the window three several times, and to his surprise and gratification, she pointed it out to him distinctly on each trial.

She spent a great part of the eleventh day looking out of the window, and spoke very little.

On the twelfth day she was advised to walk out, which recommendation pleased her much. Mr.—— called on her, and she told him she felt quite happy. Her brother walked out with her as her guide, and took her twice round the piazzas of Covent-garden. She appeared much surprised, but apparently delighted; the clear blue sky first attracted her notice, and she said, "it is the prettiest thing I have ever seen yet, and equally pretty every time I turn round and look at it." She distinguished the street from the foot pavement distinctly, and stepped from one to the other like a person accustomed to the use of her eyes. Her great curiosity, and the manner in which she stared at the variety of objects, and pointed to them, exciting the observation of many by-standers, her brother soon conducted her home, much against her will.

On the thirteenth day nothing particular took place till tea-time, when she observed that there was a different tea-tray, and that it was not a pretty one, but had a dark border; which was a correct description. Her brother asked her to look in the mirror, and tell him if she saw his face in it? to which she answered, evidently disconcerted, "I see my own; let me go away."

She drove in a carriage, on the fourteenth day, four miles on the Wandsworth road; admired most the sky and the fields, noticed the trees, and likewise the river Thames as she crossed Vauxhall bridge. At this time it was bright sunshine, and she said something dazzled her when she looked on the water.

On the fifteenth day, being Sunday, she walked to a chapel at some distance, and now evidently saw more distinctly, but appeared more confused than when her sight was less perfect. The people passing on the pavement startled her; and once when a gentleman was going past her, who had a white waistcoat and a blue coat with yellow buttons, which the sunshine brought full in her view, she started so as to draw her brother, who was walking with her, off the pavement. She distinguished the clergyman moving his hands in the pulpit, and observed that he held something in them; this was a white handkerchief.

She went in a coach, on the sixteenth day, to pay a visit in a distant part of the town, and appeared much entertained with the bustle in the streets. On asking her how she saw on that day? she answered, "I see a great deal, if I could only tell what I do see; but surely I am very stupid."

Nothing particular took place on the seventeenth day; and when her brother asked her how she was? she replied, "I am well, and see better; but don't tease me with too many questions, till I have learned a little better how to make use of my eye. All that I can say is, that I am sure, from what I do see, a great change has taken place; but I cannot describe what I feel."

Eighteen days after the last operation had been performed, I attempted to ascertain by a few experiments her precise notions of the colour, size, forms, position, motions and distances of external objects. As she could only see with one eye, nothing could be ascertained respecting the question of double vision. She evidently saw the difference of colours; that is, she received and was sensible of different impressions from different colours. When pieces of paper one and a half inch square, differently coloured, were presented to her, she not only distinguished them at once from one another, but gave a decided preference to some colours, liking yellow most, and then pale pink. It may be here mentioned, that when desirous of examining an object, she had considerable difficulty in directing her eye to it, and finding out its position, moving her hand as well as her eye in various directions, as a person when blind-folded, or in the dark, gropes with his hands for what he wishes to touch. She also distinguished a large from a small object, when they were both held up before her for comparison. She said she saw different forms in various objects which were shown to her. On asking what she meant by different forms, such as long, round and square, and desiring her to draw with her finger these forms on her other hand, and then presenting to her eye the respective forms, she pointed to them exactly: she not only distinguished small from large objects, but knew what was meant by above and below; to prove which, a figure drawn with ink was placed before her eye, having one end broad, and the other narrow, and she saw the positions as they really were, and not inverted. She could also perceive motions; for when a glass of water was placed on the table before her, on approaching her hand near it, it was moved quickly to a greater distance, upon which she immediately said, "You move it; you take it away."

She seemed to have the greatest difficulty in finding out the distance of any object; for when an object was held close to her eye, she would search for it by stretching her hand far beyond its position, while on other occasions she groped close to her own face, for a thing far removed from her.

She learned with facility the names of the different colours, and two days after the coloured papers had been shown to her, on coming into a room the colour of which was crimson, she observed that it was red. She also observed some pictures hanging on the red wall of the room in which she was sitting, distinguishing several small figures in them, but not knowing what they represented, and admiring the gilt frames. On the same day, she walked round the pond in the centre of St. James's square, and was pleased with the glistening of the sun's rays on the water, as well as with the blue sky and green shrubs, the colours of which she named correctly.

It may be here observed, that she had yet acquired by the use of her sight but very little knowledge of any forms, and was unable to apply the information gained by this new sense, and to compare it with what she had been accustomed to acquire by her sense of touch. When, therefore, the experiment was made of giving her a silver pencil case and a large key to examine with her hands; she discriminated and knew each distinctly; but when they were placed on the table, side by side, though she distinguished each with her eye, yet she could not tell which was the pencil case and which was the key.

Nothing farther occurred in the history of this lady's case worthy of notice till the twenty-fifth day after the operation. On that day she drove in a carriage for an hour in the Regent's Park, and on her way there seemed more amused than usual, and asked more questions about the objects surrounding her, such as "What is that?" it is a soldier, she was answered; "and that, see! see!" these were candles of various colours at a tallow chandler's window. "Who is that, that has passed us just now?" it was a person on horseback: "but what is that on the pavement, red?" it was some ladies who wore red shawls. On going into the Park, she was asked what she saw particularly, or if she could guess what any of the objects were. "Oh yes," she replied, "there is the sky, that is the grass; yonder is water, and two white things;" which were two swans. On coming home along Piccadilly, the jewellers' shop seemed to surprise her much, and her expressions made those around her laugh heartily.

From this period till the time of her leaving London on the 31st of March, being forty-two days after the operation, she continued almost daily to gain more information of the visible world, but she had yet much to learn. She had acquired a pretty accurate notion of colours and their different shades and names; and when she came to pay me a farewell visit, she then wore a gown, the first of her own choice, with the light purple colour of which she seemed highly gratified, as well as with her cap, which was ornamented with red ribbons. She had not yet acquired any thing like an accurate knowledge of distance or of forms, and up to this period she continued to be very much confused with every object at which she looked. Neither was she yet able, without considerable difficulty and numerous fruitless trials, to direct her eye to an object; so that when she attempted to look at any thing, she turned her head in various directions, until her eye caught the object of which it was in search. She still entertained however the same hope which she expressed soon after the operation, that when she got home her knowledge of external things would be more accurate and intelligible, and that when she came to look at those objects which had been so long familiar to her touch, the confusion which the multiplicity of external objects now caused, would in a great measure subside.

BIBLIOGRAPHY

Abbott, T. K. *Sight and touch: an attempt to disprove the received (or Berkeleian) theory of vision.* London: Longman, Roberts, and Green, 1864.

———. "Bishop Berkeley and Professor Fraser." *Hermathena,* 1879, 3, 1–39.

———. "Fresh light on Molyneux's problem. Dr. Ramsey's Case." *Mind* (n.s.), 1904, 13, 543–54.

Aitken, G. A. (ed.). *The Tatler.* Vol. 2. New York, Hadley & Mathews, 1899.

Alison, W. P. "On single and correct vision by means of double and inverted images on the retinae." *Royal Soc. Edinburgh Trans.,* 1836, 13, 472–93.

Alquié, F. (textes établis, présentés et annotés par F. Alquié). *Oeuvres philosophiques de Descartes.* Vol. 1 (1618–1637). Paris: Garnier, 1963.

Ames, A., Jr. *Some demonstrations concerned with the origin and nature of our sensations (what we experience).* Hanover: 1946 (mimeographed).

———. "Architectural form and visual sensations." In Creighton, T. H. (ed). *Building for modern man: A symposium.* Princeton: Princeton Univ. Press, 1949.

———. "Visual perception and the rotating trapezoidal window." *Psychol. Monogr.,* 1951, 65, No. 7.

Armstrong, D. M. *Berkeley's theory of vision.* New York: Cambridge Univ. Press, 1960.

Arnheim, R. *Art and visual perception.* Berkeley and Los Angeles: Univ. California Press, 1964.

Asch, S. E. and Pabst, E. (eds.). "Essays presented to Professor Wolfgang Köhler on the occasion of his 75th birthday." *Psychol. Beiträge,* 1962, Band VI, Heft 3/4.

Bailey, S. *Review of Berkeley's theory of vision: designed to show the unsoundness of that celebrated speculation.* London: Ridgway, 1842.

———. *Letter to a philosopher in reply to some recent attempts to vindicate Berkeley's theory of vision.* London: Ridgway, 1843.

———. *Discourses on various subjects.* London: Longman, Brown, Green and Longmans, 1852.

———. *Letters on the philosophy of the human mind.* 3 Vols. London: Longman, Brown, Green and Longmans, 1855–63.

Bain, A. *The senses and the intellect.* London: Longmans, Green, 1868. 3rd edition.

———. "A note on Dr. Bastian's paper 'on the physiology of thinking'." *Fortnightly Rev.,* (n. s.) 1869, 5, 493–98.

———. *Mental and moral science.* Pt. 1. London: Longmans, Green, 1872.

———. *Mind and body.* New York: Appleton, 1873.

Bastian, H. C. The physiology of thinking. *Fortnightly Rev.,* (n. s.) 1869, 5, 57–71.

Bell, C. "On the motions of the eye." *Royal Soc. London Philos. Trans.,* 1823, 113, 166–86.

Bentley, M. "The psychology of mental arrangement." *Amer. J. Psychol.,* 1902, 13, 269–93.

———. *The field of psychology.* New York: Appleton, 1928.

Bergmann, G. "Theoretical psychology." *Annual Rev. Psychol.,* 1953, 4, 435–58.

Berkeley, G. *An essay towards a new theory of vision,* 1709. See Fraser, 1891; 1901, Vol. 1; Calkins; Turbayne, 1963.

———. *Three dialogues between Hylas and Philonous,* 1713. See Calkins.

———. *Alciphron or the minute philosopher (fourth and seventh dialogues),* 1732. See Calkins.

———. *Theory of vision or visual language: vindicated and explained,* 1733. See Fraser, 1901, Vol. 2, and Turbayne, 1963.

Bernstein, J. *The five senses of man.* New York: Appleton, 1886.

Best, C. H. and Taylor, N. B. *The physiological basis of medical practice.* Baltimore: Williams & Wilkins, 1943. 3rd edition.

Blake, R. R. and Ramsey, G. V. (eds.). *Perception: an approach to personality.* New York: Ronald, 1951.

Blanshard, B. *The nature of thought.* Vol. 1. London: Allen & Unwin, 1939.

Bleuler, E. *Dementia praecox or the group of schizophrenias.* Trans. by J. Zinkin. New York: International Universities Press, 1950.

Boas, F. *The mind of primitive man.* New York: Macmillan, 1938. Revised edition.

Boring, E. G. *Sensation and perception in the history of experimental psychology.* New York: Appleton-Century-Crofts, 1942.

Bourdon, B. *La perception visuelle de l'espace.* Paris: Schleicher, 1902.

Bowen, F. *The metaphysics of Sir William Hamilton,* "Collected, arranged, and abridged." New York: Allyn, 1876.

Bowne, B. P. *Introduction to psychological theory.* New York: Harper, 1887.

Brewster, D. *Letters on natural magic.* London: Murray, 1851. 6th edition.

———. *The stereoscope.* London: Murray, 1856.

Brown, T. *Lectures on the philosophy of the human mind.* Vol. 1. Boston: Carter, 1830.

Buffon, N. *Oeuvres complètes de Buffon.* Vol. 11. Paris: Abel Pilon, 1749. (Chapter, "Des Sens")

Burloud, A. *Psychologie.* Librairie Hachette, 1948.

Burtt, E. A. *The metaphysical foundations of modern science.* New York: Doubleday, 1954.

Calkins, M. W. (ed.). *Berkeley: Essays, principles, dialogues.* New York: Scribner's, 1929.

Canestrari, R. "Osservazioni sul fenomeno del trapezio ruotante." *Rivista di Psicologia,* 1956, 50, 1–20.

Canestrari, R. and Marzi, A. "Motivazione e percezione nella psicologia della personalità." In *Il pensiero Americano contemporaneo.* Milano: Edizioni di Communita, 1958.

Cantril, H. *Understanding man's social behavior: preliminary notes.* Princeton: Office of Public Opinion Research, 1947.

———. *The "why" of man's experience.* New York: Macmillan, 1950.

———, (ed.). *The morning notes of Adelbert Ames, Jr., including a correspondence with John Dewey.* New Brunswick: Rutgers Univ. Press, 1960.

Carlini, A. (trans.). *Condillac: Trattato delle sensazioni.* Bari: Laterza, 1923.

Carmichael, L. "An evaluation of current sensationism." *Psychol. Rev.,* 1925, 32, 192–215.

Carpenter, W. B. *Principles of mental physiology.* New York: Appleton, 1875.

Carr, G. (trans.). *Condillac's treatise on the sensations.* Los Angeles: Univ. Southern California, 1930.

Carr, H. A. *Introduction to space perception.* New York: Longmans, Green, 1935.

Cassirer, E. *The philosophy of the enlightenment*. Trans. by F. C. A. Koellen and J. P. Pettegrove. Boston: Beacon Press, 1964.

Cesca, G. *Le teorie nativistiche e genetiche della localizzazione spaziale*. Padova: Drucker, 1883.

Chein, I., Lane, R., Murphy, G., Proshansky, H., and Schafer, R. "Need as a determinant of perception: a reply to Pastore." *J. Psychol.*, 1951, 31, 129–36.

Cheselden, W. "An account of some observations made by a young gentleman, who was born blind, or lost his sight so early, that he had no remembrance of ever having seen, and was couched between 13 and 14 years of age." *Royal Soc. London Philos. Trans.*, 1728, 35, 447–50.

————. "An explication of the instruments used, in a new operation on the eyes." *Royal Soc. London Philos. Trans.*, 1728, 35, 451–52.

————. *The anatomy of the human body*. Boston: J. White, 1795. 1st American edition.

Clarke, J. (trans.). *Rohault's system of natural philosophy, illustrated with Dr. Samuel Clarke's notes*. Vol. 1. London, 1729.

Clifford, W. K. *Select works of William Kingdon Clifford*. New York: Humboldt, 1889.

Condillac, E. *Essai sur l'origine des connoissances humaines*, 1746. Pt. 1, Sec. 6. See Le Roy.

————. *Traité des sensations*, 1754. See Le Roy, and Carlini.

Crafts, L. W., Schneirla, T. C., Robinson, E. E., and Gilbert, R. W. *Recent experiments in psychology*. New York: McGraw-Hill, 1938.

Crombie, A. C. (trans.) "Kepler: de modo visionis." In Cohen, I. B. and Taton, R. (eds.). *Mélanges Alexandre Koyré: L'aventure de la science*. Vol. 1. Paris: Hermann, 1964.

Darwin, C. "A biographical sketch of an infant." *Mind*, 1877, 2, 285–94.

Darwin, R. W. "New experiments on the ocular spectra of light and colours." *Royal Soc. London Philos. Trans.*, 1786, 76, 313–48.

Dashiell, J. F. *Fundamentals of objective psychology*. New York: Houghton Mifflin, 1928.

Davis, J. W. "The Molyneux problem." *J. Hist. Ideas*, 1960, 21, 392–408.

Descartes, R. *La dioptrique*. Discourses 1–6 in Alquié; complete translation in Olscamp.

————. *Discourse on the method of rightly conducting the reason*. See Haldane and Ross, Vol. 1.

————. *Meditations on first philosophy*. See Haldane and Ross, Vol. 1, and Veitch.

————. *The passions of the soul*. See Haldane and Ross, Vol. 1.

————. *The principles of philosophy*. See Haldane and Ross, Vol. 1, and Veitch.

————. *Rules for the direction of the human mind.* See Haldane and Ross, Vol. 1.

————. *Le traité de l'homme.* See Alquié.

Dewey, J. *Psychology.* New York: Harper, 1886.

Diamond, S. "Seventeenth century French "connectionism": La Forge, Dilly, and Regis." *J. Hist. Beh. Sciences,* 1969, 5, 3–9.

Diderot, D. *Letter on the blind.* In *Diderot's early philosophical works.* Trans. and ed. by M. Jourdain. Chicago: Open Court, 1916.

Elliot, H. *Modern science and materialism.* New York: Longmans, Green, 1927.

Ellis, W. D. (trans.). *A sourcebook of gestalt psychology.* New York: Harcourt, Brace, 1939.

Epstein, W. *Varieties of perceptual learning.* New York: McGraw-Hill, 1967.

Fantz, R. L. "Pattern discrimination and selective attention as determinants of perceptual development from birth." In Kidd, A. H. and Rivoire, J. L. (eds.). *Perceptual development in children.* New York: International Univ. Press, 1965.

Ferrier, J. F. "Berkeley and idealism." *Blackwood's Mag.,* 1842, 51, 812–30. See Ferrier, 1875.

————. "Mr. Bailey's reply to an article in Blackwood's Magazine." *Blackwood's Mag.,* 1843, 53, 762–70. See Ferrier, 1875.

————. *Philosophical works.* In Grant, E. and Lushington, E. L. (eds.). *Philosophical remains,* Vol. 3. London: Blackwood, 1875.

Fichte, I. H. *Contributions to mental philosophy.* Trans. and ed. by J. D. Morell. London: Longman, Green, Longman and Roberts, 1860.

Foster, M. *Lectures on the history of physiology during the sixteenth, seventeenth and eighteenth centuries.* Cambridge: Univ. Press, 1901.

Franz, J. C. A. "Memoir of the case of a gentleman born blind, and successfully operated upon in the 18th year of his age, with physiological observations and experiments." *Royal Soc. London Philos. Trans.,* 1841, 131, 59–68.

Fraser, A. C. "Berkeley's theory of vision." *North Brit. Rev.,* (n. s.) 1864, 41, 199–230.

————. *Life, letters and unpublished writings of Berkeley.* Oxford: Clarendon Press, 1871.

————, (ed.). *Selections from Berkeley.* Oxford: Clarendon Press, 1891. 4th edition.

————, (ed.). *The complete works of George Berkeley.* Vols. 1, 2. Oxford: Clarendon Press, 1901.

Giraud-Teulon, M. *Physiologie et pathologie fonctionelle de la vision binoculaire.* Paris: Bailliere, 1861.

————. "La vision binoculaire." *Revue Scientifique,* 1868, 5, 222–30.

Graham, E. C. *Optics and vision: the background of the metaphysics of Berkeley,* 1929.

Gray, P. H. "Douglas Alexander Spalding: the first experimental behaviorist." *J. Gen. Psychol.,* 1962, 67, 299–307.

Guillaume, P. *La psychologie de la forme.* Paris: Flammarion, 1937.

————. *Introduction a la psychologie.* Paris: Vrin, 1964.

Gurwitsch, A. *The field of consciousness.* Pittsburgh: Duquesne Univ. Press, 1964.

Haldane, E. S. and Ross, G. R. T. (translators). *The philosophical works of Descartes.* 2 Vols. New York: Dover, 1955.

Hall, G. S. "Muscular perception of space." *Mind,* 1877, 2, 443–58.

————. "Review of James's *The principles of psychology.*" *Amer. J. Psychol.,* 1891, 6, 578–91.

Hallowell, A. I. *Culture and experience.* Philadelphia: Univ. of Pennsylvania Press, 1945.

Hamilton, W. *Lectures on metaphysics.* Ed. by H. L. Mansel and J. Veitch. New York: Sheldon, 1880.

Hebb, D. O. *Organization of behavior.* New York: Wiley, 1949.

————. *A textbook of psychology.* Philadelphia: Saunders, 1958.

————. "Auditory-localization reflexes at birth." *Science,* 1962, 135, 998–99.

————. "The semiautonomous process: its nature and nurture." *Amer. Psychol.,* 1963, 18, 16–27.

————. *A textbook of psychology.* Philadelphia: Saunders, 1966. 2nd edition.

Helmholtz, H. *Handbuch der physiologischen optik.* Leipzig: Voss, 1867.

————. *Optique physiologique.* Trans. by E. Javal and N. Klein. Paris: Masson, 1867.

————. "Des progrès récents dans la théorie de la vision." Trans. by E. Javal. *Revue Scientifique,* 1869, 6, 210–19, 322–32, 417–28.

————. "Die neuren fortschritte in der theorie des sehens." In *Populäre wissenschaftliche Vörtrage.* Braunschweig, Viewig, 1871.

————. "The recent progress of the theory of vision." Trans. by P. H. Pye-Smith, 1873. Reprinted in *Popular scientific lectures.* New York: Dover, 1962.

————. *Treatise on physiological optics.* Ed. by J. P. S. Southall, trans. from the 3rd German edition. Optical Society of America, 1924. (Reprinted by Dover, 1962.)

Helson, H. "The psychology of *Gestalt.*" *Amer. J. Psychol.,* 1925, 36, 342–70, 494–526.

————. "The psychology of *Gestalt.*" *Amer. J. Psychol.,* 1926, 37, 25–62, 189–223.

————. "Some remarks on gestalt psychology by Kurt Koffka." *J. Hist. Beh. Sciences*, 1967, 3, 43–46.

Hering, E. *On memory*. Chicago: Open Court, 1913.

————. *Spatial sense and the movements of the eye*. Trans. by A. Radde. Baltimore: Amer. Acad. Optom., 1942.

Hicks, G. D. *Berkeley*. London: Benn, 1932.

Higginson, G. D. "The visual apprehension of movement under successive retinal excitations." *Amer. J. Psychol.*, 1926, 37, 63–115.

————. "An examination of some phases of space perception." *Psychol. Rev.*, 1937, 44, 77–96.

Höffding, H. *Outlines of psychology*. Trans. by M. E. Lowndes. New York: Macmillan, 1891.

————. *A history of modern philosophy*. Trans. from the German edition by B. E. Meyer. Vol. 1. New York: Dover, 1955.

Hooke, R. "Of an instrument to take the draught of any thing." In *Philosophical experiments and observations*. Published by W. Derham, F. R. S. London: Innys, 1726.

Houssay, B. A. (ed.). *Human physiology*. Trans. by J. T. Lewis and O. T. Lewis. New York: McGraw-Hill, 1955, 2nd edition.

Hull, C. L. "Conditioning: Outline of a systematic theory of learning." In *Nat. Soc. Study Educ.*, 41st Yrbk., Pt. II, 1942.

————. *Principles of behavior*. New York: Appleton-Century-Crofts, 1943.

————. "The discrimination of stimulus configurations and the hypothesis of afferent neural interaction." *Psychol. Rev.*, 1945, 52, 133–42.

————. *Essentials of behavior*. New Haven: Yale Univ. Press, 1951.

————. *A behavior system*. New Haven: Yale Univ. Press, 1952. (Reprinted by Wiley, 1964.)

————. "Passages from the 'idea books' of Clark L. Hull." *Perceptual and motor Skills. Monogr. Suppl.* 9–V15, 1962.

————. In Boring, E. G., Langfeld, H. S., Werner, H., and Yerkes, R. M. (eds.). *A history of psychology in autobiography*. Vol. 4. 1952. (Reprinted, New York: Russell & Russell, 1968.)

Humphrey, G. "The theory of Einstein and the *Gestalt-Psychologie:* a parallel." *Amer. J. Psychol.*, 1924, 35, 353–59.

————. *The nature of learning*. New York: Harcourt, Brace, 1933.

————. *Thinking*. New York: Wiley, 1951.

Hurwich, L. and Jameson, D. "Human color perception." *Amer. Scientist*, 1969, 57, 143–66.

Huxley, T. H. *Hume, with helps to the study of Berkeley*. New York: Appleton, 1896.

Hyslop, J. H. "Upright vision." *Psychol. Rev.*, 1897, 4, 71–73, 142–63.

————. "Binocular vision and the problem of knowledge." *Amer. J. Psychol.*, 1903, 14, 42–59.

————. "Experiments in the perception of the third dimension." *Psychol. Rev.*, 1903, 10, 47–51.

Interrelationships between perception and personality: A symposium. J. Pers., 1949, 18, 2–143, 145–266.

Ittelson, W. H. and Cantril, H. *Perception: a transactional approach.* New York: Doubleday, 1954.

Ittelson, W. H. and Kilpatrick, F. P. "Experiments in perception." *Scientific Amer.*, 1951, 185, 50–55.

Jackson, H. *Writings of Hughlings Jackson.* Vol. 1. New York: Basic Books, 1958.

James, W. "On some omissions of introspective psychology." *Mind*, 1884, 9, 1–26.

————. "The perception of space." *Mind*, 1887, 12, 1–30, 183–211, 321–53, 516–48.

————. "The psychological theory of extension." *Mind*, 1889, 14, 107–9.

————. *The principles of psychology.* 2 Vols. New York: Holt, 1890.

————. *Psychology: Briefer course.* New York: Holt, 1892.

————. *Talks to teachers on psychology.* New York: Holt, 1909.

————. *Some problems in philosophy.* New York and London: Longmans, Green, 1911.

Janet, P. "De la perception visuelle de la distance." *Revue Philos.*, 1879, 7, 1–17.

Jastrow, J. *Fact and fable in psychology.* London: Macmillan, 1901.

Jeffress, L. A. (ed.). *Cerebral mechanisms in behavior: the Hixon Symposium.* New York: Wiley, 1951.

Johnston, G. A. *The development of Berkeley's philosophy.* London: Macmillan, 1923.

Kanizsa, G. "Margini quasi-percettivi in campi con stimolazione omogenea." *Rivista di psicologia*, 1955, 49, 7–30.

Kanizsa G. and Vicario, G. (eds.). *Ricerche sperimentali sulla percezione.* Università Degli Studi Di Trieste, 1968.

Katz, D. *Gestalt psychology.* Trans. by R. Tyson. New York: Ronald, 1950.

Kilpatrick, F. P. *Demonstrations in perception: a guide to their interpretation and significance.* Hanover: Institute for Associated Research, 1952 (mimeographed).

————, (ed.). *Human behavior from the transactional point of view.* Hanover: Institute for Associated Research, 1952.

————. "The Ames oscillatory effect: A reply to Pastore." *Psychol. Rev.*, 1953, 60, 76–79.

————. "Two processes in perceptual learning." *J. Exp. Psychol.*, 1954, 47, 362–70.

————, (ed.). *Explorations in transactional psychology.* New York: New York Univ. Press, 1961.

Kline, M. *Mathematics in western culture.* New York: Oxford Univ. Press, 1953.

Klineberg, O. *Social psychology.* New York: Holt, 1940.

Koenisberger, L. *Hermann von Helmholtz.* Trans. by F. A. Welby. (Reprinted, New York: Dover, 1965.)

Koffka, K. "Perception: an introduction to the *Gestalt-Theorie.*" *Psychol. Bull.*, 1922, 19, 531–85.

————. "Mental development." In *Psychologies of 1925.* Worcester: Clark Univ. Press, 1926.

————. *The growth of the mind.* Trans. by R. M. Ogden. New York: Harcourt, Brace, 1928. Revised 2nd edition.

————. "Some problems of space perception." In *Psychologies of 1930.* Worcester: Clark Univ. Press, 1930.

————. *Principles of gestalt psychology.* New York: Harcourt, Brace, 1935.

————. "Purpose and gestalt: A reply to Professor McDougall." *Character and Personality*, 1938, 6, 218–38.

Köhler, W. "An aspect of gestalt psychology." In *Psychologies of 1925.* Worcester: Clark Univ. Press, 1926.

————. *Gestalt psychology.* New York: Liveright, 1929.

————. "The new psychology and physics." *Yale Rev.*, 1930, 19, 560–76.

————. "La perception humaine." *J. Psychologie*, 1930, 27, 5–30.

————. "Some tasks of gestalt psychology." In *Psychologies of 1930.* Worcester: Clark Univ. Press, 1930.

————. "Some notes on gestalt psychology." *International Forum*, 1931 (June), Vol. 1, 16–20.

————. "Psychological remarks on some questions of anthropology." *Amer. J. Psychol.*, 1937, 50, 271–88.

————. *The place of value in a world of facts.* New York: Liveright, 1938.

————. *Dynamics in psychology.* New York: Liveright, 1940.

————. "On the nature of associations." *Proc. Amer. Philos. Soc.*, 1941, 84, 489–502.

————. *Gestalt psychology.* New York: Liveright, 1947. Revised edition.

————. "Psychology and evolution." *Acta Psychologica*, 1950, 7, 288–97.

————. "Relational determination in perception." 1951. See Jeffress.

————. "The present situation in brain physiology." *Amer. Psychol.*, 1958, 13, 150–54.

————. "The mind-body problem." In Hook, S. (ed.). *Dimensions of mind.* New York: Collier, 1961.

————. "Unsolved problems in the field of figural after-effects." *Psychol. Rec.*, 1965, 15, 63–83.

————. "A task for philosophers." In Feyerabend, P. K. and Maxwell, G. (eds.). *Mind, matter, and method: essays in philosophy and science in honor of Herbert Feigl.* Minneapolis: Univ. Minneapolis Press, 1966.

Köhler, W. and Adams, P. A. "Perception and attention." *Amer. J. Psychol.*, 1958, 71, 489–503.

Köhler, W. and Emery, D. A. "Figural after-effects in the third dimension of visual space." *Amer. J. Psychol.*, 1947, 60, 159–201.

Köhler, W. and Fishback, J. "The destruction of the Muller-Lyer illusion in repeated trials." *J. Exp. Psychol.*, 1950, 40, 267–81, 398–410.

Köhler, W. and Held, R. "The cortical correlates of pattern vision." *Science*, 1949, 110, 414–19.

Köhler, W., Held, R., and O'Connell, D. N. "An investigation of cortical currents." *Proc. Amer. Philos. Soc.*, 1952, 96, 290–330.

Köhler, W. and Wallach, H. "Figural after-effects: an investigation of visual processes." *Proc. Amer. Philos. Soc.*, 1944, 88, 269–357.

Kuhn, T. S. *The structure of scientific revolutions.* Chicago: Univ. Chicago Press, 1962.

Külpe, O. *Outlines of psychology.* Trans. by E. B. Titchener. New York: Macmillan, 1895.

Ladd, G. T. *Elements of physiological psychology.* New York: Scribner's, 1888.

————. *Outlines of descriptive psychology.* New York: Scribner's, 1898.

Ladd, G. T. and Woodworth, R. S. *Elements of physiological psychology.* New York: Scribner's, 1911.

Lange, F. A. *The history of materialism.* 3 Vols. in one. Trans. by E. C. Thomas. London: Routledge & Kegan Paul, 1957. (Reprinted)

Lashley, K. S. "The mechanism of vision: XV. Preliminary studies of the rat's capacity for detail vision." *J. Gen. Psychol.*, 1938, 18, 123–93.

————. "Structural variation in the nervous system in relation to behavior." *Psychol. Rev.*, 1947, 54, 325–34.

————. "Persistent problems in the evolution of mind." *Quart. Rev. Biol.*, 1949, 24, 28–42.

Lashley, K. S., Chow, K., and Semmes, J. "An examination of the electrical field theory of cerebral integration." *Psychol. Rev.*, 1951, 58, 123–36.

Lashley, K. S. and Russell, J. T. "The mechanism of vision: a preliminary test of innate organization." *J. Genet. Psychol.*, 1934, 45, 136–44.

Lawrence, M. *Studies in human behavior.* Princeton: Princeton Univ. Press, 1949.

Le Cat, C. N. *Traité des sensations et des passions.* 2 Vols. Paris, 1767.

Leibniz, G. W. *New essays concerning human understanding*. Trans. by A. G. Langley. New York: Macmillan, 1896.

Le Roy, G. (ed.). *Oeuvres philosophiques de Condillac*. Paris: Presses Universitaires, 1947.

Levine, R., Chein, I., and Murphy, G. "The relation of the intensity of a need to the amount of perceptual distortion: a preliminary report." *J. Psychol.*, 1942, 13, 283–95.

Lewes, G. H. *Problems of life and mind: third series*. London: Trubner, 1879.

Linksz, A. *Physiology of the eye: vision*. Vol. 2. New York: Grune & Stratton, 1952.

Locke, J. *An essay concerning human understanding*. 2 Vols. Ed. by A. C. Fraser from the 3rd edition, 1694. Oxford: Clarendon, 1894. (Reprinted, NewYork: Dover, 1959.)

————. *An examination of P. Malebranche's opinion of seeing all things in God*, 1706. See Locke, *Works*.

————. *Some familiar letters between Mr. Locke and several of his friends*, 1706. See Locke, *Works*.

————. *The works of John Locke*. Vol. 9, 1823. (Reprinted, Germany: Scientia Verlag Aalen, 1963.)

Lotze, H. "De la formation de la notion d'espace." *Revue Philos.*, 1877, 4, 345–65.

————. *Outlines of psychology*. Trans. and ed. by G. T. Ladd. Boston: Ginn, 1886.

————. *Metaphysics*. Trans. by B. Bosanquet. Vol. 2. Oxford: Clarendon, 1887.

Luce, A. A. *Malebranche and Berkeley*. London: Oxford Univ. Press, 1934.

————. *The dialectic of immaterialism*. London: Hodder and Stoughton, 1963.

Luchins, A. S. "An evaluation of some current criticisms of gestalt psychological work on perception." *Psychol. Rev.*, 1951, 58, 69–95.

Lucretius. *On the nature of the universe*. Trans. by R. Latham. Harmondsworth: Penguin Books, 1951.

Lund, F. H. "The phantom of the gestalt." *J. Gen. Psychol.*, 1929, 2, 307–21.

McCosh, J. *An examination of J. S. Mill's philosophy*. New York: Carter, 1866.

————. *The Scottish philosophy*. New York: Carter, 1875.

————. *Psychology: the cognitive powers*. New York: Scribner's, 1892.

MacCurdy, E. (ed. and with an introduction by MacCurdy). *The notebooks of Leonardo da Vinci*. New York: Braziller, 1954.

Mach, E. *The analysis of sensations*. (Trans. by C. M. Williams from the 1st

German ed. Revised and Supplemented from the 5th German ed. by S. Waterlow.) New York: Dover, 1959.

Magendie, F. *Précis élémentaire de physiologie*. Vol. 1. Paris: Mequiqnon Maron, 1825.

Mahaffy, J. P. *The critical philosophy for English readers*. Vol. 1, Pt. 1. London: Longmans, 1872.

Maine de Biran, M. *Nouvelles considerations sur les rapports du physique et du moral de l'homme*. Paris: Ladrange, 1834.

Malebranche, N. *De la recherche de la vérité*. Vol. 2. (Edition of Bouillier.) Paris: Garnier, 1880.

———. *De la recherche de la vérité*. 3 Vols. (Edition of G. Rodis-Lewis.) Paris: Vrin, 1962–64.

———. *Dernier éclaircissement*. See Bouillier edition.

———. *Dialogues on metaphysics and on religion*. Trans. by M. Ginsberg. New York: Macmillan, 1923.

———. *Réponse à M. Régis*. See Bouillier edition.

———. *Treatise concerning the search after truth*. Trans. by T. Taylor. London, 1700.

Malinowski, B. *The sexual life of savages in northwestern Melanesia*. London: Routledge, 1929.

Mansel, H. L. *Metaphysics*. Edinburgh: Black, 1883. 4th edition.

Mayo, H. *Outlines of human physiology*. London: Burgess & Hill, 1829. 2nd edition.

Mead, M. "The primitive child." In *Handbook of child psychology*. Ed. by C. Murchison. London: Oxford Univ. Press, 1933.

Mill, J. S. "Bailey on Berkeley's theory of vision." *Westminister Rev.*, 1842. See J. S. Mill, *Dissertations and discussions*, Vol. 2.

———. "Rejoinder to Mr. Bailey's reply." *Westminister Rev.*, 1843. See J. S. Mill, *Dissertations and discussions*, Vol. 2.

———. "Bain's psychology." *Edinburgh Rev.*, 1859. See J. S. Mill, *Dissertations and discussions*, Vol. 4.

———. *Dissertations and discussions*. Vols. 2, 4. Boston: Spencer, 1865–68.

———. "Berkeley's life and writings." *Fortnightly Rev.*, (n. s.) 1871, 10, 505–24.

———. *A system of logic*. London: Longman & Green, 1872. 8th edition.

———. *An examination of Sir William Hamilton's philosophy*. London: Longmans, Green, 1889. 6th edition.

Milner, P. M. "The cell assembly: Mark II." *Psychol. Rev.*, 1957, 64, 242–52.

Molyneux, W. "Concerning the apparent magnitude of the sun and moon, or the apparent distance of two stars, when nigh the horizon, and when higher elevated." *Royal Soc. London Philos. Trans.*, 1687, 16, 314–23.

———. *Dioptrika Nova*, 1692.

Monck, W. H. S. *Space and vision: an attempt to deduce all our knowledge of space from the sense of sight.* Dublin: McGee, 1872.

Morgan, C. L. *Habit and instinct.* New York: Edward Arnold, 1896.

———. *Introduction to comparative psychology.* New York: Scribner's, 1904. 2nd edition.

Müller, J. *The physiology of the senses, voice, and muscular motion and with the mental faculties.* Trans. by W. Baly with notes. London: Taylor, Walter, and Maberly, 1848.

Murphy, G. *A briefer general psychology.* New York: Harper, 1935.

———. *Personality: a biosocial approach to origins and structure.* New York: Harper, 1947.

———. *An introduction to psychology.* New York: Harper, 1951.

———. "Affect and perceptual learning." *Psychol. Rev.,* 1956, 63, 1–15.

Murphy, G. and Hochberg, J. "Perceptual development: some tentative hypotheses." *Psychol. Rev.,* 1951, 58, 332–49.

Myers, C. S. *A textbook of experimental psychology.* Pt. 1. Cambridge: University Press, 1911. 2nd edition.

Naville, E. "Théorie de la vision." *Revue Scientifique,* 1877, 12, 943–52.

Necker, L. A. "On an apparent change of position in a drawing or engraved figure of a crystal, 1832." In Dember, W. N. *Visual perception: nineteenth century.* New York: Wiley, 1964.

Nissen, H. W., Chow, K. L., and Semmes, J. "Effects of restricted opportunity for tactual, kinesthetic, and manipulative experience on the behavior of a chimpanzee." *Amer. J. Psychol.,* 1951, 64, 458–507.

Nunneley, T. *On the organs of vision: their anatomy and physiology.* London: Churchill, 1858.

Olscamp, P. J. (trans., with an introduction by P. J. Olscamp). *Discourse on method, optics, geometry, and meteorology. René Descartes.* New York: Bobbs Merrill, 1965.

Panum, P. L. *Physiological investigations concerning vision with two eyes.* Trans. by C. Hubscher. Hanover: Dartmouth Eye Institute, 1957.

Pastore, N. "Need as a determinant of perception." *J. Psychol.,* 1949, 28, 457–75.

———. "Some remarks on the Ames oscillatory effect." *Psychol. Rev.,* 1952, 59, 319–23.

———. "Review of F. P. Kilpatrick [ed.] *Human behavior from the transactional point of view.*" Hanover: Institute for Associated Research, 1952. *Amer. J. Psychol.,* 1954, 67, 379–83.

————. "An examination of one aspect of the thesis that perceiving is learned." *Psychol. Rev.*, 1956, 63, 309–16.

————. "Form perception and size constancy in the duckling." *J. Psychol.*, 1958, 45, 259–61.

————. "Perceptual functioning in the duckling." *J. Genet. Psychol.*, 1959, 95, 157–69.

————. "Perceiving as innately determined." *J. Genet. Psychol.*, 1960, 96, 93–99.

————. "Perceptual functioning in the duckling." *J. Psychol.*, 1962, 54, 293–98.

————. "Samuel Bailey's critique of Berkeley's theory of vision." *J. Hist. Beh. Sci.*, 1965, 1, 321–37.

Pastore, N. and Klibbe, H. "The orientation of the cerebral image in Descartes' theory of visual perception." *J. Hist. Beh. Sci.*, 1969, 5, 385–89.

Pavlov, I. P. *Conditioned reflexes.* Trans. and ed. by G. V. Anrep. London: Oxford Univ. Press, 1927. (Reprinted, Dover: New York, 1960.)

————. *Selected works.* Trans. from the Russian by S. Belsky, ed. by J. Gibbons. Moscow, 1955.

Pearson, K. *The grammar of science.* New York: Scribner's, 1892.

Perry, R. B. *The thought and character of William James.* 2 Vols. New York: Braziller, 1954.

Piéron, H. "Remarques sur le perception du mouvement apparent (á propos des théories 'gestaltiste')." *L'Année Psychol.*, 1933, 34, 245–48.

————. "Quels sont les determinants de la pregnance perceptive?" *Acta Psychologica*, 1950, 7, 337–51.

Poincaré, H. *Science and hypothesis,* 1905. (Reprinted from the first English translation, New York: Dover, 1952.)

————. *The value of science,* 1913. Trans. by G. B. Halstead. (Reprinted, New York: Dover, 1958.)

Porter, N. *The human intellect.* New York: Scribner's, 1868.

Porterfield, W. *A treatise on the eye.* 2 Vols. Edinburgh, 1759.

Pratt, C. C. "The role of past experience in visual perception." *J. Psychol.*, 1950, 30, 85–107.

Prentice, W. C. H. " 'Functionalism' in perception." *Psychol. Rev.*, 1956, 63, 29–38.

Preyer, W. *The mind of the child.* Vol. 2. (Trans. by H. W. Brown). New York: Appleton, 1889.

Priestley, J. B. *History and present state of discoveries relating to vision, light, and colours.* London: Johnson, 1772.

Pritchard, R. M. Stabilized images on the retina. *Scientific Amer.*, 1961, 204, 72–78.

Proshansky, H. and Murphy, G. "The effects of reward and punishment on perception." *J. Psychol.*, 1942, 13, 295–305.

Reid, T. *Essays on the intellectual powers of man,* 1785. See Walker.

———. *Inquiry into the human mind,* 1764. In *Works of Thomas Reid.* New York: Duyckinck, 1822.

Ribot, T. *English psychology.* London: King, 1877.

———. *German psychology of today.* Trans. by J. M. Baldwin. New York: Scribner's, 1886.

Richter, I. A. (ed., with commentaries by Richter). *Selections from the notebooks of Leonardo da Vinci.* New York: Oxford Univ. Press, 1953.

Riesen, A. H. "The development of visual perception in man and chimpanzee." *Science,* 1947, 106, 107–8.

———. "Arrested vision." *Scientific Amer.,* 1950, 138, 16–19.

———. "Plasticity of behavior: psychological aspects." In Harlow, H. F. and Woolsey, C. N. (eds.). *Biological and biochemical bases of behavior.* Madison: Univ. Wisconsin Press, 1958.

Ritchie, A. D. *George Berkeley: a reappraisal.* New York: Barnes & Noble, 1967.

Rivers, W. H. R. "Vision." In Schäfer, E. A. (ed.). *Textbook of physiology.* Vol. 2. New York: Macmillan, 1900.

Robertson, G. C. "The psychological theory of extension." *Mind,* 1888, 13, 418–24.

Rock, I. and Fleck, F. S. "A re-examination of the effect of monetary reward and punishment on figure-ground perception." *J. Exp. Psychol.,* 1950, 40, 766–76.

Rohault, J. *Traité de physique,* 1671. See Clarke.

Rohrer, J. H. and Sherif, M. (eds.). *Social psychology at the crossroads.* New York: Harpers, 1951.

Ronchi, V. *Storia della luce.* Bologna: Zanichelli, 1952.

———. *Optics: the science of vision.* Trans. by E. Rosen. New York: New York Univ. Press, 1957.

———. "Complexities, advances, and misconceptions in the development of the science of vision: what is being discovered?" In Crombie, A. C. (ed.). *Scientific change.* New York: Basic Books, 1963.

Ruskin, J. *The elements of drawing and perspective.* New York: Wiley, 1887.

Russell, B. *The problems of philosophy.* London: Oxford Univ. Press, 1912.

———. *Human knowledge.* New York: Simon and Schuster, 1948.

Sapir, E. "The status of linguistics as a science, 1929." In Mandelbaum, D. G. (ed.). *Selected writings of Edward Sapir.* Berkeley and Los Angeles: Univ. California Press, 1963.

Schafer, R. and Murphy, G. "The role of autism in a visual figure-ground relationship." *J. Exp. Psychol.*, 1943, 32, 335–43.

Sechenov, I. *Selected physiological and psychological works.* Trans. by S. Belsky, ed. by G. Gibbons. Moscow.

Segall, M. H., Campbell, D. T., and Herskovits, M. J. *The influence of culture on visual perception.* New York: Bobbs Merrill, 1966.

Senden, M. v. *Space and sight.* Trans. by P. Heath with appendixes by A. H. Riesen, G. J. Warnock, and J. Z. Young. Glencoe: Free Press, 1960.

Sergi, G. *La psychologie physiologique.* Trans. by M. Mouton. Paris: Alcan, 1888.

Simon, T. C. "Can we see distance?" *Macmillan's Mag.*, 1866, 13, 429–42.

Smith, A. *Essays on philosophical subjects*, 1795. London: Murray, 1869. 6th edition. (Chapter, "External Senses")

Smith, D. E. P. and Hochberg, J. E. "The effect of 'punishment' (electric shock) on figure-ground perception." *J. Psychol.*, 1954, 38, 83–87.

Smith, N. "Malebranche's theory of the perception of distance and magnitude." *Brit. J. Psychol.*, 1905, 1, 191–204.

Smith. R. *A compleat system of opticks.* 2 Vols. To which are added remarks upon the whole, and J. Jurin "An essay upon distinct and indistinct vision." 1738.

Solley, C. M. and Murphy, G. *Development of the perceptual world.* New York: Basic Books, 1960.

Spalding, D. Instinct: with original observations on young animals. *Macmillan's Mag.*, 1873, 27, 22–93. (Reprinted in *Brit. J. Animal Beh.*, 1954, 2, 1–11 with an introduction by J. B. S. Haldane.)

Spencer, H. *The principles of psychology.* 2 Vols. New York: Appleton, 1885.

Sperry, R. W. "Neurology and the mind-brain problem." *Amer. Scientist,* 1952, 40, 291–312.

Sperry, R. W., Miner, N., and Myers, R. E. "Visual pattern perception following subpial slicing and tantulum wire implantations in the visual cortex." *J. Comp. Physiol. Psychol.*, 1955, 48, 50–58.

Sperry, R. W. and Miner, N. "Pattern perception following insertion of mica plates into visual cortex." *J. Comp. Physiol. Psychol.*, 1955, 48, 463–69.

Spitz, R. *The first year of life.* New York: International Univ. Press, 1965.

Starling, E. H. *Principles of human physiology.* Philadelphia: Lea & Febiger, 1915. 2nd edition.

Stewart, D. *Collected works.* Ed. by W. Hamilton. Vols. 1, 2, 4. Edinburgh: Constable, 1854–58.

Stratton, G. M. "Vision without inversion of the retinal image." *Psychol.*

Rev., 1897, 4, 341–60, 363–481. Extracts in Dennis, W. (ed.). *Readings in general psychology.* New York: Prentice Hall, 1949.

———. *Experimental psychology, and its bearing on culture.* New York: Macmillan, 1903.

Sully, J. *Sensation and intuition.* London: King, 1874.

———. "The question of visual perception in Germany." *Mind*, 1878, 3, 1–23, 167–95.

———. *Illusions: a psychological study.* New York: Appleton, 1881.

———. *Outlines of psychology.* New York: Appleton, 1884.

———. *Teachers handbook of psychology.* New York: Appleton, 1886.

———. *The human mind.* 2 Vols. New York: Appleton, 1892.

Taine, H. *On intelligence.* Trans. by T. D. Haye. New York: Holt & Williams, 1872.

Taylor, J. *The behavioral basis of perception.* New Haven: Yale Univ. Press, 1962.

Thorndike, E. L. *The elements of psychology.* New York: Seiler, 1905.

Titchener, E. B. *Experimental psychology of the thought process.* New York: Macmillan, 1909.

Turbayne, C. M. "Berkeley and Molyneux on retinal images." *J. Hist. Ideas*, 1955, 16, 339–355.

———. *The myth of the metaphor.* New Haven: Yale Univ. Press, 1962.

———, (ed.). *Works on vision: George Berkeley.* New York: Bobbs Merrill, 1963.

Veitch, J. (trans., with an introductory essay by Veitch). *The method, meditations and philosophy of Descartes.* New York: Tudor, 1901.

Voltaire, F. *Elémens de la philosophie de Neuton.* Amsterdam: Jacques Desbordes, 1738.

Walk, R. D. and Gibson, E. J. "A comparative and analytical study of visual depth perception." *Psychol. Monogr.*, 1961, 75, No. 15.

Walker, J. (ed.). *Essay on intellectual powers by Reid* (abridged). Boston: Phillips, Sampson, 1855.

Wallach, H. "Brightness constancy and the nature of achromatic colors." *J. Exp. Psychol.*, 1948, 38, 310–24.

———. "Some considerations concerning the relation between perception and cognition." *J. Pers.*, 1949, 18, 6–13.

Wallin, J. E. W. *Optical illusions of reversible perspectives.* Princeton, 1905.

Walls, G. L. "The problem of visual direction." *Amer. J. Optom. and Arch. Amer. Acad. Optom. Monogr.* 117, Minneapolis, 1951.

Walter, J. E. *The perception of space and matter.* Boston: Estes and Lauriat, 1879.

———. *Nature and cognition of space and time.* West Newton: Johnston and Penney, 1914.

Wardrop, J. "Case of a lady born blind, who received sight at an advanced age by the formation of an artificial pupil." *Royal Soc. London Philos. Trans.*, 1826, 116, 529–40.

Warnock, G. J. *Berkeley*. Harmondsworth: Pelican Books, 1953.

Washburn, M. F. "*Gestalt* psychology and motor psychology." *Amer. J. Psychol.*, 1926, 37, 516–520.

———. "A system of motor psychology." In *Psychologies of 1930*. Worcester: Clark Univ. Press, 1930.

Wertheimer, Max. *Experimental studies on the seeing of motion, 1912*. Condensed translation by T. Shipley. In Shipley, T. (ed.). *Classics in psychology*. New York: Philosophical Library, 1961.

Wertheimer, Michael. "Hebb and Senden on the role of learning in perception." *Amer. J. Psychol.*, 1951, 64, 133–37.

———. "Psychomotor coordination of auditory and visual space at birth." *Science*, 1961, 134, 1692.

———. Letter. *Science*, 1962, 135, 999.

Wheatstone, C. "Contributions to the physiology of vision." *Royal Soc. London Philos. Trans.*, 1838, 128, 371–94.

———. "Contributions to the physiology of vision." *Philos. Mag.*, 1852 (Series 4), 3, 241–67, 504–23.

Wheeler, R. H., Perkins, F. T., and Bartley, S. H. "Errors in the critiques of gestalt psychology II. Confused interpretations of the historical approach." *Psychol. Rev.*, 1933, 40, 221–45.

Whewell, W. *The philosophy of the inductive sciences*. Vol. 1. London: Parker, 1840.

Wight, O. W. *Philosophy of Sir William Hamilton, Bart.* "Collection of Sir Wm. Hamilton's philosophical discussions and dissertations." Arranged and edited by O. W. Wight. New York: Appleton, 1853.

Wundt, W. *Éléments de psychologie physiologique*. 2 Vols. Trans. by E. Rouvier. Paris: Alcan, 1886.

———. *Lectures on human and animal psychology*. Trans. by J. E. Creighton and E. B. Titchener. New York: Macmillan, 1907.

———. *Outlines of psychology*. Trans. by C. H. Judd. New York: Stechert, 1907.

Ziehen, T. *Introduction to physiological psychology*. Trans. by C. C. Van Liew and O. Beyer. London: Sonnenschein, 1892.

INDEX